D1602573

Cognition and Commitment
in Hume's Philosophy

Cognition and Commitment in Hume's Philosophy

Don Garrett

New York   Oxford
Oxford University Press
1997

Oxford University Press

Oxford   New York
Athens   Auckland   Bangkok   Bogota   Bombay
Buenos Aires   Calcutta   Cape Town   Dar es Salaam
Delhi   Florence   Hong Kong   Istanbul   Karachi
Kuala Lumpur   Madras   Madrid   Melbourne
Mexico City   Nairobi   Paris   Singapore
Taipei   Tokyo   Toronto

and associated companies in
Berlin   Ibadan

Copyright © 1997 by Oxford University Press, Inc.

Published by Oxford University Press, Inc.,
198 Madison Avenue, New York, New York 10016

Library of Congress Cataloging-in-Publication Data
Garrett, Don.
Cognition and commitment in Hume's philosophy / Don Garrett.
    p.   cm.
Includes bibliographical references and index.
ISBN 0-19-509721-1
1. Hume, David, 1711–1776—Contributions in theory of knowledge.
2. Knowledge, Theory of.   3. Skepticism.   4. Belief and doubt.
I. Title.
B1499.K7G37   1996
192—dc20   96-20578

9 8 7 6 5 4 3 2 1

Printed in the United States of America
on acid-free paper

For Frances,
for Bula, Matthew, and Christopher Garrett,
and in memory of Professor Barbara Lindsay,
sources of wisdom all

Acknowledgments

This book was begun under the congenial circumstances of a fellowship at the Institute for Advanced Studies in the Humanities at the University of Edinburgh in 1984 and continued during a faculty fellowship sponsored by the Research Committee of the University of Utah with the support of the College of Humanities.

I am indebted to many individuals who provided helpful comments and advice on portions of the manuscript or on the ideas in it. These include Robert Fogelin, William Edward Morris, Geoffrey Sayre-McCord, Jonathan Bennett, Elijah Millgram, David Owen, Corliss Swain, Charlotte Brown, Peter Millican, Michelle Moody Adams, Mendel Cohen, Clifton McIntosh, Virgil Aldrich, and Tom Reed.

A special debt of gratitude is due to Michael Arts, John DePompeo, Robert Dow, Susan Hickenlooper, Kristin Johnson, Albert Kostelny, David Partee, Matt Shulsen, Shawn Trauntwein, and Eric Wiseman, who provided many useful suggestions during a graduate seminar based on an earlier version of the manuscript.

Portions of chapters 2 and 3 originally appeared in "Simplicity and Separability in Hume's Empiricism," *Archiv für Geschichte der Philosophie*, vol. 67, no. 3 (September 1985), pp. 270–288. An earlier version of chapter 5 originally appeared as "The Representation of Causation and Hume's Two Definitions of 'Cause'," *Noûs*, vol. 27, no. 2 (June 1993), pp. 167–190. Portions of chapter 8 originally appeared in "Hume's Self-Doubts about Personal Identity," *The Philosophical Review*, vol. 90, no. 3 (July 1981), pp. 337–358 (copyright © 1981 Cornell University; reprinted by permission of the publisher). Permission to incorporate this material into the present volume is gratefully acknowledged.

Contents

Abbreviations

ATHN   David Hume (attributed), *An Abstract of a Book lately Published; Entitled, A Treatise of Human Nature*, in THN.

DCB   Francis Burman, *Descartes' Conversation with Burman*, translated by John Cottingham (Oxford: Clarendon Press, 1976).

DM   George Berkeley, *De Motu*, in *The Works of George Berkeley, Bishop of Cloyne*, edited by A. A. Luce and T. E. Jessop, 9 vols. (London: Thomas Nelson and Sons, 1948–1957).

E   Benedict de Spinoza, *Ethics*, in *Spinoza's Collected Works*, vol. 1, edited and translated by Edwin Curley (Princeton: Princeton University Press, 1985).

ECHU   John Locke, *An Essay concerning Human Understanding*, edited by P. H. Nidditch (Oxford: Clarendon Press, 1975).

EHU   David Hume, *An Enquiry concerning Human Understanding*, in *Enquiries concerning Human Understanding and the Principles of Morals*, edited by L. A. Selby-Bigge, revised by P. H. Nidditch (Oxford: Clarendon Press, 1975).

EPM   David Hume, *An Enquiry concerning the Principles of Morals*, in *Enquiries concerning Human Understanding and the Principles of Morals*, edited by L. A. Selby-Bigge, revised by P. H. Nidditch (Oxford: Clarendon Press, 1982).

ISM   G. W. F. Leibniz, "On What Is Independent of Sense and Matter," in *Philosophical Papers and Letters*, 2 vols., translated by L. E. Loemker (Chicago: University of Chicago Press, 1956).

LDH   David Hume, *Letters of David Hume*, 2 vols., edited by J. Y. T. Grieg (Oxford: Clarendon Press, 1932).

MFP   René Descartes, *Meditations on First Philosophy*, in *The Philosophical Writings of Descartes*, translated by John Cottingham, Robert Stoothoff, and Dugald Murdoch (Cambridge: Cambridge University Press, 1985).

NE   G. W. F. Leibniz, *New Essays on Human Understanding*, translated by

Peter Remnant and Jonathan Bennett (Cambridge: Cambridge University Press, 1981).

PC   George Berkeley, *Philosophical Commentaries,* in *The Works of George Berkeley, Bishop of Cloyne,* edited by A. A. Luce and T. E. Jessop, 9 vols. (London: Thomas Nelson and Sons, 1948–1957).

PHK   George Berkeley, *Principles of Human Knowledge,* in *The Works of George Berkeley, Bishop of Cloyne,* edited by A. A. Luce and T. E. Jessop, 9 vols. (London: Thomas Nelson and Sons, 1948–1957).

PP   René Descartes, *Principles of Philosophy,* in *The Philosophical Writings of Descartes,* translated by John Cottingham, Robert Stoothoff, and Dugald Murdoch (Cambridge: Cambridge University Press, 1985).

TDHP   George Berkeley, *Three Dialogues between Hylas and Philonous,* in *The Works of George Berkeley, Bishop of Cloyne,* edited by A. A. Luce and T. E. Jessop, 9 vols. (London: Thomas Nelson and Sons, 1948–1957).

THN   David Hume, *A Treatise of Human Nature,* edited by L. A. Selby-Bigge, revised by P. H. Nidditch (Oxford: Clarendon Press, 1978).

TIE   Benedict de Spinoza, *Tractatus de Intellectus Emendatione,* in *Spinoza's Collected Works,* vol. 1, edited and translated by Edwin Curley (Princeton: Princeton University Press, 1985).

Cognition and Commitment
in Hume's Philosophy

Introduction

In the course of his remarkable life as an author, diplomat, and government official, David Hume (1711–1776) made noteworthy contributions to many fields of inquiry, including history, economics, political science, anthropology, and psychology. But while his contributions to these fields were noteworthy, his contributions to philosophy were momentous. Indeed, most contemporary philosophers would agree that he was the greatest philosopher yet produced by the English-speaking world. Beneath this agreement about Hume's greatness, however, lies considerable disagreement and confusion concerning the meaning of his most famous philosophical doctrines, the precise nature of his philosophical greatness, and the bearing of his contributions on contemporary philosophy.

As my title indicates, it is Hume's philosophy—rather than his life, his times, or his contributions to other fields—that constitutes the primary focus of this book.[1] Specifically, this book is devoted to resolving a series of interpretive puzzles that have long stood in the way of a complete understanding and accurate assessment of Hume's philosophy. Through the resolution of these puzzles, I try to explain the meaning of some of his central philosophical doctrines, to defend an account of his greatness as a philosopher, and to facilitate a better understanding of the contemporary significance of his philosophy. Before endeavoring to explain Hume's philosophy, however, I must first explain what I mean by 'philosophy', what Hume himself meant by 'philosophy', and what the enterprise that he called by that name meant to him. I will also explain my conception of the relation of philosophy to its own history—what might be called my philosophy of the history of philosophy—and the way in which the organization and contents of this book reflect that conception. In the course of doing so, I will also be explaining why I take cognition and commitment as my central themes.

Philosophy in the Writings of David Hume

'Philosophy,' as I am using the term, simply designates the attempt to answer questions that are especially fundamental. A question is fundamental if an array of other important questions depends on the answer to it in some important way. Because there are several different ways in which one question can depend importantly on the answer to another, there are several different ways in which a question can be philosophical. Thus, a question may be philosophical because the discovery or justification of *answers* to an array of other important questions depends on the answer to it. The question, "How should moral character be evaluated?" is philosophical in this way, since the answers we give to many other important ethical questions will (at least partly) depend, for their discovery or justification or both, on our answer to it. Alternatively, a question may be philosophical because grasping the proper *interpretation* or appreciating the full *significance* of the answers to an array of other important questions depends on it. Thus, the question, "What is the causal relation?" is philosophical as well, since our understanding of how to construe or regard many important scientific truths depends on our answer to it. A question may even be philosophical because the *evaluation* of other important questions depends on the answer to it. The question, "Do we have a coherent notion of identity through time?" is philosophical in this way, since whether we take a large class of other important questions about the continuing identity of persons and things to be well formulated or not depends on our answer to it. A question may be especially fundamental in more than one of these ways or, perhaps, in other ways as well, but what distinguishes philosophical questions from others is the characteristic of being especially fundamental in at least some way. So understood, philosophy includes the most fundamental questions of the various special disciplines. It nevertheless differs from those special disciplines in at least one respect. For while the special disciplines divide the field of knowledge vertically, distinguishing themselves from one another by differences in their objects of study, philosophy divides the field of knowledge horizontally, concerning itself with those questions, whatever their objects may happen to be, that are especially fundamental.[2]

Hume uses the term 'philosophy' frequently, without ever offering a definition of it. It is reasonably clear from his usage, however, that his conception of philosophy is in one way more inclusive, and in another way more exclusive, than the one that I have just outlined. Hume does not regard philosophy as being limited only to the most fundamental questions of the special disciplines; instead, he thinks of most of those disciplines as belonging to philosophy in their entirety. He distinguishes philosophy into two main branches. The first of these is *natural philosophy*, which is concerned with the world of extended objects and includes all of what we would now call the natural sciences. The second is *moral philosophy*, which is concerned with the human mind and with human life generally, and it includes what we would now call psychology and the human or social sciences. In this respect, then, Hume's sense of the term 'philosophy' is more inclusive than mine, and that is why he can write of philosophy as "nothing but the reflections of common life, methodized and corrected" (EHU §130).

However, at various points in his writings, he distinguishes history, literature, revealed theology, and mathematics *from* philosophy—evidently, as enterprises so different in their conduct from both natural and moral philosophy as to deserve separate classification. Thus, even the most fundamental questions of these fields will apparently not be "philosophical" in his sense, unless they also belong either to natural or moral philosophy, or both. In this respect, then, his sense of the term is less inclusive than mine. It is worth noting that, in dividing philosophy into only two branches, Hume is rejecting a traditional tripartite division of philosophy into natural, moral, and metaphysical philosophy. Unlike most of his predecessors— but, he thinks, like many of his contemporaries—he uses the term 'metaphysics' not as a term for a distinct subject matter within philosophy (concerned with the ultimate nature of being) but rather as a synonym for "any difficult or abstruse reasoning," regardless of subject matter.

Because Hume used the term 'philosophy' in one sense and I use it in another, the reference to "Hume's philosophy" in the title of this book is ambiguous. This ambiguity is intentional: the phrase may be taken in both senses at once. This is possible because, of all the many questions posed by "philosophy" in his sense, the ones that interest him most are almost always "philosophical" in my sense as well. To be sure, Hume often addresses the processes of human cognition, emotion, and moral response in considerable detail. But he does so primarily because he aims to show how an understanding of these processes bears crucially on the answers to fundamental questions. In doing so, he seeks to show, in effect, that many of these topics of relative psychological detail are themselves far more fundamental than we might have supposed. At the same time, he shows how a very wide variety of the fundamental questions that concern him most can profitably be treated within what he calls "moral philosophy."

Although Hume's conception of philosophy itself remained largely constant throughout his career, his conception of his intended contribution to it underwent subtle but significant changes. His first work—and in many ways, his masterpiece—was, of course, A *Treatise of Human Nature*, published in two volumes in 1738 and 1739 while its author was still in his twenties. It is an ambitious work that, according to its subtitle, constitutes "an attempt to introduce the experimental method of reasoning into moral subjects." Hume takes as his subject the whole "science of man," and of this science he writes:

> Here then is the only expedient, from which we can hope for success in our philosophical researches, to leave the tedious lingring method, which we have hitherto followed, and instead of taking now and then a castle or village on the frontier, to march up directly to the capital or center of these sciences, to human nature itself; which being once masters of, we may every where else hope for an easy victory. From this station we may extend our conquests over all those sciences, which more intimately concern human life, and may afterwards proceed at leisure to discover more fully those, which are the objects of pure curiosity. There is no question of importance, whose decision is not compriz'd in the science of man; and there is none, which can be decided with any certainty, before we become acquainted with that science. In pretending therefore to explain the principles of human nature, we in effect propose a compleat system of the sciences, built on a foundation almost entirely new, and the only one upon which they can stand with any security. (THN xvi)

Its three books are devoted, respectively, to the "understanding," the "passions," and "morals," and in its pages Hume takes up a wide range of topics. The first book alone includes lengthy discussions of mental representation, space and time, causation, causal reasoning and probability, the belief in external bodies, the immateriality of the soul, personal identity, the characteristics of ancient and modern philosophy, and several species of skepticism. The second book takes up the nature and operations of pride and humility, of love and hatred, and of various related passions, in addition to the nature of the will. The third book considers the nature of vice, virtue, and the moral sense; justice, fidelity to promises, allegiance to governments, chastity, and modesty; and various natural virtues and abilities.

Hume's *An Enquiry concerning Human Understanding*, written as a recasting of Book I of the *Treatise* and first published in 1748, has a much more exclusive, and pragmatic, principle of organization. In this first *Enquiry*, Hume presents only as much of his theory of mind and his arguments concerning causality and causal reasoning as are necessary to draw conclusions bearing on the practical struggle against "superstition"—that is, the doctrines and practices of unphilosophical and unreflective organized religion. At the very time that his content becomes more directly subversive, however, his tone becomes strikingly more conciliatory and urbane. The first *Enquiry* also provides a treatment of skepticism that differs noticeably from that of the *Treatise*. *An Enquiry concerning the Principles of Morals*, written as a recasting of Book III of the *Treatise*, resembles the first *Enquiry* in having a narrower and more immediately practical principle of organization. This second *Enquiry* focuses on the questions of what we regard as elements of personal merit and why we find them meritorious. One of its primary aims is to draw practical moral conclusions that stand in opposition to the morality of superstitious "divines," even as it teaches its readers how to be more persuasive secular moralists themselves. An understanding of all three works is essential to an understanding of Hume's philosophy, for while the *Treatise* addresses more topics, and often provides more of his views on a given topic, the *Enquiries* provide his last, rather than his first, word on the topics they address. In addition to the philosophical topics Hume addresses in these three works, he takes up many other philosophical questions ("philosophical" in both his sense and mine) in his various essays and dissertations, in his *History of England*, and of course in his posthumously published *Dialogues concerning Natural Religion*.

From his earliest writings to his last, Hume showed a lively satirical sense concerning the pretensions and excesses of self-styled "philosophers." He also possessed a profound awareness of the confusion and difficulty in which the pursuit of philosophy, in his sense, would inevitably involve its human practitioners. He nevertheless endorsed the pursuit of philosophy, both for himself and for others who were capable of it. He did so partly because he found it to be an enjoyable and mostly innocent endeavor, but he had a more important reason as well. For he was concerned above all with virtue—with understanding it and with cultivating it. It is, he thought, chiefly through moral philosophy that we can come to understand the nature of virtue and thus come to understand, too, the ways in which virtue can be best cultivated. Moreover, of all the virtues, perhaps none concerned him more than the specifically cognitive virtue of wisdom, and he followed the ancient moralists, whom he greatly admired, in seeing philosophy as the way to wisdom.

This combination of satirical deflation and practical endorsement are evident in a well-known passage from *A Treatise of Human Nature*:

'Tis certain, that superstition is much more bold in its systems and hypotheses than philosophy; and while the latter contents itself with assigning new causes and principles to the phænomena, which appear in the visible world, the former opens a world of its own, and presents us with scenes, and beings, and objects, which are altogether new. Since therefore 'tis almost impossible for the mind of man to rest, like those of beasts, in that narrow circle of objects, which are the subject of daily conversation and action, we ought only to deliberate concerning the choice of our guide, and ought to prefer that which is safest and most agreeable. And in this respect I make bold to recommend philosophy, and shall not scruple to give it the preference to superstition of every kind or denomination. For as superstition arises naturally and easily from the popular opinions of mankind, it seizes more strongly on the mind, and is often able to disturb us in the conduct of our lives and actions. Philosophy on the contrary, if just, can present us only with mild and moderate sentiments; and if false and extravagant, its opinions are merely the objects of a cold and general speculation, and seldom go so far as to interrupt the course of our natural propensities. The CYNICS are an extraordinary instance of philosophers, who from reasonings purely philosophical ran into as great extravagancies of conduct as any *Monk* or *Dervise* that ever was in the world. Generally speaking, the errors in religion are dangerous; those in philosophy only ridiculous. (THN 271–272)

Hume saw his age as a battleground between what he called "philosophy," on the one hand, and "superstition," on the other. In that battle, Hume unequivocally chose the side of philosophy.

Philosophy and Its History

The history of philosophy in my sense—that is, the history of investigations into especially fundamental questions—is of interest partly for purely historical reasons, for its ability to illuminate the past. But the history of philosophy also matters to philosophy itself, in at least three ways. First, in coming to understand the history of philosophy, we come to understand better the current state of the enterprise: why it pursues the particular questions it does, in the manner that it does, using the methods that it does, and offering the answers that it does. Such understanding is often of considerable value for the practice and evaluation of contemporary philosophy. In this first respect, however, the relation between philosophy and its history does not differ essentially from that between other fields and their histories. Second, the history of philosophy often provides lessons, derived from past successes or failures, that are applicable to present practice. In this respect, too, however, the relation between philosophy and its history closely resembles that between other fields and their histories. Third, the writings of historical figures in philosophy—particularly the greatest such figures—are themselves consistently important objects of study as ongoing contributions to contemporary philosophical inquiry. And in this respect, the history of philosophy is an integral part of philosophy in a way that is unmatched by the case of any other field.

There are several reasons why the writings of some philosophers of the past retain this kind of special ongoing relevance to contemporary philosophy. In part, it is because the set of living questions itself—that is, the set of open questions under discussion—often changes more slowly in philosophy than in other fields. In part, it is because philosophy can often employ only relatively few resources without begging its own questions, and hence often makes progress relatively slowly in the answers that it gives. In part, it is because empirical data often support or refute philosophical claims relatively indirectly, if at all, so that philosophy by necessity relies more on its own previous conversation for inspiration than do other fields. In part, it is because the frequent density, ambiguity, openness, and richness of philosophical works make the assimilation and understanding of those works both a time-consuming and a constantly self-renewing process. In part, it is because philosophical inquiry benefits from exploring and utilizing as resources the widest possible variety of perspectives or frameworks of understanding—a variety of frameworks that philosophers of the past can often provide. For these reasons—and no doubt others as well—the history of philosophy is of special importance to philosophy.

Yet despite this importance, our temporal and cultural distance from philosophers of the past often poses serious problems of interpretation. Accordingly, those who pursue the history of philosophy primarily for its value to philosophy itself often face a difficult choice: to what extent should one's efforts be directed toward achieving historically accurate interpretations, and to what extent should one's efforts be directed toward achieving philosophically cogent evaluations? On the one hand, insufficient attention to historically accurate interpretation often leads to mere "point scoring," in which a philosopher's position is first misrepresented and then easily refuted from a contemporary standpoint. Equally often, it leads to the converse: anachronistic, self-congratulatory predecessor-hunting, in which great philosophers of the past are charitably interpreted—precisely because of their acknowledged greatness—to be expressing (in a somewhat antiquated style, of course) whatever opinions and arguments happen to be most valued by the contemporary commentator doing the interpreting. On the other hand, insufficient attention to philosophically cogent evaluation often leads to a kind of scholastic self-absorption, in which commentators expend the greatest interpretive efforts on issues that are of little philosophical importance while leaving the questions of the ultimate adequacy and significance of the philosopher's contributions no nearer to answers than they were before.

Those who place a greater emphasis in their practice on historical interpretation and those who place a greater emphasis in their practice on philosophical evaluation need not be antagonists, however. On the contrary, where abilities and interests differ among those pursuing a common endeavor, a division of labor is generally the best tactic. Those who emphasize historical interpretation may correct the misunderstandings and refine the targets of their more evaluatively inclined colleagues. Those who emphasize philosophical evaluation may direct the attention of their more interpretively inclined co-inquirers to the most important questions for historical and textual investigation and then assess more philosophically the results of those investigations. Ultimately—and especially in the case of the best philosophers of the past—neither historically accurate interpretation nor philosophically cogent evaluation is likely to be achieved in the complete absence of the other. In order to assess fully the accuracy of an interpretation of a philosopher, one must determine whether a philosopher of such ability could, in the given context, actually have found the position ascribed to him or her reasonable and convincing, and this already involves submitting the position ascribed to serious philosophical evaluation. Conversely, in order to assess fully an evaluation of a great philosopher, one must determine whether the evaluation deals adequately with the support offered by, and difficulties arising from, the philosopher's own discussion of his or her position, and this already involves accuracy in the interpretation of the philosopher's writings. Furthermore, at least in the case of the best philosophers, an interpretation that is based on an accurate understanding of the philosopher's own intentions is almost certain to be of greater purely *philosophical* interest and significance than an interpretation that is based on historical misunderstandings.

Any work whose topic falls within the history of philosophy, if it is intended to be a contribution to philosophy itself, should ultimately support assessments of the bearing of the historical texts it considers on living contemporary philosophical issues. For such assessments to be well grounded, however, they must be based on accurate interpretation of those texts. In the attempt to provide accurate interpretation, three strategic goals are of particular importance: first, to isolate and grasp the philosopher's most fundamental aims, methods, and principles; second, to understand the content and structure of the reasons or arguments by which the philosopher justifies his or her conclusions; and third, to explicate the philosopher's conclusions and their interrelations.

In the attempt to achieve these three strategic goals, in turn, three tactics are often useful. First, because a philosopher's aims, principles, and methods are often deeply influenced by his or her conception of what the process of understanding that he or she aims to utilize and produce actually *is*, it is often helpful to begin by focusing on the philosopher's views about understanding and cognition—what we might nowadays call the philosopher's views in *cognitive science* or *cognitive psychology*.[3] Second, it is often helpful, in understanding the content and structure of a philosopher's arguments, to set out the most central of them as explicitly and formally as possible, primarily in the philosopher's own words; for in making and referring to such a formulation of the arguments, we are forced to remain more attentive to the philosopher's own intentions. And third, in explicating a philosopher's conclusions, it is often helpful to focus on interpretive puzzles—apparent contradictions, paradoxes, or other surprising features of the texts—that give rise to disagreement or consternation among readers. For it is in resolving these puzzles, where possible, that we see most deeply and specifically into the use a philosopher intends for his or her own claims, and hence we can see into their real meaning and interrelations.

In particular, the philosophy of David Hume—whose writings are so often explicitly addressed to the nature of the "understanding"; whose arguments are so carefully and elaborately thought out; and whose conclusions, though presented in masterful prose, have nevertheless given rise to so many interpretive puzzles—benefits from this kind of tactical treatment. The organization of this book reflects this belief. The book begins with a chapter setting out, in the context of the philosophy and cognitive science of his era, Hume's own account of the process of understanding, emphasizing his account of the main human representational faculty, which he calls the "imagination." This chapter is followed by two chapters devoted to the primary methodological principles—which I call the "Copy Principle" and the "Separability Principle"—that Hume derives from his account of representation. The remaining seven chapters are devoted to particular philosophical topics from his *Treatise* and his two *Enquiries*, questions chosen both for their centrality to

Hume's writings and for their contemporary philosophical importance. These topics are, in order: the inductive origins of belief, the nature of causation, the freedom of human actions, belief in miracles, the nature of personal identity, the character of moral evaluations, and the status of skeptical arguments.[4] Each of the book's ten chapters explicitly and formally reconstructs, primarily in his own words, Hume's central argument about its main topic. Furthermore, each of these chapters is organized around the attempt to resolve one or more serious interpretive puzzles—most of them famous—that arise in the attempt to understand his conclusions and their interrelations. In each case, an understanding of Hume's views about the nature of cognition proves to be essential, in one way or another, to the solution of the puzzle. Thus, each of these chapters aims to do more than simply to discuss or cover some central topic. Each also aims to *solve*—indeed, to be the last word about—a particular interpretive problem or set of problems that have long stood in the way of understanding Hume's philosophy. Whether this ambitious aim is wise or foolish, of course, the reader alone must judge.

Although my primary aim is to resolve some of the main puzzles that have hindered a fuller understanding of Hume's philosophy, I begin each chapter by explaining the context of his treatment of his topic within his own philosophy and the philosophy of his time, and I conclude by considering the significance of his contribution both for the philosophy of his own time and for the philosophy of our own. In doing so, I defend a general account of Hume's philosophical greatness and of the contemporary relevance of his philosophy. Hume was one of the first, and one of the most insightful, philosophers ever to be explicitly concerned with the interrelations among philosophy, psychology, and the psychology of philosophizing. Much of his historical greatness and continuing relevance lies, I judge, in the richness of the interrelations he uncovered and in the depth and originality of the detailed contributions he made to the discussion of a wide range of significant philosophical questions in the light of his concern with those interrelations. One essential pattern within those contributions lies in his development of ways to make stable and defensible human commitments to both science and morals, while at the same time understanding—and facing uncompromisingly—the underlying animal cognitive mechanisms that produce those commitments. In his view, a better understanding of the operations of human cognition is essential to improving not only our *understanding* of our commitments but, ultimately, the *character* of those commitments as well. The example of that project—of improving the character of our commitments through understanding the underlying processes of our cognition—constitutes, I believe, the most general basis for both his historical greatness and his contemporary significance. Hume was not, of course, a philosopher who was never wrong, but he remains a philosopher about whom and from whom there is still much to learn.

Cognition and Imagination

The seventeenth and eighteenth centuries saw a renewed interest in exploring the nature of the human cognitive instrument—that is, in understanding the *human understanding*. Many thinkers proposed that such understanding *of* understanding would prove essential to refining scientific method, improving the state of human knowledge, and fostering human progress. Hume was one of these thinkers.

Book I of *A Treatise of Human Nature* is entitled "Of the Understanding." At the very outset of his attempt to explain the nature of the understanding, he presents four crucial distinctions. He goes on to employ these four distinctions frequently, both in the *Treatise* and in *An Enquiry concerning Human Understanding*, and together with his two most frequently used principles—the Copy Principle and the Separability Principle—they constitute the basis of his cognitive psychology.

The first of these distinctions is the distinction of mental objects or entities, which he calls "perceptions," into "impressions" and "ideas":

> ALL the perceptions of the human mind resolve themselves into two distinct kinds, which I shall call IMPRESSIONS and IDEAS. The difference betwixt these consists in the degrees of force and liveliness, with which they strike upon the mind, and make their way into our thought or consciousness. Those perceptions, which enter with most force and violence, we may name *impressions*; and under this name I comprehend all our sensations, passions and emotions, as they make their first appearance in the soul. By *ideas* I mean the faint images of these in thinking and reasoning; such as, for instance, are all the perceptions excited by the present discourse, excepting only, those which arise from the sight and touch, and excepting the immediate pleasure or uneasiness it may occasion. I believe it will not be very necessary to employ many words in explaining this distinction. Every one of himself will readily perceive the difference betwixt feeling and thinking. (THN 1–2)

The second is the distinction between "simple" and "complex" perceptions:

> There is another division of our perceptions, which it will be convenient to observe, and which extends itself both to our impressions and ideas. This division is into SIMPLE and COMPLEX. Simple perceptions or impressions and ideas are such as admit of no

distinction nor separation. The complex are the contrary to these, and may be distinguished into parts. Tho' a particular colour, taste, and smell are qualities all united together in this apple, 'tis easy to perceive they are not the same, but are at least distinguishable from each other. (THN 2)

The third is the distinction between "impressions of sensation" and "impressions of reflexion":

Impressions may be divided into two kinds, those of SENSATION and those of REFLEXION. The first kind arises in the soul originally, from unknown causes. The second is derived in a great measure from our ideas, and that in the following order. An impression first strikes upon the senses, and makes us perceive heat or cold, thirst or hunger, pleasure or pain of some kind or other. Of this impression there is a copy taken by the mind, which remains after the impression ceases; and this we call an idea. This idea of pleasure or pain, when it returns upon the soul, produces the new impressions of desire and aversion, hope and fear, which may properly be called impressions of reflexion, because derived from it. These again are copied by the memory and imagination, and become ideas; which perhaps in their turn give rise to other impressions and ideas. So that the impressions of reflexion are only antecedent to their correspondent ideas; but posterior to those of sensation, and deriv'd from them. (THN 7)

The first two distinctions are thus distinctions within the class of perceptions, while the third is a further distinction within the subclass of impressions. The fourth involves a distinction within the subclass of ideas—it occurs in a section entitled "Of the ideas of the memory and imagination" (THN I.i.3)—but Hume presents it as a distinction between two idea-forming faculties, memory and imagination:

We find by experience, that when any impression has been present with the mind, it again makes its appearance there as an idea; and this it may do after two different ways: either when in its new appearance it retains a considerable degree of its first vivacity, and is somewhat intermediate betwixt an impression and an idea; or when it intirely loses that vivacity, and is a perfect idea. The faculty, by which we repeat our impressions in the first manner, is called the MEMORY, and the other the IMAGINATION. (THN 8–9)

Questions may be raised about each of these four distinctions. First, no sooner does Hume draw the impression/idea distinction in terms of differing degrees of force and liveliness than he goes on to remark:

The common degrees of these are easily distinguished; tho' it is not impossible but in particular instances they may very nearly approach to each other. Thus in sleep, in a fever, in madness, or in any very violent emotions of soul, our ideas may approach to our impressions: As on the other hand it sometimes happens, that our impressions are so faint and low, that we cannot distinguish them from our ideas. But notwithstanding this near resemblance in a few instances, they are in general so very different, that no-one can make a scruple to rank them under distinct heads, and assign to each a peculiar name to mark the difference. (THN 2)

But if the difference between impressions and ideas consists only in degree of force and liveliness (which he also calls "vivacity" or, in the first *Enquiry*, "force and vivacity"), why does he write of ideas that *approach* to impressions in this regard and of impressions that cannot be *distinguished* from ideas? Why do not ideas that approach to impressions in force and liveliness simply become impressions, and why do not impressions that cannot be distinguished from ideas thereby become ideas? Second, how does Hume's example of the color, taste, and smell of an apple as simple perceptions square with the apple's spatial complexity and his own later discussion of sensory *minima* in *Treatise* I.ii and I.iv.5? Is he concerned primarily with conceptual simplicity or with perceptual simplicity—or does he simply confuse the two? Third, why does Hume say that impressions of sensation arise "from unknown causes," when the very term 'impressions of sensation' suggests that their cause is known to lie in the physical processes of sense experience?

I will try to answer each of these questions in the course of this book.[1] For the present, however, let us turn our attention to the fourth distinction and, in particular, to the second faculty that Hume distinguishes, that of the imagination. It appears, from the variety of contexts in which he refers to it and the variety of functions that he ascribes to it, that the imagination plays a major role in his philosophy. Yet his remarks about it have puzzled many readers, in at least three different ways.

First, in his original presentation of the impression/idea distinction, Hume treats the having of ideas as essential to, if not actually identical with, *thinking*. Yet in drawing the memory/imagination distinction, he goes on to imply that the only ways of having ideas—and hence, presumably, of thinking—are through memory and imagination. The term 'imagination', however, ordinarily suggests feigning, illusion, or mere supposition. How then can he maintain that all human thoughts beyond the bare recollections of memory—thus presumably including those expressed in the *Treatise* and the first *Enquiry*—are a matter of mere *imagination*?

Second, Hume confesses rather casually in a footnote midway through Book I of the *Treatise* that he actually uses the term 'imagination' in two different senses:

> When I oppose the imagination to the memory, I mean the faculty, by which we form our fainter ideas. When I oppose it to reason, I mean the same faculty, excluding only our demonstrative and probable reasonings. When I oppose it to neither, 'tis indifferent whether it be taken in the larger or more limited sense, or at least the context will sufficiently explain the meaning. (THN 117n)

Why should imagination be opposed to *memory* in one sense and to *reason* in another, and how are these two senses related to each other? Norman Kemp Smith, noting Hume's reference elsewhere (THN 265) to "imagination, or the vivacity of our ideas," suggests that the first sense of 'imagination' is concerned with feigning and the voluntary combination and separation of ideas, and hence with ideas insofar as they are *faint*, while the second sense is concerned with ideas insofar as they have *force and liveliness* (indeed, Kemp Smith suggests that the imagination in this second sense simply is vivacity of conception). Thus, Kemp Smith concludes that the two senses are "almost directly opposite [in] meaning," agreeing "only in one respect, namely, that in both the imagination has to be contrasted with reason."[2] Yet Hume says not that the two senses are opposite in meaning but that, with one exclusion, both senses apply to the same faculty, and he maintains that only the second sense is to be contrasted with reason.

Third, at *Treatise* I.iii.6, Hume opposes imagination to "the understanding"—the faculty that constitutes the primary topic of both Book I of the *Treatise* and the first *Enquiry*—when he asks "whether experience produces the idea of an object [which we call cause or effect] by means of the understanding or of the imagination" (THN 88). Yet near the end of Book I, he claims, in contrast, that the "memory, senses, and understanding are, therefore, all of them founded on the imagination, or the vivacity of ideas" (THN 265), and he then goes on to write of "the understanding, that is, . . . the general and more establish'd properties of the imagination" (THN 267). How can the understanding be opposed to the imagination while at the same time being founded on it and even consisting in certain properties of it?

These puzzles, in turn, raise several larger questions. Does Hume have any consistent conception of the imagination at all, and if so, what is it? In what relation does he think the imagination stands to memory, reason, and the understanding? And what are the consequences, if any, of his views about the imagination for the nature of his philosophy? In the first section of this chapter, I prepare to answer these questions by examining the role of imagination in several of Hume's most notable immediate philosophical predecessors. In the second section, I set out Hume's own conception of the imagination, outline his reasons for holding that memory and imagination are the only idea-forming faculties, and explain the basis of his confidence in those reasons. In the third section, I describe the relation of the faculty of imagination to the faculties of memory, reason, and understanding in Hume's cognitive psychology and, in doing so, seek to resolve the three puzzles just described. In the fourth section, I explore the role of Hume's theory of the imagination in his philosophy and discuss the significance of that theory for the common characterization of Locke, Berkeley, and Hume as "empiricists."

Imagination and Intellect in Early Modern Philosophy

Imagination and Intellect in Descartes

Hume uses the term 'idea' more narrowly than do his immediate predecessors. He uses the term 'perception' as his most general term for mental objects, using it to denote both (i) the vivid experiential contents that he calls impressions, and (ii) the representations occurring in thought that he calls ideas. Descartes, in contrast—like Spinoza, Leibniz, Locke, Berkeley, and most other early modern philosophers influenced by him—uses the term 'idea' as his most general term for mental objects, thereby including not only what Hume calls ideas but also what Hume calls impressions. Accordingly, in Descartes's usage, sensation is itself a faculty of forming ideas.

In addition to sensation, however, Descartes distinguishes two further faculties of forming representations, faculties whose representations are not sensations. These further representational faculties are (i) the *imagination*, whose representations are, in a broad sense, "imagistic" ideas (visual, auditory, gustatory, tactile, etc.) derived from the contents of sensations, and (ii) the *intellect*, a higher faculty whose representations are radically nonimagistic ideas. Descartes introduces this distinction near the end of Meditation II, in the course of his famous discussion of a piece of wax. There he asserts that he can *conceive* the substance that underlies the wax's changing properties by forming an intellectual (or "intelligible") idea of it even though he cannot *imagine* (form an imagistic idea of) it. He concludes that there is no cause for worry in the fact (noted earlier in Meditation II) that he cannot imagine the mind as an unextended thinking thing. He further elaborates the distinction at the beginning of Meditation VI:

> I remark in the first place the difference that exists between the imagination and pure intellection. For example, when I imagine a triangle, I do not conceive it only as a figure comprehended by three lines, but I also apprehend these three lines as present by the power and inward vision of my mind, and this is what I call imagining. But if I desire to think of a chiliagon, I certainly conceive truly that it is a figure composed of a thousand sides, just as easily as I conceive of a triangle that it is a figure of three sides only; but I cannot in any way imagine the thousand sides of a chiliagon, nor do I, so to speak, regard them as present [with the eye of my mind]. And although in accordance with the habit I have formed of always employing the aid of my imagination when I think of corporeal things, it may happen that in imagining a chiliagon, I confusedly represent to myself some figure, yet it is very evident that this figure is not a chiliagon, since it in no way differs from that which I represent to myself when I think of a myriagon or any other many-sided figure; nor does it serve my purpose in discovering the properties which go to form the distinction between a chiliagon and other polygons. But if the question turns upon a pentagon, it is quite true that I can conceive its figure as well as that of a chiliagon without the help of my imagination; but I can also imagine it by applying the attention of my mind to each of its five sides, and at the same time to the space which they enclose. And thus I clearly recognize that I have need of a particular effort of mind in order to effect the act of imagination, such as I do not require in order to understand, and this particular effort of mind clearly manifests the difference which exists between imagination and pure intellection. (MFP VI; see also DCB §41)

As he makes clear throughout his writings, many things—including God, infinity, substance, relations, mind, and even extension-in-general (as opposed to particular shapes or extended things), in addition to large numbers—can only be conceived by the intellect and not properly imagined.

Imagination and Intellect in Spinoza

Although he uses the term 'imagination' more broadly than Descartes does, to include not only what Descartes calls "imagination" but also what Descartes calls "sensation," Spinoza draws an otherwise similar distinction between ideas of imagination and ideas of intellect—and he makes it even more central to his philosophy. His early work *Tractatus de Intellectus Emendatione (Treatise on the Emendation of the Intellect)* has as its goals the establishment of the distinction between the intellect and the imagination and the discovery of the proper method for strengthening the former. There he writes:

[W]e have distinguished between a true idea and other perceptions, and shown that the fictitious, the false, and the other ideas have their origin in the imagination, i.e., in certain sensations that are fortuitous, and (as it were) disconnected; since they do not arise from the very power of the mind, but from external causes, as the body (whether waking or dreaming) receives various motions. . . .

Nor will we wonder why we understand certain things that do not fall in any way under the imagination, why there are some things in the imagination which are completely opposed to the intellect, and finally why there are others that agree with the intellect; for we know that those activities by which imaginations are produced happen according to other laws, wholly different from the laws of the intellect, and that in imagination the soul only has the nature of something acted on.

From this it is also established how easily they fall into great errors, who have not accurately distinguished between imagination and intellection. Such errors as: that extension must be in a place, that it must be finite, that its parts must be really distinguished from one another, that it is the first and only foundation of all things, that it occupies more space at one time than at another, and many other things of the same kind, all of which are completely opposed to the truth. . . . (TIE §§84–87)

Again in his *Ethics*, Spinoza discusses imagination and its physiological correlate in detail, defining imagination as follows: "[T]o retain the customary words, the affections of the human Body whose ideas present external bodies as present to us, we shall call images of things, even if they do not represent the external figures of things. And when the Mind regards bodies in this way, we shall say that it imagines" (E 2p17s).

He goes on in the *Ethics* (2p40s) to identify imagination with the "first," or lowest, kind of knowledge, and to identify intellect with the mind's ability to understand adequately, without reliance on images. Whereas the primary cause of ideas of imagination is always ultimately external, the mind's own intellectual power is the adequate cause of ideas of intellect. Indeed, for Spinoza, the intellect is the only part of the mind that is eternal, and to develop the intellect so as to lessen one's dependence on the imagination is an essential aspect of a human being's highest good.

Imagination and Intellect in Leibniz

Leibniz, too, adopts a version of the intellect/imagination distinction. He writes:

[T]he mathematical sciences would not be demonstrative but would consist of a simple induction or observation which could never assure us of the perfect generality of the truths found in it, if something higher, which only the intellect can provide, did not come to the aid of *imagination* and *sense*.

There are thus three levels of concepts: those which are *sensible* only, . . . those which are sensible and intelligible, . . . and those which are *intelligible only*. (ISM 891–892)

Moreover, in the *New Essays on Human Understanding*, written in response to Locke's *An Essay concerning Human Understanding*, Leibniz criticizes Locke for failing to distinguish between "images" on the one hand and "Being, Unity, Substance, Duration, Change, Action, Perception, Pleasure, and hosts of other objects of our intellectual ideas" on the other (NE 51). In particular, he asserts that Locke cannot account for our knowledge of necessary truths:

> Intellectual ideas, from which necessary truths arise, do not come from the senses . . . the ideas that come from the senses are confused . . . whereas intellectual ideas, and the truths depending on them, are distinct. (NE 81)

> [O]ur certainty regarding universal and eternal truths is grounded in the ideas themselves, independently of the senses, just as pure ideas, ideas of the intellect—e.g. those of *being, one, same* etc.—are also independent of the senses. . . . That is the distinction which ought to be drawn. (NE 392)

Imagination and Intellect in Locke

Leibniz is correct to observe that Locke does not distinguish intellect as a higher, nonimagistic representational faculty. Although he is unquestionably well familiar with the Cartesian intellect/imagination distinction, Locke employs the term 'intellect' only once in his published writings, and he does so then not in the technical Cartesian sense but simply as a synonym for human cognitive faculties in general.[3] In contrast, he often uses the term 'imagination' to designate a representational faculty, and he never mentions any representational faculties other than sensation, reflection, memory, and imagination.

Even without these frequent references to imagination, however, it would be clear that Lockean ideas are far more like Cartesian "ideas of imagination" than they are like Cartesian "ideas of intellect." With the exception of what he calls "ideas of reflection"—those derived from introspection on the mind's own operations—all Lockean ideas are originally derived from the senses, which, as we have seen, Descartes, Spinoza, and Leibniz all regard as an unsuitable source for ideas of pure intellect. Leibniz himself holds out some small rhetorical hope that Locke, in granting "reflection" as a source of ideas, is tacitly allowing intellect after all (NE 51). But Locke simply construes reflection as a kind of inner sensation that "though it be not Sense, as having nothing to do with external Objects; yet it is very like it, and might properly enough be call'd internal Sense" (ECHU II.i.4). Many "ideas of reflection," in fact, are also ideas of sensation as well, according to Locke; that is, they can be derived from either source. Indeed, of the many ideas that Locke classifies as "simple ideas," only two—those of "perception" and "willing"—are assigned to reflection alone.

Are all Lockean ideas then simply mental images of various kinds? The answer to this question depends largely on whether a representation must be fully determinate in order to be classified as an image. Certainly not all Lockean ideas are completely determinate in the ways in which the representations occurring in full-fledged sensory experiences are determinate. The process of abstraction, according to Locke, separates ideas that do not and in some cases even cannot occur separately in experience. It yields not only such moderately abstract ideas as "triangle" and "man" but also such extremely abstract or general ideas as "unity" and "existence" (ECHU III.iii). But a conception of abstraction as a process that removes some of the content from ideas of imagination and leaves behind less determinate ideas of imagination is not unfamiliar to Locke's predecessors and contemporaries. Descartes's own reference to the lack of any difference between his image of a chiliagon and his image of a myriagon naturally suggests that interpretation. And Spinoza claims quite explicitly that images need not be as determinate as actual sensory experiences. In his view, imagination can produce by "abstraction"—conceived as a process in which determinacy is lost through the combination and conflation of images—ideas of imagination as indeterminate even as that of "Being in general" (E 2p40s1). Whether we use the term 'image' or not, the relative closeness of Lockean ideas to ideas of Cartesian imagination, and their relative distance from ideas of Cartesian intellect, is indicated in Locke's description of them near the beginning of Book II of his *Essay*:

> [T]he mind is fitted to receive the Impressions made on it; either, through the *Senses*, by outward Objects; or by its own Operations, when it *reflects* on them. . . . All those sublime Thoughts, which towre above the Clouds, and reach as high as Heaven it self, take their Rise and Footing here: In all that great Extent wherein the mind wanders, in those remote Speculations, it may seem to be elevated with, it stirs not one jot beyond those *Ideas*, which *Sense* or *Reflection*, have offered for its Contemplation. . . . These *simple Ideas*, when offered to the mind, *the Understanding can* no more refuse to have, nor alter, when they are imprinted, nor blot them out, and make new ones in it self, than a mirror can refuse, alter, or obliterate the Images or *Ideas*, which, the Objects set before it, do therein produce. (ECHU II.i.24–25)

The remainder of Book II of Locke's *Essay* consists largely of chapters devoted to explaining the origin, in experiential terms suitable to the imagination, of one after another of Descartes's most important examples of ideas of intellect. Locke deploys an impressive variety of strategies for this purpose. Part of the reason for his emphasis on the distinction between simple and complex ideas, for example, is to permit the derivation of complex ideas of unperceived things from the combination or variation of previously experienced simple ideas; his most ambitious use of this strategy is in his account of the idea of God (ECHU II.xxiii.32). In several other cases, he provides a faculty whose operation on Lockean ideas allows the mind to perform tasks that would otherwise have to be performed by ideas of Cartesian intellect. The faculty of "comparing," for example, allows the mind to use *related ideas* as *ideas of relations* (ECHU II.xi). The faculty of abstraction, already mentioned, removes some specific content from sensory or reflective ideas so as to provide us with general ideas, including such general ideas as those of extension and thought (ECHU II.xi). (Descartes regards the ideas of extension and thought as intellectual because to him they clearly represent susceptibility to infinitely many specific "modifications" or determinations that cannot all be jointly "imagined.") In another case, that of "infinity," Locke simply denies that we have any positive idea as powerful as the one Descartes describes. Although Locke grants that we have an idea of the infinity of number, space, and time—that is, an idea of the absence of any limitation on their continuation—he denies that we have any positive idea of an infinite number, an infinite space, or an infinite time (ECHU II.xvii). The ideas of "causal power" and "unity," in contrast, he claims to find ubiquitous within experience (ECHU II.xxi). He seeks to obviate the need for intellectual ideas of large finite numbers that cannot be distinctly imagined—such as the number of sides in

Descartes's chiliagon—by attributing the *apparent* distinctness of the ideas to the *genuine* distinctness of the words used in reckoning numbers (ECHU II.xvi). The most difficult case for Locke is the idea of "substance-in-general" as a substratum underlying the properties of things. He does not deny the existence of such an idea, and at one early point he even allows, in apparent contradiction to his later general thesis, that it is derived from neither sensation nor reflection (ECHU I.iv.18). However, he also consistently disparages it as "unintelligible," "confused," "obscure," "relative," and lacking in any positive content, suggesting that we do not directly conceive substance-in-general itself, but only the kind of role we wish it to play. Thus, Locke in effect denies the existence of the intellect, as Descartes, Spinoza, and Leibniz describe that faculty, and he seeks instead to account for all human cognitive functions in terms of operations involving a single representational faculty that is very much like what they call the imagination.

Imagination and Intellect in Berkeley

The imagination plays a central and even more explicitly declared role in Berkeley's account of the mind. The imagination consists, he asserts, of all ideas that are not as "strong, lively, and distinct" as those occurring in sensory experience itself (PHK §30). The ideas of the imagination "copy and represent" those of sense (PHK §33), and—as his attack on Locke's theory of abstract ideas makes abundantly clear—they must all be fully determinate images, although they may be given a general application by the mind's selective attention. In contrast, intellect generally appears to play no role in Berkeley's account of cognitive processes. This elimination of intellect was noticed, and complained of, as early as a French review of Berkeley's first published work, *An Essay towards a New Theory of Vision*, in 1711. Berkeley responds noncommittally to that criticism in a letter to Jean LeClerc, writing that if there were a faculty of intellect distinct from the imagination, it would be concerned exclusively with spiritual objects. A similar comment occurs in his *Three Dialogues between Hylas and Philonous*, where, in the course of a discussion of abstraction and extension, Hylas asks, "But what say you to *pure intellect*? May not abstracted ideas be framed by that faculty?" To this Philonous, representing Berkeley, replies: "Since I cannot frame abstract ideas at all, it is plain, I cannot frame them by the help of *pure intellect* whatsoever faculty you understand by those words. Besides—not to inquire into the nature of pure intellect and its spiritual objects, as *virtue, reason, God*, or the like—thus much seems manifest, that sensible things are only to be perceived by sense, or represented by the imagination" (TDHP II.193–194).

In *De Motu*, published in 1721 and written in hopes of winning a prize offered by the Paris Academy of Sciences, Berkeley is somewhat more conciliatory toward the Cartesians, allowing that "pure intellect . . . knows nothing of absolute space . . . (but) is concerned only with spiritual and inextended things, such as our minds, their states, passions, virtues, and such like" (DM §53). In his earlier notebooks, in contrast, he writes more bluntly, "Pure intellect I understand not" (PC §810).

In fact, Berkeley sees no need at all for intellect as a faculty concerned with

ideas. The only question for him is whether the term 'intellect' should be adopted
to denote the mind's ability to have what he calls "notions" of minds and their own
activities—neither of which, he claims, can be represented by ideas. Although such
a terminological policy would clearly be politic in writing for Cartesian audiences,
Berkeley seems generally reticent to adopt it, and for good reason. The term 'intellect' is widely understood by his contemporaries to denote a representational faculty distinct from the imagination. But as Daniel Flage has convincingly argued
(Flage, 1987, chap. 5), notions are not really representations for Berkeley at all, and
thus they are not the products of any representational faculty. Rather, for Berkeley,
to speak of "notions" is simply to describe the fact that we can refer to minds and
volitions as a result of our direct, unmediated experience of ourselves and our activity. Though dissenting from Locke on many points concerning the mind and its
cognitive operations, Berkeley thus follows Locke in the rejection of intellect as a
separate representational faculty.

An Argument against the Intellect

The Argument against the Intellect Outlined

Hume defines the *imagination* as a "faculty by which we repeat our impressions" in
the form of ideas having less force and liveliness (THN 8). As this definition makes
clear, he follows his predecessors in regarding the imagination as a representational
faculty whose representations are images derived from sensory and/or reflective
experience. He differs from their common usage only in explicitly distinguishing
memory of past events as a separate representational faculty, rather than subsuming
it as a function of the imagination.

Hume follows the example of Locke and Berkeley, both in rejecting the distinction of intellect and imagination as two separate representational faculties and in
seeking to account for human cognitive functioning in terms of representational
faculties resembling the Cartesian imagination. Like Berkeley, he usually assumes
the correctness of this methodology as a given in his writing. He does, however,
fairly clearly indicate his reasons for rejecting the Cartesian intellect in a passage
near the beginning of *Treatise* I.iii ("Of knowledge and probability"):

> 'Tis usual with mathematicians, to pretend, that those ideas, which are their objects,
> are of so refin'd and spiritual a nature, that they fall not under the conception of the
> fancy [i.e., the imagination], but must be comprehended by a pure and intellectual
> view, of which the superior faculties of the soul are alone capable. The same notion
> runs thro' most parts of philosophy, and is principally made use of to explain our
> abstract ideas, and to shew how we can form an idea of a triangle, for instance, which
> shall neither be an isosceles nor scalenum, nor be confin'd to any particular length and
> proportion of sides. 'Tis easy to see, why philosophers are so fond of this notion of some
> spiritual and refined perceptions; since by that means they cover many of their absurdi-
> ties, and may refuse to submit to the decision of clear ideas, by appealing to such as are
> obscure and uncertain. But to destroy this artifice, we need but reflect on that principle
> so oft insisted on, *that all our ideas are copy'd from our impressions*. For from thence we

may immediately conclude, that since all impressions are clear and precise, the ideas, which are copy'd from them, must be of the same nature, and can never, but from our fault, contain any thing so dark and intricate. An idea is by its very nature weaker and fainter than an impression; but being in every other respect the same, cannot imply any very great mystery. (THN 72)

This argument against the existence of the intellect may be outlined as follows:

1. [A]ll our ideas are copy'd from our impressions.
2. All impressions are clear and precise.
3. The ideas . . . must be of the same nature [as impressions], and can never, but from our fault, contain anything . . . dark and intricate. (from 1 and 2)
4. [There are no] spiritual and refined perceptions . . . [that] . . . must be comprehended by a pure and intellectual view, of which the superior faculties of the soul are alone capable. (from 3)

Thus, any feature of our ideas that makes them *seem* to be in need of a superior intellectual faculty—that is, a representational faculty superior to the imagination—is in reality the result of our own carelessness or fault in dealing with representations that are naturally similar to impressions. It is because of Hume's confidence in this conclusion—equivalent to the rejection of the Cartesian intellect—that he can feel free to make an exhaustive distinction of idea-forming faculties into *memory* and *imagination*, faculties whose representations differ *not* in fundamental character or content but only in causal history and in degree of "force and liveliness" or "vivacity."

The Basis of Hume's Confidence

Why is Hume so confident of the soundness of this argument? Its crucial premise is clearly the initial one, that all our ideas are "copy'd from our impressions." This premise, as stated, is a version of one of Hume's primary principles, often called the Copy Principle. It involves both a Causal Thesis, that all ideas are *derived* from impressions, and a Resemblance Thesis, that all ideas *resemble* impressions. The present argument against the existence of the intellect, however, actually relies only on the Resemblance Thesis. Hume further specifies this thesis (using the simple/complex distinction) and provides his defense of it within the first few pages of the *Treatise*:

After the most accurate examination of which I am capable, I venture to affirm, that the rule here holds without any exception, and that every simple idea has a simple impression, which resembles it; and every simple impression a correspondent idea. That idea of red, which we form in the dark, and that impression, which strikes our eyes in sun-shine, differ only in degree, not in nature. That the case is the same with all our simple impressions and ideas, 'tis impossible to prove by a particular enumeration of them. Everyone may satisfy himself in this point by running over as many as he pleases. But if any one should deny this universal resemblance, I know no way of convincing him, but by desiring him to shew a simple idea that has not a correspondent impression. If he does not answer this challenge, as 'tis certain he cannot, we may from his silence and our own observation establish our conclusion. (THN 3–4)

Thus, there may be complex ideas that do not have exactly resembling complex impressions (because the complex idea is composed of simpler ideas that have been conjoined by the mind). There may also be complex impressions that do not have exactly resembling complex ideas (because we may never happen to recall to mind the precise complex arrangement of simpler elements). Nevertheless, all *simple* ideas resemble *simple* impressions, and the simple *elements* of complex ideas exactly resemble the simple *elements* of complex impressions.

But why, in turn, is Hume so confident that his bold challenge to find counterexamples that would undermine the Resemblance Thesis cannot be met? Perhaps he is predisposed to think that the only natural kind of representation involves resemblance.[4] But this predisposition can hardly be sufficient without further defense, for we have already seen that Descartes, Spinoza, and Leibniz (among many others) would be not only willing but eager to provide counterexamples to it. They would argue that a whole range of ideas of *intellect*, in particular, do not resemble, and do not have simple constituents that resemble, what Hume calls "impressions."

One reason for Hume's confidence must surely lie in his belief that each of the individual ideas that Descartes and others took to be examples of ideas of intellect can be explained satisfactorily in terms of the imagination. He recognizes that Locke sought to provide nonintellectual origins for these ideas; Hume claims, in fact, that his own Copy Principle constitutes the real content of Locke's more obscurely formulated denial of innate ideas (EHU §17). In some cases—for example, the idea of God (EHU §14)—Hume seems content with Locke's explanations of these alleged ideas of intellect. In other cases, however, such as the ideas of causation and substance, Hume will have other or further explanations to give (as we will see in later chapters). To some extent, then, his argument against the intellect early in the *Treatise* depends on his readers' acceptance of the general success of Locke's attempt to explain the origins of problematic ideas in Book II of the *Essay*, but to some extent it also depends on the alternative explanations of particular ideas that Hume himself gives only later in the *Treatise* and the first *Enquiry*.

We can nonetheless distinguish two further reasons for Hume's confidence that no damaging counterexamples to the Resemblance Thesis will be found. Both of them can be seen in the passage, cited previously, in which Hume offers his argument against the existence of the Cartesian intellect (THN 72).

When philosophers follow the mathematicians in claiming to have ideas of intellect, they are in fact, according to Hume, generally using this claim as an "artifice" to "cover many of their absurdities." If philosophers really did have ideas of a "spiritual and refined" nature, he implies, we should expect to see better results from the alleged employment of those ideas. Instead, however, we find the situation that Hume has described in the Introduction to the *Treatise*:

> Principles taken upon trust, consequences lamely deduced from them, want of coherence in the parts, and of evidence in the whole, these are every where to be met with in the systems of the most eminent philosophers, and seem to have drawn disgrace upon philosophy itself.
>
> Nor is there requir'd such profound knowledge to discover the present imperfect condition of the sciences, but even the rabble without doors may judge from the noise and clamour, which they hear, that all goes not well within. There is nothing which is

not the subject of debate, and in which men of learning are not of contrary opinions. The most trivial question escapes not our controversy, and in the most momentous we are not able to give any certain decision. Disputes are multiplied, as if every thing was uncertain; and these disputes are managed with the greatest warmth, as if every thing was certain. Amidst all this bustle 'tis not reason, which carries the prize, but eloquence; and no man needs ever despair of gaining proselytes to the most extravagant hypothesis, who has art enough to represent it in any favourable colours. (THN xiii–xiv)

Those philosophers whose hypotheses are the most "extravagant" and who are most in conflict with one another, Hume might be tempted to add, are precisely those who claim to be most guided by intellect. This provides a reason to doubt the existence of counterexamples to the Resemblance Thesis.

One further reason is evident in Hume's reference to "mathematicians": he believes that his own theory of abstract ideas explains the real cognitive successes that the theory of intellection was originally intended to explain, but that it does so without the need to postulate a further representational faculty. He suggests that mathematicians—unlike philosophers—do often fully establish true and valuable results when they claim to employ ideas of intellect. Because they do not understand the true nature of abstract ideas, however, they are mistaken about the nature of the representational faculty that accounts for their mathematical success. Hume believes that he has shown how this serious mistake can be avoided.

As we have seen, Locke had already tried to explain all of the generality of thought without appeal to general ideas of intellect. He did so by appealing instead to the process of abstraction that occurs within the imagination—a process that Descartes and his followers had taken to explain, at most, the generality of *inadequate* thought. According to Locke's theory, all abstract or general ideas derive their generality from their own representational indeterminacy. This indeterminacy is the result of separating or abstracting these ideas from some or all of the other ideas that sometimes or always accompany them in what Locke calls "real existence" (ECHU II.xi.9). Thus, for him, the abstract idea of a triangle is derived from ideas of sensation but is simply indeterminate with respect to the proportion of the sides or angles; similarly, the abstract idea of a human being is simply indeterminate with respect to eye color, presence or absence of hair, and facial details.

Hume, however, rejects Locke's appeal to indeterminate representations on several grounds, as he indicates in *Treatise* I.i.7 ("Of abstract ideas"). One of his arguments relies on the Copy Principle cited previously, which states that "all ideas are deriv'd from impressions, and are nothing but copies and representations of them." Hume infers from this principle that any content that is possible for ideas is also possible for impressions. Now, it is widely granted, according to Hume, that it is contradictory to suppose *impressions* existing without being determined in their degrees of quality and quantity. Hence, he argues, it must also be granted (contrary to Locke) that *ideas* cannot so exist either.

Hume's second argument for rejecting indeterminate representations relies on the inverse of the second of his two primary principles, a principle sometimes called the Separability Principle. The Separability Principle itself states that "whatever objects are different are distinguishable, and . . . whatever objects are distinguishable are separable by the thought and imagination (THN 18); its inverse states that "whatever objects are separable are also distinguishable, and that whatever objects are distinguishable are also different" (THN 18). It follows from the inverse of the Separability Principle that, if a line can be *separated* from any length—as occurs in a Lockean abstract idea of a line—then a line and its length are also *distinguishable*, and hence *different*. But Hume thinks it absurd that a line and its length should be two different objects, which provides a reductio ad absurdum of Locke's theory.

Hume's third argument for rejecting indeterminate representations is derived from what I will call his Conceivability Criterion of Possibility, namely, that "nothing of which we can form a clear and distinct idea is absurd and impossible" (THN 19–20). Since indeterminate objects are absurd and impossible, it follows that we cannot form a clear and distinct idea of any such object. But Hume claims that "to form the idea of an object, and to form an idea simply is the same thing," inasmuch as ideas can always serve to represent what they resemble. Hence, since it is impossible to form an idea *of* "an object, that is possest of quantity and quality, and yet is possest of no precise degree of either," it follows that there is an equal impossibility of forming an *idea* that is itself indeterminate in these respects. Or, to put the same argument in the form of a reductio ad absurdum: if Locke were correct in holding that we could form indeterminate *ideas*, we would be able to use those ideas to form a clear conception of indeterminate *objects*, and hence by the Conceivability Criterion of Possibility, we would be required to reach the absurd conclusion that real but indeterminate objects are possible.

Accordingly, Hume rejects Locke's theory of abstract ideas, in favor of a theory according to which "all general ideas are nothing but particular ones, annexed to a certain term, which gives them a more extensive signification" (THN 17). Upon noticing a resemblance among objects, Hume claims, we apply a single term to them all, notwithstanding their differences. This term is directly associated with the determinate idea of a particular instance. That determinate idea nevertheless achieves a general *signification*—and hence *serves as* an abstract idea—because the term also revives the "custom" or disposition to call up ideas of other particular instances. I will call this appropriate set of ideas of particular instances associated with a general term its "revival set." We are especially disposed to call up ideas of counterexamples (if we can find them) to claims that employ the term whenever we encounter such claims in the course of reasoning. Thus, for example, noticing a certain resemblance among a number of shapes, one calls them all "triangles." A particular occurrence of this term brings to mind the idea of a particular triangle, say an equilateral triangle, and *revives a custom* of calling up other ideas of triangles (the revival set) as needed. And if someone claims that all triangles have three sides of equal length, then although one's idea of an equilateral triangle does not itself happen to provide a counterexample, one will quickly find an idea of, say, a right triangle coming to mind, and one will therefore be able to reject the original claim.

We can now see why Hume lavishes such otherwise unexpectedly high praise on Berkeley's theory of general or abstract ideas, going so far as to call it "one of the greatest and most valuable discoveries that has been made of late years in the republic of letters" (THN 17). For Hume regards Berkeley as the first philosopher to propose the theory that "all general ideas are nothing but particular ones . . . [with] . . . a more extensive signification." Hume himself seeks to *explain* this "more extensive signification" by appealing to the ability of a "general term" to "revive a custom" of calling up other resembling ideas, whereas Berkeley's explanation of the phenomenon is a less specific appeal to the intent or will of the thinker. Nevertheless, in Hume's view it was Berkeley who took the crucial first step in showing how generality is achieved through the special employment of determinate images, and thus how the inadequate Lockean theory of abstract or general thought could be replaced. It is Berkeley's theory, filled out with further explanatory detail, that Hume thinks explains how the mind can think thoughts of generality without employing either indeterminate ideas of imagination or "refin'd and spiritual ideas." It thereby corrects Locke without any need to re-admit intellect as a second representational faculty, and it thus constitutes a "great and valuable discovery" in the science of human cognition.

Imagination and Other Cognitive Faculties

We are now in a position to solve the three puzzles about the Humean imagination described at the beginning of this chapter.

The First Puzzle: Imagination and Memory

Why does Hume claim that all ideas except those of memory result from the imagination? Both memory and imagination are representational faculties for Hume; and in declining to identify any other representational faculties, he is intentionally denying the existence of any higher, nonimagistic representational faculty such as the Cartesian intellect. He has, as we have seen, several grounds for this denial, and it is a denial that he shares with both Locke and Berkeley.

Hume could have expressed this denial by asserting that *all* ideas result from the imagination. Descartes, Spinoza, and Leibniz all construe memory—or at least, memory of objects and events that were perceived by sensation—as an operation of the imagination. Berkeley does also, as his broad definition of "imagination" cited previously entails. Hume, however, prefers to construe the imagination more narrowly, by distinguishing memory from it.

One likely reason for this preference is simply that the absence of a more significant intellect/imagination distinction leaves more classificatory room for this lesser distinction. A more positive reason, however, is that he has a relatively detailed theory of the *differences* between imagination and memory. One difference, for Hume, concerns the fashion in which memory and imagination's respective representations are caused: memory ideas are caused, in part, by past occurrences whose content and order have been *preserved*, whereas imaginative ideas are caused, in part, by past occurrences whose content may be *varied* (by division and/or recombination) and whose order may be *changed*. It is, in large measure, this difference in origins that justifies speaking of two different faculties for forming ideas, since there

are otherwise no fundamental differences in the kind of content that these two faculties may yield.

A second difference, for Hume, concerns the representations themselves: ideas
of memory differ from ideas of imagination in having a greater degree of *vivacity*, or
force and liveliness—conceived not as an additional perception or mental content
but rather as a "manner" in which these ideas occur. Ideas of memory are, as we
have seen him indicate, typically intermediate in vivacity between impressions and
other (nonmemory) ideas. However, it is important to realize that, as a practitioner
of the "science of man," he is interested not merely in classifying perceptions but in
identifying and distinguishing cognitive faculties that operate in characteristically
different ways. It is for this reason that the causal history of ideas is at least as important to Hume as their vivacity is in making the imagination/memory distinction. It
is because he is primarily interested in exploring the *cognitive faculties* that characteristically produce perceptions with impressionlike vivacity and idealike vivacity
that he seems so willing at the outset of the *Treatise* (THN 2) to countenance the
possibility of ideas that "very nearly approach to" impressions in vivacity, and of
impressions whose vivacity is so low that they "cannot be distinguished from" ideas.

This vivacity, or force and liveliness, is in turn the central unifying explanatory
property to which Hume's cognitive science appeals, a property parallel in some
ways (as the choice of terms suggests) to "force" in physics or mechanics. He argues
in *Treatise* I.iii and *Enquiry* V.ii that the presence of greater vivacity—though presumably still in an amount less than that provided by memory—constitutes the difference between beliefs, on the one hand, and ideas merely entertained, on the
other. And hence, he argues, the principles of the communication of force and
vivacity among perceptions serve to explain causal inference and various other phenomena involving variations in belief. Because belief is thus a feature of the manner or way in which we form nonmemory ideas, for Hume, belief is itself a feature
or operation of the imagination. The even greater force and vivacity of impressions
and memories also serves to explain why we are generally so certain of the truth of
what they represent, just as the (more limited) force and vivacity of certain ideas in
the imagination explains why we confidently accept *them* as true representations.

Thus, when Hume asserts that memory and imagination are the only idea-forming faculties, he is not making an epistemological claim to the effect that any
thoughts beyond our own recollections are in some way feigned, illusory, or merely
supposed. Rather, he is proposing, as a cognitive psychologist, a classification of
representational faculties that rejects the Cartesian postulation of a higher, nonimagistic faculty of intellect. This is the resolution of the first puzzle.

The Second Puzzle: Imagination and Reason

Why does Hume distinguish two senses of 'imagination', one opposed to memory
and the other opposed to reason? The terms 'intellect' and 'reason' are nowadays
often used interchangeably. But when Locke (in effect) rejects the existence of
Cartesian intellect, he does not thereby reject the existence of *reason*. "Reason,"
according to Locke, is the faculty of the "discovering and finding out of Proofs,"
"laying them in a clear and fit Order," "perceiving their Connexion," and "making

a right conclusion" (ECHU IV.xvii.3). Reason is thus a faculty of finding, presenting, appreciating, and being moved to belief by arguments. Whereas intellect, in
the Cartesian sense, is a *representational* faculty, reason is an *inferential* faculty.
The question at issue for Locke (as also for Berkeley) is not, of course, whether reasoning occurs, but rather how and on what kind of representations it operates. For
Descartes, Spinoza, and Leibniz, it operates primarily on representations of intellect—although Leibniz rather grudgingly allows, in the ability of beasts to learn
from experience, a kind of animal "reasoning" that operates on ideas of imagination, and of which humans are also capable (NE 50, 143, 475). For Locke and
Berkeley, of course, reason can only operate on the one kind of representation we
actually have—what Descartes would have considered to be representations of
imagination.

In Book IV of his *Essay*, Locke offers a quite specific account of the nature of
reasoning. While granting Aristotelian syllogism a very limited role in assessing or
ordering the results of reasoning, he rejects it as a model for the reasoning process
as it actually occurs in the human mind. Reasoning, in his view, is a matter of finding intermediate ideas that allow the mind to perceive the certain or probable
"agreement" or "disagreement" between two or more ideas whose agreement or disagreement the mind cannot perceive directly. There are thus two kinds of reasoning, demonstrative and probable:

§1. As Demonstration is the shewing the Agreement or Disagreement of two *Ideas*, by
the intervention of one or more Proofs [intermediate Ideas], which have a constant,
immutable, and visible connexion with another: so *Probability* is nothing but the
appearance of such an Agreement, or Disagreement, by the intervention of Proofs,
whose connexion is not constant and immutable, or at least is not perceived to be so,
but is, or appears for the most part to be so, and is enough to induce the Mind to *judge*
the Proposition to be true, or false, rather than the contrary. (ECHU IV.xv.1)

Similarly for Hume, reason is the faculty of reasoning: of making inferences, or
providing, appreciating, and being moved by arguments. Like Locke, he distinguishes two kinds of reasoning, *demonstrative* and *probable*,[5] distinguished by the
kind of evidence or certainty that they bestow on their conclusions. For Hume, as
for Locke and Berkeley, reasoning is an operation that occurs on the representations of the imagination. His account of reasoning differs from Locke's, however, in
at least two crucial respects. First, Humean reason need not involve the use of *intermediate ideas* (THN 96–97n). Second, Hume holds that the conviction or belief
typically produced by reason is nothing but the *vivacity* of the idea that constitutes
the conclusion, and so it is itself a particular *manner* of having ideas of imagination. Thus, for Hume, far more directly than for Locke or Berkeley, the inferential
faculty of reason is itself also a feature or aspect of the representational faculty of
imagination.

However, Hume recognizes that there are a large number of other operations or
aspects of the imagination in addition to argument or inference that can also serve to
augment force and liveliness—and hence to augment belief—in ideas of imagination. For example, the supposed spatial contiguity to miraculous events that is
involved in religious pilgrimages can enhance one's belief in those events, without

any additional process of argument or inference. The supposed causal relation of a religious relic to a holy person or event can have the same effect. So too, in Hume's view, can sympathy with the conviction of a fervently believing testifier, or the force of repetition involved in the process he sardonically calls "education." Thus, there is a sense in which we can *distinguish* "reason" from the many other aspects of the imagination that can also determine the nature and manner of conception of our ideas. It is these other aspects of the imagination that constitute the second, narrower, sense of 'imagination' that Hume distinguishes in the famous footnote cited at the beginning of this chapter. This second sense is the one in which the imagination is the same (representational) faculty as that whereby we form "our fainter ideas," but "excluding only our demonstrative and probable reasonings." Whereas imagination in the first sense is a faculty that includes *all* the ways and manners of forming nonmemory ideas, imagination in the second sense includes all of these ways *except* argumentation and reasoning. This is the resolution of the second puzzle.

The Third Puzzle: Imagination and Understanding

Why does Hume contrast imagination with understanding, while also insisting that the latter is founded on the former and even consists in its "general and more establish'd properties?" Again it will be helpful to compare his terminology with Locke's. Locke uses the term 'understanding' as the most general term for the faculty of performing cognitive acts, and he regularly contrasts it with the *will*, which is the faculty of volition. He defines the "understanding" as follows:

> The power of Perception is that which we call the *Understanding*. Perception, which we make the act of the Understanding, is of three sorts: 1. The Perception of *Ideas* in our Minds. 2. The Perception of the signification of Signs. 3. The Perception of the Connexion or Repugnancy, Agreement or Disagreement, that there is between any of our *Ideas*. All these are attributed to the *Understanding*, or perceptive Power, though it be the two latter only that use allows us to say we understand. (ECHU II.xxi.5)

Hume, too, treats the understanding as a general faculty of performing cognitive acts, and he also regularly contrasts the understanding with the will. However, he refers to a slightly different distinction of three acts of the understanding, and in doing so, he criticizes the manner in which those acts have been distinguished, arguing that *all* of the acts of the understanding reduce to particular manners of *conceiving* or coming to conceive. In an important footnote worth quoting in full, he writes:

> We may here take occasion to observe a very remarkable error, which being frequently inculcated in the schools, has become a kind of establish'd maxim, and is universally received by all logicians. This error consists in the vulgar division of the acts of the understanding, into *conception, judgment, and reasoning*. Conception is defin'd to be the simple survey of one or more ideas: Judgment to be the separating or uniting of different ideas: Reasoning to be the separating or uniting of different ideas by the interposition of others, which show the relation they bear to each other. But these distinctions and definitions are faulty in very considerable articles. For *first*, 'tis far from being true, that in every judgment, which we form, we unite two different ideas; since in that proposition, *God is*, or indeed any other, which regards existence, the idea of

existence is no distinct idea, which we unite with that of the object, and which is capable of forming a compound idea by the union. *Secondly,* As we can thus form a proposition, which contains only one idea, so we may exert our reason without employing more than two ideas, and without having recourse to a third to serve as a medium betwixt them. We infer a cause immediately from its effect; and this inference is not only a true species of reasoning, but the strongest of all others, and more convincing than when we interpose another idea to connect the two extremes. What we may in general affirm concerning these three acts of the understanding is, that taking them in a proper light, they all resolve themselves into the first, and are nothing but particular ways of conceiving our objects. Whether we consider a single object, or several; whether we dwell on these objects, or run from them to others; and in whatever form or order we survey them, the act of the mind exceeds not a simple conception; and the only remarkable difference, which occurs on this occasion is, when we join belief to the conception, and are perswaded of the truth of what we conceive. This act of the mind has never yet been explain'd by any philosopher; and therefore I am at liberty to propose my hypothesis concerning it; which is, that 'tis only a strong and steady conception of any idea, and such as approaches in some measure to an immediate perception. (THN 96–97n)

Since the acts of the understanding are *all of them* nothing but particular ways of conceiving or coming to conceive, and since conceiving and coming to conceive are, in turn, operations of the imagination, it follows that understanding itself turns out to be a set of operations of the imagination. The "understanding" is not, of course, all of the operations of the imagination, for it does not include the many operations that Hume opposes to reason. The understanding does include, however, those operations that are identified with reason; that is, those belief-enhancing features and operations of the imagination that are "general and more establish'd." Thus, the understanding is an *aspect* of the imagination, in the broad, first sense of 'imagination' in which imagination is opposed to memory. At the same time, the understanding can also be *opposed* to the imagination, in the narrower, second sense in which imagination is opposed to reason, for the imagination in that narrow sense does not include those operations that make up a considerable part of the understanding. This is the resolution of the third puzzle.

Five Kinds of Empiricism

Descartes, Spinoza, and Leibniz, all of whom fundamentally accept the intellect/imagination distinction, have traditionally been classified as "rationalists"; while Locke, Berkeley, and Hume, all of whom fundamentally reject the distinction, have traditionally been classified as "empiricists." What is the relation between the two competing views of human representational faculties, on the one hand, and the traditional "rationalist/empiricist" distinction, on the other? This question is made all the more pertinent by the fact that a number of other important philosophers of the early modern period who are widely associated with rationalism, including Malebranche and Arnauld, also employ the intellect/imagination distinction, while a number of other important philosophers widely associated with empiricism, including Hobbes and Gassendi, do not. As one might expect, the rejection of intellect has a considerable impact on the philosophies of those who make such a rejection, and nowhere is this impact more significant than in the case of Hume. His rejection of intellect bears on at least five different doctrines or tendencies, each of which has often been associated with the somewhat vague classificatory term "empiricism."

Methodological Empiricism

'Methodological empiricism', as I intend the term, denotes a doctrine or attitude concerning the proper relation between observation and theory; namely, that observation should be the main determinant of theory, and that, in cases of apparent conflict, theory should generally be revised to accommodate the interpreted observations, rather than the interpretation of the observations being revised to accommodate the theory. Briefly put, it is the attitude that says, "Don't say how things *must* be, but look and see." Methodological empiricism about *philosophy* (in my sense of that term) is simply the attempt to apply this attitude to the fundamental questions that constitute the subject matter of philosophy.

A thinker may be a methodological empiricist about philosophy without taking a similar attitude toward the relation between observation and theory in all other areas of inquiry. Furthermore, even in application to a single discipline, methodological empiricism is likely to be only a matter of degree: many will be willing to accord some degree of priority to at least some kinds of observations while also according at least some degree of priority to at least some kinds of theories. Moreover, the very theory/observation distinction to which methodological empiricism appeals may be highly problematic in many ways—perhaps especially so in philosophy—and quite possibly problematic to the point of complete untenability. To whatever extent the distinction is problematic, that fact will render equally problematic the attempts of those who accept methodological empiricism to put it into consistent practice.

Granting all of these points, however, it remains evident that, with respect to philosophical inquiry, Descartes, Spinoza, and Leibniz neither are nor seek to be methodological empiricists. Although Descartes aims to throw off the yoke of authority and tradition in order to pursue the truth for himself from an introspective starting point, his resulting four-part method does not emphasize observation in *philosophizing*; Spinoza's *Ethics* contains little essential use of observationally introduced premises; Leibniz's philosophizing is guided primarily by considerations of logic, explanatory strength, coherence, and unity. One need only recall Descartes's doctrine that the mind always thinks, his rejection of the possibility of a vacuum, or his denial of the possibility of thinking matter; Spinoza's deduction that all of Nature is infinitely thinking as well as infinitely extended, his certainty that substance has infinitely many attributes and that individual things are its modes, his denial of contingency, or his proof that everything acts only to preserve its own being; Leibniz's denial of substantial interaction in favor of the doctrine of preestablished harmony, his claim that every substance perceives or mirrors every other, or his affirmation of the ultimately phenomenal nature of extension. Each of these characteristic and prized doctrines is, and is intended by its author to be, a victory of high-level theoretical considerations over the deliverances of "naive" sensory observation.

In self-conscious contrast stands Locke's espousal of what he calls the "Historical, plain Method" of investigation, manifested in his repeated unwillingness to sacrifice or reinterpret what he regards as the results of plain observation for the sake of philosophical theory. Thus he writes: "All I shall say for the Principles I proceed on, is, that I can only appeal to Men's own unprejudiced *Experience* and Observation, whether they are true, or no" (ECHU I.iv.25). One particularly striking example is Locke's rejection of Descartes's claim that the mind always thinks, a claim to which Descartes is committed by his doctrine that thinking is the essential attribute of mind. Locke ridicules this claim as being at odds with human experience. After reporting that he finds himself to pass long periods in sleep without thinking, he chides the Cartesians for thinking otherwise: "[H]e, that would not deceive himself, ought to build his Hypothesis on matter of fact, and make it out by sensible experience, and not presume on matter of fact, because of his Hypothesis, that is, because he supposes it to be so . . ." (ECHU II.i.10). Similar is Locke's dismissal of Descartes's claim that the world must be a plenum—a claim to which Descartes is committed by his doctrine that extension is the essential attribute of material substance, from which it follows that whatever is extended is matter. Locke dismisses Descartes's claim in part by reporting that it is contrary to evident facts of motion (ECHU II.xiii). Anticipating a theoretical objection, he then remarks: "If it be demanded (as usually it is) whether this Space void of Body be Substance or Accident, I shall readily answer, I know not; nor shall be ashamed to own my Ignorance, till they that ask, shew me a clear distinct Idea of Substance" (ECHU II.xiii.17).

Berkeley, too, seeks (perhaps with mixed success) to present himself as a methodological empiricist about philosophy. In the Introduction to the *Principles of Human Knowledge*, for example, Berkeley asserts that his opponents' views are largely the result of a doctrine of abstract ideas that can be refuted by plain observation: "Whether others have this wonderful faculty of abstracting their ideas, they best can tell" (PHK Intr §10). He goes on to remark at the outset of the main body of the work: "Some truths there are so near and obvious to the mind that a man need only open his eyes to see them. Such I take this important truth to be, viz. that . . . all those bodies that compose the mighty frame of the world, have not any subsistence without the mind" (PHK §6). And he insists repeatedly that he is not denying anything the plain man thinks he observes; rather, in denying the existence of "material substance," he claims to be denying only a difficult and incomprehensible theory of philosophers, and to be doing so in a way that allows us to stop being imposed upon by the demands of theorizing in mathematics and physics as well. Nor is this attitude merely a public rhetorical pose, as these typical remarks from his private notebooks (the *Philosophical Commentaries*) indicate:

> I may expect to be supported by those whose minds are not so far overgrown with madness—especially Moralists, Divines, Politicians; in a word, all but Mathematicians and

Natural Philosophers. I mean only the hypothetical gentlemen. Experimental philosophers have nothing whereat to be offended in me. (PC §406)

Mem. To be eternally banishing Metaphysics, &c., and recalling men to Common Sense. (PC §751)

There are men who say there are insensible extensions. There are others who say the wall is not white, the fire is not hot, &c. We Irishmen cannot attain to these truths. (PC §392)

The mathematicians think there are insensible lines. About these they harangue: these cut in a point at all angles: these are divisible ad infinitum. We Irishmen can conceive no such lines. (PC §393)

Hume's own methodological empiricism is expressed in the very subtitle of his first work, *A Treatise of Human Nature: Being an Attempt to Introduce the Experimental Method of Reasoning into Moral Subjects.* He writes in the Introduction to the *Treatise* that "as the science of man is the only solid foundation for the other sciences, so the only solid foundation we can give to this science itself must be laid on experience and observation" (THN xvi). In the *Abstract of a Treatise of Human Nature*, he recommends himself as an author who "promises to draw no conclusions but where he is authorized by experience" and as one who "talks with contempt of hypotheses" (ATHN 646). Moreover, he regards this attitude as constituting a decisive advance over the philosophers of antiquity, whose "moral Philosophy"

> labor'd under the same Inconvenience that has been found in their natural Philosophy, of being entirely Hypothetical, & depending more upon Invention than Experience. Every one consulted his Fancy in erecting Schemes. . . . I believe 'tis a certain Fact that most of the Philosophers who have gone before us, have been overthrown by the Greatness of their Genius, and that little more is required to make a man succeed in this Study than to throw off all Prejudices either for his own Opinions or for those of others. (LDH I.16)[6]

It is clear why the rejection of intellect should provide a justification for methodological empiricism. For the intellect serves as a source of higher concepts capable of determining theory and placing constraints on the interpretation of observations. Each of the characteristic theoretical doctrines mentioned previously—Descartes's doctrines that the mind always thinks, that a vacuum is impossible, and that the mind is immaterial; Spinoza's doctrines that Nature is infinitely thinking and has infinitely many other attributes, that nothing is contingent, and that everything strives to preserve its own existence; and Leibniz's denial of substantial interaction and his doctrines of preestablished harmony, universal perception, and the ultimate unreality of extension—is explicitly derived in part from the alleged content of one or more ideas of intellection: substance, God, mind, extension, essence, or causation. Thus, Leibniz responds revealingly to Locke's attack on the idea of substance-in-general: "[T]his conception of substance, for all its apparent thinness, is less empty and sterile than it is thought to be. Several consequences arise from it; these are of the greatest importance to philosophy, to which they can give an entirely new face. . . . The true sign of a clear and distinct notion is one's having the means for giving *a priori* proofs of many truths about it" (NE 218).

Without ideas of intellect to provide this input, experience and observation seem left to drive theory alone—by default, as it were. When, for example, Locke affirms the possibility of empty space, in the passage cited earlier (ECHU II.xiii.17), he explicitly refuses to be moved by theoretical concern over whether such empty space would be a "substance" or not, precisely on the grounds of the apparent emptiness or lack of content of that idea. At the same time, of course, methodological empiricism may also be cited to support the rejection of intellect, since Locke, Berkeley, and Hume, at least—although not Descartes, Spinoza, or Leibniz— would agree that unbiased observation does or can show that there *is* no such representational faculty.

Conceptual Empiricism

In contrast to methodological empiricism, which is a view about the proper relation between observation and theory, "conceptual empiricism" is a view about concepts, namely, it is the view that the semantic content of thought is always fully derived from things or features of things as they have been encountered in sensory or reflective experience. Seventeenth- and eighteenth-century philosophy—"rationalist" and "empiricist" alike—assumes that the semantic content of thought is a function of the content of ideas. Descartes, Spinoza, and Leibniz, however, all deny conceptual empiricism, offering the concepts of "God" and "infinity," among others, as examples of concepts whose content is not derived from objects of direct experience but rather from the mind's native intellectual power, and are in that sense "innate."

Locke, Berkeley, and Hume, in contrast, effectively commit themselves to conceptual empiricism. Indeed, each declares his allegiance to it at the very beginning of a major work. Locke, for example, begins Book II of the *Essay* by declaring that "the Objects of SENSATION and . . . the Objects of REFLECTION are, to me, the only Originals, from whence all our *Ideas* take their beginnings" (ECHU II.i.4). Berkeley, too, admits no conceptual content that is not derived from objects or features directly encountered in experience. The first words of the main body of his *Principles of Human Knowledge* directly echo Locke: "It is evident to any one who takes a survey of the objects of human knowledge, that they are either ideas actually imprinted on the senses; or else such as are perceived by attending to the passions and the operations of the mind; or lastly, ideas formed by help of memory and imagination—either compounding, dividing, or barely representing those originally perceived in the aforesaid ways" (PHK §1).[7] Similarly, Hume announces his view of the origin of the content of ideas at the very outset of the main body of the *Treatise* in his Copy Principle:

> [A]ll our simple ideas in their first appearance are deriv'd from simple impressions, which are correspondent to them, and which they exactly represent. (THN 4)

The rejection of intellect clearly provides support for conceptual empiricism, as well as for methodological empiricism. To the extent that all of the semantic content of thought is representable in imagistic representations, that content can arguably be derived entirely from objects of sensory or reflective experience. Thus, although the rejection of intellect in favor of imagination does not *entail* that all of the semantic content of thought is derived entirely from objects of experience— since, for example, the content of some images might happen to occur innately—it renders the defense of conceptual empiricism much simpler. At the same time, as we have seen, the rejection of intellect by Locke and Hume depends, in part, on their confidence in the ultimate success of conceptual empiricism. Conceptual empiricism and the rejection of intellect are thus mutually supporting.

Nomological Empiricism

By 'nomological empiricism' I mean the view that the laws of nature cannot be known, even in principle, except on the basis of experience. Nomological empiricism thus differs from methodological empiricism in two crucial respects: first, it is an epistemological doctrine concerning how knowledge is possible in principle, rather than a methodological doctrine concerning the best way for human beings to proceed with respect to theory and observation; and second, its object is specifically scientific—the complete set of laws of nature—rather than more generally philosophical.

Spinoza clearly rejects nomological empiricism. So does Leibniz, at least insofar as he regards it as possible in principle for an infinite being to deduce the nature of the "best of all possible worlds" prior to experience. Descartes's general conception of causal relations is one in which causes can be seen to entail their effects, although his conception of mind-body interaction seems, notoriously, to violate this conception. Although he makes room for experimentation in practice, it is at least arguable that his fundamental ideal of natural laws is that they should be comprehensible from the geometrical nature of extension, motion, and the divine nature alone.

Berkeley, in contrast, claims that "the set rules, or established methods, wherein the Mind we depend on excites in us the ideas of Sense, are called laws of nature; and these we learn by experience" (PHK §30). Nor is this simply a claim about our own limitations; he writes in his notebooks: "I think not that things fall out of necessity, the connexion of no two Ideas is necessary. '[T]is all the result of freedom i.e., 'tis all voluntary" (PC §884). He thus seems committed to nomological empiricism. Hume's nomological empiricism, of course, is famous:

> I shall venture to affirm, as a general proposition, which admits of no exception, that the knowledge of this [i.e., the causal] relation is not, in any instance, attained by reasonings *a priori*; but arises entirely from experience, when we find that any particular objects are constantly conjoined with each other. (EHU §23)

The case of Locke is more complicated, in consequence of Locke's suggestion that "if we could discover the Figure, Size, Texture, and Motion of the minute Constituent parts of any two Bodies, we should know without Trial several of their Operations one upon another, as we do now the Properties of a Square, or a Triangle" (ECHU IV.iii.25). If Locke were to allow a deductive physics, of course, his conceptual empiricism would entail that humans would still have to derive its *concepts* from experience. But even waiving that point, the quoted suggestion of the possibility of deductive knowledge of physics is highly equivocal, for he immediately goes on much more modestly to compare our potential knowledge of the "Operations" of the "minute Constituents" to a watchmaker's anticipation of the movements of a watch. To the extent that he does seem to allow deductive physics as a theoretical possibility, his doing so seems to reflect the reticence of a methodological empiricist to prejudge exactly what kind of reasoning we might find ourselves able to engage in from *as yet unobserved* phenomena.

It is primarily because of their confidence in the rich content of the intellectual idea of extension that Descartes and Spinoza can so much as contemplate the ideal possibility of a priori knowledge of the laws of nature, and it is because of his confidence in the rich content of the intellectual ideas of God and existence that Leibniz can regard such knowledge as possible. The nomological empiricism of Berkeley and Hume, and the ambivalence of Locke, are in large part the consequences of their rejection of the intellect, and with it the possibility of such deductively fruitful ideas. At the same time, unconvincing attempts at a priori physics may be part of what Hume has in mind when he cites the many "absurdities" of philosophers claiming to employ the intellect.

Explanatory Empiricism

Jonathan Bennett uses the term 'explanatory rationalism' to designate the view that every fact has a sufficient reason or explanation, so that there are no "brute facts" (Bennett, 1984, chap. 5). By the term 'explanatory empiricism' I will mean the opposing view that some facts ultimately lack sufficient explanations and are therefore "brute facts."[8] Spinoza and Leibniz deny explanatory empiricism (see Garrett, 1990 and 1991); Descartes's doctrine of the arbitrariness of God's creative choices, in contrast, appears to commit him to explanatory empiricism, despite his "rationalism" in other respects. Locke is an explanatory empiricist at least provisionally, since he holds that there are some facts that "we cannot but ascribe . . . to the arbitrary Will and good Pleasure of the Wise Architect" (ECHU IV.iii.29). Berkeley's resolution of contingent facts into the free and voluntary actions of agents, cited previously (PC §875 and §884), seems to have the same consequence. Hume often proclaims that we must forever be in a position epistemologically indistinguishable from the truth of explanatory empiricism. Thus, he writes:

> It is confessed, that the utmost effort of human reason is to reduce the principles, productive of natural phenomena, to a greater simplicity, and to resolve the many particular effects into a few general causes. . . . But as to the causes of these general causes, we should in vain attempt their discovery; nor shall we ever be able to satisfy ourselves, by any particular explication of them. These ultimate springs and principles are totally shut up from human curiosity and enquiry. (EHU §26)

But he also goes further, as we have seen, adopting the Conceivability Criterion of Possibility that "nothing of which we can form a clear and distinct idea is absurd and impossible" (THN 19–20) or that "whatever we *conceive* is possible, at least in a metaphysical sense" (ATHN 650). And notoriously, Hume finds many alternative causal arrangements of the world conceivable.

It is easy to see why those who reject the Cartesian intellect should have at least a natural tendency toward explanatory empiricism. A completely sufficient explanation of a state of affairs must explain, in effect, why none of the possible alternatives to it occurred instead. For Hume, as for many of his contemporaries (and for many of ours), conceivability is the most obvious criterion of possibility. For those who accept the Cartesian intellect, however, "conceivable" means "conceivable by intellect"; whereas for Hume, "conceivable" can only mean "conceivable by the imagination"—that is, "imaginable." For Spinoza (to take the clearest example), nothing is ultimately conceivable by intellect except what is actual; there are therefore no unactualized metaphysical possibilities whose nonexistence must be explained. But for Hume, whose only test for possibility is *imaginability*, the number of metaphysical possibilities is multiplied. Since a fully adequate explanation for a state of affairs must explain why each of its possible alternatives did not occur instead, the denial of intellect thus involves a tendency to admit—or at least an inability to reject—"brute facts."

Reductive Empiricism

By 'reductive empiricism' I mean not any particular doctrine but rather a characteristic pattern of argumentation. This pattern of argumentation can be represented schematically as follows. One begins by inquiring into the content of a fundamental concept, asking a question of the general form, "What is meant by saying that some state of affairs S is realized?" One then describes a state of affairs, E, whose existence would generally be recognized as (at least) evidence that S is realized. Finally, one concludes that the meaning of 'S is realized' may be defined in terms of the realization of state of affairs E, on the grounds that the alternative would be a false epistemological skepticism (skepticism about whether we *know* that S is realized) and/or a false conceptual skepticism (skepticism about whether we can even *understand* 'S is realized'). Thus, a particular state of affairs is *defined* in terms of a state of affairs that is more commonly regarded only as *evidence* for it. Such a pattern of argumentation is completely unknown in Descartes, Spinoza, and Leibniz. However, something like it occurs—in application to different topics—in each of Locke, Berkeley, and Hume.

In the chapter of the *Essay* entitled "Of Identity and Diversity" (ECHU II.xxvii), Locke inquires into the "idea" or concept of identity in general and into the meaning of ascriptions of personal identity in particular. His answer to the latter question is as follows: "[C]onsciousness always accompanies thinking, and . . . in this alone consists *personal Identity*, i.e., the sameness of a rational Being: And as far as this consciousness can be extended backwards to any past Action or Thought, so far reaches the Identity of that *Person*; it is the same *self* now it was then; and 'tis by the same *self* with this present one that now reflects on it, that that Action was done (ECHU II.xxvii.9).

As his subsequent discussion confirms, Locke in effect holds that the identity of person A at time t_1 with person B at time t_2 *consists* in B's ability at t_2 to remember A's actions or state of mind at t_1, and that this is so because the idea or concept of the latter condition *is* the idea or concept of personal identity. Locke's critics were quick to accuse him of conflating the evidence of personal identity—that is, memory—with personal identity itself. But Locke does not adopt his memory-based theory through lack of familiarity with the alternatives. On the contrary, he seems to be aware of two such alternatives, each of which he rejects.

One alternative is the theory that identity may be defined as the sameness of an intelligible, inferred, underlying substantial substratum, in which the properties of the thing inhere, and which persists through phenomenal change. By the time he comes to discuss personal identity, however, Locke has already rejected the appeal to such substrata as being fruitless and unintelligible for all explanatory purposes.[9] The idea of a substratum in which qualities inhere—what Locke calls the idea of "substance-in-general"—is, he writes, "no . . . *clear* idea at all . . . but only an uncertain supposition of we know not what" (ECHU I.iv.18), "obscure and relative" (ECHU II.xxiii.3), and "confused" (ECHU III.vi.21; II.xiii.18); thus, that which its defenders "pretend to know, and talk of, is what they have no distinct *Idea* of at all, and so are perfectly ignorant of it, and in the dark" (ECHU II.xxiii.2). Any attempt to explicate personal identity in terms of such a substratum would clearly lead to conceptual skepticism.

A second alternative makes no appeal to the notion of substrata or "substance-in-general" but rather to the hypothesis of spatially located but extensionless and immaterial souls, conceived on analogy with extended material corpuscles. Locke devotes considerable attention to the suggestion that personal identity should consist in the sameness of one's immaterial thinking soul—a sameness which, like the sameness of material corpuscles, will involve spatio-temporal continuity. This second alternative has several advantages, from Locke's point of view.[10] Nevertheless, as an analysis of the idea or meaning of "personal identity," the second alternative is subject to two closely related objections. First, we do not know for certain that we have thinking immaterial souls, since God may have created us as material objects to which He "superadded" the ability to think (ECHU IV.iii.6); but we do know of our own personal identity. Second, even if we do think with immaterial souls, we know how to make perfectly good judgments of personal identity without being in any position to make judgments about the identity or nonidentity of the immaterial thinking souls with which we think. For all we know, such souls may wear out after a month or a decade and be replaced by others, or they may think in different persons at different times. Since we know many things about the identity of particular persons, but almost nothing about the identity of particular immaterial souls, it cannot be on the basis of the latter that we make judgments about the former. Hence, Locke concludes "*self* is not determined by Identity or Diversity of Substance [i.e., soul], which it cannot be sure of" (ECHU II.xxvii.23). That is to say, this alternative must be rejected because it leads to epistemological skepticism. It is chiefly to facts about memory that we have access in judging our own personal identity, and so it is only on the memory theory that we can account for the fact that we can *understand* and often *have good grounds for* claims about personal identity. It is for this reason that Locke adopts his memory account of personal identity; the argument is thus an instance of reductive empiricism.

Berkeley does not directly address the question of personal identity. But he does address the question, "What is it for a perception to be a perception of a *real* object, or an object with *real existence?*" His answer is that "what is meant" by calling the object of a perception "real" is that the perception itself is "strong," "affecting," "vivid," "distinct," has "no dependence on our will," is "orderly," "constant," "permanent," and "coherent" with others in a high degree (PHK §§29–36; and TDHP II.211–212, 215). These are (though not always by those names) the very features of ideas that Locke had offered in *Essay* IV.ix as constituting *evidence* that sense experience is of real objects.

Berkeley considers only one fundamental alternative to his own analysis, although he considers it in various versions. The rejected alternative is this: to say that a perception has a real object means that one's perception is caused by and/or resembles qualities inhering in a material substance existing outside the mind. In arguing against this alternative, Berkeley emphatically argues both that it leads to conceptual skepticism and that it leads to epistemological skepticism. It leads to conceptual skepticism, he argues, because we cannot attach any meaning to the claim that something exists outside a mind, nor to the claim that qualities "inhere" in a nonmental substance, nor to the claim that a nonmental substance could "cause" ideas, nor to the claim that a perception "resembles" something that is not a perception. And referring to the epistemological consequences of the alternative, he writes, characteristically: "This . . . hath been shown to be . . . the very root of Scepticism; for as long as men thought that real things subsisted without the mind, and that their knowledge was only so far forth *real* as it was *conformable to real things*, it follows they could not be certain that they had any knowledge at all. For, how can it be *known* that the things which are perceived are conformable to those which are not perceived, or exist without the mind?" (PHK §87).

Like Locke, Hume is a conceptual reductionist about personal identity, which he characterizes in terms of causation and resemblance among perceptions. Hume's most famous conceptual reduction, however, is his definition of causation in terms of constant conjunction, according to which a cause is either "an object precedent and contiguous to another, and where all objects resembling the former are plac'd in a like relation of priority and contiguity to those objects, that resemble the latter" (THN 170). Hume emphasizes the avoidance of conceptual skepticism, rather than the avoidance of epistemological skepticism. He argues that we cannot successfully conceive causation as involving a kind of "necessary connexion" holding between the cause and effect themselves, because "we have no idea of this connexion, nor even any distinct notion what it is we desire to know, when we endeavor at a conception of it" (EHU §60). Both the conceptual and epistemological elements are suggested, however, in his remark that, unless we regard causal necessity as he does, "we can never arrive at the most distant notion of it, or be able to attribute it either to external or internal objects, to spirit or body, to causes or effects" (THN 165).

The rejection of intellect provides a strong motivation for reductive empiricism. For to analyze a problematic and seemingly nonimaginable concept in terms of its (imaginable) empirical evidence is one prime strategy available for construing that concept as a representation in the imagination rather than the intellect.

Representation, Cognitive Psychology, and Philosophy

Hume's remarks about the imagination, as initially puzzling as they may be to many twentieth-century readers, are in fact part of a coherent theory of representational faculties. His distinction of representational faculties into memory and imagination—and no others—constitutes a rejection of the Cartesian ideal of a higher and radically nonimagistic representational faculty of intellect. His remarks about the relation of the imagination to the memory, reason, and the understanding reflect a cognitive psychology according to which the acts of the understanding—conception, judgment, and reasoning—are all regarded as *aspects of conceiving*, and hence as operations or aspects of the primary representational faculty of imagination. Hume's psychology, while not the first to deny the existence of a Cartesian intellect, was certainly the most penetrating, detailed, and consistent exploration of that alternative produced in the eighteenth century.

Despite the carefulness and coherence of Hume's cognitive psychology, however, it cannot be denied that he seriously oversimplifies cognitive phenomena in several respects. First, like practically all philosophers of the seventeenth and eighteenth centuries, he treats all cognitive operations as essentially representational—that is, as consisting entirely of operations performed with and on mental representations. Second, and again like practically all philosophers of the seventeenth and eighteenth centuries, he seeks the meaning of representations primarily in their intrinsic and introspectible content, rather than in their use. Although his theory of abstract ideas constitutes the beginning of an important shift away from this emphasis, Humean abstract ideas still function chiefly through the intrinsic and introspectible content of the array of particular ideas they dispose us to call up. *Third*, unlike most continental philosophers of the seventeenth century, but like many British philosophers of the eighteenth century, he treats all mental representations as fundamentally *imagistic*—that is, as qualitatively *resembling* the contents of sensory and reflective experience. These restrictions undoubtedly hide from Hume many facts about the psychological and social aspects of a wide variety of important cognitive operations and concepts.

Yet these oversimplifications in Hume's cognitive psychology, serious as they undoubtedly are, are less philosophically vitiating than one might expect. As we have seen, his theory of representational faculties serves both to produce and to reinforce his overall outlook of methodological, conceptual, nomological, explanatory, and reductive empiricism. These empiricisms—though in much modified forms—constitute part of the fundamental framework of a good deal of twentieth-century thought as well. This shared outlook is no accident, for the empiricist tendencies of the twentieth century are in large measure the direct causal descendants of the empiricisms of Locke and Hume. If we think of seventeenth- and eighteenth-century philosophy as involving a conflict between "continental rationalism" and "British empiricism," then we must conclude that empiricism won more permanent ground than did its counterpart. Hume's fundamental oversimplifications in cognitive psychology sometimes provide him with false premises from which he derives false conclusions. But they also produce a kind of hardheaded skepticism about the claims of intellect and hence of reason, and a resulting willingness to search for significance within the realms of experience, instinct, and sentiment, that give his work much of its continuing value. It is remarkable—and often not fully appreciated—how many insights he is able to accommodate through the clever development and exploitation of this restricted and oversimplified framework.

There is a certain amount of irony in the mitigated yet enduring popularity of empiricisms in the twentieth century. For despite the historical influence of the eighteenth-century empiricists, the cognitive psychology on which they based their empiricisms has until recently been largely either lamented or ignored. To take a particularly notable example, the logical positivists of the early twentieth century strongly endorsed Hume's methodological, conceptual, nomological, and explanatory empiricisms. Moreover, they elevated the pursuit of reductive empiricism— understood as the attempt to give logically equivalent analyses of philosophically important terms and locutions—to the status of one of philosophy's primary goals.[11] At the same time, however, they condemned Hume for mixing "mere" empirical psychology with philosophy. Along with a distinction between empirical or "synthetic" truths and conceptual or "logical" truths, they adopted a verificationist theory of meaning, which held that the meaning of synthetic propositions consists in their method of empirical verification. Yet they could not specify any method of empirical verification for the verification principle itself, even though they were rightly uncomfortable with treating it as a conceptual or logical truth that merely explicated their own concept of meaning. Hence, they could not explain the status or meaning of the verification principle itself. Because they lacked any principled theory of representational faculties—and, indeed, declined on principle to appeal to one for philosophical purposes—they were unable ultimately to *justify* their reductive empiricism. Hume, in contrast, with his theory of imagination, could have.

The resurgence of interest in cognitive psychology produced by the recent confluence of interdisciplinary interests called "cognitive science" provides an apt moment to investigate more thoroughly Hume's cognitive psychology. Not only can such an investigation shed light on perennial topics in the theory of cognition, it can also shed considerable new light on the real meaning of Hume's most central philosophical claims and arguments, which have often been misinterpreted as a result of ignorance of the theories of cognition in which they are embedded. Only when we fully understand Hume's claims and arguments in the light of those theories can we properly evaluate their philosophical value.

The Copy Principle

L ocke argues in *Essay* I.iv that there are no innate ideas; all ideas are instead derived from sensation or reflection. This denial of innate ideas — highly influential in eighteenth-century British philosophy — helps to justify Locke's de facto rejection of the Cartesian intellect, and thereby also to justify his methodological empiricism and commonsense skepticism toward a number of scholastic and rationalist metaphysical doctrines concerning both the physical and the mental realms.

The Copy Principle, which is the first of Hume's two most fundamental principles, is a direct successor to this Lockean doctrine, as Hume himself acknowledges (see EHU §17n). As first presented in the *Treatise*, the Copy Principle states:

> [A]ll our simple ideas in their first appearance are deriv'd from simple impressions, which are correspondent to them, and which they exactly represent. (THN 4)

As introduced in the first *Enquiry*, it states:

> [A]ll our ideas or more feeble perceptions are copies of our impressions or more lively ones. (EHU §13)

This principle, as we saw in chapter 1, involves both a Resemblance Thesis (that every simple idea has an exactly resembling simple impression) and a Causal Thesis (that every simple idea is at least partly caused by a simple impression).[1] Hume uses the principle to justify one of his prime methodological directives; namely, that in order "perfectly to understand any idea," we must "[trace] it up to its origin, and [examine] that primary impression, from which it arises" (THN 74–75). Even more important, the principle plays a crucial role in his arguments concerning such central topics as space, time, causation, substance, personal identity, and morality. In each case, it is used to argue that a certain supposed idea — of vacuum, of time without alteration, of necessary connection in nature, of a subject of inherence, of a unified and identical self, or of real moral relations existing in the objects alone, respectively — does not exist.

Yet it has seemed to many commentators that Hume fails to support the Copy Principle with evidence sufficient to justify the manner in which he applies it in these central arguments. Indeed, it has often been concluded that, despite the expectations aroused by his announced methodological empiricism, he effectively treats the principle as a priori, or as necessary, or both. Thus, Antony Flew writes of Hume's procedure that it

> amounts to making such sentences as "all our ideas . . . are copies of our impressions . . . " ambiguous: most of the time they are taken to express a contingent generalization; but at some moments of crisis he apparently construes them as embodying a necessary proposition. Such manoeuvres have the effect of making it look as if the immunity to falsification of a necessary truth had been gloriously combined with the substantial assertiveness of a contingent generalization.[2]

However, no sooner does Hume state the principle than he himself explicitly admits an exception, or counterexample, to it, involving the idea of a "missing shade of blue":

> There is however one contradictory phænomenon, which may prove, that 'tis not absolutely impossible for ideas to go before their correspondent impressions. I believe it will readily be allow'd, that the several distinct ideas of colours, which enter by the eyes, or those of sounds, which are convey'd by the hearing, are really different from each other, tho' at the same time resembling. Now if this be true of different colours, it must be no less so of the different shades of the same colour, that each of them produces a distinct idea, independent of the rest. For if this shou'd be deny'd, 'tis possible, by the continual gradation of shades, to run a colour insensibly into what is most remote from it; and if you will not allow any of the means to be different, you cannot without absurdity deny the extremes to be the same. Suppose therefore a person to have enjoyed his sight for thirty years, and to have become perfectly well acquainted with colours of all kinds, excepting one particular shade of blue, for instance, which it never has been his fortune to meet with. Let all the different shades of that colour, except that single one, be plac'd before him, descending gradually from the deepest to the lightest; 'tis plain, that he will perceive a blank, where that shade is wanting, and will be sensible, that there is a greater distance in that place betwixt the contiguous colours, than in any other. Now I ask, whether 'tis possible for him, from his own imagination, to supply this deficiency, and raise up to himself the idea of that particular shade, tho' it had never been conveyed to him by his senses? I believe there are few but will be of opinion that he can; and this may serve as a proof, that the simple ideas are not always derived from the correspondent impressions; tho' the instance is so particular and singular, that 'tis scarce worth our observing, and does not merit that for it alone we should alter our general maxim. (THN 5–6 and EHU §16)

But this is not all. After discussing the missing shade of blue, he seems almost immediately to go on to allow several other counterexamples without any apparent qualms. Immediately after reiterating his endorsement of using the Copy Principle (THN 33), he asserts that our idea of time "is not deriv'd from a particular impression mix'd up with others, and plainly distinguishable from them" (THN 36). In light of the immediate context, in which he has been emphasizing the parallel between the ideas of space and time, it is evident that he would affirm a similar doctrine about the idea of space.[3] And yet immediately after seeming to grant that the ideas of space and time are not copied from impressions, he concludes his discussion of the ideas of space and time by denying that there is any idea either of "vacuum" (i.e., empty space) or of "time without a changeable existence"—precisely on the grounds that there are no impressions from which these latter ideas can be copied (THN 65). He then concludes *Treatise* I.ii, a mere page later, by maintaining that our "idea of existence is not deriv'd from any particular impression" (THN 66). All of this suggests to many readers that Hume applies the Copy Principle both arbitrarily and unfairly—adopting it uncritically, insisting on it when it suits his purposes, and then allowing exceptions to it whenever he wishes.

In this chapter, I try to show that there is a consistent and principled approach behind these seemingly careless and inconsistent features of Hume's adoption and use of the Copy Principle. First, I argue that he does not, at any point, treat the principle as either a priori or necessary, and in the process, I will outline his own argument for the principle. Second, I consider Hume's admission of the missing shade of blue as an exception to the Copy Principle and argue that it does not significantly undermine his subsequent uses of the principle. I then argue that contrary to appearances, the ideas of time, space, and existence are not exceptions to the Copy Principle. Finally, I argue that Hume is perfectly consistent in using the Copy Principle to deny the existence of any idea of either "vacuum" or "time without a changeable existence," even though he admits the existence of the ideas of space and time.

The Status and Grounds of the Copy Principle

The Intended Status of the Copy Principle

As his critics are well aware, there are several strong reasons to believe that Hume does not intend to treat, and does not believe he has treated, the Copy Principle as either a priori or logically necessary. One of the most obvious of these reasons lies in Hume's explicit nomological empiricism. He repeatedly maintains that we cannot have any a priori knowledge of causal conditions (see, for example, THN 86, EHU §23); indeed, most of his uses of the term 'a priori' occur in the course of making or reiterating this very point. Yet in the course of explaining and defending the Copy Principle, he explicitly identifies it as a claim about a causal condition for the occurrence of ideas. From this characterization and his nomological empiricism, it follows immediately that the Copy Principle cannot be a priori—so immediately, indeed, that Hume could hardly miss the point.[4] Furthermore, his Conceivability Criterion of Possibility entails that the Copy Principle cannot be a necessary truth if its denial is conceivable, but he is equally insistent that the denial of *any* causal claim is conceivable. Thus, it follows unmistakably, from claims that Hume not only accepts but emphasizes, both that the Copy Principle cannot be a priori and that it cannot be necessary.

A second piece of evidence that Hume does not intend the Copy Principle to be either a priori or necessary is, of course, his own admission that the idea of the "missing shade of blue" would constitute a counterexample to the Copy Principle. He could hardly fail to notice that the discovery of even one empirical counterexample would be incompatible with the universality implicit in treating the principle as a priori or necessary. Nor is that counterexample later forgotten or rejected; on the contrary, he reproduces his entire discussion of it verbatim in the first *Enquiry*.

The Argument for the Copy Principle Outlined

A third piece of evidence that Hume does not intend the Copy Principle to be a priori or necessary is the character of the argument he provides for it. That argument, as it occurs in the *Treatise* (THN 4–5), may be outlined as follows:

1. [E]very simple impression is attended with a correspondent idea, and every simple idea with a correspondent impression.
2. Such a constant conjunction, in such an infinite number of instances, can never arise from chance.
3. [There is either a] dependence of the [simple] impressions upon the [simple] ideas, or of the [simple] ideas upon the [simple] impressions. (from 1 and 2)
4. To give a child an idea of scarlet or orange, of sweet or bitter, I present the objects, or in other words, convey to him these impressions; but proceed not so absurdly, as to endeavor to produce the impressions by exciting the ideas.
5. Our ideas upon their appearance produce not their correspondent impressions, nor do we perceive any colour, or feel any sensation merely upon thinking of them . . . [but] any impression either of the mind or body is constantly followed by an idea, which resembles it, and is only different in the degrees of force and liveliness.
6. In their first appearance . . . the simple impressions always take the precedence of their correspondent ideas, but never appear in the contrary order. (from 4 and 5)
7. [W]here-ever by any accident the faculties, which give rise to any impressions, are obstructed in their operations, as when one is born blind or deaf; not only the impressions are lost, but also their correspondent ideas.
8. [The correspondent ideas are lost likewise] where the organs of sensation . . . have never been put in action to produce a particular impression. [For example, we cannot form a just idea of the taste of a pineapple without actually tasting it.]
9. [A]ll our simple ideas in their first appearance are deriv'd from simple impressions, which are correspondent to them, and which they exactly represent. (from 3, 6, 7, and 8)

The first premise, (1), is simply the Resemblance Thesis conjoined with the parallel claim that for every simple impression there occurs a resembling simple idea.[5] We have already seen Hume's grounds for the Resemblance Thesis in chapter 1: an appeal to introspective experience together with a challenge to produce a counterexample.[6] As I argued in chapter 1, he is confident that no damaging counterexamples to the Resemblance Thesis can be produced because (i) he has confidence in Locke's and his own accounts of the origins of problematic concepts; (ii) he believes that philosophers who claim to employ counterexamples to the thesis derive implausible and conflicting results from them; and (iii) he is confident of the ability of his own theory of abstract ideas to explain fully the crucial phenomenon of generality in thought. His argument for the further causal claim—that simple ideas are derived from the corresponding simple impressions—appeals first to (1)'s implication that there is a constant correlation, and hence a prima facie causal relation, between simple impressions and resembling simple ideas (2–3). It then provides two kinds of empirical evidence to establish the nature of the causal relation. The first kind of evidence lies in the order in which impressions and ideas appear, in those cases where both do occur (4–6). The second kind of evidence lies in our inability to have ideas where the corresponding impressions have not occurred (7–8). The argument as a whole thus appears to be based entirely on empirical, contingent premises.

Reasons to Interpret the Principle as A Priori and Necessary

Although Hume evidently does not *intend* to treat the Copy Principle as either a priori or necessary, two related grounds might be offered for the claim that he nevertheless does so. First, it may be thought that the empirical evidence he actually presents for the premises of his argument is inadequate or nonexistent. Bennett, for example, writes boldly that "if we take the [copy] principle at face value, as a theory about the preconditions for having unlively 'perceptions' or quasi-sensory states," then "we cannot bring evidence to bear upon it" (Bennett, 1971, pp. 226–227; see also Flew, 1986, pp. 22–23). In support of this claim, he continues:

> Clearly, Hume will not bow to any fool or knave who claims to have a counter-example, any congenitally blind man who says "I have an idea of purple." To "produce" an idea one must not merely *say* but *show* that one has it; and Hume is confident that his challengers will fail in this larger task, e.g. that a congenitally blind man who says "I have an idea of purple" won't be able to give us reasons for believing him.
>
> But the blind man might well satisfy us that he is not lying, and then Hume's only resort would be to say that the blind man did not know what "purple" means. This, I suggest, is the source of his confidence: he is sure that the congenitally blind man would not be able to "produce" an idea of purple because he would not be able to satisfy us that he knew what "purple" means. . . .
>
> Now, what of the people whose ideas Hume counts as positive evidence for this theory? He has not asked them what ideas they have, and even if he did, why should he believe their answers? He must say: "Well, they clearly understand the word 'purple', and that is good enough for me." If he does not say this, then it is perfectly obscure how he can have any positive evidence for his theory as applied to anyone but himself. If he does say it, then anyone counts as having an idea of purple if he understands "purple" or a synonym of it in some other language. (Bennett, 1971, p. 227; see also MacNabb, 1951, pp. 27–29)

On this basis, Bennett argues that although Hume *offers* the Copy Principle as a claim about the relation between impressions and ideas, it is better *understood* as the thesis that experience is a precondition for "understanding," where the latter is construed as consisting in certain linguistic abilities. Although Bennett grants that this latter thesis has some considerable empirical warrant in its own right, he also suggests that its relation to certain "analytic" (and hence presumably a priori and necessary) truths about the connection between meaningfulness and "empirical cashability" helps in some way to explain Hume's adoption and/or use of the Copy Principle. And although Flew grants that some empirical evidence does support the Copy Principle itself—construed as a claim about Humean mental entities—

he also holds that Hume's confidence in it is due largely to a groping understanding of a related necessary truth of the kind that Bennett describes.

A second reason sometimes offered for the claim that Hume treats the Copy Principle as a priori or necessary is the appearance that Hume is unwilling to take seriously the possibility that the putative ideas he rejects on the basis of the Copy Principle are instead counterexamples to it—as he ought to do if the principle were merely based on experience. Thus Flew, for example, writes (just after the remark cited at the beginning of this chapter):

> But this—not to put too fine a point on it—is outrageous. It is all very well to support such a psychological generalization [the Copy Principle] by citing the kind of evidence which Hume does cite, and then to challenge all comers to produce a counter-example. But it simply will not do at all to turn the generalization thus supported into the supposedly sure foundation of a method of challenge: dismissing anything which might be proffered as a counter-example as being, on that ground alone, necessarily discredited. (Flew, 1986, pp. 20–21)

These two grounds, although distinct, are related. For the weaker the empirical grounds for the principle itself, the more it becomes incumbent on Hume to take putative counterexamples seriously—and the more telling his failure to do so will be as evidence for the view that he treats the principles as a priori and/or necessary.

Hume's Empirical Evidence

Does Hume offer adequate empirical support for his premises? Certainly there would often be strategic difficulties in *demonstrating* to other people that one was having a simple idea that was not preceded by a corresponding impression. For example, a person who, for whatever reason, never has and never will have an impression of purple obviously cannot say without self-contradiction, "Do you see that purple object over there? The impression that you and I both have when we look at that object corresponds to an idea for which I have not had the preceding impression." But this does not mean that we can never obtain *any* information concerning the mental images (ideas) of the sensorily deprived or the relation of those images to their remaining impressions or sense experiences.

It is a fact, for example, that the blind and the deaf do *not* report mental images—that is, Humean "ideas"—that are unrelated to any simpler elements previously experienced in sensation or feeling. If the blind or deaf did report having such images, of course, we might not be able to determine precisely what images they were experiencing, but would there be any reason to doubt that they were correct in reporting the occurrence of *some* such images? Just as one need not know the ornithologists' name for a bird in order to report that one is presently seeing a picture of *some* bird that one has never encountered before, so one need not know the name of a kind of image in order to report that one is presently having an image unlike any previous impression. The fact that the blind and deaf can and do report aspects of their mental lives but do not report such images is surely some evidence that they do not have them.

Furthermore, sensory deprivation is not always permanent. This is obvious in the cases where sensory deprivation is due to simple lack of opportunity, but it may also be the case where the organic damage of the congenitally blind or deaf person is repaired or otherwise overcome. If such persons frequently reported that they now had for the first time sensations or feelings of which they had previously had only images, Hume would certainly conclude that the Copy Principle was false. That such persons do not make such reports is surely some evidence in favor of that principle. Nor are we utterly without evidence concerning the experiences of persons whose sensory exposure is normal. If they frequently reported having simple images unrelated to their sense impressions or feelings, there need not be any reason to doubt the truth of their claims. In fact, however, they generally do not make such claims, and that, once again, is some evidence for the Copy Principle.

To treat all of this as evidence for the Copy Principle is, of course, to assume that the verbal and other behavior of other persons—so far as it goes—can be good evidence about the content of their mental images. But this assumption will be granted by everyone who is not a complete skeptic about the content of other minds. Hume himself may not have formulated an adequate specific refutation of skepticism about other minds, but in this he resembles nearly every other philosopher who claims to have information about other minds.[7] Furthermore, in order to treat others' behavior as evidence, there is no need to translate Hume's claims about ideas into claims about the linguistic ability to use terms (such as 'purple') for specific kinds of images. Indeed, even committed logical behaviorists (that is, conceptual reductionists about the mental states of themselves and others) need not make such a translation. They will, of course, propose that claims about the mental states of others are equivalent in meaning to claims about behavior, but they will still have their own (behaviorist) analyses of claims about *mental images*, and those analyses will likely remain largely distinct in meaning from their analyses of claims about the *understanding of particular words*. Thus, there is no need even for them to interpret Hume's Copy Principle as a disguised claim that understanding, construed as a behavioral linguistic capacity, requires experience.

The Copy Principle itself is the relatively straightforward empirical claim that the presented content of those mental representations that are less "lively" than (Humean) impressions is copied from the experienced content of these impressions. However, Hume also accepts his predecessors' and contemporaries' view that understanding—construed as a mental act—requires such representations and depends on their presented content. From the Copy Principle and this additional premise, it follows for Hume that understanding causally requires experience. Since he would no doubt agree that, in general, complex behavioral linguistic capacities causally require understanding, he would likely agree, too, that complex behavioral linguistic capacities causally require experience. But these further claims and consequences would be distinct from the Copy Principle itself.

Indeed, rather than offering a principle on which "evidence cannot be brought to bear," Hume himself brings (in addition to the positive evidence he cites) some evidence to bear *against* it, in the form of the missing shade of blue. Hume does not dig in his heels and refuse to grant that the person claiming to have the idea of this shade can make any successful reference to it. If anything, Hume's standards

for admitting contrary evidence are a bit too lax: he cheerfully accepts the anticipated results of a merely hypothetical experiment with color samples.

It must be granted that Hume's confidence in the Copy Principle is not based on
extensive empirical research directed toward that very question: he has not, for
example, sent out questionnaires. Rather, he thinks he has observed enough about
human nature to know that, if counterexamples to the Copy Principle were at all
common—among the blind and deaf, children, or others—then he would have
heard about them. Moreover, the publication of the *Treatise* and especially the first
Enquiry (with its specific challenge to produce counterexamples) itself constitutes a
sort of ex post facto questionnaire: if counterexamples are at all common, then
these discussions should help to elicit reports of them. Hume thinks that both his
own experience and his knowledge of what other people do and do not report provide extensive support for the Copy Principle. In the face of this support, an occasional dissenter may be questioned with respect to his or her sincerity or accuracy,
just as rare reported failures to produce otherwise widely replicable experimental
results may be questioned. But the existence of a large number of dissenters whose
dissent could not be convincingly explained as the result of natural errors would
certainly call the principle itself into question. Barring universal skepticism about
other minds, and given the general framework of representational categories he has
adopted, the evidence Hume presents is reasonable, relevant evidence for the Copy
Principle construed as an empirical generalization about the relation between two
classes of perceptions.

Applications of the Copy Principle

Even if Hume presents some genuine empirical evidence for the Copy Principle,
however, it remains possible that his critical use of the principle is more rigid than
that evidence warrants. Does he actually apply it as if it were either a priori or necessary?

He does not imply such a status for the Copy Principle when he uses it to establish his methodological directive to trace problematic ideas back to the impressions
from which they are derived. He argues only that "ideas are by nature weaker and
fainter than impressions, and thereby liable to obscurity and confusion" (THN 73),
whereas "the examination of the impression bestows a like clearness on the idea"
(THN 75; see also THN 33). Because impressions are stronger and firmer than
ideas, it is naturally useful to refer to them in problematic cases. The Copy Principle serves to justify this methodological directive by asserting that there will be such
an impression to be found. When he makes the same point in the first *Enquiry*,
Hume adds that we may also use the methodological directive in assessing the status of terms that we suspect have no corresponding idea:

> When we entertain, therefore, any suspicion that a philosophical term is employed
> without any meaning or idea (as it is but too frequently) we need but enquire, *from
> what impression is that supposed idea derived?* And if it be impossible to assign any, this
> will serve to confirm our suspicion. By bringing ideas into so clear a light, we may rea-
> sonably hope to remove all dispute which may arise, concerning their nature and real-
> ity. (EHU §17)

But again, there is no need to interpret Hume as maintaining that it is either a priori or necessary that every simple idea has a corresponding simple impression. He need only maintain that we have *found* this to be the case, thereby raising a reasonable expectation that the search for an original impression for a problematic idea will shed light (due to the greater clarity and vivacity of impressions) on whether the idea really exists and, if it does, on its nature.

In fact, when faced with an initial inability to find an impression from which our idea of necessary connection is derived, he quite explicitly declines to treat the Copy Principle as either a priori or necessary:

> Shall the despair of success make me assert, that I am here possest of an idea, which is not preceded by any similar impression? This wou'd be too strong a proof of levity and inconstancy; since the contrary principle has been already so firmly establish'd, as to admit of no farther doubt; at least, till we have more fully examin'd the present difficulty. (THN 77)

Even when Hume does argue against the existence of certain ideas by appealing to the Copy Principle and to the observed absence of any corresponding impression, the contexts of these instances provide no reason to suppose that the principle itself is intended to be a priori or necessary. For when he argues against the existence of a certain (putative) idea, he never argues *merely* that we do not find such a corresponding impression in experience; he also always argues that no impression could possibly satisfy the requirements we implicitly demand for such a perception. In the case of "vacuum" and "time without a changeable existence" (as we shall see shortly), he argues that any such impression would really have to be a nonimpression, since it would be an impression of nothing at all. In the case of necessary connection (as we shall see again in chapter 5), he argues that a perception of a necessary connection in nature would "amount to a demonstration, and wou'd imply the absolute impossibility for the one object not to follow, or to be conceived not to follow upon the other" (THN 161–162)—a demonstration that he argues we can already see to be impossible. Similarly in the case of the metaphysicians' conception of mental or physical substance (considered in chapter 8), the perception of such a thing would be the perception of something that bestowed simplicity at a given time and identity through time on what we can already see to be intrinsically complex and plural rather than simple and identical (THN 219–221; THN 252). In Book III of the *Treatise* (as we shall see in chapter 9), Hume does not argue merely that we do not actually find any distinctive moral relations (or other moral matters of fact) so long as we confine our attention to the objects or actions themselves. He also argues (THN 464–466) that no relation or matter of fact pertaining only to the objects or actions themselves could be guaranteed to exert at least some motivating or approbative force on any being who perceived its existence—as the perception of vice and virtue must.

In each of these cases, admitting a counterexample to the Copy Principle would mean not merely violating the Resemblance Thesis but violating it in such a way as to allow nonimagistic ideas that could not, even in principle, resemble impressions. It would thus require the admission of an entirely distinct representational faculty, and hence a very serious modification in the cognitive psychology that Hume thinks he finds otherwise well supported by experience. That is why he thinks it would be "too strong a proof of levity and inconstancy" on his part to admit counterexamples to the Copy Principle too hastily in such cases.

Hume intends the Copy Principle to be, and consistently treats it as, a well-confirmed empirical generalization. And indeed, the evidence for it, within the context of Hume's cognitive psychology, is reasonably strong. In view of the greater strength and firmness of impressions, the Copy Principle naturally gives rise to a methodological directive—namely, to seek the impressions from which problematic putative ideas are derived. It also creates a strong inductive presumption that where no prior impressions can be found, no idea will be found either.

Alleged Counterexamples to the Copy Principle

The Missing Shade of Blue

If the Copy Principle is indeed an empirical generalization, doesn't Hume's admission about the missing shade of blue undercut to a considerable extent the critical use he makes of the principle? He himself allows that, should anyone produce a counterexample to the Copy Principle, "it will then be incumbent on us, if we would maintain our doctrine, to produce the impression, or lively perception, which corresponds to it" (EHU §14).

Sympathetic critics have sometimes suggested that Hume could easily have avoided treating the missing shade of blue as a counterexample to the Copy Principle by treating all shades of color instead as *complex* ideas, in one of the ways suggested by color theory. Thus, the missing shade of blue might be treated as a complex composed of experienced hues of varying intensities, or as a complex composed of an experienced hue, an experienced degree of saturation, and an experienced degree of brightness. This expedient is not in fact available to Hume, for reasons I explain at the end of chapter 3. Instead, Hume cheerfully grants that the missing shade is a counterexample, and in concluding his discussions of it, he offers a reason why it does not merit an alteration in "our general maxim": it is because the "instance" is so "particular and singular" (THN 6 and EHU §16). In one sense, actually, the instance is *not* singular. Analogous counterexamples might easily be constructed around a "missing tone," a "missing degree of heat," and so on. But in another sense, *all* such counterexamples are "particular and singular"—that is, they have quite particular kinds of explanations. Hume has at least two quite specific explanations ready to hand of how an idea of the missing shade of blue can be obtained without the corresponding simple impression. Both explanations depend essentially on his doctrine of natural resemblances among simple perceptions.

Some resembling complex perceptions resemble each other in virtue of one containing, as a part, some simpler perception that is qualitatively identical to a part of the other. An idea of a lion and an idea of a chimera, for example, may resemble each other in virtue of involving the same kind of head. But for Hume, not all resemblance between perceptions is of this kind. In an Appendix note added to *Treatise* I.i.7, he writes:

'Tis evident, that even different simple ideas may have a similarity to each other; nor is it necessary that the point or circumstance of resemblance shou'd be distinct or separable from that in which they differ. *Blue* and *green* are different simple ideas, but are more resembling than *blue* and *scarlet*; tho' their perfect simplicity excludes all possibility of separation or distinction. 'Tis the same with particular sounds, and tastes and smells. These admit of infinite resemblances upon the general appearance and comparison, without having any common circumstance the same. (THN 637)

He then goes on to remark that any two simple perceptions must resemble each other at least in respect of their being simple, and yet by definition no two *simple* perceptions could have proper parts of the same kind in common.

Hume's view that perceptions can resemble each other without having any qualitatively identical parts is often either ignored or regretted by critics because it is thought to be inconsistent with his "nominalism." But if this view is inconsistent with nominalism, then Hume is no nominalist. Far from wanting to explain or to explain away the fact that even simples can resemble one another in various respects, he regards the fact as (i) undeniable by anyone, as the case of "simplicity" itself shows, and (ii) so fundamental that no further explanation is possible. In fact, if nominalism and realism are attempts to give some account of *how* instances of even simple qualities can resemble each other, then Hume (like Locke) is neither a nominalist nor a realist.[8]

Given the existence of natural resemblances among simple perceptions, Hume has available a plausible explanation for a subject's ability to form a simple idea of the missing shade of blue in the absence of an exactly corresponding impression: the subject has instead a very large number of simple impressions that naturally resemble the missing impression very closely and are even arranged in such an order as positively to *point*, given the nature of the resemblances, to the content of the missing impression. The operation of the mind in using an array of resembling shades to fill in the blank within an ordering of simple ideas—especially when it is an ordering of elements whose principle the mind understands (through the relevant abstract ideas)—is arguably quite similar to the operation of the mind when it interpolates missing elements into other series that do not require the formation of a new simple idea.

The process is also rather similar to a phenomenon that Hume describes in Book III of the *Treatise*:

Ideas may be compared to the extension and solidity of matter and impressions, especially reflective ones, to colours, tastes, smells, and other sensible qualities. Ideas never admit of a total union, but are endowed with a kind of impenetrability by which they exclude each other, and are capable of forming a compound by their conjunction, not by their mixture. On the other hand, impressions and passions are susceptible of an entire union, and, like colours, may be blended so perfectly together, that each of them may lose itself, and contribute only to vary that uniform impression which arises from the whole. Some of the most curious phenomena of the human mind are derived from this property of the passions. (THN 366)

In these cases, two distinct emotions—each of which is a simple impression for Hume—are "blended" into a third emotion, potentially similar to each. The "blending" involved is somewhat metaphorical, for the resulting emotion is itself a simple impression, and hence is not a complex impression containing the first two as parts. Instead, it is a *new* impression that both replaces, and causally results from, two previous emotions. Let us now imagine a similar process by which ideas of a lighter and darker shade could be imaginatively "blended" so as to produce a simple *idea* intermediate between them. This would differ from the blending of *impressions* only in the lesser force and vivacity of the perceptions on which it operated. And although Hume describes the blending process as one that applies to impressions rather than to ideas, he also characterizes it as one that applies specifically to colors. Hence, one might not be surprised to find the imagination having at least a limited capacity to "blend" ideas of closely resembling colors.[9]

Either—or both—of these explanations are readily available to Hume. Although the idea of the missing shade of blue need not—given very special circumstances of an ordering of similar ideas—be derived from an exactly corresponding impression, it is still ultimately derived from a set of very closely *resembling* impressions. It thus constitutes a very near miss for the Copy Principle. Moreover, Hume can have reasonable confidence that no *similar* explanation, in terms of closely resembling impressions, would be available for such cases as vacuum, eventless time, necessary causal connections, subjects of inherence, metaphysical selves, and real moral relations. The instance of the missing shade of blue and its correlatives for other sense modalities are in that way "particular and singular."[10]

The exception of the missing shade of blue may thus be admitted without fatally undermining either (i) the general usefulness of the methodological directive to search for the impressions from which an idea is derived, or (ii) the conclusion that we should view with deep suspicion any alleged idea for which we cannot find an original impression or set of impressions. The missing shade of blue itself requires at most a very slight and understandable amendment to Hume's general description of the powers of the imagination. However, to admit an idea of vacuum, eventless time, necessary causal connection, substance, the self, or moral relations would, as we have seen, violate the Resemblance Thesis in a far more radical way, a way that would require the reintroduction of an entirely different representational faculty, a faculty of *intellect* that he has already rejected on several different grounds. Hume is well aware that, on his own principles, empirical investigation could always force him to admit the existence of counterexamples to the Copy Principle that would be more philosophically significant than the missing shade of blue. But the missing shade of blue, because of its special explanations and near-miss character, has little effect on Hume's philosophical uses of the principle.

Space, Time, and Existence

Hume's available special explanations for the idea of the missing shade of blue do not seem applicable to the ideas of "space," "time," and "existence," however. Thus, if he were to admit such ideas as these without allowing corresponding impressions from which they are copied, he would be granting far more serious breaches of the Copy Principle. In fact, however, Hume does *not* say that there are no impressions of time, space, and existence from which the corresponding ideas are copied. Rather, he says that the idea of time (like, presumably, that of space) is not copied from a "particular impression mix'd up with others, and plainly distinguishable from them" (THN 36), and that the idea of existence is similarly not copied from "a particular impression" (THN 66). In order to see how this distinction makes a difference, it is essential to recall his theory of abstract ideas, set out in *Treatise* I.i.7 (and described in chapter 1). Let us apply that theory first to the idea of space.

Hume explicitly notes that the ideas of space and time are abstract ideas (THN 34–35) and that they are composed of parts (THN 34, 39). On his view, in fact, all visual (i.e., colored) and tactile perceptions are composed of *minima sensibilia* (minimum sensibles), and space is a manner in which two or more such *minima sensibilia* are ordered or arranged relative to one another. It follows from his general theory of abstract ideas that the abstract idea of *space* is some particular spatially complex idea, consisting of a number of simple colored or tangible ideas, an idea that is associated with a general term and a disposition to call up a set of spatially complex ideas (the term's revival set) when needed. Any complex idea that serves as the abstract idea of space will either be copied directly from a corresponding complex impression of various colors or tactile qualities, or will be made up of simpler ideas that have been copied directly from impressions of colors or tactile qualities. Thus, although there is no *separate* impression of space, every spatially complex impression is *an* impression of space—and of various other things as well. (I elaborate on this use of the simple/complex distinction, and on the way in which an impression can be an impression *of* more than one thing, in chapter 3.) Hume's theory thus contrasts with Locke's. For according to Locke, experience presents us with a *simple* idea (that is, what Hume would call an impression) of space, numerically different from such other simple representations as those of "extension," "figure," and "motion."

An exactly parallel account applies also to Hume's idea of time. Time is another manner in which two or more temporally minimal perceptions (which in this case need not be visual or tactile) are ordered or arranged relative to one another. One's abstract idea of time is thus a temporally complex idea, associated with a general term that revives a disposition to call up other temporally complex ideas. This temporally complex idea is—either directly or in its simpler parts—copied from corresponding impressions.[11] Once again, this contrasts with Locke's theory, according to which experience presents us with a unique simple idea (that is, what Hume would call an impression) of time or "succession," in addition to any other simple representations we might experience.

Similar considerations apply also to the idea of existence, with one important difference. To conceive of something and to conceive of it as existing are the same thing, according to Hume, so every impression whatever will at the same time be an impression of existence. The idea that serves as the abstract idea of existence, accordingly, may be either simple or complex. Once again, Hume's view contrasts with Locke's theory, according to which every experience presents us with a *separate*, and *simple*, idea (again, what Hume would call an impression) of existence, entirely distinct from all other simple representations.[12]

Thus, although there are no "separate and distinct" impressions of space, time, and existence for Hume, *every* idea of space, of time, and of existence is an idea that has been copied from previous impressions. Moreover, each of these previous impressions has been an impression *of* (among other things) space, time, and existence, respectively—that is, of spatially ordered things, temporally ordered things, and existing things.

Empty Space and Changeless Time

We have now seen why Hume allows ideas of space, time, and existence. Why does he not also allow ideas of "vacuum" and "time without a changeable existence"? The answer again depends largely on the theory of abstract ideas.

The case of the vacuum differs from that of space in a crucial respect. There are many impressions that are "impressions of space," and hence many different ideas that can serve as the abstract idea of space. There is, however, no impression that is an impression of a vacuum, and hence there is no idea that is capable of serving as the abstract idea of a vacuum. For a "vacuum" is supposed to be empty space, yet any spatial perception will be a complex impression whose parts are all either visual or tangible—and visual and tangible perceptions represent their locations as filled, not as empty. This is true whether the perception is an impression or an idea. Hence there is no idea of a vacuum and no impression from which such an idea can be derived.

This conclusion is much less philosophically pregnant than it might appear. It is a claim about representations, made within a cognitive science of representations, and it has no negative consequences for those who deny that the universe is a plenum. Hume also writes:

> [I]f it be ask'd, whether or not the invisible and intangible distance be always full of *body*, or of something that by an improvement of our organs might become visible or tangible, I must acknowledge, that I find no very decisive arguments on either side; tho' I am inclin'd to the contrary opinion, as being more suitable to vulgar and popular notions. If the *Newtonian* philosophy be rightly understood, it will be found to mean no more. A vacuum is asserted: That is, bodies are said to be plac'd after such a manner, as to receive bodies betwixt them, without impulsion or penetration. (THN 639)

How can Hume say this, if the term 'vacuum' does not stand for any idea? Our mistaken belief that we have an idea of a vacuum is the result of misunderstanding the character of an idea that we really do have in his view. We do have perceptions that we might call "spatially nondense"—that is, spatially complex perceptions, some of whose component parts are not contiguous but have no other perception between them. Hume is concerned only to deny that the unfilled "fictitious distance" between such noncontiguous perceptions is *itself another perception*. While there are perceptions—both impressions and ideas—of spatially nondense situations, there are no perceptions of the vacuum itself, as something that occupies the unfilled locations. In other words, we represent spatially nondense situations entirely with colored and tactile representations that are themselves spatially nondense; we do not and cannot utilize any uncolored and nontactile representations of the empty space itself.

It is potentially misleading, therefore, to describe Hume as denying that we can conceive any such thing as a vacuum. For as the passage cited shows, he is inclined to agree (and thereby implies that he can conceive) that there are real situations that would permit the interjection of additional bodies without either "impulsion or penetration" of the bodies already present—just as our spatially nondense perceptions suggest there might be. And this is precisely what the defenders of the vacuum have maintained. Hume's position is best expressed not as the claim that there is no such thing as a *vacuum* but rather as the claim that there is no such (conceivable) *thing* as a vacuum—that is, empty absolute space—playing a substantive role in our ontology.[13]

Similar considerations apply to the alleged idea of "time without a changeable existence," or changeless time. According to Hume, we cannot represent anything to ourselves as the *enduring content* of empty time, because we represent time by representing a succession of changing objects. Hence, no impression can be an impression of changeless time, and no idea can serve as the abstract idea of changeless time. Our mistaken belief that we have an idea of time without a changeable existence, however, is in Hume's view the result of misunderstanding the character of an idea that we really do have. For we do sometimes have perceptions of objects that remain unaltered while other objects change. By thinking of an unchanging object first in conjunction with one state of a changing object, and then in conjunction with a later state of the same object, we seem to perceive some change, and hence some alteration and temporal sequence, in the unchanging perception itself. In fact, however, the only perception of temporal sequence is our perception of the changing object. This produces the appearance of a "fictitious duration" applying to the unchanging object itself (THN 65), analogous to the "fictitious distance" between noncontiguous spatial parts that have no object separating them. Just as there are perceptions of spatially nondense situations but no perceptions of the vacuum as something existing *between* the objects, so there are perceptions of situations in which one thing changes while another does not, but no perception of *the duration of the unchanging object* as something that the unchanging object *goes through*. Just as Hume grants the possibility of new matter being created between two objects without impulsion or penetration, so he grants the possibility that an object that in fact did not change *might* instead have done so (THN 65). Hume's position about time is best expressed not as the claim that there cannot be time without change but rather as the claim that there is no such (conceivable) *thing* as changeless time playing a substantive role in our ontology.

Conceptual Empiricism and the Copy Principle

Hume's Copy Principle and his other views about the cognitive role of ideas, when taken together, imply conceptual empiricism. He does not treat the Copy Principle as a priori or as necessary, however, but instead as an empirical generalization— just as his own methodological and nomological empiricism require him to do. Hence, although the Copy Principle serves to justify Hume's conceptual empiricism in something like the way in which the verification principle justified the conceptual empiricism of the twentieth-century logical positivists, its basis and status are entirely different. Accordingly, Hume cannot and does not treat either the Copy Principle or the methodological directive that it justifies (i.e., to seek original impressions) as sufficient to demonstrate the nonexistence of a particular idea in the absence of careful investigation of the specific characteristics of the alleged idea.

Such investigations show, Hume believes, that there is no idea of a vacuum (i.e., empty absolute space), of changeless time (i.e., empty absolute time), of necessary causal connection in nature, of a substantial subject of inherence, of a unified and identical self, and of real moral qualities and relations existing in the objects alone. In each case, however, this is not the end of the story but the beginning of a careful investigation of the cognitive phenomena that are mistakenly described as the having of these ideas. Searches for impressions of space, time, and existence, in contrast, show for Hume that we have (many) impressions of each. The initial plausibility of the claim that we do not have such impressions results from the fact that these impressions are also of other things as well, so that there is no *separate or distinct* impression of them. Hume's theory of abstract ideas, however, shows how we can form ideas of space, time, and existence without their impressions being separate and distinct from impressions of other things.

Hume's philosophy would lose much of its distinctive character without the Copy Principle and the conceptual empiricism to which it leads. Yet conceptual empiricism, as a doctrine about concepts and their content, is subject to considerable vagueness and ambiguity. Hume's doctrine of the essential role of images in representation and meaning—the doctrine that provides the context in which the Copy Principle, as a claim about images, implies conceptual empiricism—serves to impose greater determinacy on the doctrine of conceptual empiricism. But it does so chiefly by oversimplifying the nature of concepts and human cognition through an identification of concepts with images (or, as in the case of abstract ideas, of concepts with images used as associative exemplars). Hume's methodological directive to clarify difficult or problematic concepts by looking for particular kinds of impressions seems, in this light, to be particularly misguided. For of all the many ways to deepen one's insights into the nature of important concepts, the mere intensification of images through concentration on particular experiences is surely neither one of the most important nor one of the most effective.

Nevertheless, Hume's discussions of such crucial yet problematic philosophical concepts as "space," "time," "cause," "substance," "person," and "virtue" played an important role in opening up both the eighteenth century and succeeding eras to new ways of thinking about these concepts, and in each of these Humean discussions the Copy Principle undeniably plays a central role. We will examine Hume's treatment of the latter four concepts in later chapters, and so I will not comment on them further here. But Hume's discussion of space and time—though somewhat less influential than the others—is illustrative enough for our purposes. His use of the Copy Principle calls into question both (i) the soundness of the Cartesians' alleged demonstrations that the world must be a plenum (since attention to the source of our idea of space shows that the denial of a plenum is perfectly representable and hence consistently conceivable); and (ii) the intelligibility and explanatory value of Newtonian metaphysicians' conceptions of empty absolute space and empty absolute time as independent metaphysical entities or quasi-entities. He thereby seeks to subject both Cartesian and Newtonian treatments of space and time to critical examination in the light of reflection on our cognitive capacities. Successful or not, this is a serious and substantive undertaking.

As this example suggests, and the case of other philosophical concepts will confirm, the primary importance of Hume's Copy Principle lies neither in its putative capacity to help establish conceptual empiricism as a general doctrine nor in its potential use as a weapon to attack particular words, propositions, or philosophical problems as "meaningless." Rather, its primary importance lies in the motivation that it provided to Hume for more detailed investigations into the cognitive processes underlying the use of central yet problematic concepts, and, more specifically, its tendency to focus those investigations in the areas of human experience and practice on which these concepts are based. The insights we gain from such particular investigations as these, Hume quite plausibly supposes, can have important consequences for the nature of our commitments to modes of both belief and action.

The Separability Principle

Unlike the Copy Principle, which has an acknowledged antecedent in Locke's denial of innate ideas, Hume's Separability Principle—the second of his two fundamental principles—has no obvious predecessors. He first explicitly states the principle as follows:

> We have observ'd, that whatever objects are different are distinguishable, and that whatever objects are distinguishable are separable by the thought and imagination. (THN 18)

Again unlike the Copy Principle, which appears explicitly within the first few pages of both the *Treatise* and the first *Enquiry*, the Separability Principle does not appear explicitly in the *Treatise* until the seventh and concluding section of *Treatise* I.i ("Of abstract ideas"), and it is not stated explicitly in the *Enquiry* at all. Like the Copy Principle, however, the Separability Principle plays a crucial role in Hume's *Treatise* arguments concerning space, time, causation, substance, and personal identity. And the parallel between the two principles does not end here. Readers have often judged Hume's Separability Principle—just as they have often judged his Copy Principle—to be undermined by a lack of positive support, by counterexamples, or by both.

John Laird, for example, describes the first conjunct of the principle (that "whatever is different is distinguishable") as "doubtful" and the second conjunct (that "whatever is distinguishable is separable") as "plainly . . . false" (Laird, 1932). Ralph Church calls the principle a "dogma" (Church, 1935). Both Laird and Church assert that, in his use of it, Hume simply begs the question against his opponents. And indeed, although Hume introduces his first formal statement of the principle by describing it as something that "we have observed," it is not immediately obvious that "we" have done any such thing. The immediate context of his formal announcement of the principle at *Treatise* I.i.7 is a discussion (concerning abstract ideas, described in chapter 1) to which the inverse of the principle is to be *applied*, not a discussion from which the principle itself could be *derived*.

Furthermore, Hume notoriously concludes the same section (THN I.i.7) with a discussion of "that distinction of reason, which is so much talk'd of, and is so little understood, in the schools." He offers three examples of distinctions of reason: (i) that between "figure and the body figur'd"; (ii) that between "motion and the body mov'd"; and (iii) that between "the figure and colour" of a body. As Hume says:

> The difficulty of explaining this distinction arises from the principle above explain'd, that all ideas, which are different are separable. For it follows from thence, that if the figure be different from the body, their ideas must be separable as well as distinguishable; if they be not different, their ideas can neither be separable nor distinguishable. What then is meant by a distinction of reason, since it implies neither a difference nor a separation? (THN 24–25)

In other words, the figure and the body (or motion and body, or figure and color) appear to be distinguishable (since they have just been distinguished!) and yet *not* separable, contrary to the Separability Principle.

Hume presents his explanation of distinctions of reason with an example concerning the color and figure (i.e., shape) of a white marble globe:

> When a globe of white marble is presented, we receive only the impression of a white colour dispos'd in a certain form, nor are we able to separate and distinguish the colour from the form. But observing afterwards a globe of black marble and a cube of white, and comparing them with our former object, we find two separate resemblances in what formerly seem'd, and really is, perfectly inseparable. (THN 25)

Commentators who discuss Hume's account of distinctions of reason have found it to be inconsistent with his statement of the Separability Principle. Kemp Smith (1941, p. 266), for example, says that Hume is "quite evidently allowing, under a new title, what he has seemed to deny in the earlier parts of the section."[1] Maurice Mandelbaum (1974) and John Bricke (1980, p. 71) each have suggested that admitting distinctions of reason constitutes an implicit and ex post facto restriction on the scope of the Separability Principle. Bricke does not specify what the revised scope of the principle might be. Mandelbaum, however, asserts that the principle must be restricted to apply only to ideas and not to impressions, on the grounds that Hume's account of the white marble globe constitutes an admission that "there are cases in which simple impressions are inseparable." He then adds that this restriction clearly vitiates Hume's crucial attempt to show by means of the Separability Principle that we never perceive (i.e., have an impression of) a necessary connection holding directly between a cause and effect.

In this chapter, I consider first whether distinctions of reason constitute counterexamples to the Separability Principle, and whether Hume could consistently restrict the scope of the principle. Next, I use the understanding of the principle developed in that consideration to consider (i) Hume's grounds for adopting the Separability Principle and (ii) his applications of it. In addition, I explain the bearing of the Separability Principle on a proposed solution, deferred from chapter 2, to the problem of the missing shade of blue.

The Separability Principle and Distinctions of Reason

The Intended Scope of the Separability Principle

There is a great deal of textual evidence that Hume did not wish to restrict, and did not believe he had restricted, the scope of the Separability Principle to ideas alone. In the passage just cited from *Treatise* I.i.7 (THN 24–25) concerning distinctions of reason, Hume writes as though it is the application of the Separability Principle to ideas that has become momentarily doubtful, not its application to impressions. Before coming to discuss distinctions of reason, of course, he states the Separability Principle with full generality (THN 18). And after discussing distinctions of reason, he repeats the full Separability Principle when discussing space (THN 27 and THN 40), time (THN 36), and substance (THN 233). When the topic turns to personal identity, he emphasizes that "there are not any two impressions which are perfectly inseparable" (THN 252). Even in the Appendix, when he comes to doubt his own account of personal identity, he retains his conviction that "the mind perceives no real connexion among distinct perceptions" (THN 636)—a conviction to which inseparable simple impressions would certainly constitute an enormous counterexample.[2]

Yet if we interpret the *color* and the *shape* of Hume's marble globe as two different simple impressions (as Mandelbaum suggests), then there is no alternative but to conclude that Hume does, after all, explicitly allow that two different simple impressions can be inseparable. Furthermore, this interpretation, though incompatible with the rest of Hume's text, is inevitable if one holds, as most commentators do,[3] that Hume's distinction between simple and complex perceptions is fundamentally the same as Locke's distinction between simple and complex ideas.

Simplicity

Locke defines a simple idea as one that is "in it self uncompounded [and] contains in it nothing but one uniform Appearance, or Conception in the mind, and is not distinguishable into different Ideas" [ECHU II.ii.1]. It is evident from his enumeration of simple and complex ideas in the *Essay* [especially ECHU II.iii–vii] that, if asked to enumerate the simple ideas of sensation that one perceives in seeing a black globe and a white cube, Locke would list at least the following: black, white, space, extension, rest, existence, unity, and (at least sometimes) figure. (Note, however, that even for Locke, ideas of *particular* shapes, such as sphericity, are not simple ideas: he describes them as "modes" of space, and he classifies all modes, even "simple modes," as complex ideas [ECHU II.xii.4–5].) Locke readily grants that some of his simple ideas are "necessarily connected" in thought with others and are inseparable from them in actual experience: the idea of "figure," for example, is necessarily connected with that of "extension," and the ideas of "existence" and "unity" are "suggested with" every other idea whatever [ECHU I.vii.7]. If Hume draws the simple/complex distinction in a Lockean way, therefore, one should expect him to grant that a simple idea of the globe's "whiteness" is necessarily connected with a simple idea of its "figure," because whatever is white must have some figure. But *is* Hume's way of drawing the distinction a Lockean one?[4]

Hume—like Berkeley, but unlike Locke—argues that our visual and tactile perceptions are composed of perceptual atoms, or *minima sensibilia*. Thus, in discussing space and time, he asserts

> that the idea we form of any finite quality is not infinitely [spatially] divisible, but that by proper distinctions and separations we may run up this idea to inferior ones, which will be perfectly simple and indivisible. (THN 27; cf. THN 38)

Furthermore, it is a distinctive feature of Hume's description of his spatial atoms that a *single* such atom has no shape (i.e., "figure") or extension, but that *combinations* of such atoms do (just as it takes two temporal atoms to produce "duration"); this is the essence of Hume's own attempted solution to the problem of infinite divisibility. As we have seen in chapter 1 and again in chapter 2, an abstract idea is a particular idea that is associated with a general term that can revive a disposition to call up other ideas of the same kind. It follows that any abstract idea of extension must be a particular idea of a particular instance of extension—that is, an idea of at least two contiguous (colored or tangible) spatial atoms.[5] And Hume goes on to pronounce the idea of extension—officially classified as simple by Locke—to be "compound" (i.e., complex) precisely because it must be an idea with more than one spatial part. He then argues that since the capacity of the mind is not infinite, the idea of extension must "resolve" itself into ideas that are "perfectly simple and indivisible" (THN 228; see also THN 38).

All of this strongly suggests that Hume draws the simple/complex distinction quite differently from Locke, especially where spatial perceptions are concerned.[6] Asked to enumerate the simple impressions perceived in the act of seeing a black globe and a white cube, Hume would reply that there are quite a large number—a definite, finite number, but one not deducible from the information given—of simple impressions. These simple impressions will, however, be of just two kinds: simple impressions of a shade of white and simple impressions of a shade of black.[7] To put the matter in somewhat more contemporary philosophical terms, there will be many simple impression-*tokens* of exactly two simple impression-*types*.

Why have Hume's critics failed to recognize that this would be his answer? At least part of the reason lies in the nature of Hume's very brief initial presentation of the simple/complex distinction in *Treatise* I.i.1 (THN 2). As noted in chapter 1, he there writes only:

> There is another division of our perceptions, which it will be convenient to observe, and which extends itself both to our impressions and ideas. This division is into SIMPLE and COMPLEX. Simple perceptions or impressions and ideas are such as admit of no distinction nor separation. The complex are the contrary to these, and may be distinguished into parts. Tho' a particular colour, taste, and smell are qualities all united together in this apple, 'tis easy to perceive they are not the same, but are at least distinguishable from each other. (THN 2)

This brief discussion is just as compatible with a standard Lockean interpretation of the distinction as it is with the interpretation I have proposed. It is only later, when Hume comes to employ the distinction, that a standard Lockean reading becomes untenable.

The sections of the *Treatise* I have cited as evidence concerning Hume's application of the simple/complex distinction—*Treatise* I.ii ("Of the ideas of space and time") and *Treatise* I.iv.4 ("Of the modern philosophy")—are read relatively seldom, and perhaps it is assumed, when they are read, that Hume is speaking of "simple" perceptions in some sense other than the sense he intends at other places in the *Treatise*. But, aside from the notion that Hume's theory of ideas must have been adopted entirely without question or serious emendation from Locke, there is no reason to make this assumption, and every reason not to do so. Oddly enough, the one commentator who suggests most clearly that Hume *might* consistently take his visual atoms as the only visual simples asserts that it is "plainly not *minima visibilia* (or *imaginabilia*) of which Hume is really thinking, as is shown by the instance he takes" (MacNabb, 1951).[8] But the instance shows nothing of the kind. For Hume is correct, on my interpretation, to imply that the color, taste, and smell of an apple are simple perceptions; they are simple perception-*types*. It is true that he does not remark, in giving the apple example, that there will likely be only one token of each of the latter two types and many tokens of the first at any given moment that one perceives an apple. But he has no need to do so in order to further his defense of the Copy Principle, which is the business immediately at hand in *Treatise* I.i.1. When it *is* important to remark that extended uniform color patches contain more than one simple impression-token—in discussing space (in *Treatise* I.ii) and extension (in *Treatise* I.iv.4)—he effectively and unequivocally does so, as we have seen. It may be granted that Hume does not always distinguish "types" from "tokens" in an explicit way, although he does quite often use the phrase 'particular perceptions' to refer to perception-tokens (THN 207, THN 252, and THN 634–635). But to the extent that he is not systematically explicit, it is because he rarely sees any likelihood of confusion arising, and surely not because he himself is confused or lacks the distinction. If he had truly failed to understand that the sense in which we may speak of "*the* perception of blue" is different from the sense in which the mind is a "bundle of perceptions,"[9] for example, then his entire cognitive psychology would lapse into unintelligibility.

Distinctions and Separations

Thus, there is convincing textual evidence for a non-Lockean interpretation of Hume's simple/complex distinction, one that treats the unextended *minima sensibilia* as the only simple spatial (i.e., visual and tactile) perceptions. Furthermore, such an interpretation allows us to avoid the view that the "color" and the "shape" of the marble globe are two different yet inseparable *simple* impressions. It remains to be seen, however, whether such a non-Lockean interpretation permits a consistent account of the relation between the Separability Principle and Hume's discussion of distinctions of reason.

As we have observed, commentators who examine Hume's discussion of distinctions of reason at all regard it as contradicting the Separability Principle or as implying, ex post facto, a large class of exceptions to it. But these readings cannot explain Hume's own attitude, which—far from being apologetic—is evidently that of someone who believes he has defended the principle in its full generality against a serious objection to its unlimited application. Hume promises, for example, to "employ the same principles [i.e., the principles mentioned in his account of abstract ideas, which include the Separability Principle] to explain that distinction of reason" (THN 24). He then repeats that to "remove this difficulty we must have recourse to the foregoing explication of abstract ideas" (THN 25). Did Hume really mistake a fatal *counterexample* to his principles for a successful *application* of them?

That unhappy conclusion can be avoided. Hume describes the color and the shape of his marble globe as not only seemingly but "really" inseparable. On the interpretation I propose, however, he has a perfect right to do so. The particular complex perception made up of a certain array of simple perceptions of white — that is, the perception of the entire globe's whiteness — is *identical* with the particular complex perception that is the perception of the globe's *shape*. Like any true identicals, these complex perception-tokens are neither separable, distinguishable, nor different, and hence they — or rather, *it* — cannot possibly violate the Separability Principle. This interpretation accords perfectly with Hume's assertion that we "consider the figure and colour together, because they are in effect the same and undistinguishable" (THN 25). It also accords with his description of "a figure" and "the body figur'd" as "being in reality neither distinguishable, nor different, nor separable" (THN 25). The perceptions involved are inseparable because they are identical — regardless of whether they are impressions or ideas.

But what then of the apparent *distinction* — and hence *distinguishability* — involved in distinctions of reason? There is certainly a sense in which a distinction has been made, but it is not a distinction between two different *perceptions* or *objects*. Instead, we have distinguished two aspects of the *one* perception-token, or as Hume puts it, two "separate resemblances" — that is, two different ways in which it may resemble others. Many writers on Hume (including Mandelbaum) use 'aspect' and 'impression' interchangeably, but that is a mistake. For although every perception — whether impression or idea — is an "object," as Hume uses the term in stating the Separability Principle, not every aspect of resemblance is or can be an object in this sense.

Until this last point is appreciated, Hume's solution to the problem posed by distinctions of reason cannot be understood. He himself saw that the point was not sufficiently clear in the original text. That is why he added an Appendix note to this section that makes the point more explicitly (THN 637) — this is the note already mentioned in chapter 2, in connection with natural resemblance and the missing shade of blue. In it, he argues that some resemblances between pairs of perceptions cannot be explained as consequences of one perception containing a simpler part that is qualitatively identical to a part of the other. He cites as examples (i) the resemblance between simple perceptions of green and blue, and (ii) the resemblance of all simple perceptions precisely in point of their simplicity. "Simplicity," at least, must be an aspect of resemblance between perceptions that is not itself a distinct perception occurring as a component part of every simple perception — for simple perceptions cannot have any component parts.[10]

Of course, the fact that a distinct perception of simplicity is not part of each simple perception does not entail that there is no idea of simplicity. The idea of simplicity — like the ideas of space, triangularity, extension, dog, or government — is an abstract idea for Hume. In this case, however, both the idea that serves as the abstract idea and the members of its revival set will all be simple ones. It is no accident that, at the beginning of his discussion of distinctions of reason, Hume says that "to remove this difficulty [i.e., the apparent inconsistency with the Separability Principle] we must have recourse to the foregoing explication of abstract ideas." For it is precisely this explication that shows how a *single* given perception may represent any one of a *number* of qualities by being associated with an appropriate class of resembling perceptions. And that is just what occurs in the case of a distinction of reason: a *single* perception-token functions as a perception *of* more than one thing (of whiteness and of globular shape, for instance; of a particular body, and of a kind of movement; or of a timbre, of a pitch, and of simplicity). The given perception will do so, of course, in virtue of its membership in various different classes of resembling perceptions.[11]

The distinctions of reason that appear to be exceptions to the Separability Principle thus prove to involve aspects of resemblance that—like simplicity—do not consist in the sharing of qualitatively identical parts. These aspects of resemblance are not themselves things or "objects," and so they are not within the intended scope of Hume's principle. This resolution may appear to be a mere verbal trick with the word 'object', but it is not. To speak of such "aspects" or "resemblances" at all is, for Hume, equivalent to speaking of the results of our fundamental capacity to associate resembling objects. And to speak of distinguishing such "aspects" or "resemblances" is merely a way of referring to the genuine distinction we find between the many different—but also distinguishable and separable—*classes* of perceptions that resemble the perceptions under discussion. Hume is thus able to maintain his Separability Principle without exception for all *objects*, including all perceptions, and it is for this reason that he regards his account of distinctions of reason as vindicating, rather than undermining, that principle.

Impressions, Ideas, and Necessary Connection

Hume does not restrict the Separability Principle to ideas. But even if he had done so, the restriction still would not have vitiated (as Mandelbaum claims it would) Hume's use of the principle to argue that we never receive an impression of a "necessary connection" holding directly between a cause and effect.

Hume does not explicitly employ the Separability Principle in the section "Of the idea of necessary connexion" (THN I.iii.14). He argues there that mere repetition or reasoning can neither produce nor discover a new connection between the cause and effect themselves. To defend the claim that we never perceive a necessary connection in our *first* observation of the objects, he relies first on his negative challenge: produce an example. But as noted in chapter 2, his confidence that no example of such a real necessary connection is forthcoming is based on more than the lack of such an impression in his own personal experience. For he argues (THN 161) that we cannot have an abstract idea of necessary connection unless we can conceive (have an idea of) some specific possible instance. This follows, of course, from his theory of abstract ideas, according to which having a general idea *is* having an idea, under certain special circumstances, of some specific possible instance. And he has more than merely experiential grounds for claiming that no such specific idea, or corresponding specific impression, is possible. For nothing, he claims, would really satisfy our requirements for such a perception unless it wou'd amount to a demonstration, and would imply the absolute impossibility for the one object not to follow, or to be conceiv'd not to follow upon the other: Which kind of connexion has already been rejected in all cases. (THN 161–162)

While he does not there explain why such a connection has already been rejected, the reason can be found in the earlier section, "Why a cause is always necessary?" (THN I.iii.3), and it does depend on the Separability Principle:

> All distinct ideas are separable from each other, and as the ideas of cause and effect are evidently distinct, 'twill be easy for us to conceive any object to be nonexistent this moment and existent the next, without conjoining to it the distinct idea of a cause or productive principle. The separation, therefore, of the *idea* of a cause from that of a beginning of existence, is plainly possible for the imagination; and consequently the *actual* separation of these objects is so far possible, that it implies no contradiction nor absurdity . . . without which it is impossible to demonstrate the necessity of a cause. (THN 79–80)

Similarly, a few pages later, in *Treatise* I.iii.5, he writes:

> There is no object, which implies the existence of any other if we consider these objects in themselves, and never look beyond the ideas which we form of them. Such an inference wou'd amount to knowledge, and wou'd imply the absolute contradiction and impossibility of conceiving anything different. But as all distinct ideas are separable, 'tis evident there can be no impossibility of that kind. (THN 86–87)

We do not in fact receive any uniform impression of sensation from all instances of causation, but this is not the essential thing for Hume. Even if we did receive one, so long as the impression of the cause and the impression of the effect were separable, *no* further impression could satisfy what, in Hume's view, we implicitly require of a perceived "necessary connexion betwixt cause and effect."[12]

It is apparent from the two passages just cited that Mandelbaum misconstrues the way in which Hume actually employs the Separability Principle. Hume does *not* argue in this fashion:

(A) The idea of the effect is distinct from the idea of the cause and therefore (by the Separability Principle) separable from it; in the same way, the impressions are distinct and therefore (by a second application of the same principle) separable as well. So there is no impression of a necessary connection in nature.

To draw the second inference would indeed be an error if (as Mandelbaum requires) the scope of the principle were restricted to ideas. But Hume's own argument concerning an impression of "necessary connexion" is rather to be paraphrased thus:

(B) The idea of the effect is distinct from the idea of the cause and therefore (by the Separability Principle) separable from it. Because the ideas are separable, it follows that the impressions—and, by the Conceivability Criterion of Possibility, the objects—are separable as well. So there is no impression of a necessary connection in nature.

Since this argument invokes the Separability Principle only with respect to ideas, it does not violate even the restricted version of the principle. Instead of making a second application of the Separability Principle, Hume simply assumes that whenever two *ideas* are separable, the *corresponding* (i.e., resembling) impressions will be separable as well.

This assumption can be grounded by the Resemblance Thesis of the Copy Principle. In his account of abstract ideas, for example, Hume argues that ideas must be just as determinate and particular as impressions, on the following grounds:

> [S]ince all ideas are deriv'd from impressions, and are nothing but copies and representations of them, whatever is true of the one must be acknowledg'd concerning the other. Impressions and ideas differ only in their strength and vivacity. (THN 19)[13]

Because the intrinsic difference between a perception's being an impression and its being an idea is not one of content but merely one of greater force and vivacity, the latter difference cannot introduce any *logical* or *metaphysical* difference between the two classes of perceptions: whatever is (metaphysically) possible or impossible for one should be (metaphysically) possible or impossible for the other. Hence, if two ideas are separable, their corresponding impressions will be as well.

In fact, the Conceivability Criterion of Possibility shows why mere difference of force and vivacity cannot introduce any logical or metaphysical difference between impressions and ideas. By the Conceivability Criterion, something will be (metaphysically) possible for impressions if it is conceivable. But because thought *about impressions* is, for Hume, formation of the corresponding (i.e., resembling) *ideas*, it follows that something is *conceivable* for impressions if and only if it is *possible* for the corresponding ideas. Hence, whatever is possible for ideas is also possible for impressions. In particular, if it is possible to separate two ideas (that is, if they are *separable*), then the separation of their corresponding impressions is *conceivable*, and hence possible.[14] That the separability of ideas is Hume's ultimate criterion for the separability of the things of which they are ideas (that is, of impressions and objects) is evident in the final phrase of the Separability Principle as quoted at the outset of this chapter: "separable by the thought and imagination." Of course, this result, namely, that whatever is possible in idea is also possible in impression, when taken together with Mandelbaum's "restricted" Separability Principle, entails the *unrestricted* Separability Principle—and this is another reason why the restriction would be unacceptable to Hume.

Status and Grounds of the Separability Principle

The Argument for the Separability Principle Outlined

If the interpretation presented thus far is correct, then distinctions of reason do not constitute exceptions to Hume's Separability Principle. That does not by itself entail, however, that the principle is well founded. As we have seen, Hume introduces it as something that "we have observ'd." But how and where can we have observed its truth?

Hume explicitly connects "difference" and "separation" only once prior to the first full statement of the Separability Principle (THN 18) cited at the beginning of this chapter. That connection occurs in *Treatise* I.i.3, "Of the ideas of the memory and imagination," where Hume is distinguishing between memory and imagination. He makes this distinction on two grounds. First, the ideas of the memory are more "lively and strong" than those of the imagination. Second, "the imagination is not restrain'd to the same order and form with the original impressions; while the memory is in a manner ty'd down in that respect, without the power of variation." Calling this latter feature of the imagination its "liberty . . . to transpose and change its ideas," he writes:

> The same evidence follows us in our second principle, *of the liberty of the imagination to transpose and change its ideas*. The fables we meet with in poems and romances put this entirely out of question. Nature there is totally confounded, and nothing mentioned but winged horses, fiery dragons, and monstrous giants. Nor will this liberty of the fancy appear strange, when we consider, that all our ideas are copy'd from impressions, and that there are not any two impressions which are perfectly inseparable. Not to mention, that this is an evident consequence of the division of ideas into simple and complex. Where-ever the imagination perceives a difference among ideas, it can easily produce a separation. (THN 10)

Supplying the content of this "division of ideas into simple and complex" from Hume's definition of that distinction (THN 2), we may outline the argument as follows:

1. [In the] fables we meet with in poems and romances . . . [nature] . . . is totally confounded, and nothing mentioned but winged horses, fiery dragons, and monstrous giants.
2. [A]ll our ideas are copy'd from impressions. (The Copy Principle)
3. [T]here are not any two impressions which are perfectly inseparable.
4. Simple perceptions or impressions and ideas are such as admit of no distinction nor separation. The complex are the contrary to these, and may be distinguished into parts. (THN 2)
5. Where-ever the imagination perceives a difference among ideas, it can easily produce a separation. (from 1–4)
6. The imagination [has a liberty] to transpose and change its ideas. (from 1, 2, 3, and 5)

The relations among the propositions in this outline call for explanation in several different respects.

I have distinguished (5) from (6) primarily because (6) is stronger: it claims not only that the imagination can separate ideas but also that the imagination can *recombine* these separated ideas so as to transpose their order and change their form. Of the two, (5) is closer in meaning to the Separability Principle, but it also differs from that principle, in two respects. In a minor respect, (5) is stronger than the Separability Principle. The Separability Principle asserts only relations among difference, distinguishability, and separability, without mention of any particular faculty or of how it operates. However, (5) specifically concerns the *imagination* and claims that where the imagination can perceive a difference, it can effect a sepa-

ration, and in fact it can do so "easily." That the imagination performs this function is, of course, part of what distinguishes this faculty from the memory. The
further claim that it does so "easily" is presumably supported partly by the empirical observations of (1). In another respect, however, (5) is weaker than the Separability Principle. For while (5) captures the Separability Principle's relation
between difference and separability, it omits any mention of the relation of either
to distinguishability.

Hume offers three lines of argument in support of (6). Each of these provides at
least some independent support for (5) as well, and hence provides support for at
least part of the Separability Principle. First, there is the purely empirical evidence
in (1) that the imagination liberally separates and recombines its ideas in such fan-
tasies as "poems and romances." Second, there is an argument from the Copy Principle, (2)—and more specifically, its Resemblance Thesis—together with (3), the
reflection that all impressions are separable. We have just seen that (3) can be
derived from the "restricted" Separability Principle (i.e., as restricted to ideas) taken
together with the Conceivability Criterion of Possibility. Because the present passage (THN 10) is *prior* to any statement of the Separability Principle, however, it is
more likely that (3) is intended here as an inductive generalization based on the
sheer variety of our experiences. Arguing from (2) and (3) to (5) and (6) presupposes that the copying of impressions as ideas preserves separability, but we have
already seen that the ultimate criterion for the separability of impressions *consists* in
the separability of their corresponding ideas. Third, and most important, however,
there is an argument from the very definition of the simple/complex distinction.
For that definition entails that there will be both distinguishability and separability
in perceptions just in case there is complexity—that is, a *difference* of parts—and
neither distinguishability nor separability otherwise. These consequences, in turn,
straightforwardly entail the Separability Principle—as well as the inverse that we
saw Hume employ, in *Treatise* I.i.7, in defense of his theory of abstract ideas (see
chapter 1). In doing so, of course, they also give strong support to the closely related
(5) and (6).

Thus, although Hume does cite, in (1) through (3), some empirical considerations supporting the Separability Principle, the principle depends crucially on the
definition of the simple/complex distinction. But how can a principle that is evidently derived largely from a definition have the kind of substantive consequences
that Hume seeks to derive from it? His ability to derive substantive consequences
from it depends on three additional factors: (i) the truth of the assumption on
which the definition is based, (ii) the clarity of the distinction drawn by the definition, and (iii) the correctness of his application of that distinction.

Distinguishability and Separability

First, it should be noted that Hume defines complexity in terms of the presence of
both distinguishability and separability, and he defines simplicity—the opposite of
complexity—in terms of the absence of both. His definition of simplicity (together
with his definition of complexity, and his treatment of them as opposites) thus
reflects a substantive assumption—namely, that distinguishability and separability

are actually coextensive. Hume does not explicitly seek to justify this assumption. However, he could well have argued (i) that the *making of distinctions* is a cognitive operation that depends essentially on the *separation* of ideas in the imagination, and conversely (ii) that whenever a separation of ideas occurs, the mind is in a position to make a distinction. Furthermore, he could argue: (i) that the only apparent counterexamples to the coextensivity of distinguishability and separability are those provided by distinctions of reason; and (ii) that he has successfully explained these apparent counterexamples away, by showing that they involve only the distinction—and possible separation—of *classes* of resembling objects.

Clarity of the Simple/Complex Distinction

Even if Hume is right to treat distinguishability and separability as coextensive, his ability to utilize the Separability Principle also depends on the clarity and consistent applicability of the simple/complex distinction. It has often been claimed that Hume's methodology is undermined by his careless adoption of Locke's simple/complex distinction.[15] In fact, however, Hume's distinction is neither careless nor Lockean. Locke's distinction permits, and sometimes even encourages, what Locke calls "necessary connexions," and Hume calls "real connexions," between simple ideas. (Hume uses the term 'necessary connexion' more narrowly, to apply only to causal connections.) By a "real connexion," Hume means a connection between some X and Y such that the existence of X entails the existence of Y, or vice versa; it is thus the opposite of a Cartesian "real distinction."[16] Some examples of "real connexions" would be: (i) the relation between a complex whole and one of its essential parts; (ii) the relation of necessary causal connection, construed as an inseparable relation between the cause and effect themselves; and (iii) the relation alleged by metaphysicians to hold between qualities and their underlying substantial substratum.

Locke's own reasons for having a simple/complex distinction do not require a prohibition on what Hume calls "real connexions" between simple ideas. As noted in chapter 1, Locke draws the distinction in order (i) to argue that certain ideas that may initially appear to be innate are really complex ideas made up of non-innate components; (ii) to explain why demands for definition sometimes are and sometimes are not appropriate (ECHU III.iv.7); and (iii) to provide a certain amount of architectonic structure for Book II of the *Essay*. When what Hume would call "real connexions" do occur between two different simple ideas—as between "figure" and "extension," for example—Locke regards them as constituting relatively rare instances of genuine, "non-trifling" knowledge of "necessary co-existence [of distinct qualities] in a Substance." By "trifling" knowledge, Locke means knowledge in which the idea meant by the predicate is contained in the idea meant by the subject (ECHU IV.viii.1–4). The "non-trifling" character of "figures supposes extension" as knowledge of "necessary co-existence" is guaranteed by the simplicity of the two ideas involved, since no simple idea can contain another as a part.

For Hume, however, such inseparable connections between simple ideas are unacceptable. He takes two steps in order to avoid them. First, he uses his theory of *minima sensibilia* to classify every nonatomic visual or tangible perception as complex.

This not only prevents simple impressions from having other simple impressions as spatial parts, it also renders such ideas as extension, space, and particular shapes complex. Second, he employs his theory of abstract ideas to avoid construing every feature or aspect of a perception as itself a different or distinct perception. Such Lockean simples as extension, space, rest, existence, and unity thereby become not distinct simple perceptions in their own right but rather *aspects* of perceptions, or ways in which perceptions may resemble or be classified with others. (The first two, moreover, are aspects only of *complex* impressions.) The ideas of them become abstract ideas, consisting of a determinate idea of an exemplar that is associated with a general term having the power to revive a custom of having similar ideas. Thus Hume, far from carelessly or uncritically adopting Locke's simple/complex distinction, draws a distinction of his own that is, given his theory of *minima sensibilia*, both clear and consistent. And far from ignoring the effect that the distinction has on the application of his Separability Principle, he draws the distinction in such a way as to help make that principle come out true.

Applications of the Separability Principle

Finally, if Hume's Separability Principle is to have the consequences that he thinks it has, it must be applied correctly to the cases in which he utilizes it. Among his most important uses of the principle are his arguments (i) that some (colored and tangible) ideas are not infinitely divisible, and hence that spatial imagination is atomistic (THN 27); (ii) that time is a "manner" of perceiving rather than a perception numerically different from the perceptions that succeed one another in time (THN 36); (iii) that there cannot be indivisible physical points if these are conceived as having extension (THN 40); (iv) that we cannot perceive any real necessary connection between causes and effects themselves (THN 80, 86); (v) that whatever can be clearly conceived, including each of our perceptions, is a "substance" in the sense of being "something which may exist by itself" (THN 233); and (vi) that there is no real connection, bond, or "perfect identity" among our various perceptions (THN 259–260). In the first two of these cases (the atomism of the imagination and the status of time as a manner of perception), Hume argues that because there is no separability, there is no distinguishability and no difference of parts. In the other cases, he argues that because there *is* difference (or "distinctness"), there are also distinguishability and separability. In each case, however, it is always open to Hume's opponents to dispute his initial characterization of the case as one of inseparability or difference (as the case may be), and thereby to dispute the correctness of his application of the Separability Principle.

Spinoza, for example, would agree with Hume that our expectations about the necessity of causal connections cannot be satisfied unless it is impossible and inconceivable that the cause should fail to produce its effect. He would also agree that these expectations are really incompatible with causation between different or separable things. However, Spinoza draws the opposite conclusion. Whereas Hume infers that our expectations about the necessary inseparability of causes and their effects must be disappointed, Spinoza concludes that all causation must take the form of the logically necessary (inconceivable-that-it-should-be-otherwise) self-development of a logically inseparable individual substance. A cause and its effect, as inseparable aspects or "modes" (in Spinoza's terminology) of this substance, are thus not different in Hume's sense.

Although it is possible that Hume was acquainted with Spinoza's metaphysical views only through Bayle's *Dictionary*, he makes it clear in his discussion of the immateriality of the soul (THN I.iv.5) that he is aware of the inseparability of Spinoza's "modes" or "modifications":

> The fundamental principle of the atheism of *Spinoza* is the doctrine of the simplicity of the universe, and the unity of that substance, in which he supposes both thought and matter to inhere. . . . Whatever we discover externally by sensation; whatever we feel internally by reflection; all these are nothing but modifications of that one, simple, and necessarily existent being, and are not possest of any separate or distinct existence. (THN 240–241)

Hume is concerned in this section not so much to refute Spinoza's view of the universe as to argue (to the detriment of "superstitious" religious philosophy) that "this hideous hypothesis is almost the same with that of the immateriality of the soul, which has become so popular" (THN 241). Nevertheless, he does indicate his reason for rejecting Spinoza's "hideous hypothesis." He notes that all "actions" or "abstract modes"—which Spinoza takes all ordinary objects to be—can be conceived only by distinctions of reason, and this for Hume implies that they are not really different. But, Hume writes:

> Our perceptions are all really different, and separable, and distinguishable from each other, and from every thing else, which we can imagine; and therefore 'tis impossible to conceive, how they can be the action or abstract mode of any substance. (THN 245)

He then asserts that "we conclude from the distinction and separability of their ideas, that external objects have a separate existence from each other" (THN 245). That is, because we can conceive various things (including causes and effects) as existing separately, their separate existence is (by the Conceivability Criterion of Possibility) possible, and they therefore constitute different things, by the inverse of the Separability Principle.

Spinoza, of course, would not accept this reply. As remarked in chapter 1, he follows Descartes in distinguishing between intellect and imagination. While he would grant our ability to *imagine* an effect as separated from its actual cause, he would deny that we can genuinely *conceive* the two separately. For him, it is intellectual conceivability, and not mere imaginability, that provides the test of possibility in general, and hence the test of possible separation—that is, separability—in particular. He would thus reject the identification of thought with imagination that is implicit in Hume's phrase "separable by the thought or imagination."

We have also seen in chapter 1 how Hume would respond to Spinoza's distinction. Although Hume distinguishes between clear and obscure thought (e.g., THN 51, THN 72, THN 232), he does not distinguish between imagining and conceiving as activities of mind. In effect, he denies that conceiving ever amounts to more than imagining, understood in the sense of having imagistic representations or ideas. His grounds, of course, are (i) the introspective absence of ideas of intellection, (ii) the obscurity and confusion of the results allegedly obtained through intellection, and (iii) the adequacy of his own account of abstraction, an account that does not require ideas of intellection but only images. Thus, the clear imaginability of a state of affairs is the only test of metaphysical possibility that Hume has. From one perspective, his version of the Conceivability Criterion of Possibility—namely, that whatever is conceivable is possible, where 'possible' means "imaginable"—is a bold thesis, permissively expanding the scope of the possible. From the complementary perspective, however, it is a highly cautious one. For Hume is following the policy of allowing as *possible* whatever cannot be conclusively ruled to be *impossible* by the only test of impossibility he has. Liberality about the possible is also conservatism about the impossible, just as the liberality about innocence implied in the policy of "innocent unless proven guilty" is also conservatism in judgments of guilt.

Although Hume's application of the Separability Principle to causation is one of his best-known uses of the principle, debates similar to the one just sketched are possible concerning the questions of whether any space can always be further separated in thought; whether time can be separated from the succession of perceptions that occur in it; whether any extended physical point must have different parts; and whether every sensible quality of an object, or each perception in a mind, is really different from every other. In each case, a crucial issue is likely to be whether there is a representative faculty, such as the intellect, that either (i) can separate what cannot be separated in imagination, or else (ii) can only conceive as inseparably unified what the imagination superficially separates. Hume's applications of the Separability Principle thus depend not only on the relation between distinguishability and separability, and on the clarity and specificity of his simple/complex distinction, but ultimately on his theory of representational faculties as well.

The Separability Principle in the First Enquiry

We are now in a position to answer the question of how Hume can fail to state the Separability Principle in the first *Enquiry*, despite the undeniable centrality that he assigns to it in the *Treatise*. The first *Enquiry* does not treat substance or personal identity at all, and it mentions space, extension, and time only briefly (EHU §§124–125). Of the many topics to which he applies the Separability Principle in the *Treatise*, therefore, only the topic of causation recurs to any considerable extent in the first *Enquiry*. And a trace of the principle does appear at *Enquiry* §25, where Hume argues:

> The mind can never possibly find the effect in the supposed cause, by the most accurate scrutiny and examination. For the effect is totally different from the cause, and consequently can never be discovered in it. Motion in the second Billiard-ball is a quite distinct event from motion in the first; nor is there anything in the one to suggest the smallest hint of the other.

Again at *Enquiry* §27, he asserts:

> When we reason *a priori*, and consider merely any object or cause, as it appears to the mind, independent of all observation, it never could suggest to us the notion of any dis-

tinct object, such as its effect; much less, show us the inseparable and inviolable connexion between them.

Finally, at *Enquiry* §58, he concludes:

> So that, upon the whole, there appears not, throughout all nature, any one instance of connexion that is conceivable by us. One event follows another; but we never can observe any tie between them. All events seem entirely loose and separate. They seem *conjoined*, but never *connected*.

Thus, Hume continues to infer from the difference or distinctness of causes and effects that they are separable, and hence that no real connection can be conceived between them. But because Hume in his first *Enquiry* seeks to streamline his presentation of his cognitive psychology, and to include only what is absolutely essential to his arguments, he forgoes the statement of, and arguments for, the Separability Principle. Indeed, he does not even formally state the nature of the simple/complex distinction from which it is ultimately derived, although he continues to employ that distinction (see, for example, EHU §49). Instead, he trusts that his readers will find his particular application of the principle to the case of causes and effects sufficiently plausible in its own right that he can dispense with an appeal to the principle's more general merits.

Separability and the Missing Shade of Blue

In chapter 2, we considered briefly a common suggestion for reconciling the missing shade of blue with the Copy Principle. That suggestion was that Hume should have treated every perception of a shade of color as a complex perception, composed of hues of varying intensity or composed of hue, saturation, and brightness. We are now in a position to see why this suggestion is misguided. First, as already argued in chapter 2, Hume *has* no very serious problem with the missing shade of blue. He is interested in the Copy Principle as a general psychological regularity that sheds light on cognitive processes of concept-formation, and as the support for a methodological directive concerning problematic ideas, but unlike Locke, he does not make the denial of "innate ideas" an end in itself. Hume believes that he has a good psychological explanation for the one technical exception he has discovered, and it turns on circumstances of natural resemblance special to that case. Hence the exception does not significantly undermine the methodology or the inductive arguments. Second, however, because hues cannot exist without some intensity, saturation, or brightness, and vice versa, treating any of these as simple perceptions would violate the Separability Principle and introduce real connections between simple perceptions. This would be a far more serious matter for him than an isolated exception to the Copy Principle, especially where the exception in question does not call for any major revision of the Resemblance Thesis or the theory of representational faculties. Instead, Hume provides an account that permits hues, intensities, degrees of saturation, and degrees of brightness to be distinguishable aspects of a single simple perception (which is *of* both, and also *of* a single shade). He does so in a way that does not violate the Separability Principle or introduce real connections among distinct perceptions.

Representational Simplicity and Separability

Distinctions of reason are not counterexamples to Hume's Separability Principle, as attention to his use of the simple/complex distinction and his theory of abstract ideas shows. Instead, they are distinctions among the different classes of resembling perceptions to which a given perception may belong—classes that are different, distinguishable, and separable. Although Hume offers some supportive empirical evidence for the principle, its primary basis lies in his definition of the simple/complex distinction. Hume's simple/complex distinction is far different from Locke's, and it allows him to avoid—as Locke could not—allowing "real connexions" between simple perceptions.

It is because the Separability Principle follows directly from Hume's conception of the simple/complex distinction that he can continue to use it while dispensing with any explicit statement of it in the first *Enquiry*. His ability to draw substantive consequences from the principle, however, depends (i) on his ability to justify treating distinguishability and separability as coextensive; (ii) on his ability to draw the simple/complex distinction clearly and consistently; and (iii) on the correctness of his application of that distinction to particular cases. Hume's theory of representational faculties, according to which imagination and memory are the only such faculties, greatly facilitates his attempt to draw a clear and consistent distinction between simple and complex perceptions, from which the Separability Principle flows. For that theory ultimately reduces the question of the simplicity and complexity of *perceptions* to the simplicity and complexity of *images*. Even the question of the simplicity or complexity of abstract ideas is clarified, becoming the question of the simplicity or complexity of the image that serves as the exemplar at a given time.

Hume's atomistic theories of spatial and temporal perceptual *minima*, in turn, are designed to facilitate this distinction between simple and complex images, by providing ultimate simples from which complexes can be constructed. Furthermore, he argues that since these perceptual *minima* actually exist, space and time can be *conceived* as being composed of atomic *minima*, and since every other way of conceiving space and time leads to contradiction or paradox, space and time must *be* composed of such *minima*. These theories, according to which a single spatial *minimum* is not extended, but two contiguous spatial *minima* are extended (and a single temporal moment lacks duration, although a succession of moments has it), are ingenious. They resolve some geometrical paradoxes, however, only at the price of engendering many others.

Consider one such paradox. For Hume, some line segments forming a right angle cannot be (and cannot be conceived to be) closed by a third to form a triangle. For on his theory, every line segment contains some definite number of spatial *minima*, and the length of a line segment is a strict function of the number of spatial *minima* it contains. Thus, if two line segments form a right angle and each segment contains ten spatial *minima*, it follows by the Pythagorean theorem that the hypotenuse that completes the triangle must contain a number of spatial *minima* equal to the square root of two hundred. Yet there is no whole number of spatial *minima* equal to the square root of two hundred, and parts or fractions of spatial *minima* are, by definition, impossible. It follows that two line segments each containing exactly ten spatial *minima* cannot both be sides of a completed right triangle. This suggests that in attempting to draw the hypotenuse of such a triangle, one will be forced to leave a very small distance between the hypotenuse and one of the sides. But what will be the size of that distance? It cannot be exactly equal to any whole number of *minima sensibilia*, for then it could be completely filled by them without remainder, contrary to the conclusion just established. Nor, however, can it be equal to any fractional part of a *minimum sensibilium*, for by definition no distance can be smaller than an unextended *minimum sensibilium*. In fact, Hume's conception of extension requires that he give up large portions of classical geometry, including such simple notions as that every line can be bisected. It is perhaps because he came to recognize such consequences that he abandoned and suppressed the now-lost essay on "the metaphisical Principles of Geometry" to which he refers in his correspondence (LDH I.223 and II. 252). Useful as it is in supporting his Separability Principle, his conception of *minima sensibilia* provides at best a problematic basis for geometry.[17]

Hume distinguishes all reasoning into two categories: (i) "demonstrative" reason, which produces genuine "knowledge," and (ii) "probable" reason, which does not produce knowledge in the strict but only probability (which he later distinguishes into proof and probability proper). Like Descartes, Spinoza, and Locke— but unlike Leibniz—Hume thinks of the logical force of demonstrative argument as primarily a function of its specific *content* rather than of its general *form*. And one chief result of Hume's imagistic and atomistic conception of mental representations is that it inevitably becomes much harder to discover and defend necessary connections *between* mental representations based on their *content*. Hence, the scope of what Hume and his predecessors call "demonstrative reason" or "reasoning a priori"—which depends for its operation on the discovery of such connections—naturally shrinks. As we shall see, it is precisely this consequence that Hume regularly exploits in his applications of the Separability Principle; indeed, the principle constitutes one of his most common routes for deriving philosophical conclusions from his theory of representation. For by restricting the scope of demonstrative, or a priori, reason, he is left free to investigate the role of other processes of human psychology in the origination and maintenance of assent. Indeed, it is his willingness to investigate these other processes, not his critical uses of the Copy Principle or Separability Principle per se, that constitute his most distinctive and important contribution to philosophical methodology. As with the Copy Principle, the primary value of the Separability Principle lies not so much in the doctrines it *forbids* as in the investigations that it *motivates*. It is to a selection of those investigations that we now turn in the chapters that follow.

4

Reason and Induction

In *An Abstract of a Book Lately Published; Entitled, A Treatise of Human Nature,* which is his anonymous review of his own *Treatise,* Hume writes:

> The celebrated *Monsieur Leibnitz* has observed it to be a defect in the common sys-tems of logic, that they are very copious when they explain the operations of the under-standing in the forming of demonstrations, but are too concise when they treat of prob-abilities, and those other measures of evidence on which life and action intirely depend, and which are our guides even in most of our philosophical speculations. In this censure, he comprehends *the essay on human understanding* [Locke], *le reserche de la verité* [Malebranche], and *l'art de penser* [chiefly Arnauld and Nicod]. The author of the *treatise of human nature* seems to have been sensible of this defect in these philosophers, and has endeavoured, as much as he can, to supply it. (ATHN 646–647)

Hume's emphasis on probabilities and nondemonstrative reasonings reflects the eighteenth century's increasing concern with these topics in the wake of Newton's consummation of the Scientific Revolution.

According to Hume, nondemonstrative inference—which he calls "probable" reasoning in the *Treatise* and "moral reasoning" in the first *Enquiry*—is always based on supposed relations of cause and effect and occurs when the mind passes from an impression or memory to a vivid idea, which latter constitutes a belief. His main conclusion about such inference seems startling. He argues in *Treatise* I.iii.6:

> When the mind . . . passes from the idea or impression of one object to the idea or belief of another, it is not determin'd by reason, but by certain principles, which associ-ate together the ideas of these objects, and unite them in the imagination. (THN 92)

A second version of the same argument comprises Section IV of the *Enquiry,* while a summary version of it occurs in the *Abstract of a Treatise of Human Nature,* fol-lowing the passage already cited.

This argument is generally regarded as constituting the essential core of Hume's philosophy. After introductory remarks and a few pages on the origin and associa-tion of ideas, it is the first main topic he takes up in the first *Enquiry,* and it is the one from which his other topics are made to flow. It concerns the status of the vast majority of human beliefs and provides the key to Hume's positive analysis of the causal relation. Hume devotes more space to it in the *Abstract* than to any other argument, and he clearly regards it as one of his most important and most original contributions to philosophy. Yet the argument is often thought to be flatly incompatible with many of Hume's own claims and methods. It has contributed perhaps more than any other single argument to his present philosophical stature, yet relatively few philosophers have actually claimed to endorse it. Indeed, although it is one of the most famous arguments in the entire history of philosophy, there has been a considerable amount of vagueness, ambiguity, and outright disagreement concerning the meaning of its conclusion.

Traditionally, the argument has been taken to provide Hume's chief grounds for a radical skepticism about the class of inferences that he calls "inferences from experience" or "reasoning from cause and effect." Since Hume, these inferences have come to be called "inductive"—that is, they are those in which conclusions about unobserved cases are reached on the basis of "projecting" their features onto observed cases, thereby treating unobserved cases as resembling observed cases. Hume himself uses the term 'induction' only three times in his published writings, and always in the most general of the various senses recognized by the *Oxford English Dictionary*, namely, as a synonym for 'inference' in general. I will nevertheless follow current practice in using 'induction' to refer to the kind of inference that Hume called "inferences from experience" or "reasonings from cause and effect."

The conclusion of Hume's famous argument is widely regarded as an extremely negative evaluation of the evidentiary value of inductive inferences, and it is often paraphrased as the claim that inductive arguments never provide any real "evidence" or "grounds" for their conclusions; that inductive inferences are "unreasonable," "irrational," and/or "unwarranted"; or that the premises of inductive arguments do not render their conclusions "more probable." D. C. Stove (1973) provides perhaps the clearest and most determinate version of the traditional interpretation. He interprets Hume's "inductive skepticism" as the claim that inductive arguments never increase the probability of their conclusions (i.e., "for all inductive arguments from e to h, $P(h,e.t) = P(h,t)$, where t is a tautology"). Stove finds Hume's explicit premises sufficient to warrant only a much weaker claim, "inductive fallibilism," to the effect that inductive arguments never raise the probability of their conclusions to the level of absolute certainty (i.e., "for all inductive arguments from e to h, $P(h,e.t) < 1$"). Stove claims that Hume erroneously inferred the doctrine of inductive skepticism from inductive fallibilism by means of a false tacit premise—the "deductivist assumption"—that only deductively valid arguments can increase the probability of their conclusions (i.e., "for all invalid arguments from e to h, $P(h,e.t) = P(h,t)$").

More recently, however, a number of commentators have maintained that Hume's argument is not a radical attack on induction at all, but is to be understood more restrictedly, as an attack only on narrow "deductivistic" or "rationalistic" *conceptions* of inductive inference. Ironically enough, in fact, the exemplary rigor of Stove's formalization has contributed substantially to this reaction against skeptical interpretations such as his. Many readers, convinced by Stove's description of

Hume's premises but unwilling to ascribe to him such an outrageous enthymeme, have concluded instead that Hume argued *only* for something like inductive falli-bilism, rather than inductive skepticism. In this chapter, I begin by considering rea-sons for doubting the traditional skeptical interpretation of the argument, and I contend that there are indeed at least two strong reasons to reject that interpreta-tion. Next, I describe four versions of the more recent nonskeptical interpretation, and I argue that they must each be rejected—for the same three reasons in each case. Finally, I propose and defend a different interpretation of Hume's conclusion, according to which it is not a direct denial of the evidential value of inductive infer-ences on *any* conception of them, but is instead a straightforward negative conclu-sion, within cognitive psychology, about the causes of the mechanism of inductive inference.

The Skeptical Interpretation

Hume's Use and Endorsement of Induction

There are a number of features of Hume's writings that seem incompatible with the traditional skeptical interpretation of his famous argument. First, the very subti-tle of the *Treatise* promises "An Attempt to Introduce the Experimental Method of Reasoning into Moral Subjects." Yet the experimental method is itself inductive. Hence, if every inductive inference is utterly lacking in epistemic value, then so, too, is the use of this method, together with any "science of man" that might be based upon it. Second, Hume himself makes inductive inferences constantly—before, during, and after the famous argument of *Treatise* I.iii.6. Third, he goes on—in the remainder of the *Treatise*, the first *Enquiry*, and elsewhere—to criticize various beliefs that result in part from superstition, enthusiasm, prejudice, pilgrim-ages, relics, overdependence on recent cases, the sheer repetition of "education," the pleasantness of surprising or amazing stories, and excessive or uncritical reliance on testimony. His stated grounds for doing so are that such beliefs are incompatible with "philosophical" standards of "reasoning concerning causes and effects"—that is, inductive reasoning. In fact, he devotes an entire section, *Treatise* I.iii.15, to providing a set of positive "Rules by which to judge of causes and effects."

Striking as these facts are, however, they are not decisive by themselves. One might seek to reconcile a traditional interpretation of Hume's famous argument with his own practice and endorsement of standard inductive inference by appeal to his doctrine that inductive inference is psychologically inevitable. For the *Trea-tise* provides not only descriptions of Hume's theories but also dramatic enactments or instantiations of them.[1] Hume's theories about the psychology of philosophizing entail that philosophers will sometimes say radically different things in radically dif-ferent moods. Thus, in *Treatise* I.iv.1 ("Of scepticism with regard to reason"), Hume first observes:

> When I reflect on the natural fallibility of my judgment, I have less confidence in my
> opinions, than when I consider the objects concerning which I reason; and when I pro-

ceed still farther, to turn the scrutiny against every successive estimation I make of my faculties, all the rules of logic require a continual diminution, and at last a total extinction of belief and evidence. (THN 183)

Yet in concluding the section, he remarks:

'Tis happy, therefore, that nature breaks the force of all sceptical arguments in time, and keeps them from having any considerable influence on the understanding. (THN 187)

Similarly, Hume begins *Treatise* I.iv.2, "Of scepticism with regard to the senses," by remarking:

We may well ask, *What causes induce us to believe in the existence of body?* but 'tis in vain to ask, *Whether there be body or not?* That is a point, which we must take for granted in all our reasonings. (THN 187)

Yet he concludes that section by observing:

I begun this subject with premising, that we ought to have an implicit faith in our senses, and that this wou'd be the conclusion, I should draw from the whole of my reasoning. But to be ingenuous, I feel myself *at present* of a quite contrary sentiment, and am more inclin'd to repose no faith at all in my senses, or rather imagination, than to place in it such an implicit confidence. . . . This sceptical doubt, both with respect to reason and the senses, is a malady, which can never be radically cur'd, but must return upon us every moment, however we may chace it away, and sometimes may seem entirely free from it. 'Tis impossible upon any system to defend either our understanding or senses; and we but expose them farther when we endeavour to justify them in that manner. As the sceptical doubt arises naturally from a profound and intense reflection on those subjects, it always encreases, the farther we carry our reflections, whether in opposition or conformity to it. Carelessness and in-attention alone can afford us any remedy. For this reason I rely entirely upon them; and take it for granted, whatever may be the reader's opinion at this present moment, that an hour hence he will be persuaded there is both an external and internal world. . . . (THN 217–218)

On an even larger scale, there is the contrast between the enthusiastic optimism of the Introduction to the *Treatise* and the skeptical despair expressed at the beginning of *Treatise* I.iv.7 ("Conclusion of this book"). This skeptical despair, produced by an intense survey of the most disturbing skeptical results of Book I of the *Treatise*, at first leads to a rejection of philosophy, yet the very reduction of skeptical anxiety that this rejection produces ultimately contributes to the author's return to philosophy at the end of *Treatise* I.iv.7, preparatory to embarking on Books II and III.

In light of these features of the *Treatise*, it may be argued, we should not be surprised to find Hume employing inductive inference throughout his work, even if he does once—in *Treatise* I.iii.6—find such inference to be devoid of evidentiary value. For Hume's theory about the psychology of causal inference entails that we will, on the whole, continue to engage in such inference, regardless of philosophical argument. Indeed, that theory arguably also entails, as a special instance, that we will, on the whole, continue to *approve* epistemically of our engaging in it, so long as such inference continues to succeed.[2] That is because projecting the observed success of observed instances of induction onto unobserved instances—and thereby coming to approve of inductive inferences—would itself be just another instance of the unavoidable cognitive mechanism of induction. This consequence parallels an important consequence that Hume derives more explicitly from the mechanism of moral evaluation in the final section of Book III of the *Treatise*. There Hume argues that, despite the temporarily disconcerting "hideousness" involved in examining the "hidden springs" of morality too closely, we must inevitably continue not only to feel the pull of morality but also—by the very mechanism of sympathy that renders our moral concern inevitable—continue to *approve* of that moral concern and the mechanism of its production.

Similarly, Hume's psychological theory requires that we will, if we reflect on the sources of our belief, come to *disapprove* of sources of just those kinds that he frequently criticizes. We will disapprove of these sources because we must judge them to be more "fluctuating and uncertain" (THN 109–110; see also THN 150) in their operations than standard induction. We are uncomfortable with the reflection that the sources of our beliefs are variable, impermanent, and unstable in this way, and hence we cannot, as a matter of psychological fact, reflectively approve of them. Thus, we should not be surprised to find him drawing invidious distinctions between standard inductive inference and other sources of belief: if he did not do so, he would provide a counterexample to his own psychological theory. Consistency with his psychological theory, it may be said, will require some inconsistency in the tone and even the content of his philosophical declamations at different times. Even if he does *conclude* that induction is without evidentiary value, therefore, it does not follow that he would or could *continue* to hold that opinion consistently. And although it might be objected that the predictions of his own psychological theory are among the class of inductively based beliefs that he has concluded to be unreasonable, Hume could cheerfully reply that he would be willing to abandon that psychological theory once and for all—just as soon as he found it to be within his power.

Hume's Expressions of Skepticism

Although Hume's use and endorsement of induction need not prevent him from also arguing for its evidential worthlessness, there remain two further objections that this proposed reconciliation cannot meet. The first is that, although the proposed reconciliation may in principle account for the *fact* of his practice and recommendation of induction, it cannot so easily account for its *manner*. Hume simply does not express the same kind of skeptical discomfort in the famous argument of *Treatise* I.iii.6 that he expresses when engaged in close examination of skeptical topics. In fact, *Treatise* I.iii.6 itself does not contain any reference to skepticism at all. Nor—with one passing exception (THN 150), which concerns not induction as a whole but the conflict between two kinds of "general rules"—do any of the remaining hundred pages of *Treatise* I.iii. The topic of skepticism, although mentioned at the outset of the *Treatise*, is discussed at length only in *Treatise* I.iv—where an entirely different set of arguments, newly introduced and explicitly labeled as skeptical, receive far more prominence than the argument of *Treatise* I.iii.6. In the crucial summation of grounds for skepticism in the final section of

Book I, Hume does allude to the earlier argument when he considers the "infirmities . . . which are common to human nature." He there remarks in connection with the inductive mechanism of belief-formation that "after the most accurate and exact of my reasonings, I can give no reason why I should assent to it; and feel nothing but a *strong* propensity to consider objects *strongly* in that view, under which they appear to me," a propensity that "seemingly is so trivial, and so little founded on reason" (THN 265). The only immediate conclusion he draws from this observation, however, is that it should not be surprising to find inductive inference to be sometimes in conflict with the belief in continued and distinct existences, a conflict he has already described in *Treatise* I.iv.2. Ultimately, the observation does seem to contribute to his assertion that "when we trace up the human understanding to its first principles, we find it to lead us into such sentiments, as seem to turn into ridicule all our past pains and industry, and to discourage us from future enquiries" (THN 266; see chapter 10). But this is a statement of an emotional reaction to a further reflection on the psychological origins of induction, not a statement about its evidentiary value. Furthermore, the reconsideration produces even this emotional reaction only when it is combined with other skeptical considerations that receive considerably more prominence.

In fact, although many commentators have found passages that they believe ought to *imply* that inductive arguments have no evidentiary value, the *Treatise* contains no passage that manifestly *states* that claim. Nor do the first *Enquiry* or the *Abstract* contain any such passages. Section IV of the first *Enquiry* is entitled "Sceptical Doubts concerning the Operations of the Understanding," and the following section begins by relating the conclusion of Section IV to "the sceptical philosophy." But skepticism is not treated at any substantial length in the first *Enquiry* until Section XII (again, one hundred pages after the famous argument), where the nature of Section IV's support for skepticism is finally explained as follows:

> [N]othing leads us to this [inductive] inference but custom or a certain instinct of our nature; which it is indeed difficult to resist, but which, like other instincts may be fallacious and deceitful. (EHU §127)

This skeptical argument, which also involves the results of Section V, and is itself at least partly an inductive inference from our experience of other instincts, does not imply that all inductive inference had already been demonstrated to be without evidentiary value in Section IV. It claims only that inductive inference had been shown to depend on *custom* or *instinct*, which is now remarked to be a problematic basis. The *Abstract* does state, at the end of the section that includes the summary of the famous argument, that "the reader will easily perceive, that the philosophy contain'd in this book is very sceptical." But the reason given is only that it "tends to give us a notion of the imperfections and narrow limits of human understanding"—a claim considerably weaker than the claim that inductive inference carries no epistemic weight at all.

The Argument concerning Reason and Induction Outlined

The second objection that the proposed reconciliation cannot meet is this: there is no reason why Hume *should* regard the famous argument as itself sufficient to establish that inductive inferences lack evidentiary value. The argument contains the following main steps. (Although I have consistently quoted from the *Treatise* [THN 87–92], the structure and language of the other versions of the argument are parallel.)

1. [It is] by Experience only . . . that we can infer the existence of an object from that of another.
2. [The relevant kind of experience is experience of the] constant conjunction [of like objects or events, with one always preceding the other].
3. If reason determin'd us [in these inferences] it wou'd proceed upon that principle [which I shall henceforth call the "Uniformity Thesis"] that instances, of which we have had no experience, must resemble those, of which we have had experience, and that the course of nature continues always uniformly the same. (from 1 and 2)
4. The arguments upon which such a proposition [the Uniformity Thesis] may be supposed to be founded . . . must be deriv'd either from knowledge or probability.
5. We can at least conceive a change in the course of nature. . . .
6. To form a clear idea of any thing, is an undeniable argument for its possibility, and is alone a refutation of any pretended demonstration against it.
7. There can be no demonstrative arguments [i.e., arguments yielding knowledge] to prove [the Uniformity Thesis]. (from 5 and 6)
8. [The relation of cause and effect is] the only one upon which we can found a just inference from one object to another.
9. The only connexion or relation of objects, which can lead us beyond the immediate impressions of our memory and senses, is that of cause and effect. (from 8)
10. [The connection or relation of cause and effect leads us beyond these immediate impressions of our memory and senses only insofar as experience informs us] that such particular objects, in all past instances, have been constantly conjoin'd with each other: And as an object similar to one of these is suppos'd to be immediately present in its impression, we thence presume on the existence of one similar to its usual attendant.
11. [All] probability is founded on [the Uniformity Thesis]. (from 9 and 10)
12. The same principle cannot be both the cause and effect of another [e.g., acceptance of a principle cannot originally result from a kind of argument whose acceptance itself depends on or presupposes that principle].
13. [The Uniformity Thesis cannot] arise from probability. (from 11 and 12)
14. Should it be said, that we have experience, that the same power continues united with the same object, and that like objects are endow'd with like powers . . . [that only renews the question] why from this experience we form any conclusion beyond those past instances, of which we have had experience.
15. [In making these inferences from experience,] the mind . . . is not determin'd by reason. (from 3, 4, 7, 13, and 14)

The general strategy is clear: to argue (i) that "determination of" inductive inferences "by reason" requires that a certain proposition (the Uniformity Thesis) be "founded" on some argument, an argument that must be of one of two kinds—demonstrative or probable (demonstrative or "moral" in the slightly revised terminology of the first *Enquiry*)—and then to argue (ii) that neither kind of argument can do the job required. If Hume's conclusion that inductive inferences are not "determined by reason" is to be interpreted as a claim that induction is unreasonable, irrational, or unwarranted, in the sense of having no evidentiary value, then Hume must be understood to hold that induction can have such value only if its "principle" can be "founded" on some further argument. But Hume has said nothing at this point in the *Treatise*, or in the corresponding parts of the *Enquiry* or the *Abstract*, to support such a claim. Indeed, beyond a broad endorsement of the experimental method, he has offered no general canons of reasonableness or evidentiary value in that sense at all.

In summary, if the traditional skeptical interpretation is correct, then Hume (i) helps himself to a controversial and undefended assumption about the conditions under which induction could have evidentiary value; (ii) concludes from it that induction has none, though without making any direct statement of that conclusion; and then (iii) continues to employ induction without in any way stopping (at least in the *Treatise*) to discuss his basis for doing so. This is unlikely on its face, and this unlikeliness justifies the search for a different interpretation.

The Nonskeptical Interpretation

Four Versions of the Nonskeptical Interpretation

There are thus substantial grounds for doubting the traditional skeptical interpretation. We may distinguish at least four different versions of the non-skeptical interpretation that has been proposed to replace it. The first version is offered by Tom Beauchamp and Alexander Rosenberg (1981).[3] Beauchamp and Rosenberg assert (quoting THN 89) that "[Hume's] intention is only to show that, 'there can be no *demonstrative* arguments to prove, *that those instances, of which we have had no experience, resemble those, of which we have had experience*'" (p. 44).

They go on to characterize Hume's argument as "a frontal assault on rationalist assumptions that at least some inductive arguments are demonstrative" (p. 41) and as intended to show that "no inductive inference can be supported and hence justified rationally, in the narrow *a priori* sense" (p. 41). They also write that he "restricts 'reason' to *a priori* reason in those contexts where he directly discusses the nature of induction" (p. 43) and that "Hume stipulatively confines the scope of reason to the discernment of ideas and their relations (i.e., to deductive reasoning and intuitive derivation of nonsynthetic *a priori* propositions)" (p. 43). Their own fullest paraphrase of his conclusion characterizes it as a claim "that inductive reasoning can provide neither self-evident certainty nor the logical necessity that uniquely characterizes demonstrative reasoning *a priori* reasoning, and also that demonstrative reasoning cannot prove matters of fact by its own resources alone" (p. 37). Thus, in their view, "it was never Hume's intent to question the entire institution of inductive procedures and standards" (p. 41).

N. Scott Arnold (1983) offers a second nonskeptical reading. He claims that Hume is to be understood as arguing only that "no conclusion of a predictive-inductive inference is (or can be rendered) certain relative to its premises" (p. 44) in a sense of 'certainty' that requires deductive validity. Arnold allows that Hume does ultimately express radical skepticism about inductive inferences, but only in *Treatise* I.iv, and then only as a consequence of quite different arguments concerning the relation between induction and belief in external objects.

A third nonskeptical reading is due to Janet Broughton (1983). She asserts that, for Hume, a "belief that p" is "determined by reason," if and only if three conditions are met. These are, in her formulation:

1. I entertain the thought that p.
2. I believe other propositions—say, q and r—such that I can entertain [i.e., conceive] the thought that (q and r and p) but not the thought that (q and r and not-p).
3. My perceptions of q and r are either intuitions, impressions, memories of impressions, or produced as above by such perceptions. (p. 10)

Accordingly, Hume's conclusion that inductive inferences are not "determined by reason" should, she holds, be interpreted as the claim that the conclusions of such inferences cannot satisfy this set of conditions. Broughton allows both that *Treatise* I.iv.7 expresses skepticism about induction on other grounds and that the argument of *Enquiry* IV is later put to some skeptical use in the *Enquiry*, but she denies that *Treatise* I.iii.6 itself reaches any skeptical conclusions.

Finally, Annette Baier (1991, chap. 3) has also recently offered a nonskeptical reading. She broadly endorses the interpretation of Beauchamp and Rosenberg (p. 307n). She adds, however, that the "reason" at issue in *Treatise* I.iii.6 is "reason in the 'demonstrative sciences.' It is the faculty which can give us 'knowledge', as it had been treated in Section I of Part III. . . . 'Reason' for Hume is often restricted to the faculty of intellectual intuition and demonstration, that which can discern 'intelligible' connections" (p. 60). She also repeatedly describes Hume's famous conclusion as concerned only with "deductive" reason, or "interdeducibility."

These four readings are by no means identical. Each of them, however, construes Hume's claim that inductive inferences are not "determined by reason" as a rejection only of narrow "rationalistic" or "deductivistic" conceptions of the relation between the premises and conclusions of inductive inferences, and not as a denial that such inferences are reasonable or carry evidentiary weight. I will argue that each of these readings is subject to three serious difficulties. These difficulties concern (i) Hume's use of the term 'reason', (ii) his later comments about his own conclusion, and (iii) the structure of his argument itself.

Reason

The first difficulty with these readings is that they do not treat Hume's use of the term 'reason' in his famous conclusion in a way that is compatible with his own use of that term elsewhere in the *Treatise, Enquiry,* or *Abstract.* Each reading requires that the "reason" of Hume's famous conclusion must be understood in a narrow, rationalistic sense: as a faculty of demonstrative, or a priori, argument (Beauchamp and Rosenberg); as a relation that renders conclusions "certain" relative to, and hence also entailed by, their premises (Arnold); as a faculty concerned with "nonentertainability," or inconceivability (Broughton); or as a faculty concerned with producing "knowledge" in a strict or narrow sense (Baier). Yet outside the context of the argument under discussion, Hume consistently uses the term 'reason' in a way broad enough to include all causal or inductive inferences, as Beauchamp and Rosenberg, as well as Arnold, explicitly acknowledge. (See, for example, Hume's uses of it in *Treatise* I.iii.16, I.iv.1, I.iv.2, II.iii.2, and III.i.1, as well as the many similar uses of 'reason' in *Treatise* I.ii and I.iii.4–5.[4]) Accordingly, Beauchamp and Rosenberg state that Hume employs a "stipulative" or "stipulated" sense of 'reason' solely in the context of this one argument at *Treatise* I.iii.6. But nowhere in the argument or elsewhere does Hume stipulate, or even imply, that he is employing a special or restricted sense of that term.

By way of contrast, consider Hume's procedure when he narrows his sense of the term 'probability' at *Treatise* I.iii.11 ("Of the probability of chances"). For the purposes of the sections following *Treatise* I.iii.11, Hume distinguishes "probability"—in the broad sense he has previously used—into "proofs" (arguments "deriv'd from the relation of cause and effect, and which are entirely free from doubt and uncertainty") and "probability" in the narrower sense ("that evidence, which is still attended with uncertainty"). Not only does he give explicit warning that he is doing so, he devotes an entire page to explaining and justifying his decision. Furthermore, he begins his explanation by noting:

> Those philosophers, who have divided human reason into *knowledge and probability*, and have defin'd the first to be *that evidence, which arises from the comparison of ideas*, are oblig'd to comprehend all our arguments from causes or effects under the general term of probability. . . . [I]n the precedent part of this discourse, I have follow'd this method of expression. . . . (THN 124)

Hume has felt no need to explain his use of the term 'probability' prior to this point because it has been in accordance with the common usage of "those philosophers" who divide human reason into knowledge and probability and who regard the former as the evidence arising from the comparison of ideas. "Those philosophers," of course, include Locke and his followers. Presumably, it is for the same reason that Hume has not explained his use of the term 'reason' up to this point either (a point that of course includes *Treatise* I.iii.6): he has been following the common Lockean usage of that term as well. That usage, as Hume here notes, treats the products of "reason" as consisting in both knowledge *and* probability. This is because, for Locke, "reason" is simply the inferential or argumentative faculty of the mind. Thus Locke he states unequivocally: "*Reason*, therefore . . . I take to be the discovery of the Certainty or Probability of . . . Propositions or Truths . . ." (ECHU IV.xviii.2; see also ECHU IV.xvii.2)[5].

The four nonskeptical readings surveyed thus entail that Hume uncharacteristically equivocates on the key term 'reason', substituting with absolutely no warning or comment a sense of that term radically different from the sense employed everywhere else in the *Treatise* and his other works, and different from that of the Lockean philosophical usage he generally professes to follow.

Having Reasons

Second, all four nonskeptical readings are at odds with Hume's later summaries of his own conclusion. He often summarizes that conclusion not only by writing of "reason" but also by writing of "having reasons." The following three passages are typical (see also THN 265, EHU §128):

[E]ven after the observation of the frequent or constant conjunction of objects, we have no reason to draw any inference concerning any object beyond those of which we have had experience. (THN 139)

We can give no reason for extending to the future our experience in the past, but are entirely determined by custom, when we conceive an effect to follow from its usual cause. (ATHN 654)

[We] cannot give a satisfactory reason, why we believe, after a thousand experiments, that a stone will fall, or fire burn. . . . (EHU §30).

Hume clearly offers each of these remarks as a recapitulation of his conclusion about induction. But the claim that we have or can give *no reason* for making inductive inferences appears considerably stronger than (i) the claim that they are not determined with the self-evident certainty, necessity, or exclusive resources of demonstrative reasoning (Beauchamp and Rosenberg); (ii) the claim that they are not absolutely "certain" in a sense requiring deductive validity (Arnold); (iii) the claim that we can conceive the denials of their conclusions in conjunction with our past impressions and memories (Broughton); or (iv) the claim that they are not produced by the deductive faculty of intellectual intuition that results in knowledge as opposed to probability (Baier). Although Arnold suggests that we might read Hume's "no reason" as meaning "no logically conclusive reason" (p. 45), the contexts of these remarks do nothing to suggest any such implicit restriction. On the contrary, Hume goes on in the *Treatise* passage just cited (THN 139) to describe his conclusion as one so radical that if people once become fully convinced of it, "this will throw them so loose from all common systems, that they will make no difficulty of receiving any, which may appear the most extraordinary."

Probable Arguments

The third difficulty is to be found in the structure of Hume's argument itself. As we have seen, his general strategy is to argue that "determination by reason" requires that a certain proposition, the Uniformity Thesis ("that instances, of which we have had no experience, must resemble those, of which we have had experience, and that the course of nature continues always uniformly the same" [THN 89]), be "founded" on some argument, which must be of one of two kinds—demonstrative or probable—and then to show that neither kind of argument can serve this purpose. The problem for the nonskeptical readings just described is that none of them can successfully account for the need to eliminate the second kind of argument. That is, they cannot adequately account for the presence of the argument beginning at (8) and leading to (13), which concludes that the Uniformity Thesis cannot "arise from" probability.

In order to appreciate this point, it is necessary to understand Hume's terminology. "By knowledge," he explains, "I mean the assurance arising from the comparison of ideas" (THN 124). Since "knowledge" and "probability" (in the broader of the two senses he carefully distinguishes, which is the sense applicable to *Treatise* I.iii.6) are meant to be exhaustive, probability must include every other kind of assurance—as we have already seen him indicate in *Treatise* I.iii.13. Both there and earlier (THN 89) he also refers to knowledge and probability as two different "degrees of evidence." Thus, "knowledge" is that kind of "assurance" or that "degree of evidence" that arises from the comparison of ideas, while the "general term" of 'probability' must be made to accommodate every other kind of assurance or lesser degree of evidence (THN 124). A *demonstrative* argument is simply one resulting in knowledge in this strict Lockean sense of "knowledge" (see THN 31, THN 161, THN 180–181), whereas a *probable* argument is one resulting in probability. For both Locke and Hume, knowledge can result from demonstration, or it can result from *intuition*, which is the immediate perception of the relation of ideas, without argument or inference.

Probable Arguments and Demonstration

As noted, Beauchamp and Rosenberg characterize Hume's final conclusion both by quoting a passage from *Treatise* I.iii.6 (THN 89) and by offering their own paraphrase. In quoting Hume, they assert that he concludes *only* that "there can be no demonstrative arguments to prove, that those instances, of which we have had no experience, resemble those, of which we have had experience." In fact, however, this passage occurs midway through *Treatise* I.iii.6 and represents only an intermediate step of the argument, not its final conclusion. This is confirmed by our outline of the argument, in which the passage appears as (7). Their own paraphrase of the conclusion is that (i) inductive inferences can provide "neither self-evident certainty nor the logical necessity that uniquely characterizes demonstrative *a priori* reasoning" and also that (ii) "demonstrative reasoning cannot prove matters of fact by its own resources alone." Yet for achievement of either of these goals, it would be sufficient to show that the Uniformity Thesis cannot be given a *demonstrative* justification—that is, it would be sufficient to establish (7). The establishment of (8) through (13) would, for this purpose, be completely superfluous. I will argue for this claim in greater detail, taking these two goals ascribed to Hume by Beauchamp and Rosenberg separately and in order.

First, even if it could be shown that the presupposed Uniformity Thesis did have a *probable* justification, that kind of justification would do nothing to show that the relation between experiential premises and inductive conclusions possesses either the "self-evident certainty" or the "logical necessity" unique to *demonstrative* arguments. For on Hume's account, as we have seen, probable arguments are defined as providing a "degree of evidence" and a "kind of assurance" *different* from those provided by demonstrative arguments. It would also show nothing about "a priori" reasoning, because Hume explicitly claims that all *probable* arguments are derived from *experience* (THN 89, EHU §30). One might try to argue that Hume derives (13) in order to show that even the inference from experiential premises *plus* the Uniformity Thesis to an inductive conclusion lacks the "certainty" or "necessity" of demonstrative reasoning. But this will not do. For as Beauchamp and Rosenberg acknowledge (p. 43), a demonstrative argument for Hume must have *only* "self-evident *a priori* premises," and the existence of a *probable* justification of the Uniformity Thesis would do nothing to show inductive inferences from experiential premises plus the Uniformity Thesis to be demonstrative, because it would not show the Uniformity Thesis itself to be either self-evident or a priori. Nor would it help matters to interpret their phrase "self-evident certainty [and] logical necessity unique to demonstrative reasoning" more weakly, as referring simply to deductive *validity*. For the inference from experiential premises plus the Uniformity Thesis to an inductive conclusion might well be deductively valid even if the Uniformity Thesis had no justification at all.

Second, a *probable* justification of the Uniformity Thesis would also be irrelevant to the question of whether demonstrative reasoning can "prove matters of fact by its own resources alone," because any use of the Uniformity Thesis that was justified by a probable argument would, by definition, involve an appeal to resources *other* than those of demonstrative reasoning. Thus, it is impossible to explain why, if his conclusion were only that which Beauchamp and Rosenberg provide, Hume should have any reason to establish (13)—that there is no probable argument to support the Uniformity Thesis. Even if there were such a supporting probable argument for the Uniformity Thesis, the existence of that argument would be irrelevant to every element of his conclusion as they construe it.

Beauchamp and Rosenberg themselves remark that the "question may be raised" of whether their account can do justice to Hume's remarks about the question-begging character of probable arguments for the Uniformity Thesis. Their response is that (i) Hume "requests, with skeptical intent, *only* a justification of the assumption that the future will be conformable to the past," and not "a rational justification for the entire institution of inductive reasoning"; (ii) he challenges this assumption only in the context of rationalistic views of induction, and not in the context of his own use of inductive arguments; and (iii) he could have challenged this assumption in the context of his own use of induction as well—in which case he would have raised the general problem of justifying induction—but that in fact he did not do so (p. 59). This response does not meet the present difficulty, however. As they construe Hume's purpose, it requires only a demonstration that the connection between inductive premises and inductive conclusions does not provide either self-evident certainty or logical necessity, and that demonstrative reasoning cannot prove matters of fact by its own resources alone. I have argued that the issue of a *probable* justification of induction does not arise within the context of such "rationalistic views of induction" at all. The question remains, then, why Hume should carefully raise an issue that is utterly irrelevant to his opponents' position, but implicitly tends to undermine his own essential uses of induction.

Probable Arguments and Certainty

Arnold's reading is subject to a similar difficulty. In his view, Hume's conclusion is that "no conclusion of a predictive-inductive inference is (or can be rendered) certain relative to its premises," where "certain relative to its premises" is used in a sense that requires deductive validity. According to Arnold, Hume's strategy is to argue for this conclusion on the grounds that (i) all such inferences "presuppose" the Uniformity Thesis, and (ii) the Uniformity Thesis cannot in turn be justified in such a way as to "cure" the original "uncertainty" of inductive conclusions relative to their premises. Now, the question of whether the Uniformity Thesis can be given a *demonstrative* justification is certainly relevant to this question. For if the Uniformity Thesis could be shown to be a *necessary truth*, then we would arguably have a demonstration that the truth of the experiential premises could not fail to guarantee the truth of the inductive conclusion. In effect, we could have a demonstration that the inductive inference had been valid all along. Once again, however, it is much less obvious why Hume should be interested in a *probable* justification of the Uniformity Thesis if his concern is only to show that inductive inferences are incurably invalid and hence "uncertain." For supplementing an invalid argument with a *nonnecessary* truth has no bearing on the validity or invalidity of the original argument. Yet only a *demonstrative*, and not a probable, argument could show the Uniformity Thesis to be *necessary*, as Arnold in effect allows (p. 39).

Arnold seems to recognize this problem, for he explains Hume's discussion of probable justifications of the Uniformity Thesis as follows. Hume, he asserts, wishes to show that the original invalidity of inductive inferences cannot be "cured" by transforming them into "deductively valid counterpart inferences," produced by adding the Uniformity Thesis as a further, "deductively well-justified" premise. Arnold notes that there are two kinds of deductively valid arguments: those all of whose premises are necessary, and those some of whose premises are only contingent. Only the former are "demonstrative" in Hume's sense; the latter must therefore be "probable," because Hume intends the two classifications "demonstrative" and "probable" to be exhaustive. Hence, Hume must raise the question of the *probable* justification of the Uniformity Principle, according to Arnold, because he wishes to show that the Uniformity Thesis cannot be justified by *any* "suitable" deductively valid argument, even one with (some) contingent premises.

This explanation does not remove the difficulty, however. Arnold claims that Hume argues for (13) because Hume does not wish only to show (i) that the conclusion of an inductive inference can never be "certain" relative to its *own* premises. Hume also wishes to show, on Arnold's interpretation, (ii) that no inductive inference can be supplemented by a "suitably supported" (p. 41) additional principle—such as the Uniformity Thesis—in such a way as to make the conclusion entailed by (and hence potentially "certain relative to") the *expanded* set of premises. By a "suitably supported" principle, Arnold means one that follows with deductive validity from experientially-available non-necessary truths. Unfortunately for this interpretation, however, showing (ii) is not really a distinct task from simply showing (i). Any experiential premises available to so justify the *additional* principle (such as the Uniformity Thesis) would also have been directly available for inclusion in the *original* inductive argument—resulting in a valid inductive argument in the first place. It must be emphasized that Hume has not tried to place any artificial or a priori restrictions on the experiential premises of inductive arguments. On the contrary, he is trying to show *how* we make inductive inferences, and in claiming that we make them on the basis of a certain kind of experience (i.e., experience of constant conjunctions), he has already claimed to have determined *the only kind of experientially available truths that are relevant* to making such inferences. Moreover, he never gives the slightest indication that his interest in probable arguments -for the Uniformity Thesis is in any way limited to deductively valid ones, as Arnold's reading requires.

Probable Arguments and Inconceivability

Broughton's reading, too, has similar difficulty in accounting for the presence of (8) through (13) of Hume's argument. On her reading, Hume concludes only that the denial of an inductive conclusion is always conceivable in conjunction with all of our impressions, memories of impressions, and intuitions. But (1) through (7) are already sufficient to show that inductive conclusions are not "determined by reason" in *that* sense. At (5), Hume has already ruled out the possibility that the Uniformity Thesis itself has an inconceivable denial on the grounds that "we can at least conceive a change in the course of nature" (THN 89). This remark already entails that the negation of an inductive conclusion can be jointly conceived with all of our impressions, memories, and intuitions. In contrast, the question of whether the Uniformity Thesis can be given a *probable* justification is entirely irrelevant to Hume's conclusion as Broughton interprets it, because the existence of such a probable justification would in no way tend to render the denial of any inductive conclusion *inconceivable*. Thus, her reading, too, is unable to account for his inclusion of (8) through (13), and, while she mentions (13), she does not offer any rationale for its presence.

Probable Arguments and Knowledge

Finally, the same problem also argues against Baier's reading. On her view, Hume's claim that causal inferences are "not determin'd by reason" concerns only the demonstrative faculty that yields "knowledge," in Hume's sense, as opposed to that which yields probability. But a merely *probable* justification of the Uniformity Thesis is once again irrelevant to the question of whether the Uniformity Thesis can play a role in a demonstrative or "knowledge-yielding argument." Indeed, Baier allows that a remark from the very outset of *Treatise* I.iii.6 already settles (what she regards as) the final conclusion:

> There is no object, which implies the existence of any other if we would consider these objects in themselves. . . . Such an inference wou'd amount to knowledge, and wou'd imply the absolute contradiction and impossibility of conceiving anything different. (p. 64, quoting THN 86–87)

As she notes, this "does prejudge the question of whether causal inference can be recast as sound deductive argument" and hence also whether it can be construed as the result of the knowledge-producing faculty (p. 63). Thus, on her view, Hume effectively and quite explicitly begs the question from the very beginning of his discussion. She suggests briefly that (8) through (13) are intended to "see whether 'reason' can get assurance of the principle of induction (i.e., the Uniformity Principle) by other means" (p. 67), but this still leaves those steps strictly irrelevant to the conclusion, which for her already follows directly from a remark offered in defense of (1).

Thus, the four proposed nonskeptical readings are all subject to the same three serious objections: (i) they are incompatible with Hume's use of the term 'reason';

(ii) they are incompatible with Hume's own later paraphrases of his conclusion; and (iii) they cannot account for the structure of Hume's argument, which gives a prominent role to establishing that the Uniformity Thesis cannot be supported by a probable argument.

A Third Interpretation

Argument, Inference, and Reason

There are serious objections to both the traditional "skeptical" and the more contemporary "nonskeptical" readings of Hume's argument. Although Hume does more than simply attack a narrow rationalistic conception of reason's role in inductive inference, at the same time he does less than pronounce all inductive inference to be completely lacking in evidentiary value.

We can find one important clue to Hume's intentions in his characterizations (cited previously) of his own argument as showing that we can give "no reason" for making inductive inferences. Compare these characterizations with his statement of the argument's main conclusion in the *Abstract*:

> [E]ven after I have had experience of many repeated effects of this kind, there is no argument, which determines me to suppose, that the effect will be conformable to past experience . . . what *reason* have we to think, that the same powers will always be conjoined with the same sensible qualities? 'Tis not, therefore, reason, which is the guide of life, but custom. . . . (ATHN 652)

The same conclusion in *Enquiry* IV reads as follows:

> [E]ven after we have had experience of the operations of cause and effect, our conclusions from that experience are *not founded on reasoning, or any process of the understanding.* (EHU §28)

Consider, too, the following passages:

> '[T]is impossible to satisfy ourselves by our reason, why we shou'd extend that experience beyond those particular instances, which have fallen under our observation. We suppose, but are never able to prove, that there must be a resemblance betwixt those objects, of which we have had experience, and those which lie beyond the reach of our discovery. (THN 91–92)

> What logic, what process of argument, secures you against this supposition [i.e., the falsity of the Uniformity Principle]? (EHU §32)

> It is not reasoning which engages us to suppose the past resembling the future, and to expect similar effects from causes which are, to appearance, similar. This is the proposition which I intended to enforce in the present section. . . . [I]f I be wrong, I must acknowledge myself to be indeed a very backward scholar; since I cannot now discover an argument which, it seems, was perfectly familiar to me before I was out of my cradle. (EHU §33)

Hume should be interpreted quite literally, as making a specific claim, within cognitive psychology, about the relation between our tendency to make inductive inferences and our inferential/argumentative faculty: he is arguing that we do not adopt induction on the basis of recognizing an *argument* for its reliability, for the utterly sufficient reason that there *is* no argument ("reasoning" or "process of the understanding") that could have this effect. There can be no such relevant demonstrative argument, because the denial of the conclusion remains conceivable, and there can be no such probable argument, because probable arguments are effective only to those who already practice inductive inference. Because these are the only two kinds of arguments, he claims, it follows that no argument at all could cause or "determine" us to engage in induction. As a result, we find that we can literally "give no reason" for our making inductive inferences.

It must be emphasized that this does not mean that inductive inferences are not themselves *instances* of argumentation or reasoning; indeed, Hume continually refers to them as both "reasonings" and "inferences" in the course of the very passages in question. His point is rather that they are reasonings that are not themselves produced by any piece of higher level reasoning: there is no argument that could lead us to accept the conclusion that inductive reasonings will be reliable if we did not *already* accept that conclusion in practice. Hence, in just this sense, they are a class of "reasonings" (inferences or arguments) that "reason" (the faculty of making inferences or giving arguments) does not itself "determine" (cause) us to make. 'Reason', here as elsewhere for Hume, is neither a normative epistemic term (as proponents of the skeptical interpretation have assumed) nor a term for some narrow aspect or conception of reasoning that Hume intends to denigrate or abuse (as proponents of the nonskeptical interpretation have supposed). Instead, it is simply the name that Hume, as cognitive psychologist, consistently employs for the general faculty of making inferences or producing arguments—just as it was for Locke.[6]

Reason and Skepticism

This absence of a determining argument for the practice of induction is, Hume implies, initially surprising. He is well aware that it leaves room for us to raise a theoretical question about the legitimacy of inductive inference. But it does not itself entail that induction must be without evidentiary value, and Hume does not ever write as though he thinks that it does. In *Treatise* I.iii.6 itself, and in its correlates in the *Enquiry* and the *Abstract*, he concludes only that we are not led to make inductive inferences by grasping a supporting argument, on the quite sufficient grounds that there is no such argument that could move us unless we were *already* inductive thinkers. Whether and in what sense induction is "reasonable" or provides "evidence" or increases "probability" in spite of this lack remains, at the close of the famous argument, an as-yet-unanswered question.[7] Indeed, at least in the *Treatise* version of the argument, it is an as-yet-*unraised* question. At no point does Hume argue, assert, or imply that induction could have evidentiary value *only* if we were or could be caused to accept it by a further argument supporting its reliability. We can observe such potentially disconcerting facts as induction's dependence on instinct, or the apparent conflict between inductive reasoning and the belief in "continu'd and distinct" bodies (THN I.iv.2), and these facts can give us some pause (as we shall see in chapter 10). But the inevitability of our commitment to the practice of induction places severe constraints on the kind of psychological effects the recognition of these facts can have.

This interpretation of Hume's conclusion—as a claim that we are not caused to engage in induction by grasping an independent argument supporting its reliability, because there is no such argument available—has a number of advantages over both the traditional skeptical and the contemporary nonskeptical interpretations surveyed earlier. It construes Hume's use of 'reason' as consistently referring to *all* argument and inference, demonstrative and probable, throughout his works. It squares with Hume's own later characterizations of his conclusion as concerned with an absence of "reasons." It accounts for the structure of Hume's main line of argument, which is equally concerned to rule out demonstrative and probable justifications. In addition, it explains why Hume seems not to treat his argument as directly entailing that induction lacks evidentiary value, and why he goes on in the *Treatise* without offering any explicit defense for his continuing use of induction.

The Probability of Inductive Conclusions

Does Hume deny, as Stove claims, that the premises of inductive arguments ever render their conclusions more probable? Hume devotes *Treatise* I.iii.11–13 and *Enquiry* VI to the topic of probability in the narrow sense, the sense in which it is opposed to "proof." I will discuss the specific content of these sections in chapter 7; for now, it is sufficient to observe that he does develop conceptions of at least two kinds of probability: (i) a kind of probability based on the ratio of equiprobable chances, and (ii) a kind of probability based on past frequency. Remarkably, Stove (1973) finds these later sections concerning probability to be entirely without value, either in their own right or for the understanding of Hume—this despite the centrality of probability theory to his own interpretation of Hume. There is, however, an explanation for this negative appraisal. Stove's interpretation of Hume as an inductive skeptic requires him to attribute to Hume a (partly mistaken) a priori theory of probability (including the "deductivist assumption" that "for all invalid arguments from e to h, $P(h,e.t) = P(h,t)$") as the foundation of the argument of *Treatise* I.iii.6. Hume's later attempt to *derive* a theory of probability from a theory of human cognition at *Treatise* I.iii.11–13 and *Enquiry* VI, can thus only appear to be a confusion to Stove. In fact, however, Hume first develops a theory of probability only in these later sections. Hence, he need not and should not be construed as utilizing or appealing to one in *Treatise* I.iii.6.

In *Treatise* I.iii.11–13 and *Enquiry* VI, Hume develops a conception of probability according to which a preponderance of past inductive evidence renders an inductive conclusion *probable*. Stove is therefore wrong to assert that Hume accepts "inductive skepticism" (defined as the claim that "for all inductive arguments from e to h, $P(h,e.t) = P(h,t)$, where t is a tautology"). Nor does Hume accept the "deductivist assumption" that Stove ascribes to him as a tacit premise. However, while Hume grants that past experience renders some predictions about the future *probable*, he would also deny that we are led by *reason* (i.e., by reasoning or any process of the understanding) to expect the actual occurrence of whatever is "probable" in this sense. Our tendency to believe what is rendered "probable" by a preponderance of past experience, like our tendency to believe what has been "proven" by a totally uniform experience, depends not on the acceptance of an argument for doing so but on a deep cognitive instinct.

Determination by Reason

Few interpretive remarks about Hume meet with more widespread agreement than the common claim that he uses the term 'reason' in several different senses in his writings.[8] If I am right, however, few interpretive claims could be further from the truth. On the contrary, the key to understanding Hume's treatment of induction is the realization that Hume uses the term 'reason' quite univocally to refer to the inferential faculty—a faculty that produces two kinds of arguments, demonstrative and probable. In arguing that inductive inferences are not "determin'd by reason," Hume is neither expressing an *evaluation* of the epistemic worth of inductive inferences nor making a claim restricted to an arbitrarily narrowed sense of 'reason'. Nor is he denying that inductive inferences are a *species* of reasoning. He is denying only that we come to engage in this species of reasoning as a result of any piece of reasoning *about* it. Instead, he claims, an instinctive idea-enlivening mechanism— which we share with the animals and is an example of "custom" or "habit"—leads us to project experienced constant conjunctions of events onto unobserved cases, and thereby to arrive at beliefs about those cases.

Hume's famous argument is formulated in terms of an archaic distinction between demonstrative and probable arguments—a distinction based, as we have seen, on the *certainty* or *degree of evidence* that an argument actually bestows on its conclusion. This distinction has now, of course, been largely replaced by the distinction between deductively valid and deductively invalid arguments, a distinction that concerns only the nature and strength of the *connection* between premises and conclusions. Thus, an argument with false or weak premises may be deductively *valid* for us, although it would not have been *demonstrative* for Hume. Nevertheless, the thrust of Hume's argument remains persuasive. It seems that our only convincing basis for making judgments about unobserved cases ultimately requires inductive projection from observed cases. But the claim that induction will be reliable is itself partly a claim about unobserved cases; hence, we cannot provide a persuasive basis for accepting the reliability of induction unless we *already* accept the reliability of induction.

Hume's conclusion, as stated, directly concerns the *causation* of inductive inferences—a question in cognitive psychology—rather than the *justification* of such inferences, which is a question in epistemology. Nevertheless, Hume's argument also provides good reason to conclude that no argument can show the reliability of induction by argument without *presupposing* that reliability. The failure of subsequent attempts to "justify" induction without begging the question, and thereby to solve "Hume's problem of induction," is convincing testimony to the strength of Hume's position.

In the second half of the twentieth century, a "dissolution" approach to the "problem of justifying induction" has become increasingly popular. (It is so-called because it seeks to "dissolve" rather than to "solve" the original problem.) According to this approach, made popular by P. F. Strawson (1952), Hume was right to argue that induction cannot be justified by argument but wrong to think that it requires any such justification. The practice of induction, on this view, is so deeply embedded in what we call rationality that no justification of it is required. But on the interpretation I am proposing, Hume is not claiming that the reliability of induction demands justification by argument, and he would agree that our evaluations of human reasoning skills, like almost all of our other dealings with the world, presuppose the correctness of induction. The fact that we accept induction without having any non-question-begging argument for doing so can certainly raise a skeptical specter for Hume: it "tends to give us a notion of imperfections and narrow limits of human understanding" (ATHN 657), and it exemplifies what he calls "the whimsical condition of mankind" (EHU §128). The wisest response to this and other skeptical specters, however, is a topic that he addresses only later, in *Treatise* I.iv.7 and *Enquiry* XII, and which we will take up in chapter 10. Whatever its use or abuse by skeptics, Hume's famous argument itself requires no apology: it is the first and still—despite its use of a now-archaic distinction—one of the most persuasive arguments for a true and fundamental thesis in cognitive psychology.

Two Definitions of 'Cause'

In *Treatise* I.iii.2 ("Of probability; and of the idea of cause and effect"), Hume sets out to "explain fully" the relation of cause and effect. By the time Hume took up this question, seventeenth- and eighteenth-century philosophy had already found an ever-increasing number of prima facie causal connections failing to meet the Cartesian ideal of intellectual intelligibility. Malebranche, for example, found Descartes's supposed causal link between mind and body unintelligible; Locke found the causal connection between primary qualities and sensations of color, sound, taste, smell, and temperature—as well as physical causal interactions other than the communication of motion by impulse—to be unintelligible. Berkeley found the production of ideas by volition to be the *only* intelligible (and hence, for him, the only genuine) form of causation. Nevertheless, Hume's explanation of the causal relation was the first to reject completely and universally the entire ideal of finding causal connections that would be "intelligible" to the mind independent of experience. He is thus the first important philosopher of the early modern era to claim that the discovery of all causal connections depends entirely on the experience of regularities in nature. Equally important, Hume's explanation of cause and effect serves as a primary basis for a number of his most famous doctrines about other philosophical topics, including liberty and necessity, testimony for miracles, and natural religion. It is also, not unintentionally, deeply analogous to his explanation of moral qualities.

Twelve sections and ninety-five pages after first setting out to explain the causal relation, at the climax of *Treatise* I.iii.14 ("Of the idea of necessary connexion"), he comes to

> collect all of the different parts of this reasoning, and by joining them together form an exact definition of the relation of cause and effect, which makes the subject of the present enquiry. (THN 169)

He then proceeds, notoriously, to give not one but "two definitions . . . of this relation." The first definition states:

> We may define a CAUSE to be 'An object precedent and contiguous to another, and where all the objects resembling the former are plac'd in like relations of precedency to those objects, that resemble the latter.' (THN 170)

The second definition states:

> 'A CAUSE is an object precedent and contiguous to another, and so united with it, that the idea of the one determines the mind to form the idea of the other, and the impression of the one to form a more lively idea of the other.' (THN 170)

Near the end of *Enquiry* VII ("Of the Idea of necessary Connexion"), Hume provides a similar pair of definitions. Although there are several minor differences between the *Treatise* definitions and their more streamlined counterparts in the first *Enquiry*[1] the similarities are sufficiently great that I will treat the *Enquiry* not as providing two additional definitions but simply as providing alternative versions of the same two definitions that occur in the *Treatise*. In both works, the first definition—which I will call "C1"—appeals to what Hume calls "constant conjunction," while the second definition—which I will call "C2"—appeals instead to a psychological process of association.

Why does Hume provide two different definitions for the same crucial concept? And which definition or definitions—if either—does he regard as correct or adequate? We cannot hope to understand his famous discussion of causation fully without the answers to these two fundamental interpretive questions. Yet although these questions have produced considerable discussion, there has been little consensus about the answers to them. My aim in this chapter is to answer them definitively. First, I describe the various considerations that make it seem so difficult to determine Hume's attitude toward the two definitions. Next, I seek to shed new light on the questions by examining the problem that the definition of causation poses within Hume's own theory of mental representation and the argument that leads him to the definitions he offers. I then develop an analogy between Hume's definitions of 'cause' and his definitions of 'virtue', explain why he offers two definitions of 'cause', and argue that he regards both definitions of 'cause' as correct.

Four Interpretations and Their Evidence

Which of his two definitions of 'cause' does Hume ultimately regard as correct? There are four possible answers to this question: both, only C1, only C2, and neither. Each of the four alternatives has its proponents among commentators.[2] We may distinguish no fewer than eight different kinds of evidence bearing on the choice among these four alternatives: (i) evidence that Hume endorses both C1 and C2; (ii) evidence that he does not endorse both C1 and C2; (iii) evidence that he endorses at least C1; (iv) evidence that he does not endorse C1; (v) evidence that he endorses at least C2; (vi) evidence that he does not endorse C2; (vii) evidence that he endorses at least one of C1 and C2; and (viii) evidence that he does not endorse either C1 or C2. I will present these kinds of evidence in order.

Does Hume Endorse Both Definitions?

There are at least two reasons to think that Hume regards both definitions as correct. First, there is the manner of their initial presentation. As already noted, he introduces them in the *Treatise* by announcing that he will "collect all the different parts of this reasoning, and by joining them together form an exact definition of the relation of cause and effect" (THN 169). He then goes on to say that because

> the nature of the relation depends so much on that of the inference, we have been oblig'd to advance in this seemingly preposterous manner, and make use of terms before we were able exactly to define them or fix their meaning. We shall now correct this fault by giving a precise definition of cause and effect. (THN 169)

Although the forthcoming definition is thus characterized as "exact" and "precise," it so far sounds as though there is to be only one such definition. However, he next asserts:

> [T]here may two definitions be given of this relation, which are only different by their presenting a different view of the same object, and making us consider it either as a *philosophical* or as a *natural* relation; either as a comparison of two ideas, or as an association betwixt them. (THN 169–170)

It seems unlikely that Hume would offer only one of these two definitions as "exact" and "precise" without telling us which one it is. Instead, C1 and C2 are apparently both intended to be definitions of the kind promised and can be treated as one because they differ "only by presenting a different view of the same object." Although Hume's introduction of the definitions in the first *Enquiry* is somewhat more apologetic, even there he implies that the two definitions are the only "just" ones that can be given. He then goes on to say that we "may" define 'cause' either by C1 or by C2, and he confirms their parallel definitional status by applying each in turn to an example; namely, what it means to say that "the vibration of this string is the cause of this particular sound" (EHU §60).

Second, Hume explicitly cites *both* definitions of 'cause' in order to justify further claims. In the *Treatise*, for example, he draws four "corollaries" from his discussion of causation. The third of these (concerning the alleged necessity of the claim that every beginning of existence has a cause) is justified entirely by appeal to the two definitions, each of which is quoted in full (THN 172). And in both the *Treatise* and the first *Enquiry*, he cites C1 and C2 in order to justify the two definitions of 'necessity' that he employs in his discussions of "liberty and necessity" (THN 409 and EHU §75; see chapter 6). These two definitions of 'necessity', in turn, play an irreplaceable role in Hume's argument that all human actions are just as necessary as the behavior of inanimate objects. Thus, the evidence so far strongly suggests that Hume endorses both C1 and C2 as correct definitions of 'cause'.

Yet there is also a serious reason to deny that Hume endorses both C1 and C2. For as J. A. Robinson (1962) was perhaps the first to insist, not only are the two definitions not logically *equivalent* to each other, it appears that they are not even *coextensive*. Robinson argues that in order to satisfy (either version of) C1, an object must be the temporally earlier member of a pair of objects that instantiates a general regularity, but in cases where instances of this general regularity have not been observed, it seems that the pair of objects will not be associated in the mind, and hence that the earlier object will not satisfy (either version of) C2. Conversely, in order to satisfy (either version of) C2, an object must be the earlier member of a pair of objects that are psychologically associated, but in cases where this psychological association results from observation of the conjunction of objects in an unrepresentative sample, it seems that the pair of objects will not instantiate any truly general regularity, and hence that the earlier object will not satisfy (either version of) C1. In short, unobserved regularities seem to prevent the set of causes defined by C1 from being even a subset of those defined by C2, while observed but unrepresentative samples seem to prevent the set of causes defined by C2 from being even a subset of those defined by C1.

If, as it appears, C1 and C2 are thus not coextensive, and if Hume is actually endorsing both of them as correct, then he must either be proposing definitions of two different causal relations or else contradicting himself by strictly implying that the very same things both are and are not causes. On the one hand, he insists that his two definitions provide "different views of the same object" (THN 169–170), exhibit "the relation of cause and effect in . . . two lights" (EHU §60), and give rise to senses of causal necessity that "are at bottom the same" (EHU §75). Moreover, he actually draws as a corollary of his discussion of causality the conclusion that "all causes are of the same kind . . . there is but one kind of cause" (THN 171). Yet on the other hand, it is difficult to accept the view that Hume, at the very climax of his most careful and sustained line of argument, in two different works, effectively contradicts himself within a single page by successively endorsing two clearly incompatible definitions of the same central term. The necessary conclusion seems thus to be that he cannot really be endorsing both definitions as correct; he must either be endorsing only one or be endorsing neither.

Does Hume Endorse at Least the First Definition?

Hume makes a number of additional remarks—both before and after the definitions, in both the *Treatise* and in the first *Enquiry*—that seem to imply the correctness of C1. Here is one example:

> We have no other notion of cause and effect, but that of certain objects, which have been *always conjoin'd* together, and which in all past instances have been found inseparable. (THN 93; see also THN 173; EHU §74n; and EHU §127)

Such passages strongly suggest that Hume either endorses C1 alone or else endorses both C1 and C2.

Yet there is also a serious reason to deny that Hume really regards C1 as a correct definition of 'cause'. Near the beginning of his investigation of the causal relation in the *Treatise*, he isolates as "essential" to it the relations of (i) contiguity in space, (ii) priority in time of the cause to the effect, and (iii) "a NECESSARY CONNEXION [which] . . . is of much greater importance, than any of the other two" (THN 76–77). Similarly, in the *Enquiry*, he implies that it is impossible to "*define* a cause, without comprehending, as a part of the definition, a *necessary connexion* with its effect" (EHU §74). C1 mentions priority and (in the *Treatise* version) spatial contiguity, but as Kemp Smith (1941, pp. 91–92) observes,[3] it makes no explicit mention of the allegedly more important element of a "necessary connexion." Furthermore, Hume asserts in both works (applying the methodological directive described in chapter 2) that in order to understand the idea of necessary connection, we should trace it to the impression from which it is derived (THN 157, EHU §49), and he eventually identifies this impression as an internal impression of "the determination of the mind to pass from any object to its usual attendant" (THN 165; see also EHU §59). Yet C1 makes no explicit mention of this impression nor of this determination. Thus, it seems that Hume either endorses C2 alone or else endorses neither C1 nor C2.

Does Hume Endorse at Least C2?

Hume makes at least one additional remark that seems to imply the correctness of C2:

> When we say, therefore, that one object is connected with another, we mean only that they have acquired a connexion in our thought, and give rise to this inference, by which they become proofs of each other's existence. (EHU §59)

This passage strongly suggests that Hume either endorses C2 alone, or else endorses both C1 and C2.

Yet there are also three serious reasons to deny that Hume really regards C2 as a correct definition of 'cause'. First, although C2, unlike C1, does refer at least obliquely to the "determination of the mind," the internal impression of which Hume claims to be the true origin of the idea of necessary connection, this mention of "determining" itself gives rise to a new difficulty, as several commentators have noted.[4] When C2 refers to an object whose idea "determines the mind" to form an idea of (or "conveys the thought to," in the *Enquiry* version) a second object, or to an object whose impression likewise "determines" the mind to form a lively idea of the second, it seems that 'determine' (or 'convey to') can only be a verbal variation of 'cause'. Yet Hume is quite explicit that it is *any equivalent causal term*, and not just a single word, that stands in need of definition (THN 77; THN 157; EHU §49; EHU §75n), and if we seek to define 'determine' as a synonym for 'cause' by appeal to C2 itself, the result will be circular. This difficulty renders it questionable whether Hume could have intended C2 to stand as a correct definition of 'cause'.

Second, it seems questionable whether Hume would or could accept the correctness of C2 in light of other doctrines to which he is committed. For example, as Wade Robison (1977) observes, Hume refers in both the *Treatise* and the first *Enquiry* to "a vast variety of springs and principles, which are hid, by reason of their minuteness or remoteness" (THN 132; EHU §67), yet such unobserved causes do not produce any association in the mind, and hence they seem, by C2, not to be causes at all. Similarly, *Treatise* I.iii.15 — "Rules by which to judge of causes and effects" — makes one's beliefs about the presence or absence of causal relations subject to considerable criticism and correction, yet it seems difficult to be mistaken about the occurrence or nonoccurrence of psychological processes of association and inference in the mind, as specified by C2.

Third, C2 seems to have a number of implications that have struck many readers as showing it to be simply too implausible for a philosopher as astute as Hume to accept: (i) that an object is a genuine cause even when it becomes psychologically associated with another solely as a result of one's observing an unrepresentative sample; (ii) that the existence or nonexistence of a causal relation is relative to each individual mind (because objects may be associated in one mind without being associated in another); and (iii) that there would be no causation at all unless there were minds. Thus it seems that Hume either endorses C1 alone or else endorses neither C1 nor C2.

Does Hume Endorse Neither Definition?

There is considerable reason to think that Hume endorses at least one of the two definitions. In both the *Treatise* and the *Enquiry*, he famously insists that we can neither understand nor meaningfully speak of causation as involving any "power," "force," "real connexion" or "ultimate principle" residing *in* or *between* the cause and effect *themselves* (THN 162; THN 168; THN 267; and EHU §60). This is a stringent limitation that both C1 and C2 satisfy, and one that would be difficult to satisfy otherwise; hence, the limitation strongly suggests that Hume endorses C1, C2, or both.

Yet there are also two serious reasons to deny that Hume regards either definition as correct. First, when offering the two definitions, he notes with apparent sympathy the objection that both of them are "defective" or otherwise problematic because "drawn from objects foreign to the cause" (THN 170; and EHU §60). Robison (1977), among others, takes these remarks to be an "explicit rejection" of the definitions.

Second, any ultimate endorsement of either C1 or C2 as a definition of 'cause' seems to many commentators, including Oswald Hanfling, John P. Wright, Donald Livingston, and Galen Strawson,[5] to be incompatible with Hume's remarks—particularly in the *Enquiry*, but also in the *Treatise*—referring to the "secret powers" or "ultimate principles" that "bind causes and effects together," powers and principles of which we must always remain ignorant (for example, THN 159; THN 169; THN 267; EHU §26; EHU §33; EHU §50; and EHU §52). These remarks seem to imply that Hume ultimately recognizes and employs a sense of the term 'cause' that presupposes such secret powers and ultimate principles, and hence is stronger than either C1 or C2. Thus, it seems that Hume rejects both C1 and C2 as definitions of 'cause'.

Two "Neighboring Fields": Definitions of Relations and the Necessary Connection Argument

Each of the four possible interpretations of Hume's attitude toward his two definitions is thus subject to serious objections. Although each interpretation has been adopted by a number of commentators, the defenses they offer for their chosen interpretation consist almost entirely of references to some of its strengths—many of which are primarily capacities to avoid objections that apply to other interpretations—with little effort to refute the objections that apply to the interpretation being defended. The attempt to understand Hume seems to reach an impasse.

When Hume's attempt to understand "the nature of that *necessary connexion*, which enters into our idea of cause and effect" reaches an impasse of its own in *Treatise* I.iii.2, he proposes that we

> proceed like those, who being in search of any thing, that lies conceal'd from them, and not finding it in the place they expected, beat about all the neighboring fields, without any certain view or design, in hopes their good fortune will at last guide them to what they search for. 'Tis necessary for us to . . . endeavour to find some other questions, the examination of which will perhaps afford a hint, that may serve to clear up the present difficulty. (THN 77–78)

He then proposes the investigation of two such questions.[6] Similarly, I propose that we beat the neighboring fields with two questions of our own. First, what does Hume think is required to define an abstract relational term, such as 'cause' presumably is? And second, what argument leads him to offer the two definitions of 'cause' that he provides?

Definitions of Relations

In *An Essay concerning Human Understanding* III.iv.5, John Locke offers to show "from the Nature of our *Ideas*, and the Signification of our Words . . . *why some Names can, and others cannot be defined*, and which they are." He then continues:

> 6. I think, it is agreed, that *a Definition is* nothing else, but *the shewing the meaning of one Word by several other not synonymous Terms*. The meaning of Words, being only the Ideas they are made to stand for by him that uses them; the meaning of any Term is then shewed, or the Word is defined when by other Words, the *Idea* it is made the Sign of, and annexed to in the Mind of the Speaker, is as it were represented, or set before the view of another; and thus its Signification ascertained: This is the only use and end of Definitions; and therefore the only measure of what is, or is not a good Definition.
> 7. This being premised, I say, that the *Names of Simple* Ideas, and those only, *are incapable of being defined*. The reason whereof is this, That the several Terms of a Definition, signifying several *Ideas*, they can altogether by no means represent an *Idea*, which has no Composition at all: And therefore a Definition, which is properly nothing but the shewing the meaning of one Word by several others not signifying each the same thing, can in the Names of simple *Ideas* have no Place.

In this passage, Locke makes four claims about definitions: first, that the purpose of a definition, and hence the measure of a good definition, lies in its showing the meaning of a term by conveying the idea that the term "signifies"; second, that the definition of a term cannot simply be one or more synonymous terms; third, that all terms signifying simple ideas are indefinable; and fourth, that only terms signifying simple ideas are indefinable.

Throughout his discussions of definitions of various terms, Hume implies that definition is an attempt to convey the idea that a term signifies, and hence he implies his agreement with the first claim (see, for example THN 50; THN 77; THN 277; EHU §48; and EPM §202). His rejection of synonyms as definitions for causal terms, mentioned previously, is evidence of his acceptance of the second claim. He also accepts the third claim, as his discussions of the indefinability of 'pride' and 'humility', 'love' and 'hatred', and 'the will', all indicate (THN 277; THN 329; THN 399).[7] Hume is considerably less committal, however, about the fourth claim—that is, the Lockean doctrine that *only* simple ideas are indefinable. Instead, he writes only that "Complex ideas may, perhaps, be well known by definition, which is nothing but an enumeration of those parts or simple ideas, that compose them" (EHU §49). Elsewhere, he asserts that mathematicians must allow that 'equality' is indefinable (EHU §124n, 1748 and 1750 editions; see also THN 637), even though, as a relation between quantities, an idea of equality must be classified as complex, for both Locke and Hume. Similarly, he argues that there can be no entirely satisfactory definitions of 'straight' or 'curved', even though these are both clearly complex ideas on his view (THN 49).[8]

Why should Hume decline to endorse the Lockean thesis that all terms representing complex ideas are definable? One good reason may be found in a respect in which Hume's theory of mental representation differs crucially from Locke's. As we observed in chapter 1, Lockean abstract or general ideas derive their generality from their own representational indeterminacy. This indeterminacy is the result of separating or *abstracting* these ideas from some or all of the other ideas that accompany them in what Locke calls "real existence" (ECHU II.xi.9). Thus, for Locke, the abstract idea of a triangle is simply indeterminate with respect to the proportion of the sides or angles, and the abstract idea of a human being is simply indeterminate with respect to build, eye color, presence or absence of hair, facial details, and so on. As we have also seen, however, Hume rejects Locke's account in favor of the theory that "all general ideas are nothing but particular ones, annexed to a certain term, which gives them a more extensive signification" (THN 17). Upon noticing a resemblance among objects, Hume claims, we apply a single term to them all, notwithstanding their differences. The term is directly associated with the determinate idea of a particular instance. This determinate idea nevertheless achieves a general *signification*—and hence serves *as* an abstract idea—because the term also revives the "custom" or disposition to call up ideas of other particular instances. We are especially disposed to call up ideas of counterexamples, if we can find them, to claims employing the term that we encounter in the course of reasoning. Thus, for example, noticing certain resemblances among a number of animals, I call them all "dogs." A particular occurrence of this term brings to mind the idea of a particular dog, say Lassie, and revives a custom of calling up other ideas of dogs as needed. If, for example, the claim is made that all dogs are collies, my idea of Lassie does not itself provide a counterexample, but I will quickly find an idea of, say, Rin Tin Tin coming to mind, and I will therefore be able to reject the claim.

In this example, my idea of Lassie, though entirely particular and determinate, serves as my abstract idea of "dog." Yet to define the term 'dog', it will clearly not be enough to produce the complex idea of Lassie in another person's mind by naming all of that idea's simpler parts. For as Hume would be well aware, the idea of Lassie can equally well represent Lassie herself, or all collies, or all mammals. (And similarly, an idea of some other dog could also serve as the abstract idea of "dog.") Thus, if a Humean definition of a term standing for an abstract idea is to succeed, it must somehow convey to other persons the ability to call up *any* member of an appropriate set of ideas of particular instances—what we are calling the term's *revival set*—so that the "custom" of doing so can be "revived" by later occurrences of the term defined. This ability to call up any member of the revival set for a term can be conveyed only by characterizing what all of the instances or their ideas have in common. In Hume's view, resemblance is sometimes, but not always, a matter of having the same kind of simpler parts in common (THN 637; see chapter 2). Where the resemblance among the particular instances is of this kind, definitions of abstract ideas will still be relatively easy; when it is not, definition may become more difficult or impossible. It is precisely because the resemblance among all straight lines and the resemblance among all curved lines are not resemblances of this kind that Hume finds 'straight' and 'curved' difficult to define.

Let us now apply these considerations to Humean definitions of terms for relations.[9] Among all the various terms that signify abstract ideas, we may expect that these terms will often pose particular problems of definition. Since conceiving a relation always requires a *comparison of two* ideas, according to Hume (THN 13–14), an abstract idea of a relation must evidently consist of an idea of a particular *pair* of objects standing in the appropriate relation, and the idea of this pair must be associated with a general term that revives the custom of forming ideas of *other* pairs of objects similarly related.[10] Because the particular idea that serves as the abstract idea will always be of (at least) two objects, the abstract idea itself will always be complex. However, an adequate definition must convey not merely this idea but the ability to call up any member of the revival set of ideas of related pairs. Hence, there is no guarantee that the relation in which the members of these pairs stand to each other can be specified in any nonsynonymous terms (i.e., by anything other than another term associated with the same "custom"), and hence there is no guarantee that the relation can be defined at all, in Hume's sense.[11]

There is, however, at least one case in which we can be confident that a relation will be definable; namely, when the respect in which the related objects are being compared consists in two or more other relations. And such appears, at least initially, to be the case with the relation of cause and effect, a relation that—as we have seen—Hume characterizes near the outset of his investigation as involving the three relations of priority, contiguity, and necessary connection (THN 76–77). Indeed, this characterization fails to *complete* the definition of cause and effect only because the idea of necessary connection is initially obscure, and so itself is in need of clarification. Appealing to his methodological directive that obscure ideas may be clarified by finding the impressions from which they are derived, therefore, he sets out an argument concerning the origin of the idea of necessary connection. At the conclusion of that argument, he immediately offers his two definitions of 'cause'. The question of how that argument gives rise to those definitions is our second neighboring field.

The Necessary Connection Argument

In both the *Treatise* and the *Enquiry*, Hume presents his two definitions as the outcome of an argument concerning the idea of necessary connection. He elegantly summarizes the *Enquiry* version of that argument immediately after he presents the two definitions (EHU §61). The argument, as summarized there, may be outlined as follows in Hume's own words:

1. Every idea is copied from some preceding impression or sentiment. (The Copy Principle)
2. [W]here we cannot find any impression, we may be certain that there is no idea. (from 1)
3. In all single instances of the operation of bodies or minds, there is nothing that produces any impression . . . of power or necessary connexion.
4. In all single instances of the operation of bodies or minds, there is nothing that . . . can suggest any idea . . . of power or necessary connexion. (from 2 and 3)
5. [W]hen many uniform instances appear, and the same object is always followed by the same event; we then begin to entertain the notion of cause and connexion.
6. [W]hen many uniform instances appear, and the same object is always followed by the same event . . . [w]e then *feel* a new sentiment or impression, to wit, a customary connexion in the thought or imagination between one object and its usual attendant. . . .
7. [T]his idea [of necessary connection] arises from a number of similar instances [of one object being followed by another], and not from any single instance. (from 4 and 5)
8. [This idea of necessary connection] must arise from that circumstance, in which the number of instances [of one object being followed by another] differ from every individual instance. (from 1 and 7)
9. [T]his customary connexion or transition of the imagination is the only circumstance in which they [i.e., the similar instances of one object being followed by another] differ.
10. [T]his sentiment [i.e., the customary connection or transition or determination of the imagination] is the original of that idea [of necessary connection] which we seek for. (from 6, 8, and 9)

Although the additional support that Hume offers for some of these points differs between the *Treatise* and *Enquiry* versions, the ten claims themselves may fairly be said to constitute the framework of the argument in both works. Step 3, as we have already seen in chapter 2 and chapter 3, depends not only on empirical observation of single instances but also on the Separability Principle. Hume argues that a perception of such a necessary connection in nature would "amount to a demonstration, and wou'd imply the absolute impossibility for the one object not to follow, or to be conceived not to follow upon the other" (THN 161–162)—a demonstration that he argues we can already see to be impossible, because the idea of the cause and the idea of the effect are different and distinguishable, and hence separable.

It may initially seem strange that Hume should treat this argument as the justification for his two definitions of 'cause', because the term 'cause' appears in it only once—in (5)—and then only tangentially. In the *Treatise*, of course, the transition from the argument to the definitions is mediated partly by Hume's earlier claim that "necessary connexion" is one of the three relations essential to the relation of cause and effect. In both works, however, the transition is also mediated by an even more specific conception of what the relation between "necessary connexion" and "cause and effect" is presumed to be. Hume expresses this conception in his tentative definitions of two terms that he reports to be synonyms for 'necessary connexion'. These are 'power', which he defines as "that very circumstance in the cause, by which it is enabled to produce the effect" (EHU §53), and 'efficacy', which he defines as "that very quality, which makes [causes] be follow'd by their effects" (THN 156).[12]

For Hume, this argument shows that, although we have both an impression and an idea of "necessary connexion" as an *internal feeling* of "transition" or "determination," we have no impression or idea of any necessary connection that is an additional relation or quality to be found *in* or *between* the members of individual cause-and-effect pairs. We mistake the internal impression for the impression of a relation or quality intrinsic to individual cause-and-effect pairs, according to Hume, because we tend to "spread" this impression of necessary connection onto the objects, much as we ascribe spatial locations to sensory qualities, such as sounds and smells, that have no location (THN 167). Thus, we have no idea of any additional relation or quality *intrinsic to* the members of individual cause-and-effect pairs by means of which priority and (in the *Treatise* version) contiguity can be supplemented to complete the definition of the causal relation; our representations of the causally related pairs themselves simply turn out to have no such further content. At the same time, however, the argument also explicitly shows what is common, beyond the relations of priority and perhaps contiguity, to the entire set of ideas of cause-and-effect pairs—that is, to the revival set whose members the term 'cause' or 'cause and effect' determines us to call up. Specifically, each cause-and-effect pair whose idea we become disposed to call up is such that all objects *similar to the first* have been followed by objects *similar to the second*, which results in a determination of the mind to pass *from the idea of the one to the idea of the other*. Thus, it seems that we can specify the membership of the revival set of ideas of cause-and-effect pairs in either of two ways, depending on whether we choose (i) to describe the shared (though not intrinsic) feature of the *pairs of objects* whose ideas become included in the revival set, or (ii) to describe the shared feature of the *ideas of pairs* that are included in the revival set themselves. That is, we can define 'cause and effect' either in terms of the *constant conjunction* that in fact produces the determination or transition of psychological association and inference, without specifying the psychological process to which it gives rise, or we can define 'cause and effect' in terms of the *association* and *inference*, without specifying the features of objects that in fact give rise to it. These two approaches provide two different "views of," or two different "lights on," the revival set of ideas signified by 'cause', and they correspond, of course, to C1 and C2. As Hume says, "We must not here be content with saying, that the idea of cause and effect arises from objects constantly united; but must affirm, that 'tis the very same with the idea of these objects . . ." (THN 405). The abstract idea of cause and effect is precisely the abstract idea that has the idea of these objects as its revival set.

The Two Definitions Reconsidered

Definitions of 'Virtue'

Our consideration of the two "neighboring fields" strongly suggests that Hume would accept both C1 and C2 as representing acceptable alternate strategies for defining the term 'cause'—that is, for specifying the revival set of ideas of cause-and-effect pairs that help to constitute a representation of the causal relation. This suggestion is further strengthened by an analogy with another notable case in which, according to Hume, we mistakenly "spread" an internal impression onto the objects. This is the case of virtue or personal merit. Here, too, Hume offers not one but two definitions, which I will call "V1" and "V2." First, he writes:

> [V1] Personal Merit consists altogether in the possession of mental qualities, *useful* or *agreeable* to the *person himself* or to *others*. (EPM §217)

And he explicitly characterizes this as a "delineation or definition" of "virtue or merit" (EPM §226). Yet he also writes just a few pages later:

> [V2] The hypothesis which we embrace is plain. . . . It defines virtue to be *whatever mental action or quality gives to a spectator the pleasing sentiment of approbation.* . . . (EPM §239; see also EPM §211)

Just as in the case of 'cause', we have a class of objects possessing a feature that produces a certain characteristic psychological effect on observers. However, in this case the objects are mental qualities of persons, rather than pairs of objects or events; their common feature is usefulness or agreeableness to the possessor or others, rather than the constant conjunction of resembling objects; and the psychological effect is the sentiment of moral approbation, rather than association and inference. Just as he does in the case of 'cause', Hume delineates the revival set of ideas signified by the general term 'virtue' in two ways. First, he provides a definition, V1, that specifies the feature of the objects (usefulness or agreeableness) that in fact produces the characteristic psychological effect, without specifying what that effect is. He then offers a second, alternative definition, V2, that specifies the class of objects by means of the characteristic psychological effect on observers (the sentiment of approbation), without specifying what feature of the objects actually gives rise to this effect. Significantly, Hume seems in this case quite clearly to endorse both definitions as correct, and the analogy thus provides at least some further reason to think that he also regards both definitions of 'cause' as correct.

We have already seen that there is considerable textual support for the interpretation of Hume as endorsing both of his two definitions of 'cause'. This support lies in (i) his manner of presenting the two definitions, (ii) his uses of them to derive further conclusions, (iii) his further remarks seeming to endorse each of them, and (iv) their conformity to his limitations on what can meaningfully be said and thought about causal relations. However, a number of serious objections remain to the view that Hume endorses both definitions. Let us now determine whether the insights gained from the two "neighboring field," and from the analogy with his two definitions of 'virtue' can shed new light on those objections.

The Incompatibility Objection

First, how can C1 and C2 represent acceptable alternate definitions of the same relation when they are not even coextensive? The analogy with Hume's two definitions of 'virtue' should make us reconsider the nearly universal assumption that the two definitions are *not* coextensive.

V2's reference to "the spectator" might easily be interpreted as a reference to some *individual* human observer. And so interpreted, V2 defines a "subjective," or person-relative, sense of 'virtue', according to which a given mental quality is a virtue for a particular person if and only if it produces approbation *in that person*. Indeed, such a sense is not without its uses for Hume. It is, for example, the only sense for him in which what he calls the "monkish virtues" of celibacy, fasting, penance, mortification, self-denial, humility, silence, and solitude (EPM §219) could actually be called "virtues." That is, they function *psychologically as* virtues for the monkish, even though people of better moral sensibility rightly (he claims) regard them as vices. Nevertheless, the "spectator" mentioned in V2 has been widely construed instead to be an *idealized* spectator—for example, one who correctly assesses the consequences of mental qualities, has a well-developed human moral sense, and suffers from no interfering biases such as those deriving from religion, special relations with persons under evaluation, or other eccentricities of perspective.[13] So interpreted, V2 defines a more "absolute" sense of 'virtue'; and—if Hume's theory of moral judgment is correct—V2 so interpreted is coextensive with V1.

Now, Hume's reference to "the mind" (or, in the *Enquiry* version, "the thought") in C2 is strikingly similar to his reference to "the spectator" in V2. As before, the reference to "the mind" may be interpreted as a reference to some individual human observer. So interpreted, of course, C2 provides a "subjective," person-relative sense of 'cause', according to which one object is a cause of another object for a particular person if and only if it is prior (and, perhaps, contiguous) to the other object and psychologically associated with it, in the way that C2 specifies, *for that person*. Such a subjective sense is, again, not without its uses for Hume. For example, when he discusses the effects of resemblance and contiguity in heightening our sympathy, he notes that "relations of blood, being a species of causation, may sometimes contribute to the same effect" (THN 318). What matters for the operation of this mechanism is not, of course, whether the object of our sympathy is *objectively* related to us by blood but whether we *take* him or her to be so related. (If people could not sympathize on the basis of mistaken beliefs about blood relationships, the plotlines of many daytime television dramas would have to be radically revised.)[14] C2, so interpreted, provides a sense in which objects function *psychologically* as causally related to other objects for the hasty or the credulous, even though the better informed and wiser may rightly judge them not to be causally related. Nevertheless, there is no reason why the "mind" (or "thought") of C2 cannot instead be construed to be an idealized mind or spectator—for example, one who accurately views all and only representative samples, has a well-developed human inferential mechanism, and suffers from no interfering biases such as those deriving from religion or eccentricities of the imagination.[15] And in fact, it is just this "idealized" construal of C2's reference to "the mind" that is demanded by Hume's discussions of "liberty and necessity." For after using C2 to generate a sense of necessity that requires "the inference of the understanding from one object to another" (as described earlier), he goes on to argue that *all* human actions are necessary in this sense, not just those human actions that happen to be observed by one or more human observers. Thus interpreted, C2 defines a more "absolute" sense of 'cause', and—if his general theory of causal judgment is correct—C2 so interpreted is coextensive with C1, at least as C1 is usually understood.

I say "at least as C1 is usually understood" because C1 itself proves to be somewhat ambiguous on closer investigation. Hume explicitly characterizes C1 as involving "constant conjunction" (THN 170), yet he generally treats "constant conjunction" as something that an *individual person* may or will already have observed at a given time.[16] Furthermore, in two of his seeming endorsements of C1, he writes:

> We have no other notion of cause and effect, but that of certain objects, which have been *always conjoin'd* together, and which in all past instances have been found inseparable. (THN 93)

> [W]e have no other idea of this relation [of cause and effect] than that of two objects, which have been frequently *conjoined* together. (EHU §127)

Moreover, in his sample application of C1 to the affirmation that "the vibration of this string is the cause of this particular sound," he writes that we mean only "that this vibration is followed by this sound, and that all similar vibrations have been followed by similar sounds" (EHU §60). Thus, it becomes doubtful whether C1 should be understood absolutely, as taking within its scope *all* times and *all* places, or whether it should be understood more subjectively, as tacitly restricted to the *past* experience of a *particular* observer. If Hume's general theory of causal judgment is correct, C1 on its absolute, unrestricted reading will be coextensive with C2 on its absolute, idealized-spectator reading; and C1 on its subjective, restricted reading will be coextensive with C2 on its subjective, person-relative reading. In short, the two definitions are coextensive on either their absolute or their subjective readings, so long as both are read in the same way.

It must be granted that Hume does not explicitly distinguish the two possible readings of each definition, nor, accordingly, does he indicate explicitly which he prefers (though I have little doubt that he would ultimately prefer the absolute reading, at least for most purposes, for reasons that will emerge shortly). But an understanding of his theory of abstract ideas helps to explain why he does not draw this distinction explicitly and why he writes sometimes in terms suggestive of the one reading and sometimes in terms suggestive of the other. I have argued that when one seeks to provide a Humean definition of a term signifying an abstract idea, one seeks to convey the ability to call up any of the members of an appropriate set of ideas associated with that term. And I defined the "revival set" of a term as the set of ideas that it is appropriate to convey for a successful Humean definition. But what exactly is the membership of that set? Is it the set of ideas that I, as the definer, am *actually* accustomed to revive when I hear the term in question—a set that thus constitutes my own present representation of the causal relation—even though there are members in that set that I would delete and other ideas that I would add, upon greater experience and reflection? Or is it rather the set of ideas that I *would* revive if I actually had greater or unlimited experience and reflection?

Given the Lockean tradition that my words mean, for me, whatever ideas I actually use them to signify, there is a sense in which conveying the former set does convey the actual signification of the term in my present idiolect, even though the latter set better characterizes the ideas that I *should* use the term to signify, and on which we will ultimately tend, with more experience and reflection, to converge. Moreover, the very distinction in question will often be hidden from me under normal circumstances; it can be disclosed only by second-order reflection on my own fallibility. If I first try to list the members of the set of ideas that I *take* to fall under a general term and then try to list the members of the set of ideas that really *should* fall under a general term, I will of course specify the same set both times—this is just a particular consequence of the tautological generalization that I do presently believe all of my present classificatory beliefs. Only when I reflect more generally on my fallibility in classifying will I conclude that the two sets probably differ, and even then I cannot actually specify the individual differences in membership. Further exacerbating this difficulty is the fact that Hume's theory of abstract ideas—like Berkeley's—is developed primarily with examples of simple geometrical shapes whose features of resemblance consist in readily observable spatial qualities, so that problems or mistakes about what to include are, in these cases, either rare or nonexistent.[17] For all of these reasons, Hume's theory of abstract ideas prevents him from focusing on the difference between the absolute and subjective interpretations of his two definitions, and hence he is not careful to eliminate the ambiguity between them in his writing. Thus, an understanding of Hume's theory of mental representation as it applies to relations shows not only how his two definitions can be reconciled but also why they initially appear to be incompatible.

It may be objected that, even if the two definitions are coextensive (on either reading), they still are not logically equivalent, and that this is a reason why Hume would not endorse them both. As we have seen, Hume's primary concern is to convey a mental representation of causation by delineating the membership of the revival set—not with doing so in logically equivalent ways. Nevertheless, unless the two definitions are not just coextensive but *necessarily* coextensive, they will diverge in application to some imagined or counterfactual situations—that is, as we might say, in application to other possible worlds.

Once again, the analogy with Hume's two definitions of 'virtue' is helpful. Given human nature *as it is*, the class of mental qualities that are useful or agreeable to their possessors or others has (Hume holds) the same membership as the class of mental qualities that produce approbation in an ideal human spectator. Now suppose we decide to treat 'idealized human spectator' as designating a particular psychological makeup *rigidly* in Saul Kripke's sense (Kripke, 1980)—that is, as designating the same psychological makeup regardless of the counterfactual circumstance, or possible world, to which we are referring. Then the two definitions (on their absolute readings) will also be *necessarily* coextensive (i.e., coextensive in every possible world). If we decide to treat "idealized human spectator" nonrigidly, however, then there will be possible worlds in which "idealized spectators" have different moral psychologies and in which they so will not feel approbation in response to all and only those mental qualities that are useful or agreeable to their possessors or others. But this still need be no serious problem for Hume. In application to such worlds, he may say (if he were to adopt possible-worlds terminology), the term 'virtue' would then be lacking certain necessary preconditions for its customary use, and it would become an arbitrary question whether to say (i) that *useful and agreeable qualities* would no longer be *virtues* in those worlds, or to say (ii) that *virtues* would no longer produce *moral approbation*.

The case of 'cause' is completely parallel: whether the two definitions are necessarily coextensive or not (on their absolute readings) depends on whether we treat 'the idealized mind' as designating a certain psychological makeup rigidly or not. If we do, then C1 and C2 will be necessarily coextensive. If we do not, then there will be possible worlds in which ideal minds have other psychologies and so will no longer *associate* objects that are *constantly conjoined*. But again, this is no problem for Hume. In application to such worlds, he may say, the concept of 'cause' would then be lacking certain necessary preconditions for its customary use, and it would become an arbitrary question whether to say that *constantly conjoined objects* would no longer be *causes and effects* in those worlds, or to say that *causes and effects* would no longer be *psychologically associated*.

The Objection from the First Definition of 'Cause'

Another objection to the interpretation that Hume endorses both definitions was derived from the fact that C1 makes no explicit mention of necessary connection or its impression, even though Hume characterizes necessary connection as "of much greater importance" than priority or contiguity (THN 77), and claims that it must be "comprehended" as a part of the definition of cause (EHU §74). We can now see from the preceding analysis of his argument concerning necessary connection, however, that both definitions "comprehend" the necessary connection. They do so in the sense that both specify the set of pairs that are taken to be related by a necessary connection—even though the idea of necessary connection itself turns out to be something other than what was expected. C2 characterizes the set of *ideas* that give rise to the internal impression of necessary connection directly, whereas C1 characterizes the same set indirectly, by characterizing the *objects* whose ideas give rise to this impression. Both definitions do, however, sufficiently "comprehend" the necessary connection for Hume. This is shown both by the fact that he uses each definition to generate its own corresponding definition of 'necessity' for use in his discussions of "liberty and necessity," and by his claim that "this constancy [i.e., constant conjunction] forms the very essence of necessity" (EHU §74n).[18] Thus, I conclude that the present interpretation can also overcome this objection.

Objections from the Second Definition of 'Cause'

Further objections to the interpretation of Hume as endorsing both definitions were derived from (i) the apparent circularity of C2, (ii) its apparent incompatibility with other Humean doctrines, and (iii) the appearance that it gives rise to implausible consequences. As we have seen, Hume's general strategy is to convey our representation of causation by delineating the revival set of ideas of cause-and-effect pairs in two different ways—first by appealing to a feature of the objects (i.e., constant conjunction), and second by appealing to a feature of the ideas (i.e., association). This general strategy is itself potentially sound, as we can see in its application to the closely related case of his two definitions of 'virtue'. The complication in the case of 'cause' derives from the fact that the relevant feature of the ideas happens to be an associative relation that is itself also a causal relation; hence, the ideas of cause-and-effect pairs are themselves cause-and-effect pairs whose own (second-order) ideas *also* belong to the revival set. It is perhaps because the threatened circularity derives from the specific case of defining 'cause', rather than from the general definitional strategy, that Hume does not seem to notice it more explicitly. In any case, he can identify cases of the mind being "determined" (or the thought being "conveyed") without a circular appeal to C2 in either of two ways. First, he can identify cases of "determination" by the occurrence of the characteristic *impression* of determination that Hume cites as the source of our idea of necessary connection, a remedy suggested by Robison (1977) and Aryeh Botwinick (1978). Alternatively, he can identify cases of mental "determination" by the *constant conjunction* of the associated ideas. To adopt the second alternative is, of course, to make the application of C2 partly dependent on the feature of constant conjunction mentioned in C1, but it would still be the case that C1 and C2 specify the revival set of ideas of cause-and-effect pairs in two different ways—that is, by appeal to a feature of the cause-and-effect pairs and to a feature of their ideas, respectively. Both definitions would thus still be correct and valuable, and both would serve their intended purposes, even though the application of C2 would depend on applying the central concept used in C1.

It should now be evident that the two remaining objections derived from C2 depend entirely on its subjective reading. When read *absolutely*—that is, as referring to an idealized mind—C2 is perfectly compatible with the existence of "a vast variety of springs and principles, which are hid, by reason of their minuteness and remoteness" (THN 132; EHU §67), and it is also compatible with the existence of, and need for, the "Rules by which to judge of causes and effects" set out in *Treatise* I.iii.15. Indeed, these rules become, in part, rules for making oneself more like an idealized mind. Furthermore, on the absolute reading, C2 implies neither (i) that objects observed to be conjoined in unrepresentative samples are always real causes, nor (ii) that the existence or nonexistence of a causal relation is relative to individual minds, nor (iii) that there would be no causation at all unless there were minds. However, these are all implications of the subjective reading of C1, just as much as they are implications of the subjective reading of C2. Thus, what originally appeared as objections to the view that Hume endorses C2 now become, instead, reasons to think that he would ultimately prefer the absolute readings of both definitions over their subjective counterparts—at least as conveying the objective or ideal use of the term 'cause'—*if* he were to focus on the ambiguity between the two readings. Hence, I conclude that the present interpretation can also overcome the objections derived specifically from C2 as well.

Objects "Foreign to the Cause" and Secret Powers

It now remains only to consider the two objections suggesting that Hume rejects both C1 and C2 as defective and/or too weak. The first of these objections appeals to his remarks concerning the fact that his definitions are "drawn from objects foreign to the cause." The definitions are "drawn from objects foreign to the cause," of course, because C1 refers not only to the cause-and-effect pair itself but also to "objects resembling" the cause and the effect, while C2 refers not only to the cause-and-effect pair itself but also to both the "mind" (or "thought") and to the ideas of the cause-and-effect pair.

However, Hume does not say in the *Treatise* that either of his definitions *is* "defective" because they are "drawn from objects foreign to the cause"; rather, he addresses himself to those who would "*esteem*" them to be defective for that reason. He challenges those who "express this delicacy" to "substitute a juster definition in its place." Such a definition would, of course, restrict itself to some relation or quality of each individual cause-and-effect pair that did not involve reference to any other objects (such objects as classes of *resembling* objects, on the one hand, or the mind and the *ideas* of the objects, on the other). But he has already argued, as we have seen, that no such relation or quality can be *represented*; hence, any attempt to convey a revival set by means of such a relation or quality must fail. Thus, after briefly reviewing his argument concerning necessary connection, he reports that he will "repose" himself on his present "sentiments" about these matters "as on establish'd maxims" (THN 170). Nor does he say in the first *Enquiry* that his definitions' reliance on "objects foreign to the cause" renders them defective. Rather, he says that it constitutes an "inconvenience" (EHU §60)—as surely it does, because we can neither *determine* whether two objects are related as cause and effect without considering other objects as well nor *convey* a representation of causation without appeal to such further objects. He also implies that our ideas of cause and effect are "imperfect" because we cannot represent any necessary connection as a quality or relation intrinsic to cause-and-effect pairs themselves, as we should like to do. And he implies that a definition that could convey such a representation would be "more perfect." But this does not entail that the two definitions that capture and convey the representation of causation we actually have are themselves defective or mistaken—on the contrary, they do convey the ideas that our terms actually signify "justly," as Hume immediately goes on to affirm.

The last remaining objection concerns Hume's frequent use, especially in the *Enquiry*, of such phrases as 'secret power' and 'ultimate principle'. Often when he uses these terms, it is in the course of arguing that we do not have any impression of, and cannot form an idea of, any secret power or ultimate principle in the cause itself that makes the cause give rise to its effect. Still, his constant reference to our ignorance of such powers and principles suggests to many readers that he does nevertheless believe that there is *something unrepresentable* in causes that somehow accounts for their causal efficacy. Recently, however, Kenneth Winkler (1991) has argued convincingly that none of Hume's remarks commit him to that view, and that Hume's position is, as it should be, skeptical or agnostic about the existence of unrepresentable and hence inconceivable objects and qualities.

As Winkler effectively points out, it would be inconsistent of Hume to claim to believe in specific unrepresentable powers and principles. That is because Humean belief is a lively idea, and hence a specific belief requires a specific representation of that which is to be believed. It is true, however, that for Hume there is no contradiction in the general supposition that there are things or qualities (nature unspecifiable) that we cannot represent. And he never denies, needs to deny, or seeks to deny, that there may be such things or qualities in causes (THN 168). His repeated and pointed failure to deny the existence of such things is part of the generally more conciliatory tone of the *Enquiry*. But none of these facts count, for him, against the acceptability of his two definitions. For his definitions are not intended to assert that constant conjunction and psychological association are the *only* relations that hold between causes and effects. Instead, they are intended to capture the revival set of ideas of cause-and-effect pairs that the term 'cause' and its related abstract idea signify. In doing so, he thinks, they successfully convey the representation of 'cause' that we actually use, which is the abstract idea for which the term stands. This they do "exactly," "precisely," and "justly" in his view, whereas any phrase to which *no representation* corresponds cannot capture this set. Thus, his remarks about "secret powers" and "ultimate principles," important as they are, do not refute the claim that Hume endorses both definitions of 'cause' as correct.

The Representation of Causation

Hume regards both of his two definitions of 'cause' as correct. He can do so without inconsistency because his theories of definition, of relations, and of abstract ideas sanction as legitimate *any* definition of the term that effectively specifies the membership of the revival set (of ideas of cause-and-effect pairs) that the term 'cause' disposes us to call up. The abstract idea of 'cause' and the revival set of ideas associated with it together constitute, in Hume's view, our representation of the causal relation. The appearance that his two definitions are not coextensive results from the fact that each can be interpreted in either an absolute or a subjective sense—senses that Hume does not clearly distinguish. As it happens, modern readers tend to interpret C1 in the absolute sense and C2 in the subjective sense, thus giving rise to the appearance of noncoextensivity. Hume's two definitions of 'cause'—derived respectively from a feature of cause-and-effect pairs and from a feature of ideas of cause and effect pairs—parallel in structure his later two definitions of 'virtue'.

As Hume himself emphasizes, most readers will feel the two definitions of cause to be inadequate, because both definitions appeal to "objects foreign to the cause."

That is, both definitions are stated in terms of features—namely, constant conjunction and psychological association—that would ordinarily be regarded merely as *evidence* of a causal relation. Since Hume also defends these definitions partly on the grounds that any other definitions would lead us into conceptual skepticism, his definitions are examples of reductive empiricism as that doctrine was defined in chapter 1.

Like most instances of reductive empiricism, Hume's definitions are subject to the objection that they leave something crucial—in this case, the real necessary connection or the tie that *explains* the constant conjunction—out of account. But although Hume's definitions are reductive in the sense that they *define* the word 'cause' in terms of occurrences that would ordinarily be taken as *evidence* for the causal relation, it is important to emphasize that he intends them as definitions only in *his* sense of 'definition'. That is to say, he intends that they should satisfactorily specify the revival set for the term that they define. As we have seen, his two definitions of 'cause' can even be interpreted as being *necessarily* equivalent (i.e., equivalent even in application to counterfactual situations). None of this entails that either definition must be *semantically* equivalent to the other, or to the term 'cause', in the very fine-grained twentieth-century sense that would license substitution of the one term for the other without "change of sense" in a wide variety of contexts. That ideal of definition—suggesting not only that a term and its definition should convey the same *representations* but that it should pick them out by identical *cognitive operations*—is simply not Hume's.

Hence, Hume's endorsement of his two definitions does not carry any implication that causes and effects are not also related in ways that human beings cannot understand. He cannot and does not claim that human cognitive faculties are the only possible cognitive faculties. For all we can know now, beings with faculties other than ours might recognize other definitions as also being adequate. However, he does maintain that his two definitions provide our only adequate ways of effectively specifying the revival set of ideas of cause-and-effect pairs that constitute our representation of the causal relation. Furthermore, we cannot conceive of how any additional pairs of objects or events can be related as cause and effect except by conceiving of them as, in effect, satisfying one or both definitions.

Many readers—even many who are generally sympathetic to reductive empiricism in one form or another—object that Hume's two definitions are too nonspecific, schematic, or vague to be adequate as definitions of the causal relation. It may be asked, for example, just how similar a class of things must be, and in what ways, in order to qualify as a class of "resembling objects" whose members can be constantly conjoined with those of another. For example, do *days* potentially constitute a class of resembling objects? If so, then as Thomas Reid famously pointed out, they seem to be the cause of nights, since days are constantly followed by nights. If we seek to avoid such problems by employing stricter standards of resemblance, then there is a danger of ruling out most or all causal relations, for few if any objects are resembling in all respects. And how closely must the effect follow the cause in time? Hume's own answer to this question is that the effect must follow at the very next *moment*—but this answer depends crucially on his flawed temporal atomism. Similarly, the idealized observer of Hume's second definition must have a human nature, but there is room for wide cognitive variation in how the constant conjunction of various "resembling" classes might affect a being with such a nature. For the same resemblance may have different salience to, and significance for, different human observers, even when the perspective of those observers is the same. More generally, Hume's definitions strike many readers as somewhat anti-quated and thus as insufficiently adapted to the conceptual needs of modern physics and other modern sciences.

It must be granted that Hume's two definitions of 'cause' are extremely general and open-ended. When viewed as attempts to specify the characteristics that all members of a revival set of particular idea-pairs must have in common, the defini-tions are undoubtedly open to the objection that the required degrees and kinds of resemblance (for the first definition) and the required features of human nature (for the second) are insufficiently specified. Only to those who already share some-thing of Hume's own sense of the salience and significance of various kinds of resemblances, and something of his own sense of what human nature is, can the definitions convey a criterion for classifying causes and effects that will correspond to Hume's own classifications.

From another point of view, however, the open-endedness of the definitions is also one of their greatest strengths. For human beings' sense of the salience and sig-nificance of resemblances can change as the result of accumulated experience and reflection. Presumably, Hume himself does not intend his two definitions to pro-vide a completely specified once-and-for-all checklist of criteria for cause-and-effect pairs. If he had, there would have been no need for him to go on to provide a list of "Rules by which to judge of causes and effects," as he does in *Treatise* I.iii.15. Those rules, he remarks, are "formed on the nature of our understanding"—that is, based on observation of our own successes and failures in causal reasoning. As such, the rules depend not on the *analysis* of some timeless idea of causality but rather on our own inductive learning from our own inductive practices. Although cause-and-effect pairs must belong to resembling classes of objects that are con-stantly conjoined, he does not specify what kinds or degrees of resemblances are sufficient to make a class of objects serve as a suitable class. Similarly, although cause-and-effect pairs must be such as to be associated in the mind of an observer, he does not specify in advance the complete set of reflective processes or rules that must characterize that observer. These are all respects in which the revival set of cause-and-effect pairs—and hence the abstract idea, or concept, of causation itself—is open to temporal change in Hume's system, as our processes of inductive inference mature and evolve through reflection on our own predictive successes and failures. Instead of trying to specify a complete set of timeless criteria for causa-tion, he seeks to ground our understanding of the evolving concept of causation in the fundamental associative and inferential cognitive mechanism that gives it force and significance. Insofar as it accommodates conceptual progress, this is not a dis-advantage but an advantage of his approach. It allows the concept of "causation" to evolve in response to the needs of developing science, while still allowing us to rec-ognize the resulting concept as a development of the concept of *causation* by its essential relation to the mechanism of association and inference based on constant conjunction.

Hume's analysis of the causal relation—difficult to accept as he acknowledges it to be—is nevertheless undoubtedly a watershed in the history of philosophical attempts to understand and conceptualize that relation. Although he still sometimes uses the generic term 'objects', his examples and definitions show him to be a pioneer of the transition to a more event-centered conception of causality. Even more important, he is the first thinker to propose unequivocally that *no* causal relation is intelligible to the mind prior to experience. As he puts it, "to consider the matter *a priori*, any thing may produce any thing" (THN 247). His analysis implies an account of explanation according to which *explanation* is essentially *assimilation* of one case to other resembling cases:

> It is confessed, that the utmost effort of human reason is to reduce the principles, productive of natural phenomena, to a greater simplicity, and to resolve the many particular effects into a few general causes, by means of reasonings from analogy, experience, and observation. But as to the causes of these general causes, we should in vain attempt their discovery; nor shall we ever be able to satisfy ourselves, by any particular explication of them. (EHU §26)

Hume's analysis also has several important consequences that he notes for the causal doctrines and distinctions of his predecessors and contemporaries: (i) that various distinctions among kinds of causes and between causes and "occasions" are without foundation, since pairs of objects either satisfy the two definitions or they do not; (ii) that there is no distinction between the necessity of moral causes (i.e., human agency) and the necessity of physical causes; (iii) that there is no intuitive or demonstrative basis for the doctrine that it is necessary for every beginning of existence to have a cause; and (iv) that we can never have reason to believe that any object exists of which we cannot form an idea, since all inferences to the existence of something are based on projections of experienced (and hence conceivable) conjunctions of objects (THN 171–172).

Hume sees value in his definitions of 'cause' for the light they shed on the concept of "cause" itself and on the whole nature of our scientific practice. At the same time, however, he sees equal value in their specific application to a variety of other philosophical topics—including the liberty and necessity of human actions and the credibility of testimony for miracles. These applications will occupy our attention in the next two chapters.

Liberty and Necessity

The Scientific Revolution demanded a rethinking of the relation between human beings and nature. The success of mechanistic explanation led to conceptions of the causal relation that take events, rather than substances, as the most fundamental relata. This change is evident in Hume's own analysis of causation in terms of constant conjunction, and even more so in his applications of it, despite his own lingering use of the broad term 'objects' to refer to potential causes and effects. Event-centered conceptions of causation led, in turn, to more precise formulations of the doctrine of causal determinism within natural science, while the explanatory successes of natural science inevitably raised questions about the applicability of its methods to human affairs. As a result, philosophers were forced to address anew the relation between natural events and human actions, the nature of human responsibility for actions, and the justice of divine rewards and punishments in a world of causal determination.

In *Treatise* II.iii.1–2, Hume takes up the topic of free will, which he calls "that long disputed question concerning *liberty and necessity*" (THN 399). These two sections of the *Treatise* begin the final part ("Of the will and direct passions") of Book II ("Of the passions") and serve to introduce his discussion of the role of reason in motivation. The two sections are generally combative in tone, often anticipating an imagined "adversary" and often seeking to establish the "doctrine of necessity" at the expense of the "fantastical system of liberty" (THN 404). After establishing the doctrine of necessity to his own satisfaction in *Treatise* II.iii.1, Hume proceeds in *Treatise* II.iii.2 to explain "the prevalence of the doctrine of liberty, however absurd it may be in one sense, and unintelligible in any other" (THN 407). He cites three factors to explain the prevalence of that doctrine: (i) a common failure to distinguish between the "liberty of *spontaneity*" (which is "oppos'd to violence") and the "liberty of *indifference*" (which "means a negation of necessity and causes"); (ii) the existence of a "*false sensation or experience* even of the liberty of indifference"; and (iii) the fact that religion "has been very unnecessarily interested in this question." He ends his discussion by arguing that morality and religion, far from being threatened by the doctrine of necessity, actually require it—

both because the efficacy of rewards and punishments presupposes it, and because persons cannot be responsible for their actions without it.

According to Hume, his first *Enquiry* is a "recasting" of Book I of the *Treatise*. It is therefore not surprising that it contains no discussion of such Book II topics as the passions or the role of reason in motivation. Yet it does contain a renewed consideration of "the question of liberty and necessity." Hume provides this renewed consideration in Section VIII of the *Enquiry*, where it immediately follows Section VII's two definitions of 'cause' and serves as a direct application of them. This second treatment of liberty and necessity is far more conciliatory in approach and tone than the corresponding sections of the *Treatise*. In particular, Hume no longer seeks to attack a "doctrine of liberty" in order to defend an opposing "doctrine of necessity." He seeks instead to reconcile "the doctrine both of necessity and of liberty," and to show that "all men have ever agreed" to both (EHU §63).

This change of conclusion results primarily from a tactical change in terminology. Hume now uses the term 'doctrine of liberty' to mean the doctrine that human beings have "*a power of acting or not acting, according to the determinations of the will*" (EHU §73). This power corresponds to what the *Treatise* had called the "liberty of spontaneity." Accordingly, in Section VIII, Part i, of the *Enquiry*, after repeating and enlarging his previous arguments for "the doctrine of necessity," he adds an argument that "all mankind have ever agreed in the doctrine of liberty as well." Part ii of Section VIII then begins by arguing that both the doctrine of necessity and the doctrine of liberty—as he now defines them—are essential to morality. Part ii continues with another element that is absent from the *Treatise*—a discussion of the problem posed by the doctrine of necessity for religion's understanding of the relation between human and divine responsibility. It ends with the "confession" that one aspect of this latter problem "exceed[s] all the power of philosophy" and an apparently disingenuous recommendation not to pursue the problem. Thus, although the *Enquiry* treatment of liberty and necessity is more conciliatory in tone and approach than the corresponding discussion in the *Treatise*, it is at the same time more subversive of religious philosophizing.

Hume's treatment of the topic of liberty and necessity, especially as it appears in the first *Enquiry*, is widely regarded as a locus classicus of what has since come to be called "soft determinism"—that is, the doctrine that (i) every event is fully determined by exceptionless causal laws, and (ii) this determination is fully compatible with human freedom and moral responsibility. The doctrine of soft determinism—so-called because the compatibility claim of the second conjunct softens the impact of the determinism of the first—became increasingly popular among philosophers in the decades after Hume. Although twentieth-century philosophy has been obliged to allow quantum indeterminacies and their potentially macroscopic consequences to mitigate strict determinism, soft determinism's claim that the causal determination of human actions is compatible with freedom and responsibility has remained perennially popular among philosophers. Accordingly, of all Hume's many treatments of philosophical topics, probably none would receive more widespread approval from contemporary philosophers than his treatment of "liberty and necessity." Yet close examination of Hume's discussion reveals several apparent contradictions.

First, Hume concludes his discussion of liberty and necessity in the *Treatise* by claiming to have shown that "all actions of the will have particular causes" (THN 412). Yet the evidence that he actually offers for his "doctrine of necessity" seems to consist only of arguments showing at most (i) that human actions are in general approximately as predictable as the behavior of nonhuman objects; and (ii) that when human actions prove unpredictable in practice, they are unpredictable in ways parallel to those in which nonhuman objects are unpredictable. This seems to fall far short of establishing that all human actions are caused, despite the fact that this latter proposition would be required for a defense of full-fledged soft determinism. Thus Terence Penelhum (1987) has objected:

> Hume both needs and asserts the claim that every event has a cause, yet he has not shown that every event has a cause or why we believe it (if we do). He needs both predictability and universal causation, and at best, he has only the former. . . . His arguments fail to rule out a "libertarian" understanding of human action—that is, one that confines the prediction of human behavior to statistical predictions, and accommodates the human power to surprise us as a matter of principle.

Second, Hume appears to equivocate in his descriptions of what people actually believe about determinism, necessity, and the liberty of indifference. Near the outset of his *Enquiry* treatment, he writes:

> It is universally allowed that matter, in all its operations, is actuated by a necessary force, and that every natural effect is so precisely determined by the energy of its cause that no other effect, in such particular circumstances, could possibly have resulted from it. The degree and direction of every motion is, by the laws of nature, prescribed with such exactness that a living creature may as soon arise from the shock of two bodies, as motion, in any other degree or direction than what is actually produced by it. (EHU §64; see also THN 399–400)

A few pages later, however, he asserts:

> [W]e may consider the sentiments commonly entertained with regard to those irregular events which appear in the course of nature, and the operations of external objects. All causes are not conjoined to their usual effects with like uniformity. . . . The vulgar, who take things according to their first appearance, attribute the uncertainty of events to such an uncertainty in the causes as makes the latter often fail of their usual influence; though they meet with no impediment in their operation. (EHU §67; see also THN 132)

A bit further on, he nonetheless asks rhetorically:

> Have we not reason, therefore, to affirm that all mankind have always agreed in the doctrine of necessity according to the foregoing definition and explication of it? Nor have philosophers ever entertained a different opinion from the people in this particular. (EHU §§69–70; see also THN 405)

Nor is this all. Having just reaffirmed the full unanimity of this agreement, he writes:

> I have frequently considered, what could possibly be the reason why all mankind . . . have yet discovered such a reluctance to acknowledge [the doctrine of necessity] in

words, and have rather shown a propensity, in all ages, to profess the contrary opinion. (EHU §71; see THN 407)

In the *Treatise*, Hume remarks, even more strongly:

I believe we may assign the three following reasons for the prevalence of the doctrine of liberty [i.e., the liberty of *indifference* that is incompatible with the doctrine of necessity], however absurd it may be in one sense, and unintelligible in any other. First, After we have perform'd any action; tho' we confess we were influenc'd by particular views and motives; 'tis difficult for us to perswade ourselves we were govern'd by necessity, and that 'twas utterly impossible for us to have acted otherwise. . . . (THN 407)

And further:

But so inconsistent are men with themselves, that tho' they often assert, that necessity utterly destroys all merit and demerit either towards mankind or superior powers, yet they continue still to reason upon these very principles of necessity in all their judgments concerning this matter. (THN 412)

Finally, Hume writes:

[W]hat is meant by liberty, when applied to voluntary actions? . . . we can only mean a power of acting or not acting, according to the determinations of the will; . . . this hypothetical liberty is universally allowed to belong to every one who is not a prisoner and in chains. (EHU §73; see also THN 407–408)

Thus, it seems that Hume characterizes as "universally allowed" a doctrine of strict physical determinism that he finds the "vulgar"—certainly the majority of people—to reject. Then, after nevertheless insisting that all humankind do assent to the "doctrine of necessity," he characterizes humankind as (i) professing, in all ages, to *deny* that doctrine; (ii) accepting instead a "prevalent" doctrine of liberty that is incompatible with that doctrine; and (iii) regarding the doctrine of necessity as incompatible with their own judgments of moral responsibility. Moreover, he grants all of this despite claiming that we "can only mean" by 'liberty' a power of action (the liberty of spontaneity) that is perfectly compatible with the doctrine of necessity. It is not surprising, then, that Penelhum (1987) finds Hume to be "ambivalent" about whether people do or do not believe themselves to have the liberty of indifference in addition to the liberty of spontaneity: "He sometimes seems to suggest that the latter is the only sort of liberty we think we have, while at other times Hume himself says we often suppose ourselves to have liberty of the other kind, namely liberty of indifference."

Third, it seems that Hume admits an objection against theism that, if sound, should count equally against his own attempted reconciliation of necessity and responsibility. Near the end of Section VIII, Part ii of the first *Enquiry*, he writes:

I pretend not to have obviated or removed all objections to this theory, with regard to necessity and liberty. I can foresee other objections, derived from topics which have not here been treated of. It may be said, for instance, that, if voluntary actions be subjected to the same laws of necessity with the other operations of matter, there is a continued chain of necessary causes, pre-ordained and pre-determined, reaching from the original cause of all to every single volition of every human creature. No contingency anywhere in the universe; no indifference; no liberty. While we act, we are, at the same time, acted upon. The ultimate Author of all our volitions is the Creator of the world, who first bestowed motion on this immense machine, and placed all beings in that particular position, whence every subsequent event, by an inevitable necessity, must result. (EHU §78)

And, after some discussion, he grants the force of this objection to theism, concluding:

[This] objection admits not of so easy and satisfactory an answer; nor is it possible to explain distinctly how the Deity can be the mediate cause of all the actions of men, without being the author of sin and moral turpitude. These are mysteries, which mere natural and unassisted reason is very unfit to handle; and whatever system she embraces, she must find herself involved in inextricable difficulties, and even contradictions, at every step which she takes with regard to such subjects. (EHU §81)

To this Barry Stroud (1977) objects:

This is an example of some theological difficulties apparently implied by the 'doctrine of necessity'—it is one of the reasons the doctrine has been thought to be dangerous to religion. Hume tries half-heartedly to deal with one of the theological problems, but he confesses a failure to resolve them all, and the tone of his remarks suggests that he regards that as so much the worse for religion and theology. But for some reason he does not even consider a non-religious form of the same kind of determinism. If the theological version can seem plausibly to lead to the conclusion that God is the only responsible agent, as Hume admits, then a fully secularized version could equally plausibly lead to the conclusion that there are no responsible agents at all. (p. 152)

Hence it seems that Hume, after all of his attempts at reconciliation, inadvertently allows that there remains a genuine conflict between necessity and responsibility. Moreover, this conflict raises anew the question of whether the doctrine of necessity itself is really as universally accepted as Hume maintains.

Fourth, as Susan Hickenlooper (1992) has pointed out, Hume's treatment of divine responsibility seems to contradict his treatment of human responsibility in a further respect. Immediately after presenting his description of the objection that determinism raises for theism in the passage just cited (EHU §78), Hume proceeds to distinguish the objection into two distinct problems:

First, that, if human actions can be traced up, by a necessary chain, to the Deity, they can never be criminal; on account of the infinite perfection of that Being from whom they are derived, and who can intend nothing but what is altogether good and laudable. Or, *Secondly*, if they be criminal, we must retract the attribute of perfection, which we ascribe to the Deity, and must acknowledge him to be the ultimate author of guilt and moral turpitude in all his creatures.

Following Hickenlooper, let N represent the proposition:

(N) Human actions can be traced up, by a necessary chain, to the Deity.

Let P represent the proposition:

(P) The Deity is perfectly good.

Let C represent the proposition:

(C) Some human actions are criminal.

Then, as Hickenlooper notes, the first problem Hume describes involves the seeming plausibility of the conditional proposition "If N then (if P then not-C)." He is, of course, assuming the truth of N—for which he has already argued—in order to explore its consequences for theism. The first problem for theism, then, arises from the fact that its central doctrine P in conjunction with N seems to imply the morally and theologically unacceptable denial of C.

Hume holds, however, that this first problem may be rejected. His solution is to reject the conditional "If P then not-C" on the following grounds:

> The mind of man is so formed by nature that, upon the appearance of certain characters, dispositions, and actions, it immediately feels the sentiment of approbation or blame; nor are there any emotions more essential to its frame and constitution. The characters which engage our approbation are chiefly such as contribute to the peace and security of human society; as the characters which excite blame are chiefly such as tend to public detriment and disturbance: Whence it may reasonably be presumed, that the moral sentiments arise, either mediately or immediately, from a reflection on these opposite interests. What though philosophical meditations establish a different opinion or conjecture; that everything is right with regard to the WHOLE, and that the qualities, which disturb society, are, in the main, as beneficial, and are as suitable to the primary intention of nature as those which more directly promote its happiness and welfare? Are such remote and uncertain speculations able to counterbalance the sentiments which arise from the natural and immediate view of the objects? A man who is robbed of a considerable sum; does he find his vexation for the loss anywise diminished by these sublime reflections? Why then should his moral resentment against the crime be supposed incompatible with them? Or why should not the acknowledgment of a real distinction between vice and virtue be reconcileable to all speculative systems of philosophy, as well as that of a real distinction between personal beauty and deformity? (EHU §80)

The second problem that Hume describes lies in the plausibility of the proposition "If N then (if C then not-P)." Once again, he is assuming N in order to explore its consequences for theism, and theism's second problem arises from the fact that its acknowledgment of C, when taken in conjunction with N, seems to imply the theologically unacceptable denial of P. In the case of this second problem, Hume writes, the "objection admits not of so easy and satisfactory an answer," for "to defend absolute decrees, and yet free the Deity from being the author of sin, has been found hitherto to exceed all the power of philosophy" (EHU §81). Thus, on the assumption of N, Hume evidently accepts the conditional "If C then not-P" in connection with the second problem, while (on the same assumption) rejecting the conditional "If P then not-C" in connection with the first. Yet as Hickenlooper rightly notes, these two conditionals are contrapositives of each other and, as such, appear to be logically equivalent. The same point may be put this way: in Hume's treatment of the first problem, he insists that, given the necessity of human actions, human criminality is perfectly compatible with perfect goodness on the part of the Deity, while in his treatment of the second problem, he insists on their incompatibility. This result might, of course, be taken as a reductio ad absurdum of N, but Hume accepts N. He thus appears to be guilty of an inconsistency—accepting the compatibility of divine goodness and human criminality when doing so suits his moral purposes and rejecting it when doing so suits his antitheological purposes.

In this chapter, I take up these four related problems in order. Appealing to Hume's theory of causal reasoning, his theory of representation, and aspects of his theory of moral judgment, I argue that in none of the four cases is he as confused as he might initially appear. Indeed, he deserves his status as an important figure in the attempt to reconcile liberty and necessity—if not quite his status as a paradigm example of the orthodox version of soft determinism.

Three Causal Doctrines

The Argument for the Doctrine of Necessity Outlined

Does Hume's argument concerning the doctrine of necessity establish less than he needs? In order to answer this question, it is necessary first to examine the argument he actually gives. As he presents it in *Enquiry* VIII.i, it may be outlined as follows:

1. Beyond the constant conjunction of similar objects, and the consequent inference from one to the other, we have no notion of any necessity or connexion.
2. If it appear . . . that all mankind have ever allowed, without any doubt or hesitation, that these two circumstances [of constant conjunction and inference, respectively] take place in the voluntary actions of men, and in the operations of mind; it must follow, that all mankind have ever agreed in the doctrine of necessity, and that they have hitherto disputed, merely for not understanding each other. (from 1)
3. It is universally acknowledged that there is a great uniformity among the actions of men, in all nations and ages, and that human nature remains still the same, in its principles and operations.
4. Mankind are so much the same, in all times and places, that history informs us of nothing new or strange in this particular.
5. [I]f we would explode any forgery in history, we cannot make use of a more convincing argument, than to prove, that the actions ascribed to any person are directly contrary to the course of nature, and that no human motives, in such circumstances, could ever induce him to such a conduct.
6. By means of [that experience, acquired by long life and a variety of business and company], we mount up to the knowledge of men's inclinations and motives, from their actions, expressions, and even gestures; and again descend to the interpretation of their actions from our knowledge of their motives and inclinations.
7. From observing the variety of conduct in different men, we are enabled to form a greater variety of maxims, which still suppose a degree of uniformity and regularity.
8. The philosopher, if he be consistent, must apply the same reasoning to the actions and volitions of intelligent agents [as he does to other cases, and admit that] the internal principles and motives may operate in a uniform manner, notwithstanding . . . seeming irregularities; in the same manner as the winds, rain, clouds, and other

variations of the weather are supposed to be governed by steady principles; though not easily discoverable by human sagacity and enquiry. (from 3–7)

9. Thus it appears, not only that the conjunction between motives and voluntary actions is as regular and uniform as that between the cause and effect in any part of nature; but also that this regular conjunction has been universally acknowledged among mankind, and has never been the subject of dispute, either in philosophy or common life. (from 3–8)

10. [People] take their measures [in conclusions concerning human action] from past experience, in the same manner as in their reasonings concerning external objects; and firmly believe that men, as well as all the elements, are to continue, in their operations, the same that they have ever found them. (from 3, 6, and 7)

11. There are even few of the speculative parts of learning to which [inference about human actions] is not essential.

12. It seems almost impossible . . . to engage either in science or action of any kind without acknowledging the doctrine of necessity, and this inference from motives to voluntary actions, from character to conduct. (from 10–11)

13. The same experienced union has the same effect on the mind, whether the united objects be motives, volition, and actions; or figure and motion.

14. [T]his experience of uniformity in human actions is a source whence we draw inferences concerning them. (from 12–13)

15. All men have ever agreed in the doctrine of necessity. (from 2, 9, and 14)

The argument's first premise, (1), relies on the discussion of causation and necessary connection in Section VII ("Of the Idea of necessary Connexion") to establish that we have no notion of causal necessity beyond constant conjunction (corresponding to definition C1 of 'cause') and the inference of the mind (corresponding to definition C2). (See chapter 5.) Hume then infers at (2) that, if humankind has always agreed to the presence of constant conjunction and mental inference in the case of human actions, then humankind has effectively agreed to the "doctrine of necessity" as he understands it. He next proceeds, in (3) through (9) to argue that mankind has always agreed that there is a constant conjunction between particular actions and volitions, on the one hand, and particular motives, characters, and circumstances, on the other. In (10) through (14), he argues that these constant conjunctions have regularly been a source of inference—and that everyone must, in practice, recognize this fact as well. Hence, he concludes in (15), humankind has "ever agreed in the doctrine of necessity."

The corresponding argument in the earlier *Treatise* version is somewhat briefer; Hume claims that, in order to show the requisite constant conjunction of human actions and volitions with "motives, tempers, and circumstances," a "very slight and general view of the common course of human affairs will be sufficient" (THN 401). It is, however, very similar to the *Enquiry* version both in its structure and in the considerations it adduces, and in some places it is nearly identical in wording as well. It, too, derives the twin conditions of necessity—constant conjunction and inference—from the two definitions of 'cause', and then argues for the satisfaction of each. Since the *Treatise* does not attempt the "reconciling project" of showing that everyone has really agreed about liberty and necessity, however, his conclusion there directly affirms "the necessity of these [human] actions," rather than the universal *agreement* to that necessity.

Strict Determination and Universal Causation

Hume does not seek to *demonstrate*, in his sense of that term, either the truth of the doctrine of necessity or the existence of universal agreement to it. As matters of fact whose denial is conceivable, these are not propositions that could be "demonstrated" in his sense. But his premises also fall obviously short of fully establishing the complete causal determination of all human actions. Does it follow that he has not established the doctrine of necessity?

It would follow if the doctrine of necessity required a complete and exceptionless "constant conjunction" between human actions and volitions on the one hand, and motives, kinds of character, and other circumstances, on the other. But Hume does not ever indicate that it does. On the contrary, he writes of "a certain degree of uniformity" (EHU §73), which everyone grants to be "as regular and uniform as that . . . in any part of nature" (EHU §69), and he consistently implies that any degree of constancy or regularity sufficienty to produce settled inference would confirm the doctrine of necessity. Thus, he states the second of the four "corollaries" he draws from his discussion of necessary connection:

> The same course of reasoning will make us conclude, that there is but one kind of *necessity*, as there is but one kind of cause, and that the common distinction betwixt *moral* and *physical* necessity is without any foundation in nature. This clearly appears from the precedent explication of necessity. 'Tis the constant conjunction of objects, along with the determination of the mind, which constitutes a physical necessity: And the removal of these is the same thing with *chance*. As objects must either be conjoin'd or not, and as the mind must either be determin'd or not to pass from one object to another, 'tis impossible to admit of any medium betwixt chance and an absolute necessity. In weakening this conjunction and determination you do not change the nature of the necessity; since even in the operation of bodies, these have different degrees of constancy and force, without producing a different species of that relation. (THN 171)

As this passage shows, Hume denies the existence of any "medium" between necessity and chance, and he is willing to classify even regularities having some exceptions on the side of "necessity." He is willing to do this because he holds that our idea of necessity is derived ultimately from the impression of necessary connection that arises when the mind is determined to perform inferences from experience. When this conjunction of event-types is constant enough to produce inference in the mind of an (idealized) observer, therefore, the events are an example of causal "necessity"; where the conjunction is not constant enough to produce this inference, they instead exhibit "chance." It is for this reason that Hume can describe the "vulgar" as allowing some considerable irregularity and indeterminacy in events without doubting the presence of "causes":

> The vulgar, who take things according to their first appearance, attribute the uncertainty of events to such an uncertainty in the causes as makes the latter often fail of their usual influence; though they meet with no impediment in their operations. (EHU §67)

It is true that Hume continues:

> But philosophers, observing that, almost in every part of nature, there is contained a vast variety of springs and principles, which are hid, by reason of their minuteness or

remoteness, find, that it is at least possible the contrariety of events may not proceed from any contingency in the cause, but from the secret operation of contrary causes. This possibility is converted into certainty by farther observation, when they remark that, upon an exact scrutiny, a contrariety of effects always betrays a contrariety of causes, and proceeds from their mutual opposition. A peasant can give no better reason for the stopping of any clock or watch than to say that it does not commonly go right: But an artist easily perceives that the same force in the spring or pendulum has always the same influence on the wheels; but fails of its usual effect, perhaps by reason of a grain of dust, which puts a stop to the whole movement. From the observation of several parallel instances, philosophers form a maxim that the connexion between all causes and effects is equally necessary, and that its seeming uncertainty in some instances proceeds from the secret opposition of contrary causes. (EHU §67; the passage is repeated nearly verbatim from THN 132)

Thus, philosophers might perhaps be said to regard events as even more fully or uniformly necessitated than the vulgar do—for they conclude that all physical causes are "equally necessary." But in light of the passage previously cited (THN 171), this difference is a mere nuance.

This interpretation of the "doctrine of necessity"—that is, as compatible with the mild indeterminism of the vulgar view—is further confirmed by the nature of Hume's argument to show that morality and religion require the doctrine. He argues that the general efficacy of rewards and punishments, on the one hand, and the attribution of actions to durable features of character, on the other, presuppose the doctrine of necessity. But, quite obviously, neither the general efficacy of rewards and punishments nor the attribution of actions to durable features of character require the *strict determinism* of the philosophers; they require only the weaker doctrine of general predictability that philosophers share with the vulgar. In fact, at no point in either of Hume's discussions of liberty and necessity does his argument concerning the interrelations among necessity, liberty (in either of the two senses of 'liberty' that he distinguishes), and responsibility demand anything stronger.

We must therefore distinguish several different doctrines bearing on causation and human action. The first, and strongest, is strict determinism, which we have defined schematically as the doctrine that every event is fully determined by exceptionless causal laws. Strict determinism entails what Penelhum calls "universal causation"—that is, the doctrine that every event is produced by a cause. Universal causation is, prima facie, weaker than strict determinism, however. For it might well be—and the vulgar might well have reason to accept—that every event has *some* cause, even if primary causes sometimes unaccountably fail to operate. In the case of the watch that Hume describes, for example, it might be supposed that background causes determine the hands of the watch to remain stationary when the mainspring unaccountably fails to exert its usual influence. D. G. C. MacNabb (1951, p. 57) has in effect claimed that universal causation entails strict determinism, arguing that the unaccountable failure of a primary cause to operate would itself always be an event without a cause. It is highly questionable, however, whether Hume would regard "the failure of a cause to operate" as a third event, in addition to the occurrence of the cause and the occurrence of whatever event showed the cause to fail in its operation. It is particularly questionable in light of

Hume's rejection (described in chapter 5) of the intelligibility of the concept of "power" as a term for "that circumstance in the cause which enables it to produce its effect."

In any case, Hume's doctrine of necessity is yet a third doctrine, distinct from both strict determinism and universal causation. It is weaker than either of them. It is weaker not simply because it is a doctrine restricted to human action and volition but (more important) because it permits irregularities and even occasional uncaused events, so long as there is a sufficient amount of constant conjunction to sustain inference.

Grounds for Determinism and Universal Causation

Although Hume's argument does not *require* anything stronger than the doctrine of necessity, as we have defined it, he does nevertheless *endorse* both strict determinism and universal causation. As noted, he even goes so far as to conclude *Treatise* II.iii.2 by claiming to have shown the truth of the latter. It is therefore worth asking why he also accepts those two doctrines.

Hume evidently regards the doctrine of universal causation—or at least its specific application to "beginnings of existence"—as a commonplace among philosophers. According to him, it is "universally allowed that nothing exists without a cause of its existence" (EHU §74); similarly, he describes the principle that "*whatever begins to exist must have a cause of its existence*" as "a general maxim in philosophy . . . commonly taken for granted in all reasonings, without any proof given or demanded" (THN 78–79).[1] If he is correct about its status, then no justification of the doctrine will ordinarily be required in the context of philosophical discussion. As the passage previously cited (THN 171) indicates, Hume believes that even his opponents will grant the principle of universal causation and choose instead to argue that some causes—namely, causes of human actions—do not *necessitate*. Furthermore, he also regards a strict determinism concerning physical events as "universally allowed," as he indicates in the passage previously cited (EHU §64). His arguments for a parallel between physical and "moral" predictions thus imply that, by parity of reasoning, we should accept a strict determinism regarding human actions as well.

Does Hume simply rest content, then, with appealing to general assent for universal causation—supplemented, in the case of strict determinism, by considerations of parity? MacNabb has claimed that the discussion of the vulgar and philosophical views of the "uncertainty of causes," cited previously (EHU §72 and THN 132), provides Hume's grounds for universal causation and determinism. Penelhum (1987) disputes this claim. As Penelhum notes, the passage that MacNabb cites presents us as already presupposing that every situation involves a *potential* cause; it simply explains why the vulgar and the philosophical draw different conclusions about whether potential causes always operate uniformly, and hence about whether the outcomes of those cases are fully determined. Hume explicitly describes how our success in finding hidden *counteracting* causes, in cases where causes have seemed to fail, leads philosophers to treat all outcomes as completely determined. But it is also reasonable to suppose that, in Hume's view, a similar success in finding hidden causes in those cases where no causes initially appear leads philosophers to the belief in uniform causation.

This supposition is confirmed by a passage from an earlier point in the *Treatise*:

> [T]ho' we are here suppos'd to have had only one experiment of a particular effect, yet we have many millions to convince us of this principle; that like objects, plac'd in like circumstances, will always produce like effects; and as this principle has establish'd itself by a sufficient custom, it bestows an evidence and firmness on any opinion, to which it can be apply'd. The connexion of the ideas is not habitual after one experiment; but this connexion is comprehended under another principle, that is habitual; which brings us back to our hypothesis. In all cases we transfer our *experience* to instances, of which we have no experience, either expressly or tacitly, either directly or indirectly. (THN 105)

Unlike the previous passages (EHU §67 and THN 132), this passage refers not merely to all *causes* but to all *objects*. It appears to say that every difference in outcomes must be produced by some difference in the antecedent conditions, which entails that whatever exists has a cause of its existence. We cannot interpret the passage as saying only that those differences that are *effects* must have a cause. For on that interpretation, a single experiment could not suffice to establish a causal relation, contrary to Hume's claim (because any difference in outcomes could be due either to a difference in the antecedent conditions or to the difference not being an effect at all). Furthermore, the final sentence of the passage makes it clear how this process works. It is by projecting observed cases onto unobserved cases that we assign particular causes to particular effects, and it is by a kind of meta-application of the same inductive procedure that we infer that all events *have* determining causes, on the basis of our experience of events whose determining causes we have been in a satisfactory position to discover.[2]

Attitudes toward Necessity and Liberty

The Vulgar and the Philosophical

We are now in a position to reconsider the four puzzles described at the outset of this chapter. First, then, how can Hume describe a doctrine of strict physical causation as "universally allowed" while also attributing to the vulgar a view that is incompatible with it? When Hume speaks of a doctrine as being "universally allowed," he means that it is universally granted in contemporary philosophical debate (in the broad eighteenth-century sense of 'philosophical'), and not that it is accepted by every human being. This interpretation is strongly suggested by the very specificity and theoretical character of the strict physical determinism that Hume describes as "universally allowed" (EHU §64). The interpretation is confirmed by his explicit statement, immediately following his account of the vulgar view, that it is only "philosophers" who "form a maxim that the connexion between all causes and effects is equally necessary, and that its seeming uncertainty in some instances proceeds from the secret opposition of contrary causes." Additional confirmation comes in Hume's willingness to characterize the principle that "nothing exists without a cause" both as "universally allowed" (EHU §74) and as "a general maxim in philosophy . . . commonly taken for granted in all reasonings, without any proof given or demanded" (THN 78–79). Thus, there is no contradiction in Hume's claim that a strict and exceptionless physical determinism is "universally allowed" even though the vulgar suppose that causes sometimes unaccountably fail to produce their usual effects. The vulgar simply do not participate in those debates in which the denial of their supposition is "allowed" as a matter of course.

Nor is there any contradiction between Hume's claim that the vulgar allow a degree of indeterminacy through the "uncertainty" of causes and his claim that all humankind accepts the doctrine of necessity. For as we have already seen, "the doctrine of necessity," as Hume intends it, requires only that human actions exhibit a *sufficient degree* of constant conjunction with motives, tempers, and circumstances—that is, a degree sufficient to facilitate inference. This doctrine is entirely consistent with the mild indeterminism of the vulgar.

Illusions of Liberty and Necessity

But what of Hume's seemingly conflicting claims about humanity's attitudes toward the doctrines of liberty and necessity? In order to understand his claims about our attitudes toward those doctrines, it is necessary to realize that he consistently regards humans in general—philosophers and vulgar alike—as ambivalent in their views about liberty and necessity. They are ambivalent, he holds, as a consequence of their confusion about the nature of necessity. He has already argued in his analysis of causation that, if we are to mean anything clear by the objective causal term 'necessity', we can only mean constant conjunction and/or inferences based on constant conjunctions. But because we mistakenly believe that physical causation can be conceived as involving what he calls a "necessary connexion in nature," we erroneously suppose that we can intelligibly mean more. In the only clear senses of 'necessity' actually available, he therefore maintains, everyone would agree to the "doctrine of necessity," a doctrine that we all acknowledge in our "whole practice and reasoning" (EHU §71). We are prevented from applying the term 'necessity' to human actions, however, by the erroneous belief that this term *ought* to denote the further condition of a "force" or "real necessary connexion in nature," a condition that we suppose to be present in physical causation but to be missing in human action. For this reason, we deny the doctrine of necessity "in words" and verbally maintain that "necessity" is incompatible with responsibility.

Correlatively, by the 'liberty of indifference', defined as the "negation of necessity and causes," we can only mean, if we are to mean anything clear, the *absence* of constant conjunction and/or inference. And in manifesting our practical acceptance of conjunction and inference, we all show our de facto rejection of the liberty of indifference in this sense. However, Hume maintains that because we suppose that there is a kind of necessity *beyond* conjunction and inference, we also suppose that there is a kind of "negation of necessity"—that is, a kind of "liberty of indifference"—that is *compatible* with conjunction and inference. For this reason, we can be tempted by our experience of our own actions to profess verbally a belief in a kind of "liberty of indifference." In fact, however, there is no clear sense of the term 'liberty of indifference' to provide the object of such a belief. Hence, he writes:

> But as long as we will rashly suppose, that we have some farther idea of necessity and causation in the operations of external objects; at the same time, that we can find nothing farther in the voluntary actions of the mind; there is no possibility of bringing the question to any determinate issue, while we proceed upon so erroneous a supposition. (EHU §72)

Thus, for Hume, we must be careful how we order the belief operator and the existential quantifier when we characterize the common beliefs of mankind. It is true to say that we tend *to believe that there is* a possible kind of "liberty of indifference" that we possess, but it is false to say that *there is* a possible kind of "liberty of indifference" such that we clearly believe ourselves to possess it. This is why Hume claims that the doctrine of liberty that opposes necessity is "absurd . . . in one sense [because everyone can see that it is false], and unintelligible in any other [because it depends on an inconceivable kind of liberty]" (THN 407). Hume thinks that we "can only mean" the liberty of *spontaneity* when we ascribe liberty to ourselves, precisely because the doctrine that we have a liberty of *indifference* is obviously false on its clear construal and unintelligible on its more common one. That is, we cannot mean anything other than the liberty of spontaneity, he thinks, if we are speaking both honestly and intelligibly. There is no contradiction or ambivalence in Hume's *account of* our beliefs—rather, he gives a consistent and univocal diagnosis of an (allegedly) widespread ambivalence *in* our beliefs.

Attitudes toward Necessity and Responsibility

Theological and Secular Necessity

Let us turn now to Stroud's objection. According to Stroud, Hume allows that the theological version of the doctrine of necessity "can plausibly lead to the conclusion that God is the only responsible agent." Accordingly, Stroud argues, Hume should admit that "a fully secularized version [of the doctrine of necessity] could equally plausibly lead to the conclusion that there are no responsible agents at all"—an admission that would run contrary to Hume's claim that the doctrine of necessity is compatible with moral responsibility and is even required by it.[3] A closer reading of Hume's discussion will show, however, that he need not allow that a fully secularized version of the doctrine of necessity would lead to the denial of human responsibility. This is because, contrary to Stroud's interpretation, Hume does not admit that a *theological* version of the doctrine of necessity can plausibly lead to the conclusion that God is the only responsible agent.

Immediately after presenting his description of the objection that the doctrine of necessity poses for theology (EHU §78, quoted previously), Hume proceeds, as we have seen, to distinguish the objection into two distinct problems. His solution to the first problem lies in his claim that the distinctions of vice and virtue are founded on "the natural sentiments of the human mind," which operate primarily

on the more *immediate* causal tendencies and consequences of features of character and of the actions that express them. Hume has already argued earlier in
Enquiry VIII.ii that persons acquire merit or demerit from their actions only insofar
as those actions are caused by enduring features of character. He now adds, in
effect, that the prospect of a theological doctrine of necessity would not affect the
judgments of character that an idealized observer would make. Indeed, the original
problem posed by a theological doctrine of necessity, as Hume sees it, lies not in its
implication that all human actions or volitions are causally *necessitated* but instead
in its implication that they are causally necessitated *by a perfect and benevolent
being*. For the latter thesis evidently implies that the actions and character of each
person must somehow be ultimately good and useful in the grander scheme—and
hence not ultimately bad—no matter how harmful and disagreeable their more
immediate effects. Hume enunciates his solution to this problem quite clearly—
namely, that such *remote* considerations cannot permanently affect our moral sentiments, and hence they have no rightful bearing on moral evaluation—and he pronounces that solution to be "obvious and convincing."

It is thus only the second of the two problems—the one concerning divine
guilt—that Hume declares to be difficult to solve. If God is the ultimate cause of
the evil actions that humans perform, then He causes them with full knowledge of
the consequences of His actions, and those consequences thereby reflect on His
character. But *God's* responsibility for human evil is not, in Hume's own view,
incompatible with *human* responsibility for the same evil. That is because responsibility for an evil act depends on whether it is indicative of the enduring character of
the person who caused it. Where one person—God—is the cause of the character
of another person, a single act may well result from, and causally express, the character of both. Thus, although Hume might well grant that the theological doctrine
of necessity leads plausibly to the conclusion that God is a responsible agent, and
even an agent responsible for all that occurs, he can deny that the theological doctrine of necessity leads plausibly to the conclusion that God is the *only* responsible
agent, or is *solely* responsible for all that occurs. The doctrine of necessity itself—
whether theological or secular—has no extenuating tendency, in Hume's view,
except through the confusion about the nature of necessity that he has already surveyed and (he believes) corrected.

It is true that Hume puts in his objector's mouth the claim:

> [W]e must therefore conclude, either that [all those actions of men, which we so rashly
> pronounce criminal] are not criminal, or that the Deity, not man, is accountable for
> them. (EHU §78)

But this is not Hume's own voice. Furthermore, it marks a contradiction in the
objector's position, since the objection began by describing the second of the two
problems thus: "if [human actions] have any turpitude, they must involve our Creator in the same guilt" (EHU §100). The objector's claim that the Deity, *and not
man*, would be accountable for criminal actions seems influenced by the immediately preceding remark that "ignorance or impotence may be pleaded for so limited
a creature as man; but those imperfections have no place in our Creator."

Divine Goodness and Human Responsibility

Hume's distinction between the two problems concerning theism and the doctrine of necessity, and his acceptance of a solution only for the first, leaves us still with the apparent inconsistency described by Hickenlooper. Does Hume equivocate on the compatibility of perfect divine goodness and human criminality in a (mildly or strictly) deterministic universe?

In his solution to the first problem, Hume asks rhetorically, "why should not the acknowledgment of a real distinction between vice and virtue be reconcileable to all speculative systems of philosophy, as well as that of a real distinction between personal beauty and deformity?" (EHU §80). Although Hume does not answer this question explicitly, it is not a question that he would likely have asked if he thought he could show that the hypothesis of divine moral perfection is logically incompatible with the existence of human criminality. And his preceding rhetorical questions illustrate why Hume does not think he can show any such logical incompatibility:

> What though philosophical meditations establish a different opinion or conjecture; that everything is right with regard to the WHOLE, and that the qualities, which disturb society, are, in the main, as beneficial, and are as suitable to the primary intention of nature as those which more directly promote its happiness and welfare? Are such remote and uncertain speculations able to counterbalance the sentiments which arise from the natural and immediate view of the objects? (EHU §80)

Precisely because moral judgments result from human moral *sentiments*,[4] the prospects for showing a *logical incompatibility* between divine perfection and human criminality are highly unpromising. This interpretation of Hume is strengthened by the admission of Philo—the most Humean character in his *Dialogues concerning Natural Religion*—that the evidence provided by the universe around us does not support, but cannot absolutely *refute*, the hypothesis of a morally good creator. We daily affirm the virtue of some human individuals and the vice of others, in Hume's view, and we do so with a strength and conviction that we see to be capable of withstanding the potential effects of any speculative convictions about the moral structure of the universe as a whole. But it is the stable moral sentiments of mankind that constitute the standard of moral judgment. Thus, the first problem can be "solved"—we can see that acceptance of the hypothesis of a morally perfect deity in a deterministic universe cannot force us, and would not lead us, to give up the drawing of moral distinctions among human characters. *If* we could convince ourselves of the former, it could not significantly undermine our commitment to the latter, which is fundamental.

But to allow that there is no logical incompatibility between divine perfection and human criminality in a deterministic universe is not to say that it is easy to provide a coherent explanation of exactly *how* both could be true in such a universe. Thus, Hume writes of his second problem that it

> admits not of so easy and satisfactory an answer; nor is it possible to explain distinctly, how the Deity can be the mediate cause of all the actions of men, without being the author of sin and moral turpitude. (EHU §81)

Given the power and knowledge ascribed to the Deity, it seems that in order to provide such an explanation it would at least be necessary to show how human criminality produces goods that cannot be produced as well without human criminality. And perhaps, if we examine our moral sentiments, even that would not be enough for us to excuse God's use of human criminality as a means. Hume does not say that no such explanation could be given, but only that it "has been found hitherto to exceed all the power of philosophy" (EHU §81). In the absence of such an explanation, human criminality in a more-or-less deterministic universe must be a weighty, if not logically conclusive, piece of evidence against the existence of divine moral perfection. For this reason, the second of Hume's two "problems" of necessity and responsibility continues to pose a serious problem for religion.

Hume accepts the conditional "If N then (if C then not-P)" because he finds the probability of not-P to be very high relative to the hypothesis of C and N. He rejects the conditional "If N then (if P then not-C)" because he finds the truth of C to be unshakable, and so he finds the probability of not-C to be very low, even on the hypothesis of P and N. Of course, if contraposition preserves logical equivalence in these two conditionals, then the two conditionals are logically equivalent, and Hume would stand convicted of contradiction in accepting one and rejecting the other. Moreover, contraposition does preserve logical equivalence for truth-functional material conditionals and for strict implication (i.e., entailment). But this simply shows that Hume's two conditionals should not be interpreted as material conditionals or as conditionals of strict implication. Rather, as indicative conditionals, they express subjective assessments of relative probability.[5]

Hume's "Reconciling Project"

If the interpretation presented here is correct, Hume's doctrine of necessity is weaker than either universal causation or strict determinism, and his grounds for thinking it important lie ultimately in his explanation of the cognitive processes of causal inference. He presents a consistent theory of popular attitudes toward liberty and necessity, an account that is grounded in his own theory of how causation and necessity must be represented in the mind. An understanding of his theory of moral judgment shows that his discussion of theological determination does not undermine his claim that the doctrine of necessity is compatible with responsibility. Nor does it undermine his attempt to subvert "superstitious" religion by posing the problem of divine responsibility for evil. So far, therefore, Hume's project of "reconciling" the doctrines of necessity and liberty, while posing problems for theism, seems successful.

Hume's arguments involving the doctrine of necessity do not, I have claimed, commit him to strict determinism or universal causation. This result is encouraging, so far as the soundness of Hume's arguments are concerned, for the weaker a conclusion is, other things being equal, the more likely it is to be true. And in at least one respect, this result also renders Hume's argument more directly relevant to contemporary philosophy. For contemporary philosophy, as already noted, has been obliged to withdraw from strict determinism. However, it may now seem that

Hume's conclusions concerning the doctrine of necessity are so weak as to have no bearing at all on contemporary disputes about free will. Contemporary opponents of the necessity of human actions—"libertarians"—will indeed agree with Hume's "doctrine of necessity" as we have described it, but they will seek to locate the absence of what *they* mean by 'necessity' in a failure of strict determinism.

As we have already seen, Hume believes that his own opponents will grant that human actions are *caused* but will deny that "moral" causes—that is, causes in the sphere of human action—*necessitate*. His twentieth-century opponents, in contrast, tend to deny that human actions are necessitated on the grounds that they are not strictly *determined* but can only be predicted probabilistically. To the extent that this represents a real historical change in strategy among opponents of necessity, it would be tempting to attribute it, at least in part, to Hume's own success against the earlier strategy. Nevertheless, his arguments remain relevant to the attempts of contemporary libertarians to defend an understanding of human freedom that relies essentially on the rejection of strict determinism.

First, Hume's comparison of the kinds and degrees of regularity in the field of human action with those in nonhuman nature establishes a prima facie case that consistency requires us to draw the same conclusions about the character and extent of causal determination in both cases. If, therefore, it is granted that the behavior of inanimate objects above the quantum level is for all practical purposes deterministic, then it is incumbent on libertarians to explain the positive *disanalogies* that lead them to suppose it likely that the same is not true of the behavior of human beings. Of course, it is one thing to argue that psychology itself is not a deterministic science and quite another to argue that human behavior is not fully governed by deterministic laws under *any* description—including a materialistic description. It is the latter, more difficult, thesis that the libertarian must establish.

Second, Hume at least suggests a prima facie case for thinking that the difference between deterministic and probabilistic (i.e., merely "statistical") laws is fundamentally irrelevant to the questions of liberty and responsibility. For if his account of necessity is correct, then the two kinds of laws manifest, at most, different degrees of the same kind of necessity; it is for this reason that Hume confidently considers the vulgar to be subscribers to the "doctrine of necessity." Why, Hume might ask, should a person be laudable for actions that he or she can be accurately predicted to perform 99.9% of the time, yet not be laudable for the very same actions if he or she can be accurately predicted to perform them 100% of the time—especially when *changing* the percentage may not be under the agent's voluntary control in either case? If causes sometimes unaccountably fail to operate, that does not entail that our actions are not caused by them when they do operate. Nor does it explain how we could be responsible for the uncharacteristic actions that we might perform when they did fail to operate (THN 410–412 and EHU §76). In short, given Hume's account of necessity, the burden is on the libertarian to explain either (i) why we should value a "liberty" that consists in the statistical possibility of individually unaccountable behavioral quirks, or (ii) how the libertarian version of "liberty" can amount to anything more.

It is often objected against Hume that his positive conception of liberty, as consisting entirely in freedom from constraint, is extraordinarily thin. It is said, for example, that it draws no distinction between the reluctant and ashamed kleptomaniac or compulsive handwasher, on one side, and the agent who acts with wholehearted commitment, on the other. In Hume's defense, it may be remarked that there is room in his theory of responsibility to draw distinctions among such cases. As Hume repeatedly emphasizes, a person's actions are relevant to his or her moral evaluation just insofar as the actions are indicators of the person's standing character. Some actions, however, reveal more about the whole tenor of a person's character than do others:

> Men are less blam'd for such evil actions as they perform hastily and unpremeditatedly, than for such as proceed from thought and deliberation. For what reason? but because a hasty temper, tho' a constant cause in the mind, operates only by intervals, and infects not the whole character. (THN 412)

Hume's example concerns hasty temper, rather than internal conflict between compulsions and considered judgments, or between strong first-order desires and second-order desires not to be moved by those first-order desires, but a similar point applies. While he draws no distinction of *freedom* between those who act from inner compulsion and those who act wholeheartedly, he can draw a distinction in the moral evaluation of the agents themselves.[6]

Hume's discussion of liberty and necessity has, of course, important consequences for his theory of moral evaluation, but it also has equally important consequences for his treatment of religion. The "unintelligible" doctrine of human liberty that he rejects has served as a bulwark against the attribution of moral evil to God through the so-called free will defense—for the doctrine can be used to deny the necessity of the causal chain that would otherwise lead us to regard the evil actions of humans as evidence of the moral character of the Deity who knowingly creates and sustains their natures. Insofar as Hume's discussion of liberty and necessity depends on his conception of causation, therefore, his discussion illustrates the philosophical application of that conception of causation to religious topics. A second—and even more famous—application of Hume's conception of causal reasoning to religious topics occurs in his notorious treatment of miracles.

Miracles

The Scientific Revolution posed questions not only about the relation between nature and human actions but also about the relation between nature and divine actions, and about the existence of divine actions in or alongside nature. In the face of a mechanistic universe from which God appeared to stand aloof, many theologians claimed that the historical occurrence of miracles in conjunction with divine revelation, as established by the testimony of scripture, was a primary source of evidence for the truth of Christianity.

Section X of *An Enquiry concerning Human Understanding*—entitled "Of Miracles"—is surely the most famous philosophical treatment of the credibility of reports of miracles ever written. Hume divides the section into two parts. Part i provides his most general argument concerning assent to miracles, an argument that appeals prominently to claims about "proof," "probability," "experience," "laws of nature," "miracles," and the relations among them. Part ii goes on to raise four separate and specific objections to the credibility of testimony for miracles, concerning (i) the quality of existing testimony for miracles, (ii) the psychological factors contributing to the offering and acceptance of testimony for miracles, (iii) the frequent origination of testimony for miracles among ignorant peoples, and (iv) the conflicts posed by the testimony for miracles of different religions. Because of the contrast between the generality of the premises of Part i and the specificity of the premises of Part ii, commentators sometimes refer to the argument of Part i as Hume's "a priori argument" concerning miracles, and to the four arguments of Part ii as his "a posteriori arguments."

There is general consensus among Hume's readers concerning the structure of the arguments and the content of the conclusions of the more specific and "a posteriori" Part ii. Furthermore, if there is not quite universal consensus about the precise degree of success that those arguments achieve, there is general agreement that the arguments are appropriate and establish at least a prima facie case against the credibility of testimony for miracles. In contrast, however, there is no consensus concerning the argument, the conclusion, or the success or failure of the more general, but crucial, Part i.

That there is no consensus about Hume's *argument* in Part i is evident from a survey of the literature. Commentators have offered a wide variety of principles as "central premises" in Hume's argument, few of which occur either in Hume's text or in the reconstructions of other commentators. These proposals for tacit or implied premises include the following: "a violated law of nature is no longer a law of nature" (Norton, 1982; Beckwith, 1989); "if E is a highly improbable event, no evidence is sufficient to warrant our belief that it occurred" (Beckwith, 1989); "to evaluate testimony that p, one must compare the [prior] probability of p with the probability that the testifiers are lying or mistaken, and take the greater probability" (Hambourger, 1980); "we cannot have an impression of a supernatural cause" (Levine, 1989); "empirical reason includes the principle that for every event there is a law that explains it" (Wilson, 1989); "if in one case the occurrence of an event within the natural causal order were not sufficient to establish that the event had natural causes, then there would be no reason for believing it would be sufficient in any case" (Ahern, 1975); and "sensory evidence is always stronger than testimonial evidence" (Yandell, 1990).

There is no greater consensus concerning Hume's *conclusion* in Part i. On the contrary, some commentators characterize Hume as arguing that miracles are impossible or *cannot occur* (Beckwith, 1989; Norton, 1982; and Fogelin, 1990); others, that one cannot *reasonably believe* that a miracle has occurred (Sorenson, 1983; Coleman, 1988; Yandell, 1990; and Fogelin, 1990); still others, that one cannot reasonably believe *on the basis of testimony* that a miracle has occurred (Lewis, 1947; Ahern, 1975; Penelhum, 1975; Hambourger, 1980; Levine, 1989; and Wilson, 1989); and yet others, only that one cannot reasonably believe on the basis of testimony that a miracle has occurred *unless* the falsehood of the testimony would be even more miraculous than the occurrence of the miracle that it allegedly reports—and that even in that case, one can reasonably accept the miracle only with a relatively low degree of assurance (Flew, 1959, 1961, and 1986; Swinburne, 1970; Basinger and Basinger, 1986; and Sobel, 1987).

Finally, there is no consensus about the *success or failure* of Hume's argument in Part i. Some commentators hold that Hume's argument is at least fairly successful (Mackie, 1982; Owen, 1987; Sobel, 1987; and Wilson, 1989). Others hold that it fails, either because it relies on one or more false premises (Ahern, 1975; Hambourger, 1980; Burns, 1981; Beckwith, 1989; Levine, 1989; and Yandell, 1990), because its premises are not adequate to its conclusion (Broad, 1916–1917; Swinburne, 1970; and Burns, 1981), or because it begs the question (Lewis, 1947; Beckwith, 1989; and Levine, 1989).

Much of this striking lack of agreement is the result of six apparent inconsistencies in Hume's discussion. More often than not, commentators attribute tacit or implied premises to Hume because they are trying to reconstruct his argument so as to avoid one or more of the inconsistencies. Frequently, when commentators revise or reinterpret Hume's stated conclusion, they do so either in order to avoid one or more of the inconsistencies directly, or in order to accommodate his conclusion to a reconstruction of the argument that is itself motivated by the same goal. Their final evaluations of the argument, in turn, generally depend on the quality of the reconstructed argument, the character of the revised conclusion, and/or the continuing unresolved status of one or more of the remaining apparent inconsistencies.

Each of the six inconsistencies is only apparent, and not real. The key to resolving them lies in an understanding of Hume's argument as he actually presents it—in the context of his cognitive psychology and of the conception of probability that he derives from it. In this chapter, I first describe the six apparent inconsistencies. I then explain several relevant aspects of Hume's cognitive psychology and of his conception of probability before going on to outline the argument of "On Miracles." Finally, I draw on the results of the previous sections in order to resolve the six apparent inconsistencies in Hume's discussion and to assess its significance.

Six Apparent Inconsistencies

Each of the six apparent inconsistencies in Hume's discussion can be elicited by means of a question. I will consider them in an order in which they might occur to a thoughtful reader of Hume's text.

Experience

First, what does Hume mean by 'experience'? Near the beginning of Part i, he argues that any judgment of the probability of human testimony must depend entirely on experience (EHU §88). It seems that, in making this argument, he must be referring only and specifically to the experience of the individual who is to judge. For to judge the probability of testimony on the basis of the merely reported experiences of *others* would appear to beg the question of the reliability of testimony. A few pages later, however, he claims that an assessment of the testimony for a miracle must take into account what he calls the "uniform experience against every miraculous event" (EHU §90), and he cites such "uniform experience" as showing what "has never been observed in any age or country." Yet the fact that something has never been observed *in any age or country* is something that could hardly be established without already relying freely on the testimony of others. Thus it seems that Hume equivocates on the central term 'experience' in such a way as to make it appear that an individual's evidence against the occurrence of a miracle is far more extensive (as involving observations at distant times and places) than it actually could be on his own theory.

Laws of Nature

Second, what does Hume mean by 'laws of nature'? This term plays the crucial role in his main definition of a "miracle" as "a violation of the laws of nature" (EHU §90).[1] Yet he does not explicitly define 'law of nature'; he simply goes on to claim that a "firm and unalterable experience has established these laws" (EHU §90). From this characterization of them, it seems natural to suppose that "laws of nature" are by definition either (i) universal generalizations to which no exceptions ever *occur*, or (ii) universal generalizations to which no exceptions are ever *observed*. On the former supposition, however, the concept of a miracle occurring would be self-contradictory from the very start, and on the latter supposition, the concept of veridical eyewitness testimony for a miracle would be self-contradictory. In either case, the rest of Hume's arguments concerning the credibility of testimony for miracles would evidently then be superfluous.

Moreover, if either one of these suppositions is correct, Hume will appear to have missed the larger point, for no event—no matter how bizarre—will *be* a miracle unless it (i) fails to occur (given the first supposition), or (ii) fails to be observed (given the second). Defenders of testimony for particular bizarre or supernatural events—such as someone rising from the dead, to take a Humean example, or parting the Red Sea—may then easily claim to elude the scope of his negative conclusion, a conclusion that concerns only the credibility of reports of *miracles*. For if laws of nature are universal generalizations to which no exceptions ever *occur*, then to suggest that a particular bizarre event has occurred will be to suggest, ipso facto, that it is not a violation of a law of nature, hence that it is not a miracle, and hence that it is outside the scope of Hume's conclusion. Similarly, if laws of nature are universal generalizations to which no exceptions are ever *observed*, then to report that a bizarre event has been observed will be to imply, ipso facto, that the event is not a violation of a law of nature, hence that it is not a miracle, and hence that it is, once again, outside the scope of Hume's conclusion. Thus it seems that Hume defines his terms in a way that obviates all of his more specific arguments about testimony for miracles, while at the same time deriving an epistemic principle that could be applied even to the most bizarre kinds of events only by begging the question of their nonexistence or failure to be observed.

The Miraculous and the Marvelous

Third, what does Hume mean by the distinction he draws between the "miraculous" and the merely "marvelous" (or "extraordinary")—or, equivalently, between events that would be "contrary" to one's experience and those that are merely "not conformable" to it? He draws this distinction in order to emphasize that testimony for the miraculous must meet an even higher standard than testimony for the merely marvelous. His example is the "Indian prince" who "reasoned justly" when he "refused to believe the first relations concerning the effects of frost" (EHU §89). According to Hume, the freezing of water in cold weather would be *marvelous* and *extraordinary* for the Indian prince, and *not conformable* to his previous experience. Nevertheless, Hume insists, it would not be *miraculous* for the prince or *contrary* to his experience, because the prince has observed water only in warm weather and has no experience of water in cold. It thus requires only "very strong" or "a pretty strong" testimony to establish for the prince that water has frozen. An event like the raising of the dead, in contrast, would be a *miracle*, and *contrary* to experience, according to Hume, and thus testimony for it must be held to a far more stringent standard.

Yet how are these two cases essentially different? For although Hume may have experience of the death of individuals whom an almighty deity did not will to raise from the dead, he has evidently no experience of the death of individuals whom an almighty deity did will to raise from the dead. Why does this latter fact not render the raising of the dead—like the freezing of water—at most merely marvelous and not conformable to previous experience for Hume, and hence subject to the weaker evidential standard that he imposes on testimony for the merely marvelous and extraordinary? It seems that Hume treats these similar cases inconsistently.

Superior Proofs and Greater Miracles

Fourth, what does Hume mean when he writes of "opposite" and "superior" proofs of the occurrence or nonoccurrence of a particular miracle—or, correlatively, of a miracle that would be "more miraculous" or a "greater miracle" than another? Near the end of Part i, he writes:

> [T]here is here a direct and full *proof*, from the nature of the fact, against the existence of any miracle; nor can such a proof be destroyed, or the miracle rendered credible, but by an opposite proof, which is superior. (EHU §90)

Yet he has already defined 'proofs' as "such arguments from experience as leave no room for doubt and opposition" (EHU §46n), and it seems that one proof could not be opposite and superior to another when neither would leave any room for doubt or opposition.

Similarly, he concludes that "no testimony is sufficient to establish a miracle, unless the testimony be of such a kind, that its falsehood would be more miraculous, than the fact, which it endeavors to establish" (EHU 91). And he ends Part i by reporting that, when considering testimony of a miracle:

> I weigh the one miracle against the other; and according to the superiority, which I discover, I pronounce my decision, and always reject the greater miracle. If the falsehood of his testimony would be more miraculous, than the event which he relates, then, and not till then, can he pretend to command my belief or opinion. (EHU §91)

Yet as we have seen, Hume defines a "miracle" as a "violation of a law of nature," and he himself insists in a footnote:

> The raising of a house or ship into the air is a visible miracle. The raising of a feather, when the wind wants ever so little of a force requisite for that purpose, is as real a miracle, though not so sensible with regard to us. (EHU §90n)

Since an event either violates a law of nature or it does not, it seems that no miraculous event could be a greater miracle, or more miraculous than any other. Thus it seems that Hume contradicts his own definitions.

Absolute Impossibility

Fifth, what does Hume mean when he refers, in Part ii, to "the absolute impossibility" of certain miraculous events? Commenting on the witnesses to a recent series of alleged Jansenist miracles, he writes:

> And what have we to oppose to such a cloud of witnesses, but the absolute impossibil-
> ity or miraculous nature of the events, which they relate? And this surely, in the eyes of
> all reasonable people, will alone be regarded as a sufficient refutation. (EHU §96)

Treating miracles as an "absolute impossibility" appears to be inconsistent with his repeated denials (e.g., in THN I.iii.14 and EHU VII) that we can have any insight into necessary connections in nature. It appears to be even more directly in conflict with his Conceivability Criterion of Possibility, namely, that "whatever is conceivable is possible, at least in a metaphysical sense" (ATHN 650; see also THN 32 and THN 241, and the discussion in chapter 1). Moreover, it seems to conflict with his approach throughout Part i of Section X. In Part i, he appears to take the *metaphysical possibility* of miracles for granted even while arguing that testimony for their occurrence must be *epistemically problematic*. Indeed, he concludes Part i by asserting only that testimony cannot establish a miracle unless the falsehood of the testimony would be even more miraculous, and he illustrates the point by citing his own willingness to weigh one alleged miracle against another. Yet nothing in the a posteriori arguments of Part ii seems to warrant any shift in attitude on the question of the absolute impossibility of miracles from Part i to Part ii. Thus it seems that Hume both violates his own general metaphysical principles and equivocates on the question of what Part i actually establishes.

The Uniformity of Nature

Finally, regardless of his other arguments, how can Hume himself criticize beliefs in miracles—as he clearly does throughout both Part i and Part ii—in light of his own views about what we would call "inductive inferences" and he calls "inferences from experience"? To treat past experience as providing a legitimate "proof" against the occurrence of a miracle seems to presuppose that the course of nature is uniform and that instances one has not observed will resemble instances one has observed. Yet as noted in chapter 4, Hume vigorously maintains that this thesis of the uniformity of nature cannot be defended by any argument that does not presuppose it (THN I.iii.6; EHU IV). Moreover, he holds that inductive inferences are "not determin'd by reason" (THN 92) and "are not founded on reasoning or any process of the understanding" (EHU §28). Thus, given these views, it seems that Hume is inconsistent in treating beliefs in miracles as worse than other beliefs about matters of fact that go beyond present experience and memory.

Cognitive Psychology and Probability

In order to understand Hume's argument in "On Miracles," and so to resolve these apparent inconsistencies, it is necessary to understand (i) his distinction of arguments into demonstrations, proofs, and probabilities; and (ii) his account of the species of probability.

Demonstration, Proof, and Probability

"Demonstrations," according to Hume, are arguments depending only on the intrinsic relations among ideas, arguments in which the "denial of the conclusion involves a contradiction" (EHU §30). As such, they do not depend on experience. "Proofs" are not demonstrations but rather "such arguments from experience as leave no room for doubt or opposition" (EHU §46n). "Probabilities" constitute the remainder of arguments from experience—that is, those that produce a lower degree of assurance (EHU §46n).

Proofs and probabilities thus differ in the degree of assurance they produce. But they resemble each other, Hume holds (EHU V–VI), inasmuch as the degree of assurance involved in both proof and probability is nothing more than the degree of a fundamental psychological magnitude that constitutes "belief" or "assent." In the *Treatise*, Hume explicitly identifies this psychological magnitude as "force and vivacity," the same magnitude that, when present in an even higher degree, also serves to distinguish impressions from ideas. In the first *Enquiry*, however, Hume does not explicitly make this identification of belief with a lower degree of "force and vivacity," although he does characterize belief as "nothing but a more vivid, lively, forcible, firm, steady conception" (EHU §40). In what follows, I will refer to the psychological magnitude that constitutes Humean belief simply as "vivacity." Both the *Treatise* and the *Enquiry* emphasize that, in both proof and probability, the characteristic constituting belief or assent is produced in an idea by an impression, ultimately as a causal consequence of an association derived from some amount of uniformity in the judger's past experience. In the case of a proof, this experience has been "entirely regular and uniform" (EHU §57), whereas in the case of probability, such entire regularity and uniformity is in some way lacking.[2]

Species of Probability

Section VI of the *Enquiry* ("Of Probability") describes two species of probability, the first of which is the probability of *chances*. In this species of probability, the projection of past experience assures us that *one* out of a certain set of alternatives will be realized in a given circumstance. At the same time, this experience gives us no expectation of one rather than another of these alternatives. Hence, an idea, or "view," of each alternative acquires a certain and similar degree of vivacity, as one of the alternatives suggested by past experience. When some of these views happen to concur in some characteristic, their force is combined in that respect, giving greater vivacity (and hence belief or assent) to the idea of an outcome possessing that characteristic. This greater vivacity varies with the number of concurring views. At the same time, however, views of those possibilities that do not concur in that characteristic will oppose or conflict with the concurring views. Accordingly, these opposing views will lessen the vivacity of the idea of an outcome possessing the characteristic in question. This lessening effect will vary with the number of opposing views. The final result is a degree of vivacity for the idea of a particular outcome that corresponds to the proportion of concurring views among all of the views. For example, if a die has one number marked on 4 of its faces, and another number marked on the other 2, we expect that the first number will come up on a roll of the die with more assurance than if that number had only been on, say, 3 out of 6 sides, but with less than if it had been on 999 out of 1,000.

The second species of probability that Hume discusses in *Enquiry* VI is the probability of *causes*. In the most common form of this species of probability, the projection of past experience once again provides us with a set of alternatives, one of which is to be realized in a given set of circumstances.[3] As before, the vivacity that constitutes belief or assent is derived from the concurrence in some characteristic of various different ideas or views, while the diminished vivacity that is characteristic of mere probability is the result of a conflict of opposing views. And as before, this vivacity increases with the number of concurring views and decreases with the number of opposing views, with the final result that the vivacity of the idea of a particular outcome corresponds to the proportion of concurring views among all of the views. In the probability of causes, however, each different view is the result of a distinct past experience, which Hume calls an "experiment." In his example, if we have experience that 19 out of 20 ships sent out have returned safely, the 20 experiments produce 19 concurring views in which a ship returns safely, and we expect that the next will return safely as well—with more assurance than if, say, only 18 of 20 had returned safely, but with less than if 999 out of 1,000 had done so.

Enquiry IX ("Of the Reason of Animals") begins with a brief discussion of a third species of probability, that of *analogy*, which the *Treatise* explains at greater length. Whereas the probabilities of chances and of causes involve imperfect *uniformity*, the probability of analogy derives from a different kind of irregularity—namely, a lack of full *resemblance* between the circumstance under consideration and those involved in one's past experiments. This lack of resemblance weakens the vivacity, and hence the belief and assurance, of the conclusion. Thus, Hume writes:

> The vivacity of the first impression cannot be fully convey'd to the related idea, either where the conjunction of their objects is not constant, or where the present impression does not perfectly resemble any of those, whose union we are accustomed to observe. In those probabilities of chance and causes above explain'd, 'tis the constancy of the union, which is diminished; and in the probability deriv'd from analogy, 'tis the resemblance only, which is affected. Without some degree of resemblance as well as union, 'tis impossible there can be any reasoning; but as this resemblance admits of many different degrees, the reasoning becomes proportionably more or less firm and certain. An experiment loses of its force, when transferr'd to instances, which are not exactly resembling; tho' 'tis evident it may still retain as much as may be the foundation of probability, as long as there is any resemblance remaining. (THN 142)

In the *Treatise*, Hume also describes four kinds of "unphilosophical probability." These include (i) the variations in vivacity that result from the temporal distance of the relevant experiments; (ii) the additional vivacity derived from whatever happens to be the most recent experiment; (iii) the variations of vivacity that result from the mere length of arguments; and (iv) the rashly formed "general rules" (such as national or ethnic prejudices) that result from applying the probability of analogy even to circumstances of resemblance that have already been determined to be causally irrelevant (THN I.iii.13). Whereas the probabilities of chances, causes, and analogy "are receiv'd by philosophers, and allow'd to be reasonable foundations of belief and opinion," unphilosophical probability comprises those kinds of probability that "have not had the good fortune to obtain the same sanction." They lack this good fortune because they involve cognitive mechanisms that, upon reflection, we find we do not approve. Those who do reflect on these mechanisms—that is, the "philosophical"—reject the first kind of unphilosophical probability, for example, because they observe that, if it were accepted, "an argument must have a different force to day, from what it shall have a month hence" (THN 143). Similarly, they reject the fourth kind of unphilosophical probability because it conflicts with those positive general "rules by which to judge of causes and effects" that we formulate for ourselves on the basis of reflection on our cognitive mechanisms and their inductive successes and failures (THN 149), and which Hume details in *Treatise* I.iii.15. Thus, he writes:

> [W]hen we take a review of this act of the mind [i.e., the fourth kind of unphilosophical probability, concerning rashly formed general rules], and compare it with the more general and authentic operations of the understanding, we find it to be of an irregular nature, and destructive of all the most establish'd principles of reasonings; which is the cause of our rejecting it. (THN 150)

The Argument against Testimony for Miracles

With this understanding of Humean probability as background, we can now understand his arguments concerning testimony for miracles. His argument in Part i may be usefully divided into three sections. The first concerns epistemological principles of proof and probability in general; the second concerns human testimony; and the third concerns testimony for miracles in particular. I will outline these sections in order. For purposes of comparison, I will then go on to outline Hume's argument as it continues in Part ii.

Epistemological Principles of Proof and Probability

The first section of Hume's argument seeks to establish three general epistemological principles on the basis of three initial premises. It may be outlined as follows:

1. [E]xperience [is] our only guide in reasoning concerning matters of fact.
2. Some events are found, in all countries and all ages, to have been constantly conjoined together: Others are found to have been more variable, and sometimes to disappoint our expectations.
3. A wise man . . . proportions his belief to the evidence.
4. In such conclusions as are founded on an infallible experience, [a wise man] expects the event with the last degree of assurance, and regards his past experience as a full *proof* of the future existence of that event. (from 1, 2, and 3)
5. In other cases [i.e., where conclusions are not founded on an infallible experience, a wise man] proceeds with more caution: He weighs the opposite experiments: He considers which side is supported by the greater number of experiments: to that side

he inclines, with doubt and hesitation; and when at last he fixes his judgement, the evidence exceeds not what we properly call *probability*. (from 1, 2, and 3)
6. In all cases [of reasoning concerning matters of fact], we must balance the opposite experiments, where they are opposite, and deduct the smaller number from the greater, in order to know the exact force of the superior evidence. (from 1, 2, and 3)

The first premise, (1), which states that experience is our only guide in reasoning concerning matters of fact, is a direct consequence of Hume's previous analysis of causal reasoning. The second premise, (2), characterizes that experience: some kinds of events are found to be conjoined with complete constancy, while others are often conjoined but with less constancy and more variability. The third premise, (3), characterizes the response of the "wise man" to this experience: he proportions his belief to the evidence. Hume's first conclusion from these premises is (4), which affirms that the wise man expects the pattern of an infallible experience to be continued in the future with "the last degree of assurance," and regards the experience itself as constituting a "proof." His second conclusion, (5), is that, where experience is more mixed or variable, the wise man "proceeds with more caution . . . , weighs the opposite experiments . . . , considers which side is supported by the greater number of experiments," and inclines to that side "with doubt and hesitation," so that the evidence "exceeds not what we properly call *probability*" (and more specifically, the probability of causes). Given Hume's cognitive psychology, (4) and (5) imply that the amount of vivacity characterizing the conclusions of the wise is a function of the uniformity of their experience concerning similar circumstances. That is, where that experience is completely uniform, the vivacity is of the highest degree (in proof), and where that experience is less uniform, the degree of vivacity varies with the degree of uniformity (in probability). The third conclusion, (6), is that in all cases of reasoning concerning matters of fact, "we must balance the opposite experiments, where they are opposite, and deduct the smaller from the greater, in order to know the exact force of the superior evidence." For example, we must allow the opposing experiments to decrease the vivacity of the conclusion in a way that varies with the number of opposing experiments, so that the final belief in the conclusion will be a function of the proportion of positive experiments or views among the class of all relevant experiments or views.

Human Testimony

The second section of Hume's argument seeks, as he says, to "apply these principles" — that is, (4) through (6) — "to a particular instance." That instance is, of course, the case of human testimony. Thus, he argues as follows:

7. [N]o objects have any discoverable connexion together, and . . . all the inferences, which we can draw from one to another, are founded merely on our experience of their constant conjunction.
8. [The connection of] human testimony . . . with any event seems, in itself, as little necessary as any other.
9. Were not the memory tenacious to a certain degree; had not men commonly an inclination to truth and a principle of probity; were they not sensible to shame,

when detected in a falsehood: Were not these . . . discovered by experience to be qualities, inherent in human nature, we should never repose the least confidence in human testimony.

10. [O]ur assurance in any argument [derived from the testimony of men and the reports of eyewitnesses and spectators] is derived from no other principle than our observation of the veracity of human testimony, and of the usual conformity of facts to the reports of witnesses. (from 7, 8, and 9)

11. [T]he evidence, derived from witnesses and human testimony . . . varies with the experience, and is regarded either as a proof or a probability, according as the conjunction between any particular kind of report and any kind of object has been found to be constant or variable. (from 4, 5, and 10)

Hume's first premise in this section, (7), is a consequence of his account of causal inference according to which there are no discoverable necessary connections in nature, and all inferences about matters of fact are based instead on the experience of constant conjunction. He then observes more specifically, in (8), that we find no necessary connection between testimony, on the one hand, and the truth of the claims made by that testimony, on the other, and he adds in (9) that if we did not find the truth of testimony to be *conjoined* with its being offered, we would not repose any faith in it at all. He concludes at (10) that the inference from any human testimony of an event to the actual occurrence of the event is based on the experienced conjunction of similar testimony with the events reported. He then appeals to his general epistemological principles concerning proof and probability. From (4), (5), and (10), he concludes, at (11), that where the conformity between facts and testimony has been constant and unalterable, we have proof; where it has not been, we have only probability.

Testimony for Miracles

The third section of Hume's argument goes on to consider the particular case of testimony for miracles, given two additional premises. It may be outlined as follows:

12. A miracle is a violation of the laws of nature. (definition)

13. [A] firm and unalterable experience has established these laws [of nature].

14. There must, therefore, be a uniform experience against every miraculous event, otherwise the event would not merit that appellation. (from 12 and 13)

15. [T]here is here a direct and full proof, from the nature of the fact, against the existence of any miracle; nor can such a proof be destroyed, or the miracle rendered credible, but by an opposite proof, which is superior. (from 4, 5, and 14)

16. [Where] the testimony of witnesses [affirms something that] instead of being merely marvellous, is really miraculous; and . . . the testimony considered apart and in itself, amounts to an entire proof; in that case, there is proof against proof, of which the strongest must prevail, but still with a diminution of its force, in proportion to that of its antagonist. (from 6, 11, and 15)

17. [N]o testimony is sufficient to establish a miracle, unless the testimony be of such a kind, that its falsehood would be more miraculous, than the fact, which it endeavors to establish; and even in that case there is a mutual destruction of arguments, and the superior only gives us an assurance suitable to that degree of force, which remains, after deducting the inferior. (from 15 and 16)

The first additional premise is (12), the definition of a miracle as a "violation of the laws of nature." The second is (13), the claim that "a firm and unalterable experience has established these laws." From these premises Hume concludes at (14) that there must be a uniform experience against every miraculous event. From this together with the characterization of "proof" in (4), and the implication of (4) and (5) that proofs are always stronger arguments than probabilities, he concludes at (15) that there is a "direct and full proof" against the existence of any miracle, and that such a proof "cannot be destroyed, or the miracle rendered credible, but by an opposite proof, which is superior." At (16), he considers the special case in which testimony for a miracle is of a kind that, considered in itself, would make the testimony a proof. He concludes, from (6), (11), and (15), that in such a case "there is proof against proof, of which the strongest must prevail, but still with a diminution of its force, in proportion to that of its antagonist."[4] This conclusion may plausibly be regarded as a special second-order application, to (11) and (15), of the "balancing" principle enunciated in (6), with conflicting proofs themselves playing the role of compound "experiments." From (15) and (16), Hume reaches his final conclusion of Part i, (17), that "no testimony is sufficient to establish a miracle, unless the testimony be of such a kind, that its falsehood would be more miraculous, than the fact, which it endeavors to establish," and that "even in that case there is a mutual destruction of arguments, and the superior only gives us an assurance suitable to that degree of force, which remains, after deducting the inferior."

"A Posteriori" Arguments

In Part ii of "On Miracles," Hume seeks to establish two further main conclusions about testimony for miracles. In order to do so, he provides four additional considerations, arguing as follows:

18. [T]here is not to be found, in all history, any miracle attested by a sufficient number of men, of such unquestioned good-sense, education, and learning, as to secure us against all delusion in themselves; of such undoubted integrity, as to place them beyond all suspicion of any design to deceive others; of such credit and reputation in the eyes of mankind, as to have a great deal to lose in case of their being detected in any falsehood; and at the same time, attesting facts performed in such a public manner and in so celebrated a part of the world, as to render the detection unavoidable: All of which circumstances are requisite to give us a full assurance in the testimony of men.
19. [P]assions incline the generality of mankind to believe and report, with the greatest vehemence and assurance, all religious miracles.
20. It forms a strong presumption against all supernatural and miraculous relations, that they are observed chiefly to abound among ignorant and barbarous nations; or if a civilized people has ever given admission to any of them, that people will be found to have received them from ignorant and barbarous ancestors, who transmitted them with that inviolable sanction and authority, which always attend received opinions.
21. [I]n matters of religion, whatever is different is contrary [in such a way that] it is impossible the religions of [e.g.,] ancient Rome, of Turkey, of Siam, and of China should, all of them, be established on any solid foundation.
22. Every miracle . . . pretended to have been wrought in any . . . [religion], as its direct scope is to establish the particular system to which it is attributed; so has it

the same force, though more indirectly, to overthrow every other system. (from 21)

23. In destroying a rival system, [a miracle] likewise destroys the credit of those miracles, on which that system was established.

24. All the prodigies of different religions are to be regarded as contrary facts, and the evidences of these prodigies, whether weak or strong, as opposite to each other. (from 22 and 23)

25. [I]t appears that no testimony for any kind of miracle has ever amounted to a probability, much less to a proof; and that, even supposing it amounted to a proof, it would be opposed by another proof derived from the very nature of the fact which it would endeavor to establish. (from 4, 5, 15, 18, 19, 20, and 24)

26. It is experience only which gives authority to human testimony, and it is the same experience which assures us of the laws of nature. (from 1, 10, and 13)

27. When . . . these two kinds of experience [i.e., that for a kind of human testimony and that for a law of nature] are contrary, we have nothing to do but to subtract the one from the other, and embrace an opinion, either on one side or the other, with that assurance which arises from the remainder. (6 and 26)

28. [T]his subtraction [of the experience for a kind of human testimony from that for a law of nature] with regard to all popular religions amounts to an entire annihilation. (4, 5, 13, 19, 20, 24, and 27)

29. [N]o human testimony can have such force as to prove a miracle and make it a just foundation for any such system of religion. (from 4, 12, and 28)

First, Hume claims at (18) that none of our actual historical testimony for miracles satisfies the conditions required to give us "a full assurance in the testimony of men." These conditions demand a sufficient number of witnesses (i) "of such unquestioned good-sense, education, and learning, as to secure us against all delusion in themselves"; (ii) "of such credit and reputation in the eyes of mankind, as to have a great deal to lose in case of their being detected in any falsehood"; and at the same time, (iii) "attesting facts performed in such a public manner and in so celebrated a part of the world, as to render the detection unavoidable."

Second, Hume claims at (19) that "passions incline the generality of mankind to believe and report, with the greatest vehemence and assurance, all religious miracles." Among the passionate mechanisms that Hume details are (i) the direct tendency of the pleasant feelings of surprise and wonder associated with miracles to encourage belief in them; (ii) the indirect tendency of these same pleasant feelings to encourage the relating of miracles, as a result of the sympathetic pleasure that results from producing the pleasant feelings of surprise and wonder in others; (iii) the tendency of the "spirit of religion" to make us suspend our critical faculties and even our honesty for the sake of a supposedly holy cause; and (iv) the tendency of the "spirit of religion" to increase the usual idea-enlivening effects of eloquence, thus producing credulity in the auditors, the perception of which increases the impudence of the reporter, which in turn overwhelms the credulity of the auditors.

Third, Hume claims at (20) that "supernatural and miraculous relations" are "observed chiefly to abound among ignorant and barbarous nations," or, if they are accepted among civilized people, "that people will be found to have received them from ignorant and barbarous ancestors, who transmitted them with that inviolable sanction and authority, which always attend received opinions." This, he asserts, forms a strong presumption against all such relations.

Fourth, Hume argues at (21) that rival religions make incompatible claims. He infers from this at (22) that, to whatever extent any miracle tends to establish one religion, it tends at the same time to overthrow other religions to the same extent. But, he claims at (23), to the extent that a miracle would *establish* a particular religion, it must to that extent be *overthrown* by any miracle that would overthrow that particular religion. Thus, he concludes at (24) that "all the prodigies of different religions are to be regarded as contrary facts, and the evidence of those prodigies, whether weak or strong, as opposite to each other."

From these four considerations—that is, from (18), (19), (20), and (24)—together with his epistemological principles (4) and (5) concerning proof and probability, Hume concludes at (25) that, to the present time, "no testimony for any kind of miracle has ever amounted to a probability, much less a proof." And, given (15), he adds that "even supposing it amounted to a proof, it would be opposed by another proof derived from the very nature of the fact which it would endeavor to establish." The conclusion, (25) constitutes one of the two main conclusions of Part ii.

The second, third, and fourth considerations, however, bear not only on the credibility of *extant* testimony for miracles but on the credibility of *future* testimony for miracles as well, at least to the extent that the alleged miracles would tend to "establish a religion." Thus, Hume remarks at (26) that it is experience alone that gives authority both to human testimony and to laws of nature, a claim that follows from (1), (10), and (13). At (27), he applies the balancing principle of (6) to conflicts between the experience for testimony and that for laws of nature, inferring that "when these two kinds of experience are contrary," we must "subtract the one from the other, and embrace an opinion, either on one side or the other, with that assurance which arises from the remainder." But (13) states that the experience for a law of nature is always a proof, while the considerations about passions, barbarous civilizations, and conflicts among miracles of different religions—that is, (19), (20), and (24)—show that human testimony for a miracle of a kind that would establish a religion *can never* amount to a proof. It should be noted that Hume here treats (4) and (5) as implying that probabilities lose all their force in the face of proof. This is a reasonable way to interpret (4) and (5), since (5) is explicitly limited to "other cases"— that is, cases in which proof is not present. Thus, by (27), he infers at (28) that in the case of "all popular religions" this subtraction "amounts to an entire annihilation." From (28), the characterization of proof at (4), and characterization of miracles at (12), he concludes that "no human testimony can have such force as to prove a miracle and make it a just foundation for any such system of religion." This is the second main conclusion of Part ii. Hume emphasizes that this last conclusion is restricted to the proof of miracles "so as to be the foundation of a system of religion," remarking that otherwise it may well be possible for human testimony to provide a proof of the occurrence of a miracle—even though, as he has already concluded at (25), no human testimony has in fact ever provided such a proof.

The Six Apparent Inconsistencies Resolved

We are now in a position to answer the six questions posed earlier, so as to resolve the six apparent inconsistencies.

Experience Reconsidered

What does Hume mean by 'experience'? When he argues at (7) through (11) that judgments of the probability of testimony must depend entirely on experience, he must indeed mean that such judgments depend ultimately on the experience of the *individual judger*, since one could not use the experiences of other persons as evidence without already effectively judging the probability of their testimony. When he writes of the uniform experience against a miracle as showing what "has never been observed in any age or country," however, he clearly intends the scope of the term 'experience' to include at least some of the experiences of others. But there is no inconsistency here. For Hume makes it clear in (11) that it is possible for *particular kinds of testimony* to achieve the level of 'proof'. The process by which a first particular kind of testimony comes to achieve this status must, of course, involve only the individual's own confirmations of that kind of testimony. Once the reliability of that kind of testimony has achieved the level of proof, however, testimony *of that kind* will bestow "full assurance," and hence it may well function itself to provide vicarious experiments and views in the cognitive process of probable judgment that Hume describes as the probability of causes. That is why Hume asserts the following in Section IX of the *Enquiry*—in the course of listing nine reasons why some persons so exceed others in reasoning, despite their having the same basic cognitive mechanisms:

> After we have acquired a confidence in human testimony, books and conversation enlarge much more the sphere of one man's experience and thought than those of another. (EHU §84n)[5]

Thus, Hume need not be equivocating on the scope of 'experience'. The probability of any given kind of testimony is ultimately dependent on the judger's own experience, but once that experience has validated a kind of testimony, the experience of others—when it is the object of that kind of testimony—can then function cognitively very much as if it were one's own. Indeed, such testimony may even be brought to bear as part of the proof against a proposition that is supported by a *second* kind of testimony that has not achieved the status of proof—as occurs in the case of testimony for miracles.

Laws of Nature Reconsidered

What does Hume mean by 'laws of nature'? Although Hume does not define the term, a good deal can be inferred from his use of it. First, the choice of the term itself suggests that laws of nature have the form of universal causal generalizations. Second, according to (12), a violation of a law of nature is by definition a miracle. Third, (13) requires that there must be a "firm and unalterable experience" in favor of any law of nature.[6] Finally, (15) requires, via (12)'s definition of 'miracle', that there be a direct and full *proof* of every law of nature. I conclude, therefore, that a law of nature is a universal causal generalization, whose violation is by definition a miracle, supported by a "firm and unalterable experience"—i. e., a universal causal generalization for which there is a *proof*, in Hume's technical sense of that term.

But what does it mean to say that there is a "firm and unalterable experience" or "proof" for something having the form of a universal causal generalization? Do we mean that there is, objectively, an exceptionless uniformity, and hence (the basis for) a proof, *whether anyone knows it or not*? Or do we mean only that the *individual judging* has an exceptionless and uniform experience, something that therefore *functions as* a proof *for that individual*?

In *Treatise* I.iii.14, and again in *Enquiry* VII, Hume offers two different definitions of the term 'cause', the first in terms of the constant conjunction of resembling events, and the second in terms of association and inference in the mind. As we have seen in chapter 5, each of these two definitions of 'cause' is ambiguous between a "subjective" reading and an "absolute" reading. (We also saw that the two definitions are coextensive on their subjective readings, and again coextensive on their absolute readings. Hume's theory of abstract ideas prevents him from distinguishing these two readings more clearly.) On the subjective reading, two things are related as cause and effect for an observer if and only if they have been observed to be constantly conjoined in the observer's experience, so that they lead to association and inference in the mind of the observer. On the absolute reading, two things are related as cause and effect if and only if they have actually been constantly conjoined in all times and places, so that they would lead to association and inference in the mind of an idealized observer. Both the subjective and the absolute readings have their uses for Hume, in different contexts. Sometimes when he discusses causes, he is interested in events that are related by "absolute" or "objective" causation, while at other times he is interested in events whose ideas function psychologically as ideas of cause and effect in the cognitive organization of an individual judger, whether the events are objectively related as cause and effect or not.

Not only the term 'cause' but also such related terms as 'proof', and hence also 'law of nature' and 'miracle', are susceptible to the same kind of subjective/absolute ambiguity in Hume. In the context of "On Miracles," however, it is clear from the structure of the argument that Hume is appealing to *subjective* senses of 'proof', 'laws of nature', and 'miracle'. For if a law of nature were understood as a completely uniform constant conjunction, or something for which an idealized observer had a firm and unalterable experience, the very notion of an exception to a law of nature would be contradictory, as we have already seen. Rather, as Hume uses the terms in "On Miracles," something has the status of "law of nature"—that is, plays the *cognitive role* of a "law of nature"—*for an individual judger* if it has the form of a universal generalization, is regarded by the judger as causal, and is something for which the judger has a firm and unalterable experience—that is, a proof. This is, of course, compatible with there actually being exceptions to it, so long as none of those exceptions have, for the judger, the status of *experiments* within his or her experience.

Thus, Hume is not arguing that the wise reject testimony for miracles because they recognize that miracles are impossible by definition. Nor is he claiming that no one could ever *observe* a miracle. He is not missing the point by defining 'miracle' in such a way that any event that actually occurs or is observed, no matter how bizarre, would fail to be a miracle. Rather, he is claiming at (14) and (15) that, if something is to have the status of "miracle" *in an individual's cognitive organization*, then by definition it is something for which the individual has, within his or her experience, a *proof*. Hence the "miracle" must be—prior to the consideration of the new testimony in favor of it—something of whose denial the individual rightly has *full assurance*.[7]

The Miraculous and the Marvelous Reconsidered

What does Hume mean by the distinction he draws between the "miraculous" and the merely "marvellous" (or "extraordinary")—or, equivalently, between events that would be "contrary" to one's experience and those that are merely "not conformable" to it? As we have seen, events that are miraculous or contrary to experience for an individual judger are events that would violate "a law of nature"—that is, a generalization, universal and causal in form, for which the individual judger has a proof. Marvelous or extraordinary events, or events not conformable to experience, are—as Hume explains them—events that, while occurring in circumstances of which the judger has no experience or proof, are contrary to "analogy" (EHU §90n). Analogy, as we have already seen, is the species of probability that arises from an *imperfect resemblance* between past experiments and the circumstance presently under consideration.

But can Hume offer any principled basis for his claim that frost is merely *marvelous* for the Indian prince, while the raising of the dead is *miraculous* for us? There is indeed a difference between the two cases, as Hume understands them. For although the prince has not experienced cold climates, considerable evidence suggests that there are such climates, and even that temperature is sometimes relevant to the state and behavior of substances (as the boiling of water and the cooling of heated metals suggest). A rational Indian prince must therefore allow that, although there may be a high probability of analogy against the sudden hardening of water even in cold climates, he has no proof that water does not harden in cold climates, and he must also grant that there is at least some probability that cold climates exist. In the case of raising the dead by divine volition, in contrast, it may be denied that there is any degree of probability that any almighty deity ever does will to raise persons from the dead. This may be denied on either of two grounds: (i) that there is no such almighty deity; or (ii) that no such deity, even if existing, ever wills to raise persons from the dead.

It is important to note that Hume does not *argue*, in Part i, that the raising of the dead is a miraculous event for us; he merely gives it as one example among many (such as the raising of houses into the air) along the way to arguing for a much more general claim about the relation between testimony and miraculous events, *whatever* events may ultimately prove to fall within the latter class. And nothing in the argument of Part i requires that all—or even any—alleged *divine actions* be miraculous. However, Hume does indicate in Part ii what his strategy would be for treating various alleged divine actions as miraculous rather than merely marvelous. He writes:

> Though the Being to whom the miracle is ascribed, be, in this case, Almighty, it does not, upon that account, become a whit more probable; since it is impossible for us to

know the attributes or actions of such a Being, otherwise than from the experience which we have of his productions, in the usual course of nature. This still reduces us to past observation. (EHU §99)

Although Hume gives some grounds elsewhere in his writings (and even, some-what obliquely, in Section XI of the *Enquiry*) for doubting the *existence* of an almighty intelligent deity, here his strategy is more restricted: he argues that we could know whether such a deity performs particular kinds of actions only on the basis of experience. The implication of this argument for the case of raising the dead is that our experience of various deaths (of individuals good and bad, pious and impious, important and unimportant, in a wide variety of circumstances, from a wide variety of causes) provides a *proof* for the claim that persons are not raised from the dead by the volitions of an almighty deity. Although there is indeed some testi-mony, as Hume must admit, to the effect that such a deity *has* done so, this testi-mony is not of a kind that constitutes a *proof*, and hence does not furnish an *experi-ment*, in Hume's technical sense of that term. On the contrary, he holds that such testimony belongs to a class of testimony that is easily discountable—on specific grounds provided in Part ii—and so it does not give rise to an opposing *view* serving to lessen our proof that such volitions do not occur. In other words, no raising of the dead enters into *the judger's experience*, where "experience" is understood in the way explained earlier in this chapter. Thus, although we can specify circumstances—such as a volition of an almighty deity—in which a raising of the dead would pre-sumably occur, this does not prevent the raising of the dead from being a miracle for us, *if* we have (what is for us) a *proof* that such circumstances do not occur.

Of course, it is likely that every death occurs in a specific set of circumstances that is not completely duplicated in any other death. And it is also likely that we can specify a concatenation of specific circumstances under which no deaths have yet happened to be observed, even though some future death may well occur under them. It might therefore be argued that our confidence that no one will ever be raised from the dead by divine volition is only a matter of analogy, and not of proof. But a similar claim could equally well be made about any other sort of event. If we have a proof that none of these circumstances is *individually* of a kind that is relevant to a divine volition for a raising of the dead, then once again this fact need not prevent the raising of the dead from being a miracle for us. Our understanding of the difference between life and death is connected with our knowledge of many other laws of nature, laws that rule out a huge number of circumstances as causally irrelevant to the difference between life and death. Similarly, our experience of the world appears to rule out a huge number of circumstances as causally irrelevant to the production of divine volitions. And as we have seen, it is precisely the tendency to attach continuing weight to circumstances already shown to be causally irrele-vant that reflective and philosophical persons reject in the fourth species of unphilosophical probability (namely, that drawn from hasty general rules). Thus, by appealing implicitly to an experiential proof that divine volitions to raise the dead do not occur, Hume appears to have at least the basis for a principled distinc-tion between (i) frost in cold climates, as assessed by the Indian prince, and (ii) the raising of the dead by divine volition, as assessed by ourselves.

Superior Proofs and Greater Miracles Reconsidered

What does Hume mean when he writes of "opposite" and "superior" proofs of the occurrence or nonoccurrence of a particular miracle—or, correlatively, of a miracle that would be "more miraculous" or a "greater miracle" than another? First, we must understand how proofs can be "opposite," when both are by definition such as to leave no room for "doubt or opposition."

How can a proof oppose another proof that leaves no room for opposition? We have already seen that, where past experiments involving a given kind of circumstance provide incompatible *views* of what has happened or will happen in such a circumstance, these incompatible views do indeed prevent proof and instead produce mere probability. In the case of proofs for two different laws of nature, however, the experiments do not all present views of *the same circumstances*. The experiments against raising the dead, for example, all produce views of dead persons and the subsequent behavior of their bodies. If these experiments are uniform, the result is a proof. The experiments in favor of a certain species of testimony, in contrast, produce views of testimony of that kind being given in conjunction with the experienced or proven truth of the testimony. If these experiments are uniform, the result is another proof. Because of the difference in kinds of circumstance, views of the first kind do not *directly* conflict with views of the second. They produce an (unexpected) conflict only when an instance of the particular kind of testimony occurs for the claim that a dead person has risen. This certainly produces a cognitive conflict, but it is not a *direct* opposition between the views supporting the law of nature and the views supporting the testimony—for these are still not opposing views of the same circumstance but of two different circumstances, namely deaths and testimonies. Rather, the views supporting the law of nature produce a *further* idea, with a maximal degree of assurance, that the raising of the dead reported did not occur, while the views supporting the testimony produce a *further* idea, with a maximal degree of assurance, that the raising of the dead did occur. It is these composite or *second-level* ideas or views, resulting from the initial experiments and views, that are in opposition or conflict, because they are incompatible projections from past experiences onto the present case. The resolution of this conflict may indeed prevent these two second-order views from *maintaining* their maximal degrees of assurance, but that does not mean that both did not result from what were, in themselves, proofs.

How are such conflicts to be resolved? When a proof conflicts with a probability, Hume in effect concludes at (15), the proof will always be superior.[8] But conflict resolution can take this form only when the conflict is between a proof and a probability. Where the conflict is between opposing proofs, some other means must be employed to resolve the conflict. Hume holds, at (16), that in a conflict between proofs, each must lose a considerable portion of its vivacity from the conflict. But this does not entail that each will lose the *same* portion. On the contrary, there are at least two ways in which one proof can be superior to another, and so be better able to maintain a relatively greater amount of vivacity.

First, one proof may include *more* experiments than another. We may perhaps read Hume as allowing that proofs supported by more experiments and views have greater initial vivacity than proofs supported by fewer experiments and views. For although he writes of proof as providing a maximal degree of belief or assent, perhaps he means only that the vivacity of a "proof" must fall somewhere above a certain line that divides the assent of proof from the assent of probability. (See LDH II.350, a passage called to my attention by William E. Morris.) Even if he does not mean this, however—so that the assent produced by every proof is initially of the very same degree—the number of experiments may still help to determine the ability of a proof to *resist loss* of vivacity to another proof. (In a similar way, the ability of a set of previously uniform experiments to resist the loss of vivacity resulting from a new *direct* opposing experiment is, for Hume, a function of the number of uniform experiments to which the new experiment is opposed.) As already suggested, allowing the number of experiments to play this role would be a plausible application of Hume's "balancing" principle of (6) to the special case of competing proofs.

Second, other experiments besides those contributing directly to the two opposing proofs may nevertheless contribute to the ability of one to resist the force of the other. In particular, this will be so if some additional experiments support the conclusion of one of the proofs *by analogy*. Thus, Hume writes the following concerning a hypothetical conflict between a proof that there cannot be eight days of total darkness, on the one hand, and a proof of the veracity of very extensive and uniform human testimony, on the other:

> The decay, corruption, and dissolution of nature, is an event rendered probable by so many analogies, that any phenomenon, which seems to have a tendency towards that catastrophe, comes within the reach of human testimony, if that testimony be very extensive and uniform. (EHU §99)

As Hume indicates, this strengthening of one proof, in its conflict with another, by a consideration of somewhat resembling experiments, is an instance of what he calls the probability of analogy. It is another plausible second-order application of the "balancing principle" of (6) to the special case of opposing proofs.

Thus, some Humean proofs can indeed be *opposite* and *superior* to others. Furthermore, the same considerations also explain how one miracle can be a *greater* miracle, or *more miraculous*, than another. A miracle will be a greater miracle, or more miraculous, than a second if and only if the proof against the first is superior to the proof against the second. Hume is not contradicting his own definitions of 'proof' and 'miracle' in writing of opposite and superior proofs and greater miracles; rather, he is alluding to what he believes is the ability of some proofs to better resist loss of vivacity, in cases where proofs derived from views of different circumstances come into unexpected conflict.

Absolute Impossibility Reconsidered

What does Hume mean when he refers, in Part ii, to "the absolute impossibility" of certain miraculous events? As we have seen, Hume's Conceivability Criterion of Possibility holds that "whatever we *conceive* is possible, at least in a metaphysical sense" (ATHN 650). Thus, he cannot consistently hold that miracles are impossible "in a metaphysical sense" unless he holds that they are inconceivable. But his own cognitive psychology demands that, in order to treat them as *inconceivable*, he would have to argue that the concept of a miracle is somehow *contradictory*—and this, we have seen, he does not do. In his *Treatise* discussion of the probability of causes, however, he writes, "there is no probability so great as not to allow of a contrary possibility; because otherwise 'twou'd cease to be a probability, and wou'd become a certainty" (THN 135). He goes on to argue that the "component parts of this possibility and probability are of the same nature, and differ in number only" (THN 136). That is to say, the *possibility* opposed to every probability of causes is itself a compound of one or more different *views*, derived from opposing *experiments*.

Thus, we see that there is a *second* sense of 'possibility' in Hume, one derived not from mere conceivability but rather from the lack of uniformity in experience. Hence there is a correlative kind of impossibility that is opposed not to the knowledge produced by intuition or demonstration (which shows the denial of a conclusion to be a contradiction) but rather to the certainty of *proof*. (These dual senses of 'possible' and 'impossible' correspond to dual senses of 'separable' and 'inseparable' noted in note 2 of chapter 3.) When Hume claims, in Part ii, that the alleged Jansenist miracles he mentions are "impossible," he is alluding to a consequence of Part i; namely, that in the nature of the case, we have an experiential *proof* against them. In adding that they are "absolutely" impossible, he is likely also thinking of his argument, given earlier in Part ii, that because of their religious character, no testimony in favor of them can itself ever amount to another, contrary, proof. Since he is pronouncing the miracles impossible not in the "metaphysical sense" in which their existence is a *contradiction* but in the practical sense in which their existence is ruled out by a *proof*, he is neither violating his metaphysical principles nor equivocating on his earlier conclusion.

The Uniformity of Nature Reconsidered

Finally, regardless of his other arguments, how can Hume himself criticize beliefs in miracles—as he clearly does throughout both Part i and Part ii—in light of his own views about what we would call "inductive inferences," or what he calls "inferences from experience"? As we have seen in chapter 4, when Hume argues that the thesis of the uniformity of nature cannot be defended by any argument that does not presuppose it, and when he goes on to infer that no inductive inferences from experience are "determin'd by reason" or "produced by any argument or process of the understanding," he is not thereby denying or doubting the thesis of the uniformity of nature, nor is he passing a negative epistemic judgment on inductive inferences from experience. Rather, he is making a claim in cognitive psychology about the causal origin of such inferences; namely, that it is not as a result of our inferential faculty or of any argument that we are caused to engage in them. Deflating and discomforting as the intense contemplation of this claim may admittedly be, acceptance of it does not preclude Hume, logically or psychologically, from engaging in such inferences or from accepting the thesis of the uniformity of nature. Nor do the skeptical considerations that Hume elaborates in *Treatise* I.iv.7 and *Enquiry* XII, considerations that we will take up in detail in chapter 10. On the contrary, he holds that he, like every other human being, must perform such inferences and accept the thesis in practice, given his and our shared inductive cognitive mechanisms. Moreover, he holds that when these cognitive mechanisms are turned reflectively on themselves and the consequences of their own operations, they generate a set of "rules by which to judge of causes and effects" (THN 149, THN 173–176). He and other human beings who so reflect will be causally determined, he thinks, to come to *approve* of inferences that conform to those rules as constituting the best way to the truth about matters of fact that go beyond our present perceptions and memories.

Indeed, Hume not only approves *epistemically* of those who make inductive inferences from experience in accordance with the rules for judging of causes and effects, he also approves of them *morally*. According to Hume's general theory of virtue or personal merit, as set out in Book III of the *Treatise* and again in *An Enquiry concerning the Principles of Morals*, virtues are mental characteristics that are useful or agreeable to their possessors or others, producing a pleasing sentiment of approbation in those who consider them. Among these virtues is that of "wisdom," as he indicates explicitly in *Treatise* III.iii.4 (THN 611). As we have already seen, Humean wisdom involves, among other things, "proportioning one's belief to the evidence" in the way described in (4) through (6). Because he cannot help thinking that wisdom leads to truth, which he regards as generally useful (especially to its possessor, but also to others), Hume himself *approves morally* of wisdom, and he holds that other reflective individuals will do so also. It is because he holds that wisdom is typically productive of *truth* that he draws inferences from premises about what the wise man does to a conclusion about what is and is not (epistemically) "sufficient" to establish a miracle. However, it is his view that wisdom is a *virtue* that gives this conclusion its ultimate practical force.

Just as his claims in cognitive psychology about the causal origin of inductive inferences from experience do not preclude Hume from engaging in such inferences or from accepting the thesis of the uniformity of nature, so those claims do not preclude him from disapproving of those cognitive mechanisms that, upon reflection, appear to be distortions of those inferences, hindering or preventing reasoning from operating in accordance with the philosophical rules for judging of causes and effects. He disapproves epistemically of such mechanisms as obstacles to the pursuit of truth, and he disapproves morally of those whose beliefs are frequently produced or colored by them. Among these distorting mechanisms are the four kinds of unphilosophical probability that he describes in the *Treatise*. Also among them, he finds, are the passionate mechanisms that he describes—in Part ii of "On Miracles"—as contributing to belief in miracles despite the weight of contrary experiments. To let these distorting mechanisms govern one's beliefs is, in Humean terminology, not wisdom but *folly*.

There should be no misunderstanding about the basis of Hume's position. He does not have, and does not believe that anyone has, an argument that would convince beings with a cognitive nature radically different from ours to engage in inductive inferences from experience, or to accept the thesis of the uniformity of nature, or, a fortiori, to adopt our philosophical rules for judging of causes and effects. Nor does he believe that *we* are caused to engage in such inferences or to accept that thesis as the result of argument (although arguments presupposing the

uniformity of nature may serve to confirm us in them and will lead the philosophical among us to the rules for judging of causes and effects). Similarly, Hume does
not have, and does not believe that anyone has, an argument that would convince
beings with a moral nature radically different from ours to value wisdom as a
virtue—even if they were already convinced that it was the most effective way to
truth. Nor does he believe that *we* are caused to value wisdom as a virtue solely as
the result of argument (although argument may convince us of its *utility*). He
believes that moral sentiments of approval must intervene in order to produce that
result.

But arguments binding on beings with radically different cognitive or moral
natures are not required for Hume's purposes, since his readers all share the same
fundamental human cognitive and moral mechanisms. When these mechanisms
are turned upon our cognitive mechanisms themselves—at least in a world like
ours—they produce an epistemic and moral valuing of wisdom. Reflective individuals will thus come to desire to proportion their belief to the evidence, just as
Hume desires to do.[9] Such individuals are Hume's intended primary audience in
"Of Miracles," as he indicates early in Part i:

> Nothing is so convenient as a decisive argument of this kind, which must at least
> *silence* the most arrogant bigotry and superstition, and free us from their impertinent
> solicitations. I flatter myself, that I have discovered an argument of a like nature,
> which, if just, will, with the wise and learned, be an everlasting check to all kinds of
> superstitious delusion, and consequently, will be useful as long as the world endures.
> (EHU §86)

Moreover, because even foolish and unreflective human beings share these same
fundamental cognitive and moral mechanisms, Hume holds that his arguments
should at least silence their impertinence, even if it does not change the way they
manage their beliefs.

Hume is thus not guilty of inconsistency in opposing belief in miracles, even
though he holds that the thesis of the uniformity of nature cannot be defended by
any argument that does not presuppose it, and that any inferences that go beyond
the content of present experience and personal memory are "not determin'd by reason." In nevertheless accepting the thesis of the uniformity of nature and performing inductive inferences from experience, he is consistently instantiating his own
theory of human cognitive psychology. In seeking to govern his inferences "wisely,"
by proportioning his belief to the evidence in accordance with philosophical rules
for judging of causes and effects, he is seeking to be the kind of person of whom he
can epistemically and morally approve. In arguing that others should do the same,
he is appealing to premises that—if his human cognitive and moral psychology is
correct—should be shared or shareable by all of his readers.

The Probability of Miracles

The six apparent inconsistencies in Hume's discussion of miracles in *Enquiry* X.i
can each be resolved by careful attention to the theory of proof and probability that

Hume derives from his more general cognitive psychology. We can now look again at the nature of Hume's argument, the content of his conclusion, and the success or failure of his undertaking in Part i.

Hume's argument in Part i proceeds from a set of premises about the cognitive functioning of the wise man to a set of general epistemological principles concerning proof and probability. It then applies these principles to the case of human testimony in general. From this application, in turn, together with a general characterization of the role of "laws of nature" and "miracles" in human cognitive organization, he reaches a conclusion concerning the kind of testimonial evidence that would be required to establish the occurrence of a miracle. That argument is complete as he presents it in Part i, and it does not require supplementation by any of the additional premises proposed by commentators.

Hume's intended conclusion in Part i is precisely the one he states:

> [N]o testimony is sufficient to establish a miracle, unless the testimony be of such a kind, that its falsehood would be more miraculous than the fact, which it endeavors to establish; and even in that case there is a mutual destruction of arguments, and the superior only gives us an assurance suitable to that degree of force, which remains, after deducting the inferior. (EHU §91)

In that conclusion, the term 'miracle' should be understood subjectively, as relative to an individual's own cognitive organization—that is, as referring to a universal generalization, regarded by the individual judger as causal, and for which the individual judger has a proof. The long qualification concerning *opposing* miracles is an essential part of that conclusion. It is not merely an ironic superfluity, as some commentators have suggested. Although one might guess what Hume's attitude would be toward such evidence as seeming personal sensory experience of a miracle—namely, that one should be skeptically alert to the likelihood of illusion or delusion—his own argument in Part i concerns only testimonial evidence. Finally, it is important to realize that the argument of Part i does not, by itself, show that all or any divine actions would be miracles. Hence it does not, by itself, establish that no testimony is sufficient to establish the occurrence of a divine action, or even that the occurrence of such actions would be epistemologically problematic. Hume does suggest grounds in Part ii, however, for thinking that our experience includes proofs against the occurrence of a wide variety of divine actions. He also provides several reasons in Part ii for thinking that testimony of divine actions will always be of especially low evidential quality.

Hume's argument is careful, detailed, and well thought out. It does not beg the question in any way, and its premises, if true, provide strong support for the conclusion. However, the argument's premises depend on his cognitive psychology, which is not only outdated in its general overreliance on images but is also questionable in its details.

One unintended consequence, for example, of Hume's description of these mechanisms is that the *sufficiency* of evidence can depend on the order in which it is received. Suppose that person A testifies to the occurrence of an event, E, that would violate regularity R, and that person A's testimony is of a kind T. Suppose that no other examples of violations of R are ever perceived by anyone, and that no other examples of false testimony of kind T are ever discovered by anyone. Is A's testimony credible? If the recipient has had enough experience of veridical instances of T to establish that kind of testimony as proof but has not yet observed enough instances of R, then A's testimony will constitute an *experiment* against R, and R can at best achieve probability, not proof, no matter how much further experience accumulates for it. However, if the recipient has had enough experience of R to establish it as a law of nature but has not yet observed enough instances of T, then the observed instances of R will constitute an *experiment* against the reliability of T, and T can at best achieve probability, not proof, no matter how much further evidence accumulates for its reliability. Finally, if the recipient has already had enough experience of R and of T to render them both sources of proof, then the recipient will experience the kind of conflict between proofs that Hume describes in the case of the "eight days of darkness." Yet this variability of evidential force with the order in which evidence is received is closely related to the second kind of unphilosophical probability (in which the most recent experiment carries extra weight), a kind of probability of which Hume disapproves. Clearly, some additional reflection on ways to correct this consequence is called for within Hume's epistemology.

Somewhat more generally, it might be argued that Hume's distinction between proofs and probabilities is artificially sharp and that he is wrong to maintain that proofs should always outweigh probabilities. In his defense, however, it should be emphasized that "proof" may be a very difficult status to achieve, and it is likely to characterize only or chiefly our most *fundamental* beliefs about the ways in which the world works—beliefs that serve to organize all of our thinking and are typically supported by enormous amounts of human testimony, among other kinds of evidence. It is precisely because reports of miracles violate *these* beliefs that they are so striking. Surely the burden of proof lies with those who claim that it can be wise to abandon these beliefs on the basis of individual human testimony. Hume is not arguing that testimony should never lead us to revise our conception of what the laws of nature are; repeated independent testimony might well lead us to abandon one conception of a regularity instantiated by our past experience for an alternative conception. Hume's quarrel is only with the project of believing, on the basis of testimony, an event that *simultaneously* retains the status of *miracle* in the cognitive organization of the believer.

Hume's overall project in the *Treatise* and in the first *Enquiry* is to understand human cognitive functioning in such a way as to better enable us to arrive together at a reflective assessment concerning which features of that functioning we wish to approve and encourage, and which we do not. That assessment, he hoped, would lead us to recognize the cognitive mechanisms supporting what he regarded as "superstitious" religion—including belief in miracles—as irregular and pernicious ones, deserving to be classified as a species of "unphilosophical probability." Certainly—as Hume himself would have expected—reflection about probability has advanced considerably since he wrote. For one thing, Bayesian considerations now play a much greater role in our reflections than they seem to have done for him. Nevertheless, his overall project of seeking reflective assessments about probability in general, and miracles in particular, remains attractive. It is still worth examining how, *and* to what extent, we may be in a position to go beyond Hume in our own reflective judgments about the cognitive processes that are involved in the evaluation and acceptance of miracles. Indeed, over two hundred years after he wrote, such a comparison of our standpoint with Hume's remains one of the most rewarding ways to begin our own attempt to assess the wisdom or unwisdom of believing in miracles. In his humbler moments, at least, Hume would have hoped for no more than this for his discussion of miracles—and also, no less.

Personal Identity

For the eighteenth century, the nature of personal identity was not simply a metaphysical puzzle. Rather, it was a philosophical problem with consequences not only for temporal moral responsibility but also for the justice of divine rewards and punishments in the afterlife. Skepticism concerning the existence of nonphysical, substantial souls exacerbated the problem. It was largely in order to defend the justice of divine rewards and punishments in the face of his own relative agnosticism about substantial souls that Locke offered his reductive empiricist analysis of personal identity in terms of consciousness and memory.[1]

In *Treatise* I.iv.6, entitled "Of personal identity," Hume presents with considerable pride his own explanation of why we regard human minds as entities having an identity through time. His explanation depends on his previous account (presented in *Treatise* I.iv.2) of how we arrive at the idea of identity as a *relation*, something more than unity, therefore, and yet still less than number or plurality. According to that account, the idea of identity is the idea of something persisting "invariable and uninterrupted" through a "supposed variation in time." Since human minds are not invariable or uninterrupted, the persons to whom we attribute identity are not entities with a "perfect" or "strict" identity. That to which we seek to attribute a perfect identity is in fact only a bundle of perceptions, "bundled" by their interrelations of resemblance and causation. The actual relation among these perceptions is thus only a "fictitious" or "imperfect" identity. Furthermore, Hume maintains, it is only because a series of varying objects related by resemblance and causation itself resembles an invariable and uninterrupted object that we confuse the former with the latter and ascribe an "identity" at all. The same relations of resemblance and causation also account for our tendency to attribute simplicity (as opposed to complexity) to the distinct perceptions in a bundle at a single time.

There are several evident reasons for Hume's pride in this explanation. First, he accounts for our tendency to think of ourselves as having a continuing identity through time by utilizing essentially the same mental mechanism of identity-ascription that gives rise to the belief in "continu'd and distinct existences" (THN

202–204), thereby confirming the existence of this mechanism while avoiding the need to introduce another one. Second, he is able to answer the question of whether memory "produces" personal identity (as Locke held) or only "discovers" it (as Locke's critics claimed) with a diplomatic compromise, by noting that while memory *discovers* resemblances and causal relations already existing among perceptions, in doing so it also serves to *produce* additional resemblances (THN 260–262). Third, he finds himself able to dismiss all "nice and subtle questions" concerning particular instances of personal identity as "grammatical" rather than substantive (THN 262). Of course, this dismissal calls into question the determinacy of many of the eschatological questions concerning the justice of divine rewards and punishment that originally motivated philosophical interest in the question of personal identity. But this unspoken antireligious consequence was far from disturbing to Hume.

Yet in the Appendix to the *Treatise*, Hume confesses dissatisfaction with his own previous account:

> But upon a more strict review of the section concerning *personal identity*, I find myself involv'd in such a labyrinth, that, I must confess, I neither know how to correct my former opinions, nor how to render them consistent. (THN 633)

Why did Hume become so dissatisfied? Perhaps no question in the interpretation of Hume has received as many distinct answers as this one. Although he devotes several pages in the Appendix to stating his misgivings, Hume does not succeed in clearly stating any specific problem with his earlier account. And no trace of the topic recurs in the first *Enquiry*, nor in any of Hume's other writings.

In order to answer this question, I begin by outlining Hume's argument for his original characterization of personal identity and summarizing his confession of misgivings as it occurs in the Appendix. I then survey a number of common explanations of Hume's second thoughts and argue against each of them. Next, I describe my own explanation, defend it against potential objections, and explore the underlying causes of Hume's difficulties with personal identity.

Hume's First Account and Second Thoughts

The Personal Identity Argument Outlined

Hume's argument for his analysis of personal identity has five main parts. First, he argues that the human mind lacks the "perfect identity"—that is, invariability and uninterruptedness—that metaphysicians have ascribed to the self, and so he concludes, via the Copy Principle, that we have no idea of the mind as something invariable and uninterrupted. Second, he argues, via the Separability Principle and the Conceivability Criterion of Possibility, that the human mind consists instead of nothing more than a bundle or collection of perceptions. Third, he argues that there must be some relations that constitute the "imperfect" or "fictitious" identity of human minds, for we attribute identity to a collection lacking "perfect" identity only when the collection is a succession of related objects. Fourth, he argues that the relations among perceptions that cause us to ascribe identity to the human mind—and thereby constitute its "imperfect" identity—cannot be "real connexions" discovered by the understanding and must therefore be relations that lead us to associate these perceptions in the imagination. Fifth, and finally, he argues that these relations are, in fact, resemblance and causation.

These five parts of the argument correspond to (1) through (4), (4) through (7), (7) through (10), (10) through (17), and (17) through (20), respectively, of the following fuller outline (THN 251–260):

1. [Perfect identity is] the invariableness and uninterruptedness of any object, thro' a supposed variation of time. (from THN 201)
2. It must be some one impression, that gives rise to every real idea. (from the Copy Principle)
3. There is no impression constant and invariable.
4. There is no such idea [as that of the self, considered as something having perfect identity and simplicity]. (from 1–3)
5. All our particular perceptions . . . are different, and distinct, and distinguishable, and separable from each other, and may be separately consider'd, and may exist separately, and have no need of any thing to support their existence. (from the Separability Principle and the Conceivability Criterion of Possibility)
6. [W]hen I enter most intimately into what I call myself, I always stumble on some particular perception or other. . . . I never can catch myself at any time without a perception, and never can observe any thing but the perception.
7. [The human mind is] nothing but a bundle or collection of different perceptions, which succeed each other with an inconceivable rapidity, and are in a perpetual flux and movement. (from 4–6)
8. [We have a] great . . . propension to ascribe an identity to these successive perceptions.
9. All objects, to which we ascribe identity, without observing their invariableness and uninterruptedness, are such as consist of a succession of related objects.
10. The identity, which we ascribe to the mind of man, is only a fictitious [imperfect] one [i.e., the mind to which we ascribe identity consists of a succession of related objects]. (from 1, 7–9)
11. The identity, which we ascribe to the mind of man . . . is of a like kind with that which we ascribe to vegetables and animal bodies.
12. [The identity which we ascribe to vegetables and animal bodies] proceeds from certain operations of the imagination.
13. The identity, which we ascribe to the mind of man . . . must proceed from a like operation of the imagination. (from 11–12)
14. [T]he identity which we attribute to the human mind, however perfect we may imagine it to be, is not able to run the several different perceptions into one . . . [i.e.,] every distinct perception, which enters into the composition of the mind, is a distinct existence, and is different, and distinguishable, and separable from every other perception, either contemporary or successive. (from 5, 10)
15. [If the mind is only a succession of related objects, then] the relation of [fictitious/imperfect] identity [uniting our perceptions is either] something that really binds our several perceptions together, or only associates their ideas in the imagination.
16. [T]he understanding never observes any real connexion among objects, and . . . even the union of cause and effect, when strictly examin'd, resolves itself into a customary association of ideas.

17. [I]dentity is nothing really belonging to these different perceptions, and uniting them together; but is merely a quality, which we attribute to them, because of the union of their ideas in the imagination, when we reflect upon them. (from 10 and 13–16)
18. [T]he only qualities, which can give ideas an union in the imagination are . . . resemblance, contiguity, and causation.
19. [C]ontiguity . . . has little or no influence on the present case [of personal identity].
20. [The mind is a bundle of perceptions related by resemblance and causation]. (from 17–19)

Hume's Self-Doubts

As we have seen, when Hume comes to review this account in the Appendix, he finds himself "involv'd in . . . a labyrinth," knowing neither how to "correct" his former opinions, "nor how to render them consistent" (THN 633). Promising to "propose the arguments on both sides, beginning with those that induc'd me to deny the strict and proper identity and simplicity of a self or thinking being," he proceeds to offer a battery of old and new arguments intended to show (i) that we have no idea of a substantial self possessing perfect identity or simplicity, and (ii) that there is no difficulty in conceiving our various perceptions as ontologically self-sufficient without the need for any such substantial support. He then remarks:

> But having thus loosen'd all our particular perceptions, when I proceed to explain the principle of connexion, which binds them together, and makes us attribute to them a real simplicity and identity; I am sensible, that my account is very defective, and that nothing but the seeming evidence of the precedent reasonings cou'd have induc'd me to receive it. If perceptions are distinct existences, they form a whole only by being connected together. But no connexions among distinct existences are ever discoverable by human understanding. We only *feel* a connexion or a determination of the thought, to pass from one object to another. It follows, therefore, that the thought alone finds personal identity, when reflecting on the train of past perceptions, that compose a mind, the ideas of them are felt to be connected together, and naturally introduce each other. However extraordinary this conclusion may seem, it need not surprize us. Most philosophers seem inclin'd to think, that personal identity *arises* from consciousness; and consciousness is nothing but a reflected thought or perception. The present philosophy, therefore, has so far a promising aspect. But all my hopes vanish, when I come to explain the principles, that unite our successive perceptions in our thought or consciousness. I cannot discover any theory, which gives me satisfaction on this head. (THN 635–636)

Instead of explaining why he is now dissatisfied with his earlier explanation of the "uniting principles" as consisting of resemblance and causation, however, he concludes by asserting:

> In short there are two principles, which I cannot render consistent; nor is it in my power to renounce either of them, viz. *that all our distinct perceptions are distinct existences*, and *that the mind never perceives any real connexion among distinct existences.* Did our perceptions either inhere in something simple and individual, or did the mind perceive some real connexion among them, there wou'd be no difficulty in the case. For my part, I must plead the privilege of a sceptic, and confess, that this difficulty is too hard for my understanding. (THN 636)

The two propositions that Hume reports he can neither reconcile nor renounce are not, of course, strictly incompatible with each other. They do, however, constitute his fundamental grounds for thinking that personal identity arises from associative principles of the imagination rather than from "real connexions," and it is presumably their conjunction with a serious and newfound difficulty for his earlier associative account—namely, the account in terms of resemblance and causation—that produces the real inconsistency. But he does not say what this newfound problem is. Unless we can locate the inconsistency, therefore, we must also plead the privilege of a skeptic and confess that discovering his difficulty is too hard for *our* understandings.

Five Theories of Hume's Second Thoughts

Impressions of the Self

According to Kemp Smith's well-known interpretation, it is "an awareness of personal identity" that Hume finds to be inconsistent with the two principles (Kemp Smith, 1941, pp. v, 555–558). In Kemp Smith's view, Hume's denial in Book I of the *Treatise* that we have an impression of the "self" is incompatible with passages in Book II describing the indirect passions. The most explicit of these passages occurs in Hume's description of the origin of sympathy:

> 'Tis evident, that the idea, or rather impression of ourselves is always intimately present with us, and that our consciousness gives us so lively a conception of our own person, that 'tis not possible to imagine, that any thing can in this particular go beyond it. Whatever object, therefore, is related to ourselves must be conceived with a like vivacity of conception, according to the foregoing principles. (THN 317)

Hume's problem, Kemp Smith argues, is that Book II requires an awareness of personal identity that his own theory in Book I will not allow, and his second thoughts in the Appendix are, Kemp Smith infers, a belated recognition of this fact.

One reason for doubting this explanation of Hume's misgivings is that he seems to express continued satisfaction in the Appendix with the relations among personal identity, consciousness, and memory, as they are described by his own theory. He repeats that there is no notion of the self as something distinct from our particular perceptions, and that thought "finds" personal identity in memory. Furthermore, he thinks that this latter doctrine illuminates what "most philosophers seem inclin'd to think," namely, that personal identity "*arises* from consciousness," which is itself "nothing but reflected thought or perception"—that is, a matter of memory. (Locke's theory of personal identity, of course, construes being the "same person" as a matter of having the "same consciousness," which is in turn a matter of memory.) Kemp Smith does not recognize that "reflected thought or perception" refers to memory, and so he claims that the nature of this "reflection" is the subject of Hume's despair. But according to Hume himself, his theory has "so far a promising aspect" (THN 635). He seems quite convinced that his theory as originally stated could account for the manner of our "finding" or becoming aware of personal identity—indeed, that would be its best feature—but that it fails on the quite separate matter of explaining what the connection or tie really is among the perceptions that are felt to be parts of this identity.

Even more fundamentally, however, there simply is no inconsistency between Books I and II to be the object of Hume's concern. He is quite entitled to write in Book II of both an idea and an impression of "ourselves." Certainly, Book I requires that there be no real idea of an underlying substantial self. But Book I also requires that there *must* be an idea of a bundle of perceptions that are related by resemblance and causation—"the true idea of the human mind" (THN 261). Moreover, Hume makes it clear at the outset of Book II (THN 277) that it is to such a bundle—or, more broadly, to such a bundle together with one's body (THN 303)—that he is now applying the term 'oneself'. Because the ideas making up this bundle cannot all be present to the mind at one time, the idea of oneself can only be a general or *abstract* idea, consisting, as such, of a particular (perhaps fairly complex) idea of a particular perception, associated (via a general term) with a custom or disposition to call up memories (and other ideas) of perceptions related to that particular perception by a certain kind of resemblance and/or causation.[2] It is this idea that our human cognitive nature has an unphilosophical and erroneous tendency to construe as an idea of a "perfectly identical" object, in much the same way that human nature has an erroneous tendency to regard the genuine idea of necessary connection as the idea of a "real necessary connexion in nature." Hume certainly denies that any idea has all the characteristics we are uncritically inclined to attribute to the idea of ourselves, but he does not and could not deny that we have any idea of ourselves. To deny that we have any idea of ourselves would be to deny that his cognitive psychology, or "science of man," has an intelligible subject matter.

Nor does Hume ever deny that we have impressions of ourselves, in the sense required by Book II. As a close reading of both the section "Of personal identity" and the Appendix shows, he denies only the existence of an "impression of self or substance, as something simple and individual" (THN 633), something "simple and continu'd" (THN 252), "constant and invariable" (THN 251), from which could be derived "the idea of self, after the manner it is here explained," that is, as the idea of something possessing "perfect identity and simplicity" (THN 251). But even though there is no impression corresponding to a substantial self, there may still be "impressions of ourselves" of some other kind, corresponding to, and serving as the origins of, the "true idea of the human mind" as a bundle of related perceptions.

What would such impressions be? Recall Hume's analogous account of space and time, considered in chapter 2. Because Hume asserts that we have ideas of space and time yet denies that we have any *distinct* impressions of space or time, he has been accused of violating his own Copy Principle. And he has been accused of this in spite of the fact that he begins his discussion of the origin of these ideas (THN 33) by asserting that we must employ this very principle. But as we have also seen, such an accusation misconstrues Hume's principle and thereby fails to recognize the way in which his theory of abstract ideas is meant to vindicate it.

There is, of course, no such impression as *the* impression of space, but many complex impressions are impressions of spatially arranged simple impressions, and thus have the feature of spatiality. The ideas of such complex impressions are therefore among those one is disposed to call up (i.e., are within the appropriate *revival set*) when having an abstract idea of space. Furthermore, the idea of *any* such impression can be made to serve as the abstract idea itself: because all impressions with spatial relations are members of the class of spatial things, the idea of any such impression may, given the appropriate disposition, serve as the particular idea representing the whole class of resembling things. Similar considerations apply in the case of time. And these considerations are sufficient, for Hume, to explain the existence of the ideas in question. As we have already observed, he recognizes that not every aspect in which perceptions may resemble one another is itself a separate or distinct perception (THN 637). If it were, simple perceptions—which resemble each other in their simplicity—could not be simple, because each would have to have a separate and distinct perception of simplicity as a part. The Copy Principle, as he presents it, does not require that every abstract idea representing a class of things with a common quality be preceded by an impression that is *the* separate and distinct impression of that quality. For the generation of an abstract idea to occur, it is sufficient that the idea be preceded by impressions that are impressions *of* the quality in the sense of exemplifying it. And in this sense, there are *many* impressions of space and time, as there are also of simplicity.

Now, in just the same way that there are many impressions of space, time, and simplicity, in the sense required by Hume's Copy Principle, even though there are no separate or distinct impressions of them, so there are impressions that satisfy that principle's demand for *impressions* of oneself able to give rise to the *idea* of oneself. *All* of our own impressions are impressions exemplifying the feature necessary for inclusion in the class of those perceptions that are the parts of oneself. That feature is, on Hume's theory, a certain relation of causation and/or resemblance to certain other perceptions. The idea of *any* such impression could therefore serve as one of the ideas disposed to be called up when having the abstract idea of oneself; or it could serve as that abstract idea itself.

Every impression one has is, in this sense, an impression of oneself. But in the present context, the class of impressions of oneself may be broader still. For consider why Hume is forced to correct himself when he appeals to "the idea, or rather impression of ourselves." It is because sympathy requires the infusion of vivacity into an idea, and the only source for such vivacity in this theory is an "impression"—a mere idea of ourselves would not do. But for the purposes of transferring vivacity, he classifies memories as impressions (THN 83–85).[3] Thus, in the description of sympathy cited previously, Hume is saying only that the mental mechanism of sympathy is triggered by the recognition of resemblance between ourselves and others, and that the force and vivacity needed for this mechanism are derived from our impressions or memories of ourselves—in a sense in which there clearly are such impressions and memories.

The Active Self

A second interpretation of Hume's confession has been offered by Wade Robison (1974). In his view, Hume comes to see in the Appendix that his explanations of mental phenomena—including particularly his explanation of how we come to have an idea of personal identity—appeal "to the existence of an active self distinct from any bundle of perceptions and propensities." Robison notes, for example, that the mind is said, at various points in the *Treatise*, to associate, to mistake one perception or propensity for another, to "spread" the impression of necessary connection onto the objects themselves, and to notice or intuit resemblances among perceptions.[4]

However, Hume can explain each of these mental activities as a tendency or propensity of perceptions to occur in particular ways. He clearly holds, for example, that "the mind" associates two ideas just in case a token of one tends to be followed by a token of the other. Similarly, one perception is mistaken for another when an occurrence of the one later causes a seeming-memory idea of the other; when the first tends to be called by a name that, after further thought, would be acknowledged to apply only to the other; when inappropriate beliefs (lively ideas) follow the occurrence of one perception, beliefs that would have been appropriate following the other; and so on. One propensity is mistaken for another when observation of the one tends to produce an incorrect belief in the activity of the other, or when the idea of one is mistaken for the idea of the other. The impression of necessary connection is spread onto the objects themselves when mistaken beliefs tend to occur about the cause of that impression and when the idea of that impression is mentally associated with other ideas with which it does not truly belong (as may also be seen after further reflection).

Perhaps the most problematic mental "act" for Hume to explain may be our noticing of the resemblances and other "relations of ideas" in which, he holds, genuine *knowledge* consists. Unlike belief, knowledge is not described as an idea enlivened by a present impression (although he does call knowledge a kind of "assurance"). Hence, the difference between noticing a relation of ideas and having the related ideas *without* noticing the relation need not be construed as a difference in the vivacity of those ideas. But here again Hume may say that the difference is rather one of resulting propensities: a tendency to associate the related ideas; a tendency to have further appropriate ideas and beliefs; an ability to name the relation if one wills to do so; a tendency to feel no surprise if the relation is pointed out by others; and so on.

Hume can thus reduce any given kind of "action" of the mind simply to the occurrence of particular kinds of perceptions (as he does with will and judgment) or, failing that, to propensities of perceptions to occur in particular patterns. It has been argued that reductions of the latter kind would not be adequate, because even "to have an idea of a self with propensities is to have an idea of a self which is more than a bundle of perceptions" (Nathanson, 1976), but again there is little reason to think that Hume would or should have any such worry. The fact of what propensities there are—like the fact of what causal laws there are—is for Hume a function of what past, present, and future nondispositional events actually occur. It is true that he often explicitly attributes propensities to "the mind" rather than to perceptions themselves. But this alone should not be surprising, for his own theory entails that there is no real difference between attributing propensities to the mind and attributing them to perceptions. More seriously, it is questionable whether the psychological laws Hume actually proposes are deterministic enough to support ascriptions of propensities to individual minds, particularly in cases in which these propensities do not actually manifest themselves. But while many of his own psychological explanations tend to be weakly probabilistic—the laws of association, for example, constitute only a "gentle force"—he maintains that all ultimate causal laws are deterministic. (For a discussion of his grounds, see chapter 6.) Although he identifies the idea of the mind with the idea of a set of bundled perceptions, he is not forbidden by his empiricist principles from postulating the existence of unperceived deterministic mechanisms that would underlie the propensities of perceptions to appear in particular ways. He is forbidden by his principles only from trying to specify the nature of those mechanisms beyond what experience can warrant.

Brute Mental Facts

Although Hume's bundle-theory is *consistent* with the existence of mental propensities, it seems still to leave these propensities *unexplained* in terms of any underlying mechanism, even though some may be explained as instances of others. This suggests yet a third approach to Hume's confession, one that emphasizes the main verb in his remark that he cannot "explain the principles, that unite our successive perceptions." On this view, he is satisfied with his explanation that our tendency to ascribe identity to a given bundle of perceptions is due entirely to their relations of causation and resemblance; he is complaining only that either (i) he cannot give a further or deeper explanation of why and how these relations function associatively as they do (as Beauchamp, 1979, suggests), or (ii) he cannot explain why perceptions should come in more than one causally discrete bundle, each with its own interrelations of causation and resemblance (as Stroud, 1977, proposes).[5]

Any approach of this kind, however, faces a dilemma. Hume would not be distressed by his inability to offer ultimate explanations for these brute causal facts. Indeed, it is an important part of his explanatory empiricism that causal explanations must always lead eventually to some brute facts. And yet Hume despondently declares four times in less than four pages of the Appendix that he has found a contradiction or inconsistency. Beauchamp takes one horn of this dilemma, suggesting that Hume is registering only a minor complaint and is not really worried about a contradiction. Stroud takes the other horn, writing: "To say it [the existence of separate bundles] is 'inexplicable' for Hume is to say that it is inconsistent with the theory of ideas, which he takes to be the only way to make sense of psychological phenomena" (p. 140).

Stroud is right to this extent: Hume's problem is related to the possibility of there being more than one bundle. But the problem cannot be simply that Hume has no explanation at hand for why there are many causally discrete bundles (that is, bundles whose members for the most part do not causally interact). Hume freely admits that there may be causal explanations of the ultimate sources of our perceptions that are essentially beyond our reach (THN 7, THN 84), and Stroud offers no reason to think that the explanation for the discreteness of bundles should not be of this kind. The dilemma is real, and neither alternative can be accepted: Hume is worried about a contradiction, and the mere unavailability to us of further causal explanations does not produce one.

Failures of Resemblance and Causation

A fourth explanation has been proposed by A. H. Basson (1958) and S. C. Patten (1976) and is considered also by Stroud. It interprets Hume's confession—namely, that he cannot explain the principles that unite our perceptions—as the result of a realization that causation and resemblance alone are simply not, as a matter of fact, adequate to the scope of the job. On the one hand, these two relations do not seem sufficient because, as Basson and Stroud urge, a perception in one person's mind might cause a perception (even a resembling one) in some *other* person's mind. And on the other hand, they do not seem necessary, for, as Patten and Stroud argue, not all of our perceptions seem to be related by causation and resemblance—particularly not our impressions of sensation. An impression of a coffee cup, in Patten's example, neither resembles nor causes the succeeding impression of a pen. Furthermore, we can conceive of a person's mind exhibiting fewer relations of resemblance and causation than ours do—or even none at all—and nevertheless remaining the mind of one person.

These are not trivial objections. Difficulties of this kind may even be a part of what Hume has in mind when he pronounces himself caught in a "labyrinth." But I am not convinced they are the whole of his problem, for Hume has a number of resources available to him to account for these apparent counterexamples.

In response to Basson's objection, Hume may admit that a perception in one mind could cause a perception in another. For any perception in another mind must already be part of one interrelated bundle. If a perception in one bundle causes a perception in another, the only alternatives will be either to (i) regard these bundles as a single large bundle, or (ii) continue to regard them as two different bundles in spite of the causal connection. If (he may say) there is only a single direct causal relation between the two bundles (as Basson and Stroud envision), then no doubt the latter alternative would remain the more natural, but should the direct interrelations multiply in number and complexity, then the former would indeed become more natural, as Hume's own theory suggests.

Hume can reply to Patten's objection as well. It does seem that explaining the ownership of impressions of sensation provides the most difficult case for Hume. Ideas are generally caused by other perceptions, and they are always at least partly caused by the impressions of which they are copies, whereas impressions of reflection are always caused "in a great measure" by ideas (THN 7). But even in the case of impressions of sensation, which Hume allows "arise from unknown causes" (THN 7, THN 84), he can make the following points. First, we often observe causal interactions among objects, and the "vulgar"—that is, nearly all of us, most of the time—do not distinguish objects from perceptions. Hence, causal interactions among objects will not be distinguished by the mind from causal interactions among perceptions. Second, what impressions we will perceive at any given time is nearly always *partly* dependent on our wills, that is, on our impressions of will or volition (THN 399), and these impressions of will are in turn caused by other prior perceptions. There is no reason to think that one perception must be the *whole* cause of another in order for them to have the needed causal relation. Indeed, to suppose that it must would be to set the theory of personal identity at odds with

Hume's own remarks concerning the unknowability of the ultimate causes of our impressions of sensation. Third, a bundle of perceptions need not involve *direct* or *immediate* causal relations between each perception and every other, or between each perception and its successor, so long as there is a web of interrelations that eventually extends to them all. All ideas and all impressions of reflection are, ultimately, causally dependent on prior impressions of sensation, and, because these ideas and impressions of reflection interact causally in numerous ways, this produces an indirect causal relation among the impressions of sensation as well. Moreover, the mere fact that memory is a causal relation in which a perception produces a later idea entails that one can never *remember* an impression that has no causal connection with an idea.

Finally, regarding the conceivability of minds without interrelations of causation and resemblance, Hume may argue that such "minds" would not have any tendency to ascribe personal identity to themselves, and that our own willingness to ascribe personal identity to such imagined collections of perceptions would decrease upon serious consideration. Furthermore, he may observe, it is only an empirical fact of human psychology that collections of perceptions related by causation and resemblance—rather than other kinds of collections of perceptions— should be mistaken for strict identities and thereby give rise to the belief in personal identity. Thus, we can *imagine* personal identity without causation and resemblance because, given a different psychology, perceptions unrelated by causation and resemblance could give rise to the ascription of such an identity. Moreover, he can also invoke the common "fiction" of an underlying unifying substantial substratum to explain the specious plausibility of the proposal that minds could contain perceptions unrelated by either resemblance or causation.

Therefore, while Hume's theory certainly requires more defense against the objections of Basson, Patten, and Stroud than he explicitly provides, it is not obvious that these objections alone are so inescapable as to make all Hume's hopes "vanish." Although Hume is genuinely dissatisfied with the ability of causation and resemblance to unite our perceptions, it may be doubted whether we have yet found the most important reason for that dissatisfaction.

The Necessary Ownership of Perceptions

Like Basson and Patten, David Pears locates the cause of Hume's dissatisfaction with his own theory of personal identity in the inadequacy of causation and resemblance as relations for binding our perceptions into bundles (Pears, 1993; see also Pears, 1990 and 1975). Unlike them, however, he describes the problem not simply as a failure of these relations to draw boundaries among bundles that match the boundaries we actually draw but as a failure of these relations to do justice to the necessity of perceptions' membership in the bundles of which they are members. Thus, he writes:

> When an impression of sense occurs in my series of perceptions, it does not hold its place in the series by possessing any property, or by standing in any specific relation to any other perception in the series (except, of course, the relation of being co-experi-

enced). Consequently, when I review the series, I do not find that the sensation is anchored by anything other than the fact of its contingent occurrence at the point where it occurred. Nevertheless, there is a strong modal statement that can be made about it: It, *the very same sensation*, could not conceivably have occurred in any other series. . . . However, in Hume's system, perceptions are treated like stars which form constellations, but only form them contingently, and it is obvious that the discovery of additional contingent relations between perceptions would never provide any support for the strong modal statement. Yet in Hume's system the only possible relations between perceptions are contingent relations. The other alternative, that the self is a substance, would, perhaps, do the trick, but for Hume it is unthinkable.

It may seem fanciful to suggest that Hume's problem was the difficulty of accounting for the necessary ownership of perceptions within the framework of his system. But it is hard to see what other reason he could have had for requiring stronger relations between the perceptions of a single mind than those allowed in the main text of the *Treatise*. (Pears, 1993, p. 290)

Although Hume's original account of personal identity may not be able specifically to explain the alleged necessary ownership of perceptions, it seems unlikely that concern over this lack caused his recantation of that theory, since he shows no signs, either in the main body of the *Treatise* or in the Appendix, of being attracted to any doctrine of the necessary ownership of perceptions. He continues to assert in the Appendix, of course, that "all perceptions are distinct . . . [and] are, therefore, distinguishable, and separable, and may be conceived as separately existent, and may exist separately, without any contradiction or absurdity." But beyond that, it is also an essential aspect of his explanation of the "vulgar" view about the "continu'd and distinct existence of bodies" (THN I.iv.2) that perceptions can be conceived to exist, for parts of their duration, outside of the mind in which they occur at other times. The vulgar do so conceive some of their impressions of sensation, according to Hume, since they do not distinguish impressions from bodies, and so attribute a "continu'd and distinct" existence to their own impressions. Nor is there any evident reason why he should regard it as *inconceivable* or *impossible* for such impressions to be related to another mind while unperceived by one's own. Had Hume become convinced that it was a *necessary* fact about each individual perception that it exists in the bundle of which it is a part, he would have been driven to second thoughts about his theory concerning the origin and nature of the belief in the external world as well. In fact, however, he betrays no hint of any such second thoughts about his theory of belief in continued and distinct bodies.

It should be emphasized that Hume's only criterion of possibility is conceivability in the imagination. Hence, if one's perceptions can be *conceived* to have bundling relations different from their present ones, Hume must and will conclude that it is *possible* for them to enter into those relations. A contemporary reader influenced by Kripkean essentialism (see Kripke, 1980) might argue that *this very perception of mine* could not maintain its identity across possible worlds if it were supposed to belong to another mind instead, due to the conditions for cross-world identity of perceptions. But both the concern for, and the notion of, such conditions for identity across possible worlds is alien to Hume's thought.

Three Further Theories of Hume's Second Thoughts

Identity through Change

Robert J. Fogelin, in his excellent book on Hume's skepticism (Fogelin, 1985), takes up the question of Hume's second thoughts about personal identity in some detail. Expressing dissatisfaction with previous explanations, he proposes for consideration not just one but three original, and ingenious, explanations. The first explanation concerns a problem of identity through change; the second concerns a problem of local conjunction; and the third concerns a problem of separability and unity.

Fogelin's first proposed diagnosis focuses on Hume's claim that our ascriptions of identity to successions of variable or interrupted objects are always the result of our *mistaking* them for invariable and uninterrupted (i.e., "perfectly" identical) objects. Thus, in the case of personal identity, we have a "propension to ascribe an identity to these successive perceptions" because we "suppose ourselves possest of an invariable and uninterrupted existence thro' the whole course of our lives" (THN 253). Fogelin writes:

> To see how this conception of identity could lead Hume into immediate trouble, consider the case of a person ascribing identity over time to himself. He might say of himself that he had in no way changed since winning the Grand Prix. That, however, is just false, and he cannot but know that it is false. Of course, Hume is fond of attributing false beliefs to the mass of mankind and then proposing *fictions* behind which they can be hidden. In the present case, however, the falsehood of unchangingness is so palpable that it seems inconceivable that it could be concealed by a fiction. Thus, starting from his curious conception of identity, Hume is led to the paradoxical result that human beings universally accept a belief that should strike them all as false. This, in turn, would lead him to feel uneasy about his account of our *belief* in personal identity. (pp. 105–106)

There are two difficulties with this explanation. The first concerns the fact—suggested in Fogelin's remark that Hume is fond of attributing false beliefs to the mass of mankind—that the tendency to accept palpable falsehoods about unchangingness is not unique to Hume's account of *personal* identity. In his parallel account of the "imperfect" identity of plants, animals, and inanimate objects, Hume emphasizes that we have a tendency to accept a wide variety of palpable falsehoods—such as the falsehoods that a sapling undergoes no change at all in becoming a giant oak, and that a church made of freestone is an invariable and uninterrupted continuation of an earlier church built of brick on the same site and then fallen into ruin. That Hume does regard these falsehoods as palpable is indicated by his remark that we "incessantly correct ourselves by reflection" (THN 254). But he argues that their obvious falsehood alone is not enough to prevent our entering into them, so long as they appeal to features of the imagination. (The fiction of a unifying substance enters in not so much to "hide" the evident *changes*, as it does to disguise the existence of a contradiction *between* these evident changes and our recurring ascriptions of identity.) Thus, if Hume does later come to doubt whether we could be seduced into the palpable falsehoods of unchangingness required by his original account of ascriptions of *personal* identity, then unless he finds some crucial difference between those falsehoods and the falsehoods involved in ascribing identity to other things, he ought to express dissatisfaction with his entire account of object identity in general. Yet the dissatisfaction expressed in the Appendix is explicitly restricted to the topic of personal identity alone.

Would Hume be likely to find the palpable falsehoods involved in ascribing personal identity crucially different from those involved in ascribing identity to other things? The contents of the human mind do often change more quickly, if not ultimately more radically, than do trees and churches, caterpillars and republics. But Hume lists four features of successions of related objects that induce the imagination to ascribe identity: (i) low proportion of changed parts to unchanged parts, (ii) gradualness of change, (iii) reference of the parts to a common end, and (iv) sympathy or interaction of the parts. Although the human mind scores relatively low on the first two criteria, it scores relatively high on the latter two. Moreover, Hume claims, we are "less scrupulous" about the difference between numerical and specific identity when "the first object is in a manner annihilated before the second comes into existence"—which, we may note, is generally the case with the succession of perceptions. Furthermore, he claims, we are also less scrupulous about the identity of those successions "where the objects are in their nature changeable and inconstant" (THN 258), such as are the parts of a river—or, we may note, a mind. This, he asserts, is because *expected* changes have less influence on the imagination.[6] Thus, it appears that in *Treatise* I.iv.6 Hume already provides the grounds on which he would argue that we can be seduced into ascribing perfect identity to the human mind—its evident variability notwithstanding—through the same mechanisms of the imagination that produce our ascriptions of identity to other things.

The second difficulty with this proposal is even more fundamental: the problem it cites is not one that would lead Hume, even if he conceded it, to characterize himself as caught in a "contradiction," unable to render his "former opinions . . . consistent." Perhaps it *is* implausible to say that we ever mistake a human mind for something invariable and uninterrupted. But even if Hume granted that point, he would have no particular reason to despair of resemblance and causation as "the principles, that unite our successive perceptions in our thought or consciousness," and hence he would have no serious reason to doubt his account of what personal identity actually consists in. If he were to grant the implausibility of mistaking minds for perfect identities, he would have to give up his explanation of part of the *specific mechanism* by means of which these two associative relations induce us to ascribe an identity to the mind. That we do ascribe an identity of some kind, however, no one can doubt. Given Hume's prior argument against the substantial self, there is no reason to doubt that the identity is an "imperfect" one—that is, a relation holding among a succession of related objects. Hume would then still go on to conclude, for the same reasons as before, that the connecting principles producing such an imperfect identity are resemblance and causation, the only two associative relations remaining. To put the point in terms of the outline of Hume's original argument provided earlier in this chapter, Fogelin's first proposal raises a difficulty for part of Hume's explanation of *why* (9) is true, but it does not call the truth of (9) itself into serious question. It may also call into question the *depth* of the analogy with vegetable and animal identity expressed in (11), but (11) through (13) constitute only one line of argument for (17). Hume explicitly indicates that (14) through (16)—together, presumably, with (10)—constitute an *independent* argument for (17), one that is "still closer and more immediate" (THN 259). Hence, the problem, even if granted, does not seriously undermine Hume's ability to derive his final conclusion. The resulting lacuna of explanation might be an embarrassment, but given Hume's general willingness to accept the reality of facts that he cannot yet explain causally, it does not seem to constitute a "contradiction" or an inconsistency, nor anything sufficient in itself to make him despair of his entire account of "the uniting principles" of personal identity.

Local Conjunction

Fogelin's second proposal is that Hume's problem derives from his claim in *Treatise* I.iv.5 ("Of the immateriality of the soul"): "All our perceptions are not susceptible of a local [i.e., spatial] union, either with what is extended or unextended; there being some of them of the one kind, and some of the other." Fogelin writes, referring to *Treatise* I.iv.5:

> Hume there argued that both the materialists and the immaterialists will be embarrassed when asked to explain how extended perceptions and extensionless perceptions can be locally conjoined. . . . Later Hume may have realized that the very same considerations cut against the intelligibility of the *wholeness* (including both the *simplicity* and the *identity*) of the self. Invoking causal relations between the extended and the extensionless ideas will not relieve this difficulty, for it is the *intelligibility* of conjoining the extended with the extensionless that is at issue, and this is prior to any inquiry concerning the supposed source of the conjunction. If Hume saw that his arguments intended to show the unintelligibility of a *unified* substantial self would apply equally well against *any* notion of a unified self, then we can understand his despair at giving an adequate account of this fiction. (p. 106)

This proposal, too, may be questioned. First, like the previous proposal, it describes a problem that, even if granted, Hume would not regard as unique to *personal* identity. In the very section just cited, Hume not only allows but emphasizes that all sounds, smells, and tastes are literally located "no where." For example, he writes:

> [W]hatever confus'd notions we may form of an union in place betwixt an extended body, as a fig, and its particular taste, 'tis certain that upon reflection we must observe in this union something altogether unintelligible and contradictory. (THN 238)

If the lack of "local union" or "conjunction" among some of our perceptions were to cause Hume to despair of explaining their unification into one *person*, then the parallel lack of local conjunction among some sensible qualities would presumably lead to a similar despair about explaining the unification of those sensible qualities into one *physical object*. In fact, however, Hume shows no tendency to take back his earlier claim that "a particular colour, taste, and smell are qualities all united together in this apple" (THN 2).

But second, and more important, there is no reason why an absence of local conjunction or contiguity among perceptions *should* undermine Hume's account of personal identity in terms of resemblance and causation—especially given that in (19) Hume explicitly declares "contiguity" to be unnecessary and inapplicable as a principle of union for personal identity (THN 260). It is crucial to note that Hume does not say that *every* union of the extended and the unextended is unintelligible, but only that their "union in place" is unintelligible. In *Treatise* I.iv.5, Hume declares that he can explain why the taste or smell of an apple constitutes "part" of the apple solely by appealing to the relations of "causation, and contiguity in the time of their appearance, betwixt the extended object and the quality, which exists without any particular place" (THN 237). Similarly, in *Treatise* I.iv.6, he thinks that he can explain why our various perceptions constitute parts of the same mind solely by appealing to the relations of resemblance and causation among them. To put the matter in Fogelin's terms, Hume's project in *Treatise* I.iv.6 is precisely to explain the "wholeness" of the mind without appealing to a local spatial conjunction of all of its perceptions, and to do so by utilizing instead the relations of resemblance and causation. Fogelin has not provided a reason why Hume should, in the Appendix, suddenly expect this latter project to fail. Thus, unless Hume sees some further, independent reason to question the adequacy of his previously identified uniting principles of resemblance and causation, his views about local conjunction will pose no threat to his account of personal identity.

Separability versus Unity

Fogelin's third and final proposal—and the one that he says he prefers—takes as its starting place Hume's attempt in *Treatise* I.iv.2 ("Of scepticism with regard to the senses," already mentioned in connection with Pears's proposal) to show that the "vulgar" do not believe a contradiction—though they do believe an empirical falsehood—when they suppose that their perceptions sometimes exist without being perceived by them. Hume must show this, because, as we have seen, literal belief in a contradiction is impossible on his own theory of belief: it would require a lively yet inconceivable idea. Hume argues as follows:

> [W]e may observe, that what we call a mind, is nothing but a heap or collection of different perceptions, united together by certain relations, and suppos'd, tho' falsely, to be endowed with a perfect simplicity and identity. Now as every perception is distinguishable from another, and may be consider'd as separately existent; it evidently follows, that there is no absurdity in separating any particular perception from the mind; that is, in breaking off all its relations, with that connected mass of perceptions, which constitute a thinking being. (THN 207)

Fogelin comments:

> The passage concludes by speaking about the "*connected mass* of perceptions, which constitute a thinking being." Now in the Appendix it is just this connectedness that Hume finds himself unable to explain, and this does lead Hume into profound difficulties. Hume's argument against Berkeley [for the possibility of unperceived perceptions] depends upon the notion of an *individual* mind from which a perception may be separated, but Hume provides no principle for individuating heaps of perceptions into

minds. Strictly speaking, each perception is itself an individual substance and, again strictly speaking, a collection or heap of individual substances is not an individual substance. More remarkably, on Hume's principles, each perception is an individual *mind*, and a collection of minds is not itself a mind. Less strictly, for Hume, perceptions must be connected together loosely enough to allow separation, while at the same time they must be connected together closely enough to constitute a mind from which things can be separated. Hume's radical atomism guarantees the first result, but precludes the second. Without both features (separable perceptions and a unified mind), Hume's theory of perception no longer contains a response to Berkeley's claim that it is self-contradictory to suppose that a perception can exist unperceived. (p. 107)

Fogelin is certainly correct to say that Hume needs both the logical separability *and* the unity or connectedness of the mind's perceptions to account for the belief that our perceptions can exist unperceived by us. He is also correct in saying that Hume's atomism provides a separability of perceptions sufficient for the purpose. It permits: (i) the logical possibility that some perceptions exist without ever being appropriately related to other perceptions; and (ii) the logical possibility that some perceptions exist without being appropriately related to certain other perceptions for some temporal portion of their existence, so that they could be said to be, for that period of time, existing "unperceived" by the mind to which they are related at another time. Again, Fogelin is clearly correct in saying that Hume finds himself, in the Appendix, unable to explain the unity or connectedness of our perceptions; that he is unable to do so is perhaps the clearest and most specific single thing that Hume says about the nature of his difficulty. But once again the question is *why* Hume now finds himself unable to explain this connectedness, which he had explained to his own satisfaction earlier in the *Treatise*. Fogelin's remarks, in the passage just cited, suggest three possibilities.

Is it that Hume "provides no principle for individuating heaps of perceptions into minds?" But he clearly does provide such a principle, in the associative relations of resemblance and causation. Furthermore, both of these associative relations, as Hume understands them, are compatible with the logical separability of their relata. Indeed, the causal relation as Hume understands it *always* involves such separability (THN 79–80).

Is it then that the human mind must be an "individual substance," while for Hume "each perception is itself an individual substance and . . . a collection or heap of individual substances is not an individual substance?" But he defines a substance simply as "something which may exist by itself," a definition that, as he asserts, "agrees to everything which can possibly be conceived" (THN 233), presumably *including* collections and heaps. A church building—to take a Humean example—can surely be an "individual substance," despite being a collection of (related) bricks that are themselves individual substances. If the rejoinder is made that the church cannot be an *individual* substance precisely because it is a complex of parts, then of course Hume would justly reply by denying that a mind is or need be an "individual" substance either, in *that* restricted sense.

Or, finally, is the problem more specifically that "on Hume's principles, each perception is an individual *mind*, and a collection of minds is not itself a mind"? But first, it is not obvious that a single perception can ever be a mind on his principles. Hume characterizes the human mind, at least, as a "heap or collection of different perceptions," which are "united together by certain relations"; a single perception is neither a heap nor a collection. In a footnote, Fogelin cites the following passage as evidence that Hume would allow a single perception to be a mind:

> We can conceive a thinking being to have either many or few perceptions. Suppose the mind to be reduc'd even below the life of an oyster. Suppose it to have only one perception, as of thirst or hunger. Consider it in that situation. Do you conceive any thing but merely that perception? Have you any notion of *self* or *substance*? If not, the addition of other perceptions can never give you that notion. (THN 634)

Hume's remarks in this passage do not entail, however, that a perception unrelated to all others would constitute a mind. At most they imply that a mind can contain a single perception at a single time, not that a single perception entirely unrelated to earlier or later perceptions would count as a mind. And even that implication may be questioned: Hume may be read as asking the reader to consider "reducing" a mind to a condition in which it would be so impoverished as to be no longer a mind.

But suppose that Hume *would* regard a single perception, when unrelated to all others, as a rudimentary or limiting-case mind. That concession does not entail that a single perception would itself still be a mind when it is suitably related to others, nor that a *collection* of suitably related perceptions could not *also* be a mind. Consider an analogous case. It is not obvious that a single flower can be a bouquet. But even if a single flower, when unrelated to all others, can be regarded as a rudimentary or limiting-case bouquet, it still does not follow that the same flower is itself a bouquet when that flower is suitably related to others, nor that a collection of suitably related flowers cannot also be a bouquet.

Thus, although Fogelin's third proposal is right to insist that Hume needs the unity or connectedness as well as the separability of the mind's perceptions, I conclude that the proposal, as it stands, does not provide a compelling reason why Hume would or should have become dissatisfied with his own earlier account of that unity or connectedness.

Real Connections and the Representation of the Self

A Humean Contradiction

What, then, is the heart of Hume's problem? The most fundamental difficulty with his account, and the one that I believe to be the most likely cause of his second thoughts, is that he would assent to each of the following jointly inconsistent propositions:

(A) All of our distinct perceptions are distinct existences.

(B) The mind never perceives any real connection among distinct existences.

(C) The ownership of any perception is determined either by its causal relations and its relations of resemblance or by its perceived real connection to (i.e., inherence in) a distinct substantial self.

(D) The causal roles of qualitatively identical objects (distinct existences) can differ only in virtue of differences in spatial or temporal location, unless the mind perceives a real connection between at least one of them and some other distinct object.

(E) Many kinds of perceptions are "no where."

(F) It is possible that two numerically distinct but qualitatively identical perceptions of any kind, including perceptions that are "no where," should occur in different minds at the same time.

I will briefly explain how I understand these propositions and why I attribute them to Hume.

The first two are, of course, the two principles Hume cites in the Appendix. Together, they entail that the mind never perceives any real connection between different perceptions or between perceptions and other objects. By 'real connexion' used as a technical term, Hume means (at least) a connection between two objects that is more than simply an associative relation in the imagination.[7] The relation between a perception and a mental substance in which it is necessarily to inhere, and the relation of necessary connection understood as a relation between the cause and effect themselves, would both constitute "real" connections in this sense. Thus, (B) follows directly from the Separability Principle. It is not a corollary of (A), despite Kemp Smith's oft-cited claim to the contrary; (A) simply states that perceptions fall within the scope of (B).

The third proposition (C), is entailed by Hume's view that his own theory of personal identity provides the only correct alternative to the theory that we ascribe personal identity by perceiving the relation of our perceptions to a substantial self. The fourth proposition, (D), follows from his two definitions of 'cause', which he offers as the only alternatives to the failed attempt to conceive causal relations as involving "real" necessary connections. It clearly follows from Hume's first definition of 'cause' (i.e., the definition in terms of constant conjunction) that qualitatively identical perceptions can differ in their causal roles only in virtue of differences in their spatial or temporal locations. The same conclusion follows from the second definition (i.e., the definition in terms of inference and association involving the ideas of the cause and the effect) as well, because an idea can be *of* one rather than the other of two qualitatively identical perceptions only in virtue of having a causal relation to one that it does not have to the other. As we have just seen in connection with Fogelin's second proposal, Hume asserts (E) just prior to the section "Of personal identity" (THN 235), on the grounds that only visual and tangible perceptions have genuine spatial locations: passions, sentiments, and even sounds, tastes, and smells do not. Finally, (F) is a basic commonsense belief about the very nature of persons—a belief that we may expect Hume, like anyone else, both to hold and to be reluctant to give up. In Hume's cognitive psychology, an idea of a mind other than one's one is, presumably, structurally similar to one's idea of one's own, the difference lying in the believed or supposed relations of causation and resemblance of that mind's perceptions to one's own. Thus, an idea of another mind is fundamentally an idea of one or more perceptions that one believes (as the result of observations of another human body) or supposes to have occurred, even though that perception or those perceptions are not themselves causally integrated with one's own—together with a willingness to include, as falling under a term for that person, any other perceptions that may be related by causation and resemblance to the perception or perceptions in question. To deny (F) would, after all, be to allow a "real" causal connection of sorts, because the existence of one perception would then be sufficient to entail the simultaneous *nonexistence* of any other of the same kind.

Although this may seem a fairly long list of propositions, the problem they pose is simple. Any two qualitatively identical perceptions must share exactly the same resemblance relations with other objects, and—given (A) and (B)—they can be conceived as having different causal relations only in virtue of their different spatial or temporal locations. Yet many such perceptions have no spatial location, and so they cannot differ in that respect, and perceptions of the kind mentioned in (F) will share the same temporal location as well. A pair of such perceptions cannot, accordingly, be distinguished either by their relations of resemblance or by their relations of causation. Hence, either both of them will belong to a given bundle of perceptions or neither of them will. It would be both impossible and inconceivable that one impression of the smell of lilacs should exist in one mind at the same time that a second but qualitatively identical impression of the smell of lilacs existed in another.

The problem is not easily overcome. It has sometimes been suggested (e.g., by MacNabb, 1951, pp. 149–150) that Hume would do well to recognize an empirical relation of "copresentation" holding among the perceptions of a single mind at a given time. But the recognition of such a nonspatial analogue of spatial contiguity would at best solve only the problem of the "simplicity" of a mind at one time and not the problem of its identity through time. Copresentation would either supplement or (more likely) replace resemblance and causation as a means of conceiving simultaneous perceptions as collected into *momentary* bundles, but the problem of conceiving momentary bundles as collected into *durational* ones would remain. It is unlikely that a mere difference of "copresented" companion perceptions would always be able to determine which of two qualitatively identical perceptions should be assigned a particular causal role. And in any case, it is always possible that two momentary bundles should themselves be qualitatively identical in all their contents, as in the case of two individuals engrossed in watching the same movie to the exclusion of all other thoughts.

Furthermore, the same problem of conceiving momentary bundles as collected into durational ones remains even if all perceptions are granted full Humean spatial locations. This is so because, for Hume, the spatial locations of perceptions consist in their spatial relations to other spatial perceptions of the same kind (i.e., impression or idea) in the same mind at the same time;[8] the identity of such locations *through* time is dependent on the identity of minds, and not vice versa. It is true that a perception may be given a further, derivative, spatial location by locating it with respect to the "continu'd and distinct" human body with which it is believed to be causally related. But the possibility of derivative locations of this kind is no solution to the present difficulty. For we cannot say which of two simultaneous and qualitatively identical perceptions is the effect of a physiological process in a given body, unless one of the perceptions has already been bundled with the perceptions constituting the mind associated with that body—and if the copresented or contiguous perceptions do not happen to provide a way to choose, this is precisely what cannot be done. If, for example, two total momentary perceptions consist entirely of uniform fields of a shade of green, it will be impossible to attribute one of these perceptions to one mind or body and the other perception to another. Thus, even if (E) is weakened or eliminated, the conjunction of Hume's views about the spatiality of perceptions with (A) through (D) and a version of (F) strengthened to apply to total momentary mental states will preserve the contradiction.

It has been argued (Biro, 1976 and 1979) that there is no real difficulty with Hume's account of personal identity once we recognize the "intentionality of memory." But in fact, as we now see, the problem is rather that Humean memory and other psychological causal relations are not intentional *enough*. When two similar perceptions, P_1 and P_2, occur at a given time, and a later idea, P_3, of the same kind occurs with the force and vivacity appropriate to memories, it simply remains indeterminate whether P_3 is a memory of P_1 or of P_2. We cannot, therefore say, or even conceive, that one rather than the other has been collected into the same bundle as P_3. As Hume says, "did our perceptions either inhere in something simple and individual, or did the mind perceive some real connexion among them, there wou'd be no difficulty in the case" (THN 636, quoted previously). If our perceptions inhered in something that was simple at one time and identical through time (thus providing a real connection between perceptions and nonperceptions), we could say that P_3 was a memory of P_1 rather than of P_2 just in case P_1 rather than P_2 inhered in the same substance as P_3. And if there were a genuine necessary connection between causally related perceptions (thus providing a real connection among the perceptions themselves), we could say that P_3 was a memory of P_1 just in case there was a real necessary causal connection between P_1 and P_3.

Hume is not prepared to grant the existence of such connections. But he is also not prepared, if my interpretation is correct, to accept it as a logical consequence of the "true idea of the human mind" that whenever two perceivers have the same experience—whether impression of sensation, passion, or idea—at the same time, they are in fact sharing the numerically same perception. He allows that perceptions could exist outside any mind, and he would presumably allow that a perception could in principle be shared by more than one mind. It is nevertheless quite another thing to maintain that the existence of one perception literally *entails* the nonexistence of any simultaneous resembling perceptions in the face of the doctrine that all perceptions are distinct existences. He therefore pleads the "privilege of a sceptic" to profess ignorance, holding out the hope that the problem of the inadequacy of causation and resemblance might be solved with further reflection, but suspecting it to be evidence of a serious mistake.

Possible Objections

It may fairly be objected against my interpretation that Hume nowhere describes his problem as one involving the perceptions of other minds. However, this objection is not by any means fatal. Although the problem that Stroud describes is indeed one that would entirely disappear if there were no other minds, the problem I have described would exist whether there were actually any other minds or not. This is because I find Hume's problem not in the fact that the *actual* existence of discrete causal bundles is simply causally inexplicable but in the fact that, on Humean principles, the *possible* existence of such bundles becomes incoherent. The essence of the problem is that, given Hume's views about causation, the relations of causation and resemblance are *necessarily* insufficient to provide an "idea of the human mind" as strong as our actual idea, even after our idea has been purged of its vague association with metaphysical substance. That is to say, he has failed to explain adequately the nature of our representation of the human mind and hence has failed to describe how we represent ourselves to our ourselves. For if we did represent ourselves to ourselves in the way that he describes in *Treatise* I.iv.6, we could *not* conceive, or represent to ourselves as a genuine possibility, something that clearly *is* conceivable—namely, the existence of other perceivers with similar and simultaneous perceptions. Although the insufficiency can thus be best demonstrated (and perhaps even can only be demonstrated) by appealing to the *possibility* of other perceivers with similar perceptions, the heart of the problem is the inability of causation and resemblance sufficiently to bind our perceptions in the way required by a "true idea" of the identity of the human mind. This latter description of his problem is precisely the one Hume gives.

Fogelin (1985) considers an earlier presentation of the present interpretation (Garrett, 1981). He does not dispute that the problem I have described is a serious one that *should* have concerned Hume. However, he offers two objections to the suggestion that it *did* concern Hume and caused his second thoughts. The first is that "no text is cited to show that Hume was even remotely worried about the ingenious problem . . . posed" (p. 104). To this, it may be replied that the proposed explanation fits everything that Hume does say about the cause of his dismay in the Appendix: (i) that it renders his former opinions inconsistent; (ii) that it is an inability to "explain the principles, that unite our successive perceptions in our thought or consciousness"; and (iii) that it would be resolved "if our perceptions either inhered in something simple or individual, or the mind perceived some real connexion among them" (such as a "real" causal connection between individual causes and effects themselves, so that we could reject Hume's analysis of causation, an analysis that is essential to the problem). With the exception of the common-sense view that two minds can have different but qualitatively identical perceptions at the same time—which Hume may be supposed to hold as a matter of course— all of the elements of Hume's theory that give rise to the problem I have described occur in the main body of the *Treatise*, including the account of causation and the doctrine that some perceptions are "no where." It is true that there is no anticipation of the problem itself in the main body of the *Treatise*, but the language of the Appendix suggests that whatever his problem is, it has arisen suddenly in Hume's mind. Although it has been provoked "upon more strict review" of the section on personal identity, he does not imply that it was in any significant way *anticipated* there. In fact, no plausible difficulty with Hume's account of personal identity can be said to be anticipated in the main body of the *Treatise*.

Fogelin's second objection is that the problem I have described does not seem to be something that Hume was likely to worry about: "Hume was uncritically wedded to the way of ideas. He thought that he had immediate access to his own ideas and he simply took it for granted that these ideas were *his*" (p. 104). It is certainly true that Hume thinks that he has immediate access to his own *present* ideas. But he finds it deeply problematic to determine why certain past ideas, to which "someone" had immediate access, count as "his," and, correlatively, he finds it problematic to determine what the "he," who has this immediate access, actually is and how this individual can be conceived in the imagination. In finding these matters problematic, it may be noted, he is following another practitioner of the way of ideas, John Locke, and if Hume and Locke had not found these matters so problematic, then they would not have written about personal identity as they did. Hume's project in *Treatise* I.iv.6 is precisely to investigate what relations produce associative connections among perceptions—the latter considered as logically independent, noninhering, and often unlocated entities—sufficient to make them count as the mind of one person. Hume himself says that his explanation will have to "take the matter pretty deep" (THN 253), and the problem I have described is just the sort of problem one does encounter in taking Hume's project "pretty deep." I conclude, therefore, that the present proposal can withstand the two objections just canvassed.

It is possible, of course, that Hume had more than one problem, or some other problem, or even no clear problem in mind when he wrote the Appendix. But I am convinced that the present explanation of his confession is to be preferred, because it alone meets both of the following conditions: (i) it accounts for each element of Hume's description of his problem, and (ii) it describes, at the same time, a problem that would and should have worried Hume if he had seen it. It is in fact, regardless of the actual cause of his second thoughts, the single most fundamental problem in his account of personal identity.

The Representation of Self

Hume's argument for his analysis of personal identity is grounded in his cognitive psychology. Although there have been many attempts to specify the problem that caused Hume's confession in the Appendix, only the interpretation proposed here describes a serious problem that need have caused Hume serious concern if he had recognized it. On this interpretation, Hume's problem is fundamentally a failure within his cognitive psychology: it is a failure to describe adequately our own representation of ourselves. For on Hume's original theory, we could not successfully represent to ourselves the existence of qualitatively identical but numerically distinct perceptions existing in the minds of different individuals at the same time.

The philosophical moral to be drawn from Hume's confession is thus not that he could not consistently dispense with an "active" or substantial self, or with a transcendental ego. Nor is it that there could not be personal identity without a personal physical body; that common suggestion, while it may be true, is more materialistic than Hume's own dilemma demands. Rather the moral is simply that if we are to conceive of two minds as having similar but distinct contents at the same time, they must somehow be given either a spatial location or some substitute for it that can serve the same purpose of individuation. Since Hume has already rejected the notion of a quasi-spatial spiritual location for minds,[9] he correctly sees inherence in mental substance and real necessary connections among perceptions as the only apparent ways out of his dilemma.

Reductive empiricists claim that a state of affairs S may be defined in terms of the holding of certain *evidence* for S (see chapter 1). Although Hume readily grants the possibility of unseen mechanisms behind our perceptions, he is a reductive empiricist about the self, defining the self as a bundle of perceptions related by causation and resemblance. He defends this definition, in part, by rejecting the intelligibility of the self construed as a subject or substratum in which perceptions inhere. As we have seen in chapter 5, he is also a reductive empiricist about causation, defining causation in terms of constant conjunction and in terms of inference. He defends these latter definitions, in part, by rejecting the intelligibility of the causal relation construed as a relation or relational property inherent in the cause and effect themselves. Having made these rejections, he cannot explain the concept of personal identity in a way that will distinguish the contents of one mind from those of another when those contents are similar and simultaneous. It seems that the representational resources of his cognitive psychology are ultimately inadequate to the self-referential task of explaining the representation of one's own mind as an entity potentially distinct from others.

Moral Evaluation

The eighteenth century's heightened interest in understanding human cognitive processes was by no means restricted to the role of cognitive processes in the development of natural philosophy and metaphysics. In the Introduction to the *Treatise*, Hume remarks that several "late philosophers in *England*" have "begun to put the science of man on a new footing, and have engaged the attention, and excited the curiosity of the public" (THN xvii). Of those he mentions by name— Locke, Shaftesbury, Hutcheson, and Butler—all but Locke devoted most of their attention to the role of human psychological faculties in morality. One central question concerned the role of the faculty of reason in morals.

Hume devotes the first section of Book III of the *Treatise* to establishing that "moral distinctions (are) not deriv'd from reason." His discussion of this thesis, however, seems to most readers to involve contradictory claims about the meaning and cognitive status of moral evaluations.[1] His own further remarks about moral evaluations, both in the remainder of the *Treatise* and in the *Enquiries*, have tended not to ameliorate but to exacerbate the appearance of inconsistency. In consequence, he seems to have given no clear theory of the nature or meaning of moral distinctions at all, leaving it obscure what he means by saying that reason does *not* discover such distinctions. Commentators have dealt with Hume's apparent inconsistency in various ways. Some writers have simply attributed one or another competing theory of the meaning of moral evaluations to him. In the face of this diversity, both Jonathan Harrison (1978) and J. L. Mackie (1980) argue that Hume's writings contain expressions or indications of a considerable number of competing and mutually incompatible theories. Stroud (1978), largely in order to avoid countenancing such a plurality of incompatible theories in Hume, urges that Hume has no theory of the meaning of moral evaluations. The topic of moral evaluation thus appears to be a classic instance for L. A. Selby-Bigge's well-known complaint about Hume:

> His pages, especially those of the *Treatise*, are so full of matter, he says so many different things in so many different ways and different connexions, and with so much indifference to what he has said before, that it is very hard to say positively that he taught, or did not teach, this or that particular doctrine. He . . . is often slovenly and indifferent

about his words and formulae. This makes it easy to find all philosophies in Hume, or, by setting up one statement against another, none at all. (Editor's Introduction to the *Enquiries*, EHU and EPM, p. vii)

In this chapter, I begin by explaining why commentators have found incompatible theories of the meaning of moral evaluations in Hume. I then outline and describe Hume's main argument for the conclusion that moral distinctions are not derived from reason. Next, I describe three aspects of Hume's cognitive psychology that provide the context needed to understand his theory of the meaning of moral evaluations, and I utilize this psychology to develop a Humean cognitive history of moral evaluations. Finally, I will use these results to resolve the seeming inconsistencies in his pronouncements about the meaning of moral evaluations, the origin of moral distinctions, and their relation to reason.

Nonpropositional and Propositional Theories

Nonpropositional Theories

Commentators have found a wide variety of incompatible theories of the meaning of moral evaluations in Hume. These theories can be easily divided into two groups, however, based on the answer they give to a single question. That question is whether moral evaluations do or do not affirm genuine propositions—that is, do they make assertions that are susceptible of truth or falsehood and that could therefore provide the objects of genuine beliefs? (I will use these terms—'genuine proposition', 'assertion that is susceptible of truth or falsehood', and 'object of genuine belief'—interchangeably.)

There are several reasons to think that Hume does not regard moral evaluations as affirming genuine propositions. First, his announced purpose in *Treatise* III.i.1 is to show that moral distinctions are not derived from reason. He begins by arguing:

Since morals, therefore, have an influence on the actions and affections, it follows, that they cannot be deriv'd from reason; and that because reason alone, as we have already prov'd, can never have any such influence. Morals excite passions, and produce or prevent actions. Reason of itself is utterly impotent in this particular. The rules of morality, therefore, are not conclusions of our reason. (THN 457)

Hume remarks only a page later, "Reason is the discovery of truth or falshood" (THN 458). If moral evaluations were true or false, therefore, it would seem that they could, at least sometimes, be discovered by reason—in apparent contradiction to what he has just claimed to have established. Thus, it seems that moral evaluations cannot be true or false, and that they are therefore not genuine propositions.

Second, according to Hume, "Truth or falsehood consists in an agreement either to the *real* relations of ideas, or to *real* existence and matter of fact" (THN 458). But after arguing that morality does not consist in a relation of ideas, he goes on to assert:

Nor does this reasoning only prove, that morality consists not in any relations, that are the objects of science; but if examin'd, will prove with equal certainty, that it consists not in any *matter of fact*, which can be discover'd by the understanding. . . . But can there be any difficulty in proving, that vice and virtue are not matters of fact, whose existence we can infer by reason? Take any action allow'd to be vicious: Wilful murder, for instance. Examine it in all lights, and see if you can find that matter of fact, or real existence, which you call *vice*. In which-ever way you take it, you find only certain passions, motives, volitions and thoughts. There is no other matter of fact in the case. The vice entirely escapes you, as long as you consider the object. (THN 468–469; for a related passage, see EPM §240)

Thus, Hume seems to claim that moral evaluations state neither relations of ideas nor matters of fact, and hence that they are not susceptible of either truth or falsehood.

Third, Hume concludes *Treatise* III.i.1 ("Moral distinctions not deriv'd from reason") with this now-famous passage:

In every system of morality, which I have hitherto met with, I have always remark'd, that the author proceeds for some time in the ordinary way of reasoning, and establishes the being of a God, or makes observations concerning human affairs; when of a sudden I am surpriz'd to find, that instead of the usual copulations of propositions, *is*, and *is not*, I meet with no proposition that is not connected with an *ought*, or an *ought not*. This change is imperceptible; but is, however, of the last consequence. For as this ought, or ought not, expresses some new relation or affirmation, 'tis necessary that it shou'd be observ'd and explain'd; and at the same time that a reason should be given, for what seems altogether inconceivable, how this new relation can be a deduction from others, which are entirely different from it. But as authors do not commonly use this precaution, I shall presume to recommend it to the readers; and am persuaded, that this small attention wou'd subvert all the vulgar systems of morality, and let us see, that the distinction of vice and virtue is not founded merely on the relations of objects, nor is perceiv'd by reason. (THN 469–470)

How strongly this passage supports nonpropositional interpretations of Hume is subject to dispute. For example, it uses the term 'proposition'—which Hume elsewhere applies only to assertions that are true or false—in application to moral evaluations, and he refers to *ought* propositions as "express[ing] some new relation or affirmation." Taken literally, moreover, the passage says only that it "seems" inconceivable how *ought* propositions could be inferred from *is* propositions, not that it really is inconceivable. However, most readers take these features of the passage to be ironic. And if Hume holds that *ought* propositions do *not* affirm genuine propositions, then it is easy to see why he should find them so "difficult" to infer from *is* propositions—for they could not properly be *inferred* at all. This "difficulty" would certainly subvert any "vulgar" system of morals that supposed that they could be.

Finally, the penultimate paragraph of Hume's first *Enquiry* states:

Morals and criticism are not so properly objects of the understanding as of taste and sentiment. Beauty, whether moral or natural, is felt, more properly than perceived. Or if we reason concerning it, and endeavor to fix its standard, we regard a new fact, to wit, the general taste of mankind, or some such fact, which may be the object of reasoning and enquiry. (EHU §131)

Once again, if moral evaluations are not genuine propositions, susceptible of truth and falsehood, then it is easy to see why morals should be a matter not of the understanding but of taste; if moral evaluations are either true or false, however, then it seems hard to see why morals should be a matter of taste rather than of the understanding.

These passages suggest several possible interpretations of Humean moral evaluations. Many commentators interpret Hume as an emotivist—that is, as holding that moral evaluations only *express* moral feelings or sentiments, without making any assertions.[2] However, Harrison and Mackie also suggest that Hume might have endorsed prescriptivism—that is, the view that so-called moral evaluations fundamentally express not propositions or feelings but imperatives. Similarly, Harrison suggests that Hume might treat evaluations as expressions of wishes. In addition, he suggests that Hume sometimes treats moral evaluations as *identical* with the having of moral sentiments, omitting any significant role for moral *utterances* as a kind of moral evaluation.[3]

Propositional Theories

There are, nevertheless, many passages in which Hume does seem to treat moral evaluations as genuine propositions. First, and perhaps most notoriously, the previously cited passage about willful murder continues as follows:

> You never can find it [i.e., the vice], till you turn your reflexion into your own breast, and find a sentiment of disapprobation, which arises in you, towards this action. Here is a matter of fact; but 'tis the object of feeling, not of reason. It lies in yourself, not in the object. So that when you pronounce any action or character to be vicious, you mean nothing, but that from the constitution of your nature you have a feeling or sentiment of blame from the contemplation of it. (THN 469)

To say that, from the constitution of one's nature, one has a feeling or sentiment of blame from the contemplation of an action or character, is certainly to affirm a definite matter of fact.

Second, in *Treatise* III.iii.1 ("Of the origin of the natural virtues and vices"), Hume describes various ways in which we "correct" our moral sentiments by reflection:

> We blame equally a bad action, which we read of in history, with one perform'd in our neighbourhood t'other day: The meaning of which is, that we know from reflexion, that the former action wou'd excite as strong sentiments of disapprobation as the latter, were it plac'd in the same position. (THN 584)

He thereby seems to imply that moral evaluations, at least sometimes, make assertions not about actual moral sentiments but about the moral sentiments that we *would* feel if we were more closely related to the agent than we actually are.

Third, when Hume returns in *Treatise* III.iii.3 ("Of goodness and benevolence") to the topic of the "correction" of moral sentiments, he writes of us as

> confin[ing] our view to that narrow circle, in which any person moves, in order to form a judgment of his moral character. . . . We are quickly obliged to forget our own interest in our judgments of this kind. . . . In like manner, tho' sympathy be much fainter than our concern for ourselves, and a sympathy with persons remote from us much fainter than that with persons near and contiguous: yet we neglect all these differences in our calm judgments concerning the characters of men. (THN 602–603)

But throughout Hume's writings, he uses 'judgment' to refer to the faculty that bestows assent on *propositions* or *assertions* (see, for example THN 96n)—that is, on items that are either true or false—and for the products of that faculty. It is in this spirit that he uses such phrases as "judgment or opinion" (THN 415) and "sound judgement of truth or falsehood" (EPM §134). In *Treatise* III.i.1 ("Moral distinctions not deriv'd from reason") itself, he refers to "any judgment, true or false" (THN 561).

Fourth, as noted in chapter 5, Hume seems to offer a definition of 'virtue' in Section IX of *An Enquiry concerning the Principles of Morals*:

> Personal Merit consists altogether in the possession of mental qualities, *useful* or *agreeable* to the *person himself* or to *others*. (EPM §217)

Shortly thereafter, he explicitly describes this characterization as a "delineation or definition" of "virtue or merit" (EPM §226). But if evaluating a person as virtuous is equivalent to ascribing the possession of useful or agreeable mental qualities to that person, then such an evaluation seems to state a matter of fact that is either true or false.

Fifth, a few pages later, he seems to offer a second definition of 'virtue':

> The hypothesis which we embrace is plain. It maintains that morality is determined by sentiment. It defines virtue to be *whatever mental action or quality gives to a spectator the pleasing sentiment of approbation.* . . . (EPM §239; see also EPM §211n)

But if evaluating persons as virtuous is equivalent to asserting that their mental actions or qualities give rise to approbation in a spectator, then such an evaluation seems to state a matter of fact that is either true or false.

Finally, *Treatise* III.i.2, which immediately follows the famous "is/ought" passage, ostensibly seeks to show that moral distinctions are "deriv'd from a moral sense." But attributing moral distinctions to a moral sense seems to imply that there really is some matter of fact whose presence we *sense* in making moral evaluations, and thus that a moral evaluation recognizes, reports, or affirms the presence of this matter of fact.

Accordingly, Hume's writings have also inspired several mutually incompatible propositional interpretations of Humean moral evaluations. For example, commentators have proposed that he seems to treat moral evaluations (i) as reports of one's own moral sentiments; or (ii) as assertions about what one's sentiments would be under certain circumstances; or (iii) as assertions about what the sentiments of humankind, or an ideal human, would be, under certain circumstances; or even (iv) as reports of special, irreducible moral qualities of a sort that could be detected by a special sense.[4]

"Moral Distinctions Not Deriv'd from Reason"

The Argument concerning Moral Distinctions Outlined

In *Treatise* III.i.1, Hume gives several arguments to show that moral distinctions are "not deriv'd from reason." (He gives a similar but expanded set of arguments in Appendix I to *An Enquiry concerning the Principles of Morals*, although there the tone is more respectful toward the limited role of reason—a role that was nonetheless also recognized in the *Treatise*.) Although he considers a number of objections and specific alternatives, there are three main lines of argument: (i) that reason is concerned with assessing truth or falsehood, and hence does not evaluate actions, which are the objects of moral evaluation; (ii) that reason alone cannot produce moral evaluations because the former is, while the latter are not, motivationally inert; and (iii) that morality cannot be discovered by either of the two kinds of reason, namely, demonstrative reasoning and reasoning concerning matter of fact ("probable reasoning"). These correspond to (1) through (5), (6) through (8), and (9) through (17) of the following outline:

1. Reason is the discovery of truth or falshood.
2. Truth or falshood consists in an agreement or disagreement either to the *real relations* of ideas, or to *real* existence and matter of fact.
3. Whatever . . . is not susceptible of this agreement or disagreement, is incapable of being true or false, and can never be an object of our reason. (from 1–2)
4. Our passions, volitions, and actions are not susceptible of any such agreement or disagreement.
5. 'Tis impossible [that our passions, volitions, and actions] can be pronounced either true or false, and be either contrary or conformable to reason. (3–4)
6. Our actions do not derive their merit from a conformity to reason, nor their blame from a contrariety to it. (from 5)
7. Reason can never immediately prevent or produce any action by contradicting or approving of it. (from 6)
8. Morals excite passions, and produce or prevent actions.
9. The operations of human understanding divide themselves into two kinds, the comparing of ideas, and the inferring of matters of fact.
10. If the thought and understanding were alone capable of fixing the boundaries of right and wrong, the character of virtuous and vicious either must lie in some relations of objects, or must be a matter of fact, which is discovered by our reasoning. (from 9)
11. Were virtue discover'd by the understanding; it must be an object of one of these operations, nor is there any third operation of the understanding, which can discover it. (from 10)
12. If you assert that vice and virtue consist in relations susceptible of certainty and demonstration, you must confine yourself to these four relations [resemblance, contrariety, degrees in quality, proportions in quantity or number], which alone admit of that degree of evidence.
13. There is no one of those relations [which alone admit of demonstration] but what is applicable, not only to an irrational, but also to an inanimate object.
14. If . . . vice and virtue consist in relations susceptible of certainty and demonstration . . . it follows, that even such [irrational and inanimate] objects must be susceptible of merit or demerit. (from 12–13)
15. [It is absurd that irrational or inanimate] objects must be susceptible of merit or demerit.
16. Morality lies not in any of these [four demonstrable relations], nor the sense of it in their discovery. (from 14–15)
17. Morality . . . consists not in any matter of fact, which can be discover'd by the understanding.
18. Moral distinctions are not derived from reason. (from 5, 7–8, 11, and 16–17)

Hume expresses this final conclusion in a variety of other ways as well:

Moral distinctions are not the offspring of reason. (THN 458)

'Tis impossible, that the distinction betwixt moral good and evil, can be made by reason. (THN 462)

Morality is not an object of reason. (THN 468)

The distinction of vice and virtue is not founded merely on the relations of objects, nor is perceiv'd by reason. (THN 470)

Vice and virtue are not discoverable merely by reason, or the comparison of ideas. (THN 470)

Reason and Morality

Two important points may be noted from careful attention to Hume's argument and to the ways in which he expresses his conclusion. First, when Hume denies that moral distinctions are derived from reason, he does not use the term 'reason' in a vague or merely honorific sense. Rather, he uses it as a technical term in his cognitive psychology. It is, here as elsewhere throughout his writings, the term that specifically designates the faculty of making inferences. He is not, therefore, asking whether moral distinctions are warranted or justifiable; instead, he is asking whether their occurrence can be explained as a *product of inference operating on representations of the objects of evaluation,* or whether we must instead recognize the occurrence of some specifically moral *non*inferential element. It is for this reason that he thinks he can treat the question of whether moral distinctions are derived from reason as interchangeable with the question of whether we make such distinctions "by means of our impressions or our ideas" (THN 456). Given his Copy Principle—that ideas must be copied from impressions—he thinks that such a noninferential element would require the existence of distinctively moral impressions.[5]

Second, Hume's arguments are directed toward answering the general question of whether the *origin* of the capacity to make moral distinctions depends only on *reason* or on something else (such as distinctively moral impressions). He is not addressing the more particular question of whether or not someone who already has this capacity, based partly on his or her noninferential endowments, could ever infer the correctness of a moral evaluation.

Three Aspects of Hume's Cognitive Psychology

The Correction of Sentiments

In order to reconcile the seeming contradictions in Hume's account of moral evaluations, we must combine three different elements of Hume's cognitive psychology: (i) his theory of the correction of sentiments (especially moral sentiments); (ii) his theory of the development of abstract ideas; and (iii) his theory of the nature of definitions.[6] The first of these three topics must be explored in some detail; the second and third have been considered in previous chapters and need only be summarized.

Hume argues in *Treatise* III.i.2 ("Moral distinctions deriv'd from a moral sense") that moral distinctions depend on moral sentiments. These sentiments consist of a particular species of pleasure (moral approbation) and a particular species of pain (moral disapprobation or blame). We find the moral sentiments to arise when we consider the mental characteristics of persons—that is, features of their characters—and, derivatively, the actions that manifest them. Thus:

> To have the sense of virtue, is nothing but to *feel* a satisfaction of a particular kind from the contemplation of a character. The very *feeling* constitutes our praise or admiration.
> . . . We do not infer a character to be virtuous, because it pleases: But in feeling that it pleases after such a particular manner, we in effect feel that it is virtuous. (THN 471)

In *Treatise* III.iii.1 ("Of the origin of the natural virtues and vices"), however, and again in *Treatise* III.iii.2 ("Of goodness and benevolence"), Hume describes several ways in which we come, as he says, to "correct" these moral sentiments. These corrections are of at least three different kinds. They result from the conjunction of a number of distinctive features of human nature with a number of distinctive features of the human situation.

First, Hume emphasizes that we often feel "sentiments of blame" toward others when we find that others stand in opposition to our own self-interest (THN 583), so that "it seldom happens, that we do not think an enemy vicious" (THN 472). However, such feelings of blame tend to decrease or disappear when we reflect that "a certain degree of selfishness" is "inseparable from human nature." Furthermore:

> We are quickly oblig'd to forget our own interest in our judgments of this kind, by reason of the perpetual contradictions, we meet with in society and conversation, from persons that are not plac'd in the same situation, and have not the same interest with ourselves. (THN 602)

Second, "all sentiments of blame and praise are variable, according to our situation of nearness or remoteness, with regard to the person blam'd or praised" (THN 582). This is because the moral sentiments are the results of sympathizing with persons who are or would be affected by the person whose character we evaluate—and we sympathize more strongly with those who are near to us than with those who are remote.[7] But this variability produces considerable disparity, both among the moral sentiments of *different* persons who happen to be differently situated and among the moral sentiments of the *same* person at different times. Thus, Hume writes:

> Besides, that we ourselves often change our situation in this particular, we every day meet with persons, who are in a different situation from ourselves, and who cou'd never converse with us on any reasonable terms, were we to remain constantly in that situation and point of view, which is peculiar to us. The intercourse of sentiments, therefore, in society and conversation, makes us form some general inalterable standard, by which we may approve or disapprove of characters and manners. (THN 603)

This standard involves our taking on, in our thoughts, a "*steady* and *general* point of view" that aims at sympathy with all those who are or would be most immediately affected by the person being evaluated, regardless of their relations to ourselves.[8]

Third, our moral sentiments—toward different persons of similar character, or the same person with unchanged character at different times—can also vary with variations in persons' fortunes. Thus, when a person is found in circumstances where his or her good character is "attended with good fortune, which renders it really beneficial to society," we find that "it gives a stronger pleasure to the spectator, and is attended with a more lively sympathy" (THN 585). This variation tends to diminish or disappear, however, when we reflect that "an alteration of fortune [for example, imprisonment] may [very easily] render the benevolent disposition entirely impotent," while preserving the character intact.

Three points must be emphasized about these corrections of sentiment in Hume. First, correction of this general kind is not unique to the case of moral sentiments. Hume emphasizes that corrections of moral sentiments are similar to the corrections we make with regard to the senses and with respect to beauty. Thus, he writes:

> The case is here the same as in our judgments concerning external bodies. All objects seem to diminish by the distance; But tho' the appearance of objects to our senses be the original standard, by which we judge of them, yet we do not say, that they actually diminish by the distance; but correcting the appearance by reflexion, arrive at a more constant and establish'd judgment concerning them. In like manner, tho' sympathy be much fainter than our concern for ourselves, and a sympathy with persons remote from us much fainter than that with persons near and contiguous; yet we neglect all these differences in our calm judgments concerning the characters of men. (THN 603)

> In like manner, external beauty is determin'd merely by pleasure; and 'tis evident, a beautiful countenance cannot give so much pleasure, when seen at the distance of twenty paces, as when it is brought nearer us. We say not, however, that it appears to us less beautiful: Because we know what effect it will have in such a position, and by that reflexion we correct its momentary appearance. (THN 582)

Second, corrections of moral sentiments (particularly those of the first two kinds, involving self-interest and situation) are essential for the use of moral language. Thus, Hume writes, "indeed 'twere impossible we cou'd ever make use of language, or communicate our sentiments to one another, did we not correct the momentary appearances of things, and overlook our present situation" (THN 582).

Finally, the corrections we make are more efficacious with regard to our language than with regard to our sentiments themselves. Hume makes this point repeatedly, writing, for example:

> The passions do not always follow our corrections; but these corrections serve sufficiently to regulate our abstract notions, and are alone regarded, when we pronounce in general concerning the degrees of vice and virtue. (THN 585; see also THN 582 and THN 603)

Abstract Ideas and Definitions

The correction of moral sentiments thus brings us to the topic of language. Language must use at least some general terms, and of course for Hume, general terms have meaning by signifying abstract ideas. As we have had several occasions to observe, Hume rejects Locke's well-known theory of abstract ideas in favor of the theory that "all general ideas are nothing but particular ones, *annexed to a certain term*, which gives them a more extensive signification" (THN 17). Upon noticing a resemblance among objects, Hume holds, we apply a single term to them all, notwithstanding their differences. The term is directly associated with the determinate idea of a particular instance. This determinate idea nevertheless achieves a general signification—and hence serves *as* an abstract idea—because the term also revives the "custom" or disposition to call up ideas of other particular instances.

As we have also seen (in chapter 5), Hume's rejection and replacement of Locke's theory of abstract ideas demands a corresponding change in the theory of definition. Specifically, he must reject the Lockean doctrine that *only* terms standing for simple ideas are indefinable. This is because, in order to define a term standing for an abstract idea, it will clearly not be enough to produce in another person's mind the particular complex idea that is *serving as the abstract idea* by naming all of *that* idea's simpler parts. If a definition of a term standing for an abstract idea is to satisfy Hume's own requirement for a successful definition, it must somehow convey to other persons the ability to call up any member of an appropriate *set of ideas of particular instances*, so that the "custom" of doing so can be "revived" by later occurrences of the term defined. This ability to call up any member of the revival set of a term can be conveyed only by characterizing what all of the instances or their ideas have in common.[9]

A Cognitive History of Moral Evaluation

Moral Feelings

By seeing Hume's remarks about moral evaluation in the light of his theories of sentiment correction, abstraction, and definition, we can distinguish three distinct processes in the development of moral distinctions and at least two kinds of moral evaluations.

Hume insists that to *feel* a moral sentiment is itself a moral evaluation and the making of a moral distinction (e.g., at THN 471). Making such moral distinctions and evaluations does not depend on the possession of language—at least, not on the possession of moral language.[10] In order to feel moral sentiments, and hence to make moral evaluations in this sense, it is not necessary to command any such terms as 'virtue', 'vice', or 'ought'. These moral sentiments are what Hume calls "impressions of reflexion" (THN 7–8; see the beginning of chapter 1). Because they are impressions rather than ideas, they cannot literally be moral *beliefs*, and they cannot be products of reason. Instead, having moral sentiments is *feeling* approval or disapproval for a feature of character, just as one feels heat from a fire, or aesthetic appreciation for a sunset.

When persons feel heat from a fire, of course, they typically include the *idea* of heat—copied from the impression of heat—in their complex idea of fire (THN 15–17). Hume remarks that moral taste "has a productive faculty, and gilding or staining all natural objects with the colours, borrowed from internal sentiment, raises in a manner a new creation" (EPM §246). So it might be supposed that we have, on Hume's view, at least some tendency to incorporate an idea copied from our moral sentiments into our idea of the persons and/or features of character that we evaluate. To do so would, of course, risk treating the moral sentiments as impressions of sensation rather than as what they really are—namely, impressions of reflection. Even if we do incorporate, or "project," a copy of the moral sentiment into our idea of a person or of a person's character, however, the moral evaluation itself, in this sense—as the feeling of approbation or disapprobation—consists in having the impression and not in having the idea.[11]

Moral Judgments

Since all of our moral terms are general terms, it follows for Hume that they stand for abstract ideas. On his theory, we begin to form abstract ideas when we effectively notice that a number of things are resembling. Now, it is certainly very likely that the various personal characteristics that produce immediate moral approbation (or, in the opposite case, disapprobation) in us will naturally tend to strike us as resembling, and that we will accordingly seek a way of referring to them all. This will be particularly likely, of course, if we have incorporated a copy of that sentiment into our complex idea of the person, but it will still be likely even if we have not treated the moral sentiment in that way. At the outset, we will no doubt seek to use these newly coined general terms—for example, 'virtue', 'vice', 'ought'—to cover just those mental characteristics or actions of particular persons that actually do produce moral approbation or (in the opposite case) disapprobation in us, and we will form abstract ideas of more specific degrees of "virtue" and "vice" in accordance with the degrees of moral approbation that we feel.

As his account of the correction of sentiments has already shown us, however, Hume thinks that such an attempt will be subjected to two related kinds of pressure. First, we will find that we often cannot get other people to use these terms in application to the same set of instances—the same *revival set*—for which we use it. Second, we will find that we often cannot even get ourselves to use these terms in application to the same set of instances at different times. In response to these pressures, the revival sets associated in our minds with such terms as 'virtue' and 'vice' (and terms for various degrees of these) tend naturally to undergo the various alterations already described—migration toward what *would be* approved from a steady and general point of view, the neglect of *actual* consequences for *typical* ones—which allow us to achieve a degree of stability in the use of these terms. To some extent, we even find that, as we imaginatively alter our situation and our focus, our moral *feelings* change to correspond with the *judgments* that we make with these abstract ideas. Thus, Hume's choice of the term 'abstract' is quite intentional when he remarks, "The passions do not always follow our corrections; but these corrections serve sufficiently to regulate our abstract notions" (THN 585).

Once we have functioning abstract ideas of vice, virtue, and their various degrees and species, we can formulate propositional judgments or beliefs to the effect that a particular person *is virtuous*, or that a particular mental characteristic *is especially vicious*, or that an action *ought to be done*. Such judgments need not differ in fundamental cognitive structure from nonmoral judgments ascribing general characteristics—for example, judgments that an object is "square" or "dangerous." These moral judgments constitute a second kind of moral evaluation in addition to moral feelings, and they may, of course, occur either with or without a corresponding moral feeling. Although such judgments are propositional in character, they are nevertheless dependent on the existence of moral feelings in two ways. First, the most common way of making such a judgment involves, as a preliminary, imaginatively taking up a steady and general point of view, so as to have moral feelings as a result of the sympathetic reactions that are elicited. Second, and even more fundamentally, no person could have the necessary abstract moral ideas in the first place unless that person had previously had moral sentiments from which such abstract ideas could be developed. Moreover, it is moral feelings, not the moral judgments that result from them, that are directly and independently motivating.

Applications of Moral Definitions

After we have developed abstract moral ideas, such as those of virtue, vice, and their various degrees, and thereby come to use general moral terms and to make moral judgments, philosophers might begin to wonder whether these moral terms are definable or not. There must, of course, be *something*—however attenuated, dispositional, or disjunctive it may be—that the members of even the "corrected" revival set of the abstract idea of virtue (or of vice) have in common; otherwise, our ability to use the corresponding general terms would simply be causally inexplicable. But, as we have seen, this alone does not guarantee that terms for abstract ideas such as 'virtue' and 'vice' will be *definable*, by Hume's lights. The best way to determine whether a term for a complex abstract idea is definable or not is simply to try to define it. An adequate Humean definition of 'virtue' or 'vice', it will be recalled, would be one that conveys, in terms that are not themselves mere synonyms for 'virtue' or 'vice', what all members of the appropriate revival sets have in common.

As we have already observed (in chapter 5), Hume's second *Enquiry* identifies two such definitions of 'virtue'.[12] The first defines 'virtue' as "mental qualities, *useful* or *agreeable* to the *person himself* or to *others*" (EPM §217), while the second defines 'virtue' as "*whatever mental action or quality gives to a spectator the pleasing sentiment of approbation*" (EPM §239). Both of these definitions fulfill the conditions for a satisfactory definition of the general term 'virtue', since both capture something that all and only members of the appropriate revival set have in common.[13] Once these definitions have been suggested, of course, it is simple enough to perform the further act of judging:

> Mother Teresa has mental characteristics that are useful and/or agreeable to herself and/or others.

or the act of judging:

> Mother Teresa has characteristics that produce the pleasing sentiment of moral approbation in an observer.

Furthermore, if one is convinced that one or both of Hume's two definitions of *the term* 'virtue' are correct, then one could also infer:

The term 'virtue' correctly describes Mother Teresa.

In other words, one could infer the quasi-lexicographic proposition:

Mother Teresa can truly be called "virtuous."

All of the judgments just described would, however, be mental acts of judgment different, for Hume, from the distinctively *moral judgment* that "Mother Teresa is virtuous," in the sense of 'moral judgment' we have elaborated. For in making a *standard* moral judgment that someone's character is virtuous, we do not employ the concepts (i.e., abstract ideas) of "agreeableness," "utility," "approbation," "powers to produce," or "observer." We simply place that person's character among the revival set of our abstract idea of 'virtue', a revival set that we acquired not through mastering any specified list of *criteria* but through the conversational and reflective honing and adaptation of the abstract idea of virtue that was originally derived from our moral sentiments. Although a *moral judgment* (properly so-called) and an *application of a moral definition* may place the same object under the same predicate, they will do so in cognitively different ways. Only those who have *felt* moral sentiments and have developed abstract ideas of virtue and vice from them could make *moral judgments*, as we have used that term, whereas anyone who understood the terms in which the definitions were couched could make applications of moral definitions, even if they themselves possessed no moral sense. Applications of moral definitions ascribe nonmoral qualities to persons and/or describe the correct usage of moral terms. They are not, in that sense, a kind of moral *evaluation* at all.

Inconsistencies Resolved

Evidence for Nonpropositional Interpretations

With an understanding of (i) Hume's argument that moral distinctions are not derived from reason and (ii) his cognitive history of moral evaluations, we can now offer a coherent interpretation of Hume and reconcile the apparent contradictions in his remarks cited at the outset of this chapter. On the interpretation I propose, Hume recognizes both nonpropositional moral evaluations (moral feelings) and propositional moral evaluations (moral judgments) as distinct psychological events. Moral judgments are, however, dependent and even parasitic on moral feelings in two different ways. This dependence justifies Hume's claim that moral distinctions are not derived from reason. Let us now apply this interpretation to the puzzling passages with which we began.

Of the four passages cited as evidence that Hume holds a nonpropositional theory of the meaning of moral evaluations, all but the last occur in *Treatise* III.i.1. The first passage introduces Hume's argument that reason alone cannot discover or produce moral distinctions—on the grounds that reason by itself only produces ideas that are themselves motivationally inert, whereas moral distinctions are independently motivating. On my interpretation, moral judgments are propositional, and hence can sometimes be inferred by reason. For example, one might infer from the testimony of the *New York Times* that Mother Teresa is virtuous. But the possibility of arriving at such a conclusion by probable reasoning concerning the reliability of the *New York Times* does not show that morality itself can be derived solely from reason, as Hume understands that claim. For in order to be able to make this judgment about Mother Teresa, one must oneself have had many moral feelings so as to develop the abstract idea of "virtue" (and, in addition, one must also be supposing that others have or would have such feelings about Mother Teresa).

At several places Hume compares the perception of morality to the perception of sensory characteristics, and the analogy is particularly apt here. Just as he claims that moral distinctions are not derived from reason, so too it is easy to imagine him remarking that *color* distinctions, or *shape* distinctions are not "derived from reason" either. By this he would mean, of course, that abilities to make color and shape discriminations are not a matter simply of making *inferences* from information about other features of objects. Rather, they are abilities that depend on our capacity to have colored or spatial *impressions*. He would not mean this to imply that we, who do possess the relevant senses, could never *infer* that a box was red or square—say, as the result of someone else's testimony that it was. He would mean, rather, that the capacity to make and understand such distinctions depends on and is derived from the ability to have specific kinds of *impressions*.

In the second nonpropositional passage cited previously, Hume claims that reason alone cannot find the viciousness of an act of willful murder in a consideration of the murder itself. This remark is compatible with the present interpretation. On this interpretation, Hume is arguing that moral distinctions cannot be discovered by the *inferential faculty operating on representations* of the object of evaluation itself, but instead require a distinctively moral internal impression. Hume does not claim that the viciousness of the act does not consist in *any* matter of fact, but rather that it "consists not in any *matter of fact*, which can be discover'd by the understanding"[14] and that it is not a matter of fact "in the case," so that "the vice escapes you as long as you consider the object" (THN 468). His point is that the mere operation of *reason* on representations of the object cannot by itself discover that willful murders are vicious until *after* humankind has felt moral sentiments in response to them. This is why Hume continues the passage: "You never can find it [i.e., the vice], till you turn your reflexion into your own breast, and find a sentiment of disapprobation, which arises in you, towards this action. Here is a matter of fact; but 'tis the object of feeling, not reason."

The third passage offered in defense of nonpropositional interpretations of Hume is the famous passage in which Hume says that it "seems inconceivable" how *ought* propositions can be "deductions from" (i.e., inferred from)[15] *is* propositions. If by *ought* propositions he were to mean only moral *feelings*, then of course his remark could be interpreted ironically, since as moral sentiments they cannot be inferred at all, but only felt. If, as is more likely, he means *ought* propositions to include what I have called moral judgments, then the possibility of inferring particular *ought* propositions from *is* propositions must remain open. But although the literal caution of the passage is widely interpreted as ironic understatement, there is no compelling reason why it must be so interpreted. On the contrary, since Hume has not yet provided his own account of moral judgments, a tone of caution is just what the case calls for.[16] There is, in the end, a manner in which moral judgments can sometimes be inferred from other judgments, as in the case of Mother Teresa and the *New York Times*. However, since these judgments arise from moral *senti-ments* through a complicated process of correction that Hume takes himself to be the first to explain adequately, he can still express confidence that attention to the question of *how* such inferences are possible would "subvert all the vulgar systems of morality"—none of which contain any such account.

The final nonpropositional passage comes from the end of the first *Enquiry*, where Hume asserts that morals are not so properly an object of the understanding as they are of taste. But this, too, is perfectly compatible with the view I have attrib-uted to Hume—namely, that the first moral evaluations are moral feelings or senti-ments, and that even moral judgments depend on and are regulated by moral senti-ments that are not produced by reason or the understanding.[17] Hume himself confirms that he does not mean to rule out moral judgment when he completes the passage by adding: "Or if we reason concerning it [i.e., moral or natural beauty], and endeavor to fix its standard, we regard a new fact, to wit, the general taste of mankind, or some such fact, which may be the object of reasoning and enquiry" (EHU §165).

Evidence for Propositional Interpretations

The passages seeming to favor nonpropositional interpretations can thus be recon-ciled with the interpretation I propose. What of the propositional passages on the other side, many of which seem incompatible not only with the nonpropositional passages but also with one another? The first two passages cited previously are pas-sages in which Hume uses the term 'mean' or 'meaning'. In the first, he asserts that "when you pronounce any action or character to be vicious, you mean nothing, but that from the constitution of your nature you have a feeling or sentiment of blame from the contemplation of it." In the second, he adds, in reference to our equal blame for bad actions in history and bad actions in our own neighborhood, "the meaning of which is, that we know from reflexion, that the former action wou'd excite as strong sentiments of disapprobation as the latter, were it plac'd in the same position."

As literal analyses of meaning, these are incompatible, and neither is at all plau-sible. The first would make moral evaluations express *causal* claims about the rela-tions among a character, a sentiment, and one's own nature. The second would make them express claims *about* our own possession of reflective knowledge of counterfactuals. But it would be highly anachronistic to take either or both of these as attempts to provide expressions that are logically equivalent to moral utterances. Hume uses 'mean' 'or 'meaning' when referring to the relation between words and ideas, but this is only an example of a much more general conception of "significa-tion." It is in this broader sense that Hume recommends, for example, that we "ask the sceptic, 'What his meaning is?'" (EHU §128; for other examples, see THN 25 and THN 623). In the passages in question, Hume is telling us only what we *signify*, or *show*, about ourselves when we make moral utterances; he is not offering logically equivalent analyses of those utterances.

The third passage cited previously concerns Hume's use of the term 'judgment' in application to moral evaluations in which our sentiments have been corrected. I have already argued that an understanding of his theories of the correction of sentiments and of abstraction shows how such judgments are possible as genuine objects of belief. Their occurrence is not incompatible with, but is rather dependent on, prior moral evaluations that are feelings rather than beliefs or judgments.

The final two passages cited in defense of propositional interpretations of Hume are his two definitions of 'virtue'. His theory of definition, as applied to abstract ideas, shows why these definitions are both adequate by Hume's lights—each adequately conveys the revival set of the general term 'virtue'. As I have argued, however, the statement that a given person is *virtuous* does not, for Hume, express the same judgment, or the same *cognitive act*, as the statement that the person has useful and agreeable mental qualities, or as the statement that the person produces the sentiment of approbation in an observer. The Humean adequacy of these definitions does not, therefore, entail that we can use them to show that moral judgments are really judgments about *nonmoral* qualities. Humean moral judgments are uniquely and distinctively about moral qualities. What we believe when we believe that Mother Teresa is virtuous is not that she is useful or that she produces moral approbation; her usefulness and ability to produce moral approbation are only the causes of our belief. *What* we believe can only be expressed by saying that she is *virtuous*.

Thus, we can now see why Hume claims not only that moral distinctions are *not* derived from reason but that they *are* derived from a moral sense. We begin with moral feelings of approbation or disapprobation, collect together the objects that produce them, and then hone the resulting abstract ideas through conversational and reflective pressures. In doing so, we come to create a revival set of ideas of persons or characters that all have something in common. This something in common is, of course, their virtue or their vice, respectively. In this way, we find that our mere moral *sentiments* become a genuine moral *sense*—as Hume says, "raising in a manner, a new creation."

Another Reconciling Project

If the interpretation developed here is correct, then much of the commentary on Hume's metaethics has been misguided. Hume's doctrine that moral distinctions are "not deriv'd from reason" is no more a claim about the illegitimacy of its subject than is his parallel claim that inference from past experience is "not determin'd by reason." Both are claims within cognitive psychology, concerning the role of the inferential faculty. Hume's two definitions of 'virtue', like his two definitions of 'cause', are each adequate by the standards of his own theory of definition. He is not committed by them or by his other pronouncements to any of the implausible logical analyses of moral statements that have been ascribed to him on the basis of his remarks about the "meaning" of moral utterances. He does, however, regard moral judgments—though not moral feelings—as propositional. A claim that color or shape distinctions are derived from sensation rather than reason would not be incompatible with the propositional character of color and size judgments, and in a similar way, his claim that moral distinctions are derived from sentiment rather than reason is not incompatible with the propositional character of moral judgments. When we understand Hume's theories of sentiment correction, abstraction, and definition, we are in a position to see how he thinks we begin with moral sentiments and, by a self-adjusting social linguistic process, construct moral ideas and beliefs that apply them.

In claiming that morality is not derived from reason, Hume is not denying that reason plays a significant role in morality. In the second *Enquiry*, his tone regarding the reason/sentiment debate in morals becomes markedly more conciliatory than it was in the *Treatise*, in a way that is very reminiscent of his change in tone regarding "liberty and necessity" from the *Treatise* to the first *Enquiry*. As in the case of the liberty/necessity debate, however, it is only Hume's rhetorical tactics, and not his underlying doctrine, that changes. In both the *Treatise* and the second *Enquiry*, he allows a role to reason in discovering features of character in others, in assessing the typical consequences of various features of character on the possessor and others, and in "correcting" the moral sentiments that result from sympathy with others. But in neither work does he waver in his doctrine that moral distinctions cannot be made or grasped without the capacity to feel the impressions of reflection that are the moral sentiments—just as causal necessity could not be fully grasped without the capacity to feel the impressions of reflection that are the impressions of necessary connection.

In making moral distinctions dependent on human psychology, Hume is quite intentionally propounding a doctrine that calls into question the reasonableness of supposing that a deity would be concerned with right and wrong, and hence also of supposing that a deity is morally admirable. The doctrine thus provides another one of the ways in which he uses the science of man to undermine the forces of religious "superstition." But this does not mean that Hume intends his doctrine to undermine the seriousness of our own commitment to morality. On the contrary, he believes that confronting and understanding the mechanism of moral evaluation within our own psychology will, in the long run, serve to improve and strengthen our moral commitments.

It will improve our moral commitments, he thinks, because we will more easily recognize the "irregular" and unstable influences on our moral assessments that we must reflectively come to disapprove, just as we come reflectively to disapprove of the various mechanisms of "unphilosophical probability" (see chapter 7). Thus, in the second *Enquiry*'s analogue to the rejection of belief in testimony to the miraculous, Hume rejects what he calls the "monkish virtues":

> And as every quality which is useful or agreeable to ourselves or others is, in common life, allowed to be a part of personal merit; so no other will ever be received, where men judge of things by their natural, unprejudiced reason, without the delusive glosses of superstition and false religion. Celibacy, fasting, penance, mortification, self-denial, humility, silence, solitude, and the whole train of monkish virtues; for what reason are

they everywhere rejected by men of sense, but because they serve to no manner of purpose; neither advance a man's fortune in the world, nor render him a more valuable member of society: neither qualify him for the entertainment of company, nor increase his power of self-enjoyment? We observe, on the contrary, that they cross all these desirable ends; stupify the understanding and harden the heart, obscure the fancy and sour the temper. We justly, therefore, transfer them to the opposite column, and place them in the catalogue of vices; nor has any superstition force sufficient among men of the world, to pervert entirely these natural sentiments. A gloomy, hair-brained enthusiast, after his death, may have a place in the calendar; but will scarcely ever be admitted, when alive, into intimacy and society, except by those who are as delirious and dismal as himself. (EPM §219)

Understanding the mechanism of moral evaluation within our own psychology will ultimately strengthen our commitment to morality as well, since it will lead us to see that the mechanism itself is one of which we, as human beings, can and must approve:

> All lovers of virtue (and such we all are in speculation, however we may degenerate in practice) must certainly be pleas'd to see moral distinctions deriv'd from so noble a source, which gives us a just notion both of the *generosity* and *capacity* of our nature. It requires but very little knowledge of human affairs to perceive, that a sense of morals is a principle inherent in the soul, and one of the most powerful that enters into the composition. But this sense must certainly acquire new force, when reflecting on itself, it approves of those principles, from whence it is deriv'd, and finds nothing but what is great and good in its rise and origin. Those who resolve the sense of morals into original instincts of the human mind, may defend the cause of virtue with sufficient authority; but want the advantage, which those possess, who account for that sense by an extensive sympathy with mankind. According to the latter system, not only virtue must be approv'd of, but also the sense of virtue: And not only that sense, but also the principles, from whence it is deriv'd. So that nothing is presented on any side, but what is laudable and good. (THN 619)

Since the possession of a moral sense is itself a feature of character whose possession is useful and agreeable to its possessor and others, we must approve and value its possession and cultivation in ourselves, as well as in others. Furthermore, far from undervaluing the sense of morals in comparison with scientific reasoning, Hume recognizes that it is only because of our possession of such a sense that we recognize wisdom as a virtue, and so come to approve of scientific reasoning at all. Examination of the fundamental mechanisms of our commitments need not undermine, but instead can improve, the quality and strength of those commitments.

Skepticism and Commitment

While the Scientific Revolution offered new answers to some questions, it also raised new questions and reinstated old ones, questions concerning both the structure of the universe, on the one hand, and the powers of the human cognitive instrument, on the other. As the authority of Aristotelian explanations decayed and the writings of ancient skeptics became better known, European philosophy became increasingly interested in the uses of skepticism and the status of skeptical arguments. Descartes used such arguments strategically, to motivate his own epistemological innovations and to certify their superiority. Some philosophers arrayed skeptical arguments against religion, while others used them fideistically, to defend religion against the encroachments of science. David Hume stands among the post-Cartesian philosophers most concerned with the uses and status of skepticism.

In previous chapters, we have examined some of the ways in which Hume uses reflective reasoning about human cognitive processes to improve the operations of those processes and to enhance commitment to their refined results. Some of these reflexive applications of reasoning to itself are constructive, such as his development of the "Rules by which to judge of causes and effects" (THN I.iii.15). Others are proscriptive, such as his rejection of the four species of "unphilosophical probability" (THN I.iii.13); his rejection of the belief-strengthening influences of resemblance, contiguity, and repetition (THN I.iii.9); and his rejection of the irregular influences on belief that lead to the acceptance of miracles (EHU X.ii). Such constructive and proscriptive applications of reason to itself are each thoroughly in keeping with his aim, stated in the Introduction to the *Treatise*, of proposing "a compleat system of the sciences, built on a foundation almost entirely new, and the only one upon which they can stand with any security" (THN xvi).

In *Treatise* I.iv ("Of the sceptical and other systems of philosophy"), however, Hume considers a number of skeptical arguments that seem, when taken together, entirely destructive of any "system of the sciences." He reports, "[W]hen we trace up the human understanding to its first principles, we find it to lead us into such sentiments, as seem to turn into ridicule all our past pains and industry, and to discourage us from future enquiries" (THN 266). Upon viewing what he calls the "manifold contradictions and imperfections in human reason," he pronounces himself "ready to reject all belief and reasoning," and writes that he "can look upon no opinion even as more probable or likely than another" (THN 268–269). He closes Book I of the *Treatise* by identifying himself as a "sceptic"—a self-characterization that he reinforces in his *Abstract* of the *Treatise*, where he asserts of the *Treatise* that "the philosophy contain'd in this book is very sceptical" (ATHN 657). In the final section of the first *Enquiry*, he again considers a variety of skeptical arguments and recommends in the final part of that section a "*mitigated* scepticism." The conception of Humean reason as improving, purifying, and strengthening itself by reflective self-application is thus called into grave question by his use and apparent endorsement of destructive skeptical arguments concerning the capacities and operations of the human understanding.

Can Hume's positive "system of the sciences" properly withstand his own skeptical arguments and conclusions? This is perhaps the most fundamental question in the interpretation of his entire philosophy. Generations of his readers have concluded that there is indeed a fundamental incompatibility between his claim to develop a "science of man," on the one hand, and his treatment of skeptical arguments, on the other. John Passmore (1952) expresses this judgment clearly: "In the *Treatise*, the scepticism which Hume learnt from Bayle simply overlays the positivist-associationist structure of his original argument; in consequence, Hume lapses into inconsistencies of the most startling character" (p. 133). He concludes: "[Hume's] scepticism constantly moved beyond its subordinate role, threatening the security of the social sciences, undermining common sense as well as metaphysics. . . . Hume could not succeed in the impossible—a science founded on scepticism no degree of ingenuity can successfully construct" (p. 151). More recently, Antony Flew (1986) has expressed the same view: "[T]he reports of the findings of Hume's scientific enterprise are somewhat awkwardly bound up together with [skeptical] discussions of a very different kind. It is difficult—indeed impossible—to reconcile these with claims to possess any sort of scientific knowledge" (p. 109). As Passmore observes, the common conclusion that Hume's treatment of skeptical arguments is incompatible with his positive scientific program has led many readers to study his philosophical writings solely for the brilliance of their individual parts, and to abandon the project of understanding them as a systematic whole.

Even the individual parts in which Hume's skeptical arguments are expressed contain their own measure of paradox, however. For example, he concludes in *Treatise* I.iv.1 that "all the rules of logic require a total diminution, and at last a total extinction of belief and evidence," yet he writes a paragraph later that the question of whether he sincerely assents to the argument for this conclusion "is entirely superfluous, and that neither I, nor any other person was ever sincerely and constantly of that opinion" (THN 183). Again, in *Treatise* I.iv.2, he begins his investigation of belief in the "continu'd and distinct existence" of external objects by claiming that the truth of that belief is "a point, which we must take for granted in all our reasonings" (THN 187). Yet he concludes that investigation by writing that he cannot "conceive how such trivial qualities of the fancy, conducted by such false suppositions, can ever lead to any solid and rational system" (THN 217)—only to remark a few lines later that he will nevertheless proceed upon the supposition that "there is both an external and internal world." In *Treatise* I.iv.4, he concludes, "[T]here is a direct and total opposition . . . betwixt those conclusions we form from cause and effect, and those that persuade us of the continu'd and independent existence of body" (THN 231), yet he does not propose that we give up one set of conclusions in favor of the other. No sooner does he conclude that we have "no choice left but betwixt a false reason and none," than he remarks that such "[v]ery refin'd reflections have little or no influence upon us"—a remark that, in the very next paragraph, he nevertheless "can scarce forebear retracting" (THN 268). As these instances suggest, it is less than obvious (i) what evaluative and prescriptive epistemological implications, if any, Hume takes the conclusions of his own skeptical arguments to have; and (ii) to what extent, if any, he accepts or endorses those arguments or their conclusions. In this chapter, I seek to answer the question of whether Hume can reconcile his constructive project—that of grounding a system of the sciences on human cognitive psychology—with his use of skeptical arguments. In order to answer this question, I also seek to explain the meaning and implications of his various skeptical conclusions, the nature of his own attitude toward those conclusions, and the content of his recommendations concerning the use of human reason.

The *Treatise's* definitive survey and assessment of skeptical arguments occurs in *Treatise* I.iv.7 ("Conclusion of this book"). Hume begins that section by reflecting on the difficulty of his previous investigations. In doing so, he is particularly haunted by "memories of past errors and perplexities." The "wretched condition, weakness, and disorder" that these memories cause him to ascribe to his own faculties, together with the apparent "impossibility of amending or correcting" these faculties, reduce him "almost to despair" (THN 264). Thus, his "melancholy" at the outset of this concluding section of Book I of the *Treatise* is first generated by awareness of his own personal—though unenumerated—cognitive failings and difficulties in the past. He remarks of melancholy that "'tis usual for that passion, above all others, to indulge itself," so that "I cannot forbear feeding my despair, with all those desponding reflections, which the present subject furnishes me with in such abundance" (THN 264).[1] Accordingly, he proceeds to indulge his melancholy with a second personal observation; namely, that his own distinctive doctrines stand in opposition to those of humankind in general, leaving him intellectually isolated and insecure. A further, and less personal, source of melancholy indulgence lies, however, in considering that "beside those numberless infirmities peculiar to myself, I find so many which are common to human nature" (THN 265). It is this third reflection that leads to Hume's sustained consideration of skeptical argumentation.

Hume illustrates these "infirmities common to human nature" by considering five skeptical arguments, each drawn in whole or in part from discussions that occur in earlier sections of the *Treatise*. Each of these arguments relates, in one way or another, to the distinctive influences of features of the imagination—our primary representational faculty—on the human understanding; the fifth draws, for some of its essential premises, on each of the previous four. Each of the five skeptical arguments tends to support an observation that Hume offers as a conclusion of the third:

> When we trace up the human understanding to its first principles, we find it to lead us
> into such sentiments, as seem to turn into ridicule all our past pains and industry, and
> to discourage us from future enquiries. (THN 266)

These five arguments concern, respectively: (i) the origins of belief in three seemingly trivial idea-enlivening mechanisms that are not "founded on reason" (drawing on THN I.i.3, I.iii.6–7, and I.iv.2); (ii) the conflict between causal reasoning and the belief in "continu'd and distinct" existences (drawing on THN I.iv.4, which draws in turn on THN I.iii.6 and I.iv.2); (iii) our inability to know or conceive real or ultimate causal powers residing in the causes themselves, an inability that is generally hidden from us only by an illusion of the imagination (drawing on THN I.iii.14); (iv) the natural tendency of reason to subvert itself through reflection on its own fallibility, in a manner leaving "not the lowest degree of evidence in any proposition" (drawing on THN I.iv.1); and (v) the inability of reason alone to defend any satisfactory principle for determining which seemingly trivial belief-influencing features of the imagination to accept and which to reject (drawing on THN I.i.3, I.iii.6–7, I.iii.14, and I.iv.1–3).

I begin by outlining and interpreting each of these five skeptical arguments in turn. In calling these arguments "skeptical," I mean no more and no less than what Hume means by that term; namely, that these arguments in some way concern or tend to produce doubt and uncertainty. Although Hume clearly holds that some common human beliefs are false, I argue that in no case does he claim that an entire class of *fundamental* human beliefs is false or unworthy of belief, nor that such a class of beliefs should be rejected or suspended. On the basis of these results, I proceed to analyze (i) the problem that his skeptical arguments and conclusions pose for his own philosophy, and (ii) the solution that he presents to that problem in the discussion of skepticism that follows the review of skeptical arguments in *Treatise* I.iv.7. I conclude that Hume—audaciously enough—regards his skeptical arguments as essential preparation for a satisfactory grounding and reconfirmation of our commitment to reason and its products, at the same time that he also uses the arguments to chasten and moderate our own cognitive self-confidence. Moreover, I argue that his strategy for putting the arguments to this combined use is a coherent one.[2] Finally, I compare his treatment of skepticism in the *Treatise* with his later treatment of that topic in the first *Enquiry*, arguing that, although many details of his treatment change from the earlier work to the later one, the most fundamental aspects of his intentions and his conclusions remain constant. I conclude that Hume can, indeed, reconcile his aim for a positive system of the sciences based on human cognitive psychology with his use of skeptical arguments, and that he does so in a way that facilitates an improved, if also chastened, commitment to the historically developing products of human reason.

The Enlivening of Ideas

Hume begins his recital of skeptical considerations drawn from our common human nature by reviewing the role of vivacity, or the liveliness of ideas, in our cognitive operations. Drawing on sections of *Treatise* I.i, I.iii, and I.iv, he argues that "the memory, senses, and understanding are . . . all of them founded on the imagination, or the vivacity of our ideas," even though "the quality, by which the mind enlivens some ideas beyond others . . . seemingly is so trivial, and so little founded on reason" (THN 265).[3]

Lively Ideas and the Understanding

The aspect of the "understanding" to which Hume alludes is the process of inductive inference, without which, he states, "we cou'd never assent to any argument, nor carry our view beyond those few objects, which are present to our senses." Chapter 4 has already outlined and examined his famous argument in *Treatise* I.iii.6 for the conclusion:

> A1. [In making inductive inferences,] the mind . . . is not determin'd by reason. (THN I.iii.6)

His further explanation of the mechanism of inductive inference in Treatise I.iii.7 is based on the claim that experience of constant conjunctions (as already described in Treatise I.iii.6) sets up a custom or habit that can transfer a share of vivacity from an impression to an idea, thereby producing belief. In Treatise I.iv.7, he summarizes these earlier results by asserting (THN 265):

> A2. Experience is a principle, which instructs me in the several conjunctions of objects for the past. (from THN I.iii.6)
>
> A3. Habit is another principle, which determines me to expect the same for the future. (from THN I.iii.7)
>
> A4. Both [experience and habit conspire to] operate upon the imagination [to make] me form some certain ideas in a more intense and lively manner, than others, which are not attended with the same advantages. (from THN I.iii.7)

But as he has also argued in *Treatise* I.iii.7:

> A5. An opinion . . . or belief may be most accurately defin'd, A LIVELY IDEA RELATED TO OR ASSOCIATED WITH A PRESENT IMPRESSION. (THN I.iii.7)

Hence, Hume concludes:

> 6. [A]fter the most accurate and exact of my reasonings, I can give no reason why I shou'd assent to it; and feel nothing but a strong propensity to consider objects strongly [i.e., vividly] in that view, under which they appear to me. (from A1–A5)

Lively Ideas and the Senses

Inductive inference is not, however, the only psychological mechanism by which ideas can be enlivened into beliefs. In *Treatise* I.iv.2 ("Of scepticism with regard to the senses"), Hume investigates the origins of our beliefs that certain objects have a "continu'd and distinct existence"—in other words, that these objects (i) continue to exist when unperceived by the mind, and (ii) have an existence that is external to, and causally independent of, the mind. He begins this investigation with a number of arguments[4] intended to show (THN 192):

A7. The opinion of a continu'd and of a distinct existence never arises from the senses.

After establishing that the senses themselves (alone, or narrowly construed) cannot give rise to these beliefs, he argues that reason cannot lead us from our impressions to these beliefs either. In arguing for this claim, he distinguishes between two views, or "systems," concerning continued and distinct objects. The first is that of the "vulgar," who believe in the existence of continued and distinct objects without distinguishing impressions from objects; the second is that of the "philosophical," who do draw this distinction. He argues first that the understanding, via reason, is not the cause of the *vulgar* belief in continued and distinct objects. His argument is as follows (THN 193):

A8. [W]hatever convincing arguments philosophers may fancy they can produce to establish the belief of objects independent of the mind, 'tis obvious these argument are known but to very few, and that 'tis not by them, that children, peasants, and the greatest part of mankind are induc'd to attribute objects to some impressions, and deny them to others.

A9. Philosophy informs us, that every thing, which appears to the mind, is nothing but a perception, and is interrupted, and dependent on the mind.

A10. [T]he vulgar confound perceptions and objects, and attribute a distinct continu'd existence to the very things they feel or see.

A11. [A]s long as we take our perceptions and objects to be the same, we can never infer the existence of the one from that of the other, nor form any argument from the relation of cause and effect; which is the only one that can assure us of matter of fact.

A12. This sentiment [of the vulgar, that the very things they feel or see have a continued and distinct existence] is entirely unreasonable. (from A8–A11)

A13. This sentiment [of the vulgar, that the very things they feel or see have a continued and distinct existence] must proceed from some other faculty than the understanding. (from A12)

According to Hume, then, the vulgar do not in fact attain the belief in continued and distinct existences through reason, nor could they do so. They falsely attribute continued and distinct existence to (some of) their own perceptions, and, because they do not distinguish, even implicitly, between perceptions and objects, they cannot make any causal inference from one to the other. Instead, as Hume explains it, the human mind has a tendency to ascribe a perfect identity—that is, an absence of change and interruption through a supposed variation in time (see chapter 8)—to its interrupted but resembling perceptions. In order to maintain this ascription, the mind hides the interruptions in its perceptions from its own attention by supposing that the perceptions continue to exist even when it does not perceive them. Its ideas of these perceptions as having an unperceived existence during these intervals acquires vivacity from its memories of the impressions that are interrupted, and these enlivened ideas constitute the beliefs of the vulgar (a group that includes each person at least most of the time, in Hume's view) in the *continued* existence of the objects. From this continued existence, the vulgar naturally infer the *distinct* existence of the objects as well.

The "philosophical" (e.g., Lockean) theory of "double existence" arises when philosophers notice that the vulgar ascription of a continued and distinct existence to our very impressions is false. According to Hume, "a little philosophy" is sufficient for this purpose, as when we press an eyeball and produce a double image of an object (THN 210–211). Such experiments show that our impressions are causally dependent for their existence and operation on the mind (or rather, they show our impressions to be causally dependent on the sensory system affecting the mind, from which we presumably infer that they are also dependent on the mind). From this, in turn, the philosophical infer that these impressions are not external to the mind, and hence also that they lack a continued existence when unperceived. The philosophical system then postulates that there are other objects, distinct from our impressions, that cause our impressions and that do have a continued and distinct existence. Hume argues, however, that this opinion—although motivated partly by the discovery of the falsity of the vulgar view—is not fundamentally produced by reason either (THN 212):

A14. The only existences, of which we are certain, are perceptions, which being immediately present to us by consciousness, command our strongest assent, and are the first foundation of all our conclusions.

A15. The only conclusion we can draw from the existence of one thing to that of another, is by means of the relation of cause and effect, which shews, that there is a connexion betwixt them, and that the existence of one is dependent on that of the other. (from THN I.iii.2)

A16. The idea of this relation [i.e., cause and effect] is deriv'd from past experience, by which we find, that two beings are constantly conjoined together, and are always present at once to the mind. (from THN I.iii.6)

A17. [W]e may observe a conjunction or a relation of cause and effect between different perceptions, but can never observe it between perceptions and objects [that are not perceptions]. (from A14)

A18. 'Tis impossible . . . that from the existence of any of the qualities of the former [perceptions], we can ever form any conclusion concerning the existence of the latter [continued and distinct objects beyond our perceptions], or ever satisfy our reason in this particular. (from A15–A17)

The crucial premise (A15) depends, of course, on Hume's argument in *Treatise* I.iii.2 ("Of probability; and of the idea of cause and effect") that any reasoning concerning an existence beyond our own present perception and memory must be based on the relation of cause and effect. Such inferences depend on *experience of constant conjunction* of the supposed cause and effect, and hence cannot proceed from experienced perceptions to the existence of never-experienced objects. Instead, the philosophical system of external objects arises when the realization of the falsity of the vulgar view meets the irresistible psychological mechanism that produced belief in continued and distinct existence in the first place. Since the realization of the falsity of the vulgar view cannot destroy the force of this mechanism, philosophers seek to remove the resulting contradiction by arbitrarily postulating a second group of objects to which continued and distinct existence can be ascribed without fear of experimental disconfirmation. The persuasiveness of the philosophical system is thus parasitic on that of the vulgar system. In addition to having "no primary recommendation . . . to reason" (THN 212), it also has "no primary recommendation . . . to the imagination," because it derives all of its persuasiveness from its status as a revision of or a replacement for the vulgar system, a revision that allows us to maintain a belief in continuity and distinctness that has no basis in reason. Hume's argument concerning the philosophical system helps to establish two further conclusions, which he had already stated in anticipation of it (THN 193):

A19. [O]ur reason neither does, nor is it possible it ever shou'd, upon any supposition, give us an assurance of the continu'd and distinct existence of body. (from A13 and A18)

A20. That opinion [of the continued and distinct existence of body] must be entirely owing to the IMAGINATION. (from A7 and A19)

In denying that our assurance concerning continued and distinct existences is produced by reason, Hume thus offers a conclusion that, to a considerable extent, parallels his conclusion concerning the process of inductive inference. In one important respect, however, it is an even stronger conclusion. As we have seen in chapter 4, Hume consistently regards *individual* inductive inferences as products of probable (i.e., nondemonstrative[5]) reason; it is only the crucial *mechanism* of making inductive inferences that is not itself a product of reason. But Hume is not merely claiming that the general mechanism leading to belief in continued and distinct existences is not a product of reason; he also holds that *individual* beliefs in continued and distinct existences are not, generally speaking, produced by reason either.[6]

Near the conclusion of *Treatise* I.iv.2, Hume summarizes his account of the origin of beliefs in continued and distinct existences (THN 217–218) and argues that the process depends on principles of the imagination that are seemingly "trivial," as well as ungrounded in reason:

A21. They are the coherence and constancy of our perceptions, which produce the [vulgar] opinion of their continu'd existence.

A22. [The coherence and constancy] of perceptions have no perceivable connexion with such [a continued] existence.

A23. 'Tis a gross illusion to suppose, that our resembling perceptions are numerically the same.

A24. [It is this supposition] that our resembling perceptions are numerically the same . . . which leads us into the [vulgar] opinion, that these perceptions are uninterrupted, and are still existent, even when they are not present to the senses.

A25. Philosophers deny our resembling perceptions to be identically the same, and uninterrupted; and yet have so great a propensity to believe them such [through the operations of constancy and coherence on the imagination], that they arbitrarily invent a new set of perceptions, to which they attribute these qualities [of identity and uninterruptedness].

A26. [Both vulgar and philosophical beliefs in continued and distinct existences depend on] trivial qualities of the fancy [i.e., of the imagination], conducted by . . . false suppositions. (from A20–A25)

In light of this conclusion, Hume reports in *Treatise* I.iv.2 that he "cannot conceive how such trivial qualities of the imagination, conducted by such false suppositions [e.g., the numerical identity of our interrupted and merely resembling perceptions] can ever lead to any solid and rational system" (THN 217). Yet he also remarks, in *Treatise* I.iv.7, that without the idea-enlivening mechanism based on these seemingly trivial qualities, "even to those objects [that are present to our senses] we could never attribute any existence, but what was dependent on the senses; and must comprehend them entirely in that succession of perceptions, which constitutes our self or person" (THN 265).

Lively Ideas and Memory

In addition to inductive inference ("the understanding") and the mechanism by which we attribute continued and distinct existence ("the senses," more broadly construed), Hume also considers a third belief-enlivening mechanism. This third mechanism is memory, already discussed in *Treatise* I.i.3 ("Of the ideas of the memory and imagination"). As he indicates there, ideas of memory are distinguished from ideas of mere imagination by their higher degree of vivacity—a degree of vivacity that is, moreover, sensitive to the order in which the ideas are presented. This greater vivacity is a remnant of the initial vivacity of the impression from which the memory was derived. In his earlier discussion (THN 8), Hume asserts:

> A27. [W]hen any impression has been present with the mind, it again makes its appearance there as an idea; and this it may do after two different ways: either when on its new appearance it retains a considerable degree of its first vivacity, and is somewhat intermediate betwixt an impression and an idea; or when it intirely loses that vivacity, and is a perfect idea. (THN I.i.3)

As Hume now notes, without this idea-enlivening mechanism "we cou'd only admit of those perceptions, which are immediately present to our consciousness, nor cou'd those lively images, with which the memory presents us, be ever receiv'd as true pictures of past perceptions" (THN 265). Although he had not previously noted that the mechanism of memory is "little founded on reason" nor judged it to be "seemingly trivial," he now clearly includes this mechanism, along with those of inductive inference and attributions of continued and distinct existence, within the scope of those assessments. Thus, upon consideration of these three mechanisms, he draws two related conclusions:

> A28. The memory, senses, and understanding are . . . all of them founded on the imagination, or the vivacity of our ideas. (from A6, A20, and A27)[7]
> A29. [The] quality, by which the mind enlivens some ideas beyond others . . . seemingly is so trivial, and so little founded on reason. (from A6, A19, A26, A27)

Skepticism concerning the Enlivening of Ideas

Hume remarks that it is "no wonder" that a principle "so inconstant and fallacious"[8] as the enlivening of ideas should sometimes lead us into error. However, it is important to observe what Hume does *not* conclude or claim about the three mechanisms

of belief-enlivenment that he discusses. First, he does not claim that the most fundamental beliefs to which they give rise are, as a class, *false*. It is, of course, entirely to
be expected that the conclusions of some inductive inferences, some beliefs about
the continuity and distinctness of objects, and some apparent memories will prove to
be mistaken; no one supposes that these mechanisms are infallible. But it does not
follow, and Hume does not argue or assert, that *most or all* of the beliefs produced
by any one of these mechanisms are false. He does argue that an additional implication of the vulgar system—namely, that continuity and distinctness are features of
the very items we immediately perceive—is false. He also holds that the philosophical system, like the vulgar one, arises *through* false suppositions, or illusions, concerning the numerical identity of resembling impressions. But at no point does he
argue or assert that there are no continued and distinct bodies in existence.[9]

Nor does Hume argue or assert that (i) inductive conclusions, (ii) claims of continued and distinct existence, or (iii) memories are unworthy of belief. Fogelin
draws an important distinction between what he calls "theoretical" and "prescriptive" skepticism:

> Quite simply, a theoretical skeptic calls into question the supposed *grounds* or *warrant*
> for some system of beliefs. A radical skeptic will argue that the challenged system of
> beliefs is wholly ungrounded, whereas a more moderate skeptic will argue that the
> beliefs in question are less well-grounded than commonly thought. A prescriptive skep-
> tic (perhaps on the basis of theoretical skepticism) calls for a suspension of belief or,
> more moderately, calls for more caution in giving assent than is common. A practicing
> skeptic is one who follows or adheres to such prescriptions. (Fogelin, 1985, p. 5)

Fogelin himself interprets Hume as combining a "wholly unmitigated" radical theoretical skepticism concerning all topics beyond the immediate contents of sensory
awareness with a "carefully circumscribed prescriptive skepticism."

Fogelin's definition of theoretical skepticism conceals a crucial ambiguity, however. On the one hand, "warrant" and "grounding" may be understood as terms of
cognitive psychology, referring to the origin or basis that certain beliefs have in
inferential or other ratiocinative processes. On the other hand, they may be understood as terms of *evaluative epistemology*—that is, as synonymous with "epistemic
merit" or "belief-worthiness."[10] As we saw in chapter 4, Hume's conclusion that
inductive inferences are not "determin'd by reason" is a claim in cognitive psychology, not in evaluative epistemology. The same is true of his parallel claims about
memory and about belief in continued and distinct existences—for example, such
claims as (A20), (A26), (A27), and (A29). Insofar as Hume emphasizes (i) that the
underlying mechanism of inductive reasoning is not *itself* produced or adopted as a
result of argument or reasoning, and (ii) that this doctrine of his is a surprising or
uncommon one, he satisfies Fogelin's definition of (at least) a "moderate" theoretical skeptic *in the sense relevant to cognitive psychology*. Insofar as Hume emphasizes that memories and beliefs in continued and distinct existences do not origi-
nate in reasoning, he appears to be a "radical" theoretical skeptic about each of
these matters in the sense relevant to cognitive psychology. But it does not follow
from this that he is a theoretical skeptic *in the sense relevant to evaluative epistemology*. That conclusion would not follow unless Hume also adopted a generalization

to the effect that *only* beliefs produced by antecedent reasoning were worthy of belief, but he adopts no such generalization. On the contrary, at the outset of *Enquiry* V.i, he suggests that whatever "principle" engages us to engage in causal inference—a principle that turns out later in the section to be "custom or habit"— must be "of equal weight and authority" to argument and "processes of the under- standing."

As we shall see, Hume eventually concludes from his survey of skeptical argu- ments that human reason is indeed subject to many infirmities, and from this con- clusion he ultimately derives what Fogelin calls a "moderate" prescriptive skepti- cism—that is, a prescription that we should use (in Fogelin's apt phrase) "more caution in giving assent than is common." Hume applies this moderate prescriptive skepticism with universal scope, and hence he also applies it to the results of the three idea-enlivening mechanisms of the "understanding," "senses," and "memory." At no point, however, does he endorse a *radical* prescriptive skepticism concerning the beliefs resulting from any of these three mechanisms—that is, a prescription to the effect that such beliefs should be *rejected* or *suspended*. Nor, as a survey of the outlined argument for (A28) and (A29) will confirm, does he offer any set of premises entailing such a prescriptive conclusion.

To be sure, when an already melancholy Hume reviews, in *Treatise* I.iv.7, the actual mechanisms of idea-enlivening that produce belief, he carefully reports that he finds them to be "seemingly trivial." In a similarly melancholy but temporary mood at the conclusion of *Treatise* I.iv.2, he had already expressed what he called a "sentiment" that the mechanism underlying belief in contin- ued and distinct objects relies on "trivial" qualities of the imagination (THN 217). In reporting an inability to conceive how such seemingly trivial features of the imagination could lead to truth, while expressing a lack of surprise that they should sometimes lead us into errors, he expresses a temporary feeling of dimin- ished confidence in the three idea-enlivening mechanisms. But when he does so, he does not offer or defend any epistemic evaluation of that feeling nor any recommendation concerning the future treatment of the beliefs that result from those mechanisms. On the contrary, his strictly reportorial language concerning his own sentiments quite carefully refrains from making any such evaluations or recommendations.

The "Contradiction" of the Modern Philosophy

Hume's remark that it is "no wonder" that our idea-enlivening mechanisms should sometimes lead us into error (THN 265–266) serves also to introduce a second skep- tical argument. The particular case of "error" that Hume has in mind is one that he describes in *Treatise* I.iv.4, where he seeks to deflate a pretension of what he calls the "modern philosophy." This is the pretension to propose a system of belief concern- ing bodies that will be superior in consistency to that of the "antient philosophers," with "their substance and accident, and their reasonings concerning substantial forms and occult qualities" (THN 226).

The Status of Secondary Qualities

The main argument of *Treatise* I.iv.4 may be divided into two subarguments. First, Hume provides his version of a "modern" argument concerning the status of secondary qualities—that is, such qualities as colors, sounds, tastes, smells, heat, and cold. The argument begins from the observation that the perception of these secondary qualities varies among persons and perspectives. It proceeds from this observation to the conclusion that secondary qualities do not exist as such in bodies outside the mind—in other words, that no qualities in bodies "resemble" secondary qualities, which are therefore only impressions in the mind. He remarks at the outset that this argument provides the only one "of the reasons commonly produc'd for this opinion" concerning secondary qualities that he finds "satisfactory" (THN 226). This argument, as Hume presents it, may be outlined as follows:

B1. A man in a malady feels a disagreeable taste in meats, which before pleas'd him the most.

B2. That seems bitter to one [person], which is sweet to another.

B3. Colours reflected from the clouds change according to the distance of the clouds, and according to the angle they make with the eye and luminous body.

B4. Fire . . . communicates the sensation of pleasure at one distance, and that of pain at another.

B5. [There are] variations [in the impressions of colors, sounds, tastes, smells, heat, and cold] even while the external object, to all appearance, continues the same. (from B1–B4)

B6. [T]he same object cannot, at the same time, be endow'd with different qualities of the same sense.

B7. [T]he same quality cannot resemble impressions entirely different.

B8. [M]any of our impressions have no external model or archetype . . . [but are] internal existences, and . . . arise from causes, which no ways resemble them. (from B5–B7)

B9. These impressions [which have no external model or archetype] are in appearance nothing different from the other impressions of colour, sound, &c.

B10. [F]rom like effects we presume like causes.

B11. [Our impressions of colors, sounds, tastes, smells, heat, and cold] are, all of them, derived from a like origin. (from B9–B10)

B12. Colors, sounds, tastes, smells, heat, and cold . . . [are] nothing but impressions in the mind . . . without any resemblance to the qualities of the objects. (from B8 and B11)

The Status of Primary Qualities

Hume next offers a version of a Berkeleian line of argument to the effect that bodies cannot be conceived as having primary qualities (i.e., "extension and solidity, with their different mixtures and modifications; figure, motion, gravity, and cohesion" [THN 227]) unless they are also conceived as having at least some secondary quality. In Hume's version of this argument, an object can be conceived as having primary qualities only if it can be conceived as having motion, extension, or solidity. But motion can only be conceived as the motion of an extended or a solid body, and extension can only be conceived by conceiving space as occupied by solidity or color. We can conceive of solidity, however, only by conceiving of bodies as having some definite quality that excludes the qualities of other bodies, and it would be circular to try to conceive of this excluding quality as motion or extension. Hence, we cannot conceive of bodies having primary qualities without conceiving them as also being colored. Because color is a secondary quality, however, Hume concludes that we cannot form a "just," "consistent," or "satisfactory" idea of bodies as existing in the manner dictated by the previous ("modern") conclusion concerning secondary qualities. By this he presumably means that, although we may perhaps have a merely "relational" idea of unknown *somethings*—as simply whatever they are that cause our perceptions, leaving their qualities undetermined—we cannot form any specific idea of such bodies as having primary qualities without conceiving them as also having some specific secondary qualities. (And according to Locke's definition of "body," at least, nothing qualifies as a *body* unless it has primary qualities—specifically, solidity, extension, and mobility [ECHU II.xiii.11].) Thus, the causal conclusion of the modern philosophers stands in conflict with the cognitive mechanism that leads us to attribute specific qualities to continued and distinct bodies.

This second part of Hume's argument may be outlined as follows:

B13. [U]pon the removal of sounds, colours, heat, cold and other sensible qualities, from the rank of continu'd independent existences, we are reduc'd merely to what are called primary qualities, as the only real ones, of which we have any adequate notion.

B14. These primary qualities are extension and solidity, with their different mixtures and modifications; figure, motion, gravity, and cohesion.

B15. [Our idea of a moving body] must resolve itself into the idea of extension or of solidity.

B16. The reality of motion depends upon that of these other qualities [i.e., extension and solidity]. (from B15)

B17. 'Tis impossible to conceive extension, but as compos'd of parts, endow'd with colour or solidity.

B18. The idea of solidity is that of two objects, which being impell'd by the utmost force, cannot penetrate each other; but still maintain a separate and distinct existence.

B19. Solidity . . . is perfectly incomprehensible alone, and without the conception of some bodies, which are solid, and maintain this separate and distinct existence. (from B18)

B20. The ideas of colours, sounds, and other secondary qualities are excluded [as real qualities of bodies having continued and distinct existence]. (from B12)

B21. [To suppose that the idea of solidity] can depend on either [the idea of motion or the idea of extension] wou'd be to run in a circle, and make one idea depend on another, while at the same time the latter depends on the former. (from B16–B17, and B20)

B22. 'Tis impossible . . . that the idea of solidity can depend on either [the idea of motion or the idea of extension]. (from B21)

B23. When we reason from cause and effect, we conclude, that neither colour, sound, taste, nor smell have a continu'd and independent existence. (from survey of B1–B12)

B24. If colours, sounds, tastes, and smells be merely perceptions, nothing we can conceive is possest of a real, continu'd, and independent existence. . . . [i.e.,] after the exclusion of colours, sounds, heat and cold from the rank of external existences, there remains nothing which can afford us a just and consistent idea of body. (from B13–B14, B16–B17, B19–B20, and B22)

Hume's final conclusion in *Treatise* I.iv.4 is:

B25. There is a direct and total opposition betwixt our reason and our senses; or more properly speaking, betwixt those conclusions we form from cause and effect, and those that persuade us of the continu'd and independent existence of body. (from B23–B24)[11]

When he returns to this topic in *Treatise* I.iv.7, he characterizes this same argument as showing that "in some circumstances" it is not "possible for us to reason justly and regularly from causes and effects, and at the same time believe the continu'd existence of matter" (THN 266).

Skepticism concerning the Modern Philosophy

How skeptical does Hume intend this conclusion to be? It seems to be a very skeptical conclusion indeed, for it seems to entail that one set of fundamental beliefs — either our causal conclusions or our beliefs in continued and distinct bodies — must be false. Closer examination reveals, however, that he does *not* assert that at least one of these sets of beliefs must be false. He does, of course, present an inductive, causal argument for the conclusion that secondary qualities are not real qualities of bodies, and he does pronounce this argument to be "satisfactory," the result of "just" and "regular" causal reasoning. He also argues that we cannot justly *conceive* of, and hence believe in, continued and distinct bodies as having specific conceivable qualities in a fashion that is strictly compatible with that conclusion. That is because we cannot form a "just" or "satisfactory" idea of bodies as having primary qualities but no secondary qualities, even though primary and secondary qualities together constitute all of the qualities that we can specifically conceive bodies to have. But to *believe*, according to Hume's cognitive psychology, is simply to have a lively idea or conception. It follows that if we, and the modern philosophers themselves, do nevertheless conceive and believe in continued and distinct bodies as having full complements of specific conceivable qualities, then we, and they, conceive and believe in bodies as having secondary qualities — contrary to the central tenet of the modern philosophy. This is why he writes of finding a "contradiction" within the modern philosophy. Hume himself, however, does not ever assert the *truth* of the modern philosophers' conclusion about the unreality of secondary qualities. Instead, he restricts himself to reporting it as *their* conclusion, and it is only modern philosophers, not ordinary people or himself, that he claims to be involved in accepting a "manifest contradiction." For his own part, he holds that "many objections might be made to that system" (i.e., the modern philosophy) (THN 227) in addition to the "very decisive" difficulty that he details in *Treatise* I.iv.4 — even though "all the other doctrines of that philosophy seem to follow by an easy consequence" from its conclusion about the unreality of secondary qualities.

Yet how can Hume doubt the modern *doctrine* that secondary qualities are not real qualities of bodies while at the same time characterizing the modern *argument* for it—that is, (B1) through (B12)—as "satisfactory" and "just"? In order to understand how this is possible, we must note that, for Hume, even *satisfactory* causal arguments sometimes yield false conclusions. Thus, the fact that the argument of the modern philosophers is "satisfactory" does not entail, for him, that secondary qualities must be unreal.

The argument of the modern philosophers depends essentially, in Hume's formulation of it, on (B10), the causal maxim that "from like effects we presume like causes." This causal maxim is, in fact, the fourth of Hume's own "rules for judging of causes and effects" (THN 173)—a rule that is, as he says, a "principle we derive from experience" of past inductive successes and failures. Nevertheless, he must allow that it is entirely *possible*—not only logically but practically—for an application of the rule to lead us to a false conclusion. Indeed, he himself remarks that his rules "are very easy in their invention, but extremely difficult in their application" (THN 175). One particular way in which the fourth rule can lead us astray is evident from the immediately following rule, which states that "where several different objects produce the same effect, it must be by means of some quality, which we discover to be common amongst them." As this fifth rule makes clear, the fourth rule does not require that the causes of like effects be similar in *all* respects but only that they be similar in *at least one*. The "satisfactory" argument of (B1) through (B12) concludes that the causes of our impressions of secondary qualities are all alike in one particular respect; namely, *having no resemblance to the impression*. But for all that the fourth rule actually requires, the causes of impressions might vary in their resemblance to the impressions themselves—so long as those causes all had some *other* feature in common. In that case, the central doctrine of the modern philosophy concerning the unreality of secondary qualities—despite its basis in a satisfactory argument—could easily be false. Moreover, Hume's remark that the modern philosophy is subject to "many" objections in *addition* to a "very decisive" one suggests that he thinks the central doctrine of the modern philosophy may well *be* false.

There are, in fact, four logical possibilities that Hume must consider. The first is that at least some continued and distinct objects do have both secondary and primary qualities, even though the modern philosophy has a good probable argument—drawn from a plausible though fallible application of a sound causal maxim—against it. The second is that continued and distinct objects do not have any secondary qualities but *do* have primary qualities—just as the modern philosophy asserts. If so, however, we cannot conceive these objects accurately or "justly," because we happen to lack ideas of the *other* qualities that fill the extension of bodies, so that we must supply color in order to conceive the primary qualities. But our inability to conceive such additional qualities, resulting from our lack of impressions of them, cannot guarantee that such qualities do not exist. It simply prevents us, and the modern philosophers, from believing in them "justly" and "consistently"—that is, in a way that endows our idea of the object of belief with the object's actual set of properties. The third possibility is that continued and distinct objects have neither secondary nor primary qualities[12] but do nevertheless exist with qualities entirely different from those that we can specifically conceive. However, such objects—lacking all primary qualities and so not occupying space—would presumably not qualify as "bodies" or "matter."[13] The fourth possibility is that there are no continued and distinct existences at all.

None of these four alternatives involves any internal contradiction, and hence none is demonstrably false.[14] Furthermore, Hume offers no causal arguments against the latter three, and the one "satisfactory" causal argument against the first is offset, he suggests, by many unspecified "difficulties." But only the fourth alternative involves the falsity of the general view that there *are* continued and distinct existences. The second and third only undermine our attributions of certain qualities to objects as real qualities in the objects themselves, and the first does not undermine even this. Furthermore, none of these four alternatives requires that all or most of our "regular" arguments from cause and effect have false conclusions—although the first requires that one such argument, discovered and employed almost exclusively by modern philosophers, has a false conclusion.

We may go considerably further. Nowhere does Hume claim that most of our beliefs in the existence of continued and distinct existences are unworthy of assent, nor that such beliefs should be rejected or suspended. Nor, despite his presentation of the "satisfactory" argument of the modern philosophers, does he himself make any such claims about most of our beliefs in the real existence of particular sensible qualities. Nor does he make any such claims about most of the beliefs resulting from inductive inference. Furthermore, he offers no premises from which any such claims about any of these topics follow—with the exception of the merely probable argument of the modern philosophers against the reality of secondary qualities, an argument whose approach he generally approves but whose conclusion he pointedly refrains from endorsing.

Our inability to conceive of the specific qualities of bodies in a fashion that accords with the conclusion of the "satisfactory" and "just" causal argument of the modern philosophy—an inability that Hume takes his own cognitive psychology to establish conclusively—does, however, lead him to pose a set of rhetorical questions that express a feeling of diminished confidence in the human cognitive faculties whose investigation gives rise to this unhappy result:

> How then shall we adjust those principles together? Which of them shall we prefer? Or in case we prefer neither of them, but successively assent to both, as is usual among philosophers, with what confidence can we afterwards usurp that glorious title, when we thus knowingly embrace a manifest contradiction? (THN 266)

In raising these questions, resulting from what he takes to be a real difficulty of modern philosophers, Hume is expressing feelings of skeptical discomfort. But in raising them he does not make or defend any epistemic evaluation of those feelings, nor does he make or defend any recommendation concerning our response to them.

The Inconceivability of Real Causal Connections

Hume derives the third skeptical argument from his conclusion—reached in *Treatise* I.iii.14 and outlined in chapter 5—that our idea of the "necessary connexion" between causes and effects is copied from the impression of the mental transition that results from constant conjunction. Because the imagination tends to "spread" this impression onto the objects, he explains in *Treatise* I.iii.14, we mistakenly take ourselves to be acquainted with a circumstance in the cause that necessitates its effect. But because causes and effects are always distinct objects or events, we can always conceive of one without the other, and hence we cannot genuinely conceive of necessary connections as features that prevent the possibility of such a separation.

The Illusion of Ultimate Causal Principles

In *Treatise* I.iv.7, this natural proneness to error and illusion concerning the necessary connection of causes becomes the occasion for further discouragement about what Hume calls the "solidity" of our faculties and about the influence of the imagination. There, he argues as follows:

C1. [The necessary] connexion, tie, or energy [of causes] lies merely in ourselves, and is nothing but that determination of the mind, which is acquir'd by custom, and causes us to make a transition from an object to its usual attendant, and from the impression of one to the lively idea of the other. (from THN I.iii.14)

C2. We wou'd not willingly stop [our inquiries into the causes of every phenomenon] before we are acquainted with that energy in the cause, by which it operates on its effect; that tie, which connects them together; and that efficacious quality, on which the tie depends. (from THN I.iii.14)

C3. [W]hen we say we desire to know the ultimate and operating principle, as something, which resides in the external object, we either contradict ourselves, or talk without a meaning. (from C1 and THN I.iii.14)

C4. [The discovery that] the connexion, tie, or energy of causes lies merely in ourselves . . . not only cuts off all hope of ever attaining satisfaction, but even prevents our very wishes. (from C1–C3)

Because awareness of (C1) prevents "our very wishes" to discover a real efficacy in causes themselves, or a real causal connection residing between causes and effects, Hume in *Treatise* I.iii.14 calls it "the most violent" of "all the paradoxes, which I have had, or shall hereafter have occasion to advance" (THN 166). If we speak of a determination of the mind as lying in the causes themselves, we "contradict ourselves." If we seek to avoid this contradiction by refusing to identify the necessary connection with this determination of the mind, then we have no idea of the necessary connection at all, and so we "talk without a meaning." Although we are not usually aware of this difficulty, that is only because of the following:

C5. [The fact that we are not] sensible, that in the most usual conjunctions of cause and effect we are as ignorant of the ultimate principle, which binds them together, as in the most unusual and extraordinary . . . proceeds merely from an illusion of the imagination. (from THN I.iii.14)

Hume takes this failure of our cognitive ambitions, and the illusion that hides it from us, as support for a general conclusion to which we have already alluded:

C6. When we trace up the human understanding to its first principles, we find it to lead us into such sentiments, as seem to turn into ridicule all our past pains and industry, and to discourage us from future enquiries. (from C4–C5)

Skepticism concerning the Illusion of Ultimate Causal Principles

Although Hume asserts (C6) in the context of the third skeptical argument, its generality suggests that all five of his skeptical arguments are intended to constitute at least some support for it. In any case, however, (C4) and (C5) certainly provide one reason to suppose that tracing the human understanding up to its first principles gives rise to skeptical "sentiments." For we learn that we cannot, as we usually suppose, conceive real necessary connections in nature; that our desire to conceive of them is accordingly unsatisfiable; and that the imagination typically operates to hide these realizations from us.

Yet while Hume claims that one common construal of the *nature* of our idea of necessary connection is false, this does not entail that any *other* common beliefs are false or unworthy of belief, nor that they should be rejected or suspended. In particular, it has no negative implications for our beliefs in the existence of causes or causal relations themselves—as his continued reference in (C5) to "the most usual conjunctions of cause and effect" makes clear. We have already seen, in chapter 5, that Hume regards his own two definitions of 'cause'—definitions that do not presuppose any real necessary connection lodged in the causes themselves, or between causes and effects—as "precise" and "just." Pairs of events that satisfy these definitions are, therefore, rightly classified as causes and effects, in his view, even though our only idea of necessary connection is copied from an impression of reflection rather than "that very circumstance in the cause, by which it is enabled to produce the effect" (EHU §53). Although Hume in (C6) *reports* the initial sentiments produced by an investigation of the first principles of the human understanding, he again pointedly refrains from offering any epistemic evaluation of those sentiments or any recommendations concerning the rejection or suspension of beliefs in the future.

Reason's Reflective Subversion of Belief

The fourth skeptical argument that Hume mentions in *Treatise* I.iv.7 is the argument that he sets out in *Treatise* I.iv.1 ("Of scepticism with regard to reason"). That argument may be naturally divided into two parts: (i) an argument that the force of demonstration degenerates, by a process of reasoning, into probability; and (ii) an argument that the force of probability would naturally degenerate, by repeated applications of a similar process of reasoning, into nothing. Thus, in *Treatise* I.iv.7, he claims to have already "shewn, that the understanding, when it acts entirely alone, and according to its most general principles, entirely subverts itself, and leaves not the lowest degree of evidence in any proposition, either in philosophy or common life" (THN 267–268).

Demonstration Degenerates into Probability

Hume begins the first subargument of *Treatise* I.iv.1 by noting that demonstrative argument is a natural process, and he observes that our employment of it sometimes goes awry, so that it produces the truth frequently but not unerringly. Thus, although demonstrative reasoning itself may provide us with complete "assurance" concerning each of its conclusions, reflection on its successes and failures also provides a natural basis for ordinary probable reasoning, and this probable reasoning provides us with some doubt, based on past failures of demonstrative reasoning, concerning the truthfulness of any particular conclusion of demonstrative reasoning. Reason thereby lessens its own assurance of its demonstrative conclusions. Hume's argument to this point may be outlined thus:

D1. [W]hen we apply [the rules of demonstrative sciences], our fallible and uncertain faculties are very apt to depart from them, and fall into error.

D2. Our [demonstrative] reason must be consider'd as a kind of cause, of which truth is the natural effect; but such-a-one as by the irruption of other causes, and by the inconstancy of our mental powers, may frequently be prevented. (from D1)

D3. We must . . . in every [demonstrative] reasoning form a new judgment, as a check or controul on our first judgment or belief; and must enlarge our view to comprehend a kind of history of all the instances, wherein our understanding has deceiv'd us, compar'd with those, wherein its testimony was just and true. (from D2)

Thus far, it is an open possibility that the failures of demonstrative reasoning cited in (D1) can be restricted to some particular subset of such reasonings, so that some demonstrative reasoning will not be subject to doubt based on probable reasoning. Accordingly, Hume tries to show that no such restriction can be made. He does so by taking the addition of two single numbers as examples of "the most simple question" that we can conceive, so that if errors occur in such additions, they can be supposed to occur in every kind of case. In fact, such simple additions are not themselves examples of *demonstrations* (since demonstrations require steps and intermediate ideas) but rather of the immediate *intuitions* (THN 70) that make up the steps of demonstrations. Intuitions and the demonstrations built from them are, for Hume, the only two sources of knowledge (THN 79) in the strict sense of "knowledge" that he opposes to probability. Accordingly, Hume intends his argument concerning simple additions to extend the scope of his conclusion not merely to demonstration but to *both* knowledge-producing faculties. This intention is confirmed by the language of his conclusion, (D11), which concerns "all knowledge." This portion of the argument may be outlined as follows:

D4. None will maintain, that our assurance in a long numeration exceeds probability.

D5. 'Tis easily possible, by gradually diminishing the numbers to reduce the longest series of additions to the most simple question, which can be form'd, to an addition of two single numbers.

D6. Upon this supposition [that the longest series of additions can be reduced to an addition of two single numbers, which is the most simple question], we shall find it impracticable to shew the precise limits of knowledge and of probability, or discover that particular number at which the one ends and the other begins.

D7. Knowledge and probability will not divide, but must be either entirely present, or entirely absent.

D8. Knowledge and probability are of such contrary and disagreeing natures, that they cannot well run insensibly into each other. (from D7)

D9. If any single addition were certain, every one wou'd be so, and consequently the whole or total sum.

D10. There is scarce any proposition concerning numbers, of which we can have a fuller security [than probability]. (from D4–D6 and D8–D9)

D11. All knowledge resolves itself [degenerates] into probability, and becomes at last of the same nature with that evidence, which we employ in common life. (from D2, D3, D5, and D10)

It is sometimes objected to premise D9 of this argument that errors in long calculations may result from failures to remember at some particular point what numbers are to be added next, rather than from the failure of a single simple addition. For Hume's purpose, however—which is to explore the consequences of the general "inconstancy of our mental powers"—such failures of memory or retention *are* failures in adding two single numbers. That is, such cases may be construed as attempts to add two single numbers, attempts that fail due to our inability to retain the idea of one or both of the numbers to be added long enough to carry out the addition correctly. Failures of retention constitute one kind of "inconstancy of our mental powers" affecting our attempts to perform simple additions.

Probability Degenerates into Nothing

The second part of Hume's argument in *Treatise* I.iv.1 extends the same general strategy to probable reasoning itself. Probable reasoning, too, often produces false conclusions through the "irruption of other causes, and . . . the inconstancy of our mental powers"; hence, probable reasoning concerning probable reasoning shows the proneness of probable reasoning itself to error. Hume treats this reflection as weakening the original evidence of each probable judgment:

D12. In every judgment, which we can form concerning probability, as well as concerning knowledge, we ought always to correct the first judgment, deriv'd from the nature of the object, by another judgment, deriv'd from the nature of the understanding.

D13. [Even] the man of the best sense and longest experience . . . must be conscious of many errors in the past, and must still dread the like for the future.

D14. [There is] in every probability, beside the original uncertainty inherent in the subject, a new uncertainty deriv'd from the weakness of that faculty, which judges. . . . (from D12–D13)

Thus, we reach a revised and weakened state of assurance by taking into account the weakness of our faculties, as well as the mixed or inadequate character of our experience of the subject matter of the original judgment. But now, we may reflect, our very judgment about the extent to which our faculty of probable reasoning functions reliably is itself a probable judgment. Hence it is subject to the principle elaborated in (D14), which entails that that judgment must itself be weakened by a new uncertainty or doubt derived from a consideration of the weakness of the faculty by which we have made that assessment:

> D15. [Any] decision [concerning the possibility of error in the estimation we make of the truth and fidelity of our faculties], tho' it should be favourable to our preceding judgment, . . . [is] founded only on probability.
>
> D16. [W]e are oblig'd by our reason to add [in every case of probability] a new doubt deriv'd from the possibility of error in the estimation we make of the truth and fidelity of our faculties. (from D14–D15)
>
> D17. [In every case of probability, a new] doubt [deriv'd from the possibility of error in the estimation we make of the truth and fidelity of our faculties is one] which immediately occurs to us, and of which, if we wou'd closely pursue our reason, we cannot avoid giving a decision. (from D16)

Furthermore, Hume assumes that reason would transfer this additional weakening influence to the original judgment. Presumably, he is thinking as follows. Whereas our initial judgment was made with a felt degree of probability x, and our first reflection on our faculties led only to a felt degree of probability y that our first judgment was actually probable to (at least) degree x, our second reflection results in only a felt degree of probability z that it is probable to (at least) degree y that our initial judgment was actually probable to (at least) degree x. And it is plausible to suppose that this second reflection will cause us to have less confidence in our original judgment than we had at either of the preceding stages. (In thus contrasting "actual" and "felt" probability, I mean to contrast the *actual* proportion of positive instances among all the instances in the observed sample with the *felt* degree of vivacity or belief. Normally, of course, Hume thinks that the former produces a precisely corresponding quantity of the latter. When this correspondence is not produced or maintained, "the inconstancy of our mental powers" has prevented our probable reasoning from operating normally.)

With this assumption of the transitivity of the weakening force of probabilistic reflection, he continues:

> D18. [Any] decision [concerning the possibility of error in the estimation we make of the truth and fidelity of our faculties] . . . must weaken still further our first evidence. (from D15 and D17)

But this is not all. For this third judgment, as a probable judgment, is itself subject to precisely the same kind of reflection, and the resulting fourth judgment must for the same reason pass its weakening force to the second, and hence also to the original judgment:

> D19. [Any] decision [concerning the possibility of error in the estimation we make of the truth and fidelity of our faculties] . . . must itself be weaken'd by a fourth doubt of the same kind, and so on *in infinitum*. (from D15 and D17)

Hume argues in his treatment of space that finite objects must contain only a finite number of parts, on the grounds that infinite divisibility entails an infinite extent. He now proceeds to apply a more general version of this principle to belief or assent.[15] He holds that this belief, being finite in quantity (because the human mind can contain only finite quantities), cannot survive a continually repeated process of diminution without ultimately being annihilated:

D20. No finite object can subsist under a decrease repeated in infinitum.

D21. [E]ven the vastest quantity, which can enter into human imagination, must . . . [by a decrease repeated in infinitum] be reduc'd to nothing. (from D20)

D22. Let our first belief be never so strong, it must infallibly perish by passing thro' so many new examinations [as we are obliged by our reason to make], of which each diminishes somewhat of its force and vigour. (from D17–D19, and D21)

Finally, combining the results of his two subarguments, Hume concludes:

D23. When I reflect on the natural fallibility of my judgment, I have less confidence in my opinions, than when I only consider the objects concerning which I reason; and when I proceed still farther, to turn this scrutiny against every successive estimation I make of my faculties, all the rules of logic require a continual diminution, and at last a total extinction of belief and evidence. (from D11 and D22)

Skepticism concerning Reason's Subversion of Belief

In order to understand Hume's conclusion, we must understand what he means by (i) "all the rules of logic," and (ii) "a total extinction of belief and evidence." Let us consider these questions in order.

What does Hume mean by "all the rules of logic"? He cannot mean simply the rules of demonstrative reasoning, for his argument primarily concerns the application of probable reasoning, both to demonstrative reasoning and to itself. Nor can he mean the rules of an a priori theory of probability. As we have seen in chapters 4 and 7, he propounds no a priori theory of probability; rather, he develops his conception of various kinds of probability from his investigation of the cognitive mechanisms of probable reasoning.

A more promising place to look for Hume's "rules of logic" is in the "Rules for judging of causes and effects" set out in *Treatise* I.iii.15 — rules that he calls "all the LOGIC I think proper to employ in my reasoning" (THN 175). These rules, he writes, are directed toward allowing us to determine when two events or objects "really are" related as cause and effect. Both (D2) and the parallel claim about probable reasoning implied by (D13) are claims precisely about *causation* — namely, that reason is a cause that produces truth as its natural effect, but it is a cause that is subject to the interference of other causes. These causal claims are indeed mandated by the application of the first six of the eight rules for judging of causes and effects that Hume supplies. Given these causal claims, the doctrines of (D3) and (D12) — namely, that the operations of probable reasoning are to be turned onto reasoning itself — function as particular instances of the generalization that probable reasoning operates on (apparent) causal relations. Since reason is a cause that does not produce truth invariably — because it is subject to the disturbing influences of other causes — reason will necessarily subject itself to what he calls "the probability of causes" (see chapter 7). The result of reason's doing so, being itself an example of reasoning, must in turn be subjected to the same "probability of causes," and so on. The natural result of such repeated self-application of reason's "rules of [probable] logic" to itself, according to Hume, would be the extinction of all belief.

But although Hume reaches the conclusion that "all the rules of logic" require an extinction of belief, there is no reason to suppose that this conclusion is an epistemic evaluation of either the truth or the final worthiness of our beliefs. That is because there is no reason to suppose that 'logic' is a term of epistemic evaluation in this context. In his Introduction to the *Treatise*, for example, Hume treats 'logic' straightforwardly as a term of cognitive psychology, writing that "the sole end of logic is to explain the principles and operations of our reasoning faculty, and the nature of our ideas" (THN xv). In contexts in which we are effectively *assuming* that our reasoning faculties are reliable and their results are to be approved—perhaps, that is, in nearly all ordinary contexts, since our reasoning faculties are, after all, the primary means by which we have arrived at our own beliefs—the assertion that an outcome is required by "all the rules of logic" might well be taken to imply some epistemic approval of that outcome on the part of the speaker. In the context of considering the argument of *Treatise* I.iv.1, however, it is precisely the assumption of the reliability and worthiness of our reasoning faculties that is undergoing scrutiny. Hume's conclusion that an extinction of belief is required by the rules of logic is—as close examination of his argument shows—simply a conclusion of cognitive psychology concerning the natural consequences of the understanding's own natural operations.[16] He immediately goes on to cancel any conversational implication that he himself accepts the loss of belief to which a complete application of the "rules of logic" would lead, by writing:

> Shou'd it here be ask'd me, whether I sincerely assent to this argument, which I seem to take such pains to inculcate, and whether I be really one of those sceptics, who hold that all is uncertain, and that our judgment is not in *any* thing possest of *any* measures of truth and falshood; I shou'd reply, that this question is entirely superfluous, and that neither I, nor any other person was ever sincerely and constantly of that opinion. (THN 183)

Hume's purpose in presenting the skeptical argument, he emphasizes, is simply to reinforce his previous conclusion that belief depends on "some sensation or peculiar manner of conception [i.e., vivacity]."[17] He explains our ability to retain a sufficient degree of belief in the face of this skeptical reasoning as due to the "forc'd and unnatural" character of the successive reflections, which make the ideas used in the skeptical argument "faint and obscure," and so without their usual force (THN 185).

The realization that Hume's conclusion concerning "all the rules of logic" is a conclusion of cognitive psychology, rather than a conclusion of epistemic evaluation, helps to blunt some of the force of criticisms to the effect that other ways of considering the frailty of our faculties might not lead to the extinction of all belief. As we have seen, his argument proceeds by inviting us to realize that it is only probable that any given initial judgment is at least as probable as we felt or supposed it to be, and that it is only probable that this second judgment is at least as probable as we felt or supposed *it* to be, and so on. Thus, reason replaces its own original judgment with a new judgment of a certain felt degree of probability that it is only

probable to at least a certain degree that it is probable to at least a certain degree
... that our original judgment is probable to at least the degree with which we originally felt it. At each iteration, Hume holds, the natural operation of reason would
lessen our confidence in the original judgment, were it not for the imagination's
difficulty in following the "subtle and refin'd reasoning" of such repeated reflections. But suppose we reflect instead that there is some probability that the original
felt degree of probability was *too low* to match our evidence, and suppose we add
the reflection that our estimate of the probability that our original felt probability
was too low might *itself* be too low, and so on.[18] This line of thought, it seems,
would tend to *increase* our confidence in our original judgment. However, the
fact—if it is a fact—that a second way of reflecting on the fallibility of our faculties
would increase (or at least not lessen) our degree of belief in a judgment through
an operation of reason does not entail that reason would not lessen our degree of
belief *when operating in the way that Hume describes*. When reason is considered as
a natural faculty to be described by cognitive psychology, there is no presumption
that reason will not produce conflicting outcomes when it operates in two different
ways. If reason were in fact to produce such conflicting outcomes through different
operations, that would simply provide the basis of yet a further skeptical argument.[19]

It may be granted, then, that Hume offers no epistemic evaluation in concluding
that "all the rules of logic" require a total extinction of *belief*. His full conclusion, however, is that these rules require a "total extinction of belief and evidence." Does not
this reference to "evidence" introduce an epistemic evaluation into his conclusion?

We may observe first that it would be an error to identify Hume's *total extinction
of evidence* with a *decrease in the probability of all propositions to 0*, in the sense
employed by the contemporary probability calculus. In that calculus, any proposition with a probability of 0 has a negation with a probability of 1, and this is clearly
not what Hume intends by a "total extinction of evidence." In fact, however, a
much stronger claim is warranted: Hume does not use 'evidence' as a term of epistemic evaluation at all. On the contrary, he consistently uses it to mean "evident-
ness"—that is, as equivalent to "belief," "assurance," or "vivacity," construed as
properties of ideas (THN 83, THN 104, and THN 124, for example). Particularly
revealing in this regard is his discussion of "unphilosophical probability" (THN
143–144), where he refers to one species of unphilosophical probability as "weakening the evidence" of past instances, at the same time that he specifically refuses
to grant that it *ought* to do so. Similarly, he writes of the need to have a "very strong
and firm imagination to preserve the evidence" through a long series of inferences
(THN 144). In no case does he use the term 'evidence' to mean the belief-worthiness or support of a proposition, as opposed to its vividness or strength of assent.

Thus, close examination of Hume's argument for, and terminology in, his conclusion at (D22) shows it to be a conclusion of cognitive psychology; namely, that
an extinction of belief would naturally result from repeated self-applications of
causal and probable reasoning to reasoning itself, were reason left to operate alone.
Nowhere in the course of the argument does he assert that the results of reasoning
are, as a class, false or unworthy of belief, nor does he recommend anywhere in the
argument that they be rejected or suspended.

Refined and Elaborate Reasoning

At the outset of *Treatise* I.iv.4 ("Of the modern philosophy"), Hume seeks to "distinguish in the imagination betwixt the principles which are permanent, irresistible, and universal," such as inductive inference, and "the principles, which are changeable, weak, and irregular," such as those responsible for the obscurities and absurdities of the "antient philosophy" (THN 255). The implication is that we might choose to endorse the former principles and reject the latter. Hume's final skeptical argument in *Treatise* I.iv.7, however, constructs a dilemma for the attempt to determine which aspects of the imagination should be accepted and which rejected. Although it draws on conclusions from each of the previous four arguments to support its premises, the dilemma itself is posed for the first time in *Treatise* I.iv.7, where it serves as a culmination of Hume's skeptical argumentation.

Imagination and "Elaborate Reasoning"

Hume initiates his final skeptical argument with two considerations against accepting the trivial suggestions of the imagination:

E1. [The trivial] suggestions of the fancy [i.e., imagination] are often contrary to each other. (from THN I.iii.9–10)

E2. Nothing is more dangerous to reason than the flights of the imagination, and nothing has been the occasion of more mistakes among philosophers. (from A25–A26, B26, C5, THN I.iii.9–10, and THN I.iv.3)

E3. [The trivial suggestions of the fancy] lead us into such errors, absurdities, and obscurities, that we must at last become asham'd of our credulity. (from E1–E2)

Hume does not stop to mention any cases of "contrary suggestions" of the imagination. However, his earlier discussions of the ways in which such things as resemblance, contiguity, education (i.e., sheer verbal repetition), and passion play upon features of the imagination to enhance religious and other kinds of belief (THN I.iii.9–10) suggest at least some likely examples. He also does not stop to mention any specific instances of philosophical "mistakes" at this point, but a number of them are presumably still fresh in his readers' minds. For example, like the vulgar, the philosophical are led by their imaginations to suppose falsely that our interrupted perceptions are numerically identical, and, when subsequently forced to deny that supposition, they arbitrarily invent new objects whose existence they mistakenly expect to be able to defend by reasoning (A25–A26). The philosophical belief in continued and distinct existences depends on the imagination, yet it conflicts with a result of causal reasoning, leading to the inconsistency of the modern philosophy (A26 and B25). It is only the imagination that hides from philosophers the realization that they do not and cannot conceive necessary connections as features of causes themselves (C5). In addition, Hume's discussion of the "antient philosophy" in *Treatise* I.iv.3 details the ways in which its various fictions and incoherences result from features of the imagination. Finally, the discussion of belief in *Treatise* I.iii.9–10 describes the unfortunate effects of resemblance, contiguity, education, and passion on the imagination (including the imaginations of philosophers), and observes that "a lively imagination very often degenerates into madness or folly" (THN 123).

Nonetheless, Hume argues in *Treatise* I.iv.1 for the conclusion that reason, acting through its own natural tendencies, would operate reflexively upon itself until it produced a complete loss of belief (D22), and he asserts that we avoid this loss of belief only because of a trivial feature of the imagination—namely, our inability to enter fully into "refined reasonings" and "remote views":

> E4. We save ourselves from . . . total scepticism [resulting from a refined and elaborate argument] only by means of that singular and seemingly trivial property of the fancy, by which we enter with difficulty into remote views of things, and are not able to accompany them with so sensible an impression, as we do those, which are more easy and natural. (from THN I.iv.1)

It thus appears that we cannot, after all, simply endorse those "general and more establish'd properties of the imagination" that we call "the understanding," while rejecting the other properties—for it is these general and more established properties themselves that would lead to reason's reflexive subversion of belief. The discovery of the further property of the imagination that ultimately forestalls this subversion suggests that we might save ourselves from a commitment to the correctness of total skepticism by endorsing a principle to the effect that we should reject "all refin'd and elaborate reasoning."

Here, at last, Hume takes up the long-deferred normative question of what epistemic principle, if any, should be adopted in light of the argument of *Treatise* I.iv.1. However, he immediately presents three reasons why the proposed principle should not be adopted. First, the proposed principle would *prohibit* many beliefs that we approve and wish to keep:

> E5. [If] we . . . establish it for a general maxim, that no refin'd or elaborate reasoning is ever to be receiv'd . . . [we] cut off entirely all science and philosophy.

Second, the proposed principle would effectively *license* many beliefs that we disapprove and wish to prohibit (many of which are also in conflict with one another):

> E6. [If] we . . . establish it for a general maxim, that no refin'd or elaborate reasoning is ever to be receiv'd . . . [we] proceed upon one singular quality of the imagination. (from E4)
>
> E7. [If] we . . . establish it for a general maxim, that no refin'd or elaborate reasoning is ever to be receiv'd . . . [then we] by a parity of reason must embrace all of them. (from E6)

Third, the only argument that reason can offer in favor of the principle of rejecting all refined and elaborate arguments is evidently one that leads us through consideration of the argument of *Treatise* I.iv.1 and of the psychological reason why we do not entirely succumb to the extinction of belief that it describes. Yet any such argument would itself be extremely "refin'd and elaborate," and hence it appears that reason could lead us to *adopt* the principle only by first *violating* it:

E8. [If] we . . . establish it for a general maxim, that no refin'd or elaborate reasoning is ever to be receiv'd, . . . this maxim must be built on the preceding reasoning [i.e., D1–D22, plus E4], which will be allow'd to be sufficiently refin'd and metaphysical.

For these three reasons, Hume concludes:

E9. If we embrace this principle [that no refin'd or elaborate reasoning is ever to be receiv'd], and condemn all refin'd reasoning, we run into the most manifest absurdities. (from E3, E5, E7, and E8)

Endorsing the proposed principle of *rejecting* all refined and elaborate reasoning would thus leave us with an artificially constrained version of reason that leads to falsehoods and absurdities: it would be what Hume calls "a false reason." However, it appears that a policy of rejecting the proposed principle and instead *endorsing* the results of all refined and elaborate reasoning would leave us with no defense against the conclusion that reason should be allowed to annihilate all belief. Acting in accordance with this endorsement of all refined and elaborate reasoning would thus mean allowing reason to erase its own initial tendency to be an inferential (i.e., belief-producing) faculty, leaving us with what Hume therefore calls "no reason at all." Thus, he concludes:

E10. If we reject [this principle that no refin'd or elaborate reasoning is ever to be receiv'd], in favour of those reasonings, we subvert entirely the human understanding. (from E4)

E11. We have . . . no choice left but betwixt a false reason and none at all. (from E9–E10)

Skepticism concerning Refined and Elaborate Reasoning

Hume's "rules for judging of causes and effects" (THN I.iii.15) are specific rules of reasoning that are themselves produced and supported by reasoning. That is, inductive reasoning concerning the particular circumstances of past successes and past failures of inductive reasoning leads to the conclusion that reasoning in accordance with these rules will tend to be more successful than reasoning that is not in accordance with them. Reason cannot and does not produce or support the proposed principle of rejecting all refined and elaborate reasonings in this way. On the contrary, reason applied to what we discover about human cognitive processes produces the conclusion that the proposed principle would lead to "manifest absurdities." Yet a principle of endorsing all refined and elaborate reasoning means endorsing the extinction of all belief.

Even at the conclusion of this argument, however, Hume does not claim that any of our most fundamental beliefs are false—although he has referred to cases in which philosophers are led into error by their imaginations. He still endorses no general canons of belief-worthiness—although he considers and rejects two such canons (one that approves and one that disapproves of refined and elaborate reasonings)—and he expresses no opinion as to whether any fundamental class of beliefs is or is not worthy of belief. Far from recommending that fundamental classes of beliefs should be rejected or suspended, he remarks instead that he knows "not what ought to be done in the present cause" but "can only observe what is commonly done," which is that "this difficulty" concerning the status of refined and elaborate reasoning "is seldom or never thought of"—and, when it is thought of, it is quickly forgotten, leaving little impression behind (THN 268).

Despite his observation that "reflections very refin'd and metaphysical" generally have little influence, Hume goes on to report that his present "intense" view of the "manifold contradictions and imperfections in human reason" revealed by his review of skeptical arguments has "so wrought upon me, and heated my brain, that I am ready to reject all belief and reasoning, and can look upon no opinion even as more probable or likely than another" (THN 268–269). Yet even this intense psychological product of his five skeptical arguments taken together is not a *recommendation* to reject belief and reasoning, as examination of its carefully crafted language shows. Rather, it is a cognitive psychologist's report of strong but temporary skeptical sentiments—a report expressed, in fact, in terms of the effect of reasoning on the *brain*. It is only after this report that Hume begins to develop what he takes to be a satisfactory answer to the crucial question of what attitude should be taken toward the skeptical sentiments that his report expresses.

From Melancholy to Commitment

The expression of intense skeptical sentiments that follows Hume's review of skeptical arguments starkly manifests the central problem that his recognition of these arguments poses. Having investigated the operations of human reason—using, of course, human reason itself—can we recommit ourselves to the continued use of that faculty in light of what we have, or think we have, discovered about it? Or must the various "infirmities and imperfections" of reason to which reason itself appears to testify return fatally upon the investigative project itself, undermining any confidence that we may have acquired about our conclusions in the system of the sciences based on the "science of man"?

In *Treatise* I.iii, Hume reaches at least two conclusions with potentially skeptical applications: his conclusion about the basis of inductive inference in custom rather than reason, and his conclusion about the imaginative illusion of real necessary connections. Prior to *Treatise* I.iv, however, he discusses primarily the implications for cognitive psychology of these conclusions, resolutely avoiding any discussion of their skeptical applications.[20] Only in *Treatise* I.iv does he begin to allow himself to consider the potentially skeptical implications of any of his discoveries; only in the first half of *Treatise* I.iv.7 does he survey these implications systematically; and only in the latter half of *Treatise* I.iv.7 does he explore the question of what cognitive attitude should be taken toward those implications. That exploration begins obliquely, however, with a further set of psychological observations. What immediately follows his recital of skeptical arguments is not additional argumentation about them but rather the simple description of an ordered succession of natural moods—what he calls "bents of mind"—resulting from his consideration of skeptical arguments and the "imperfections" of human reason that they reveal.

From Melancholy and Delirium to Indolence and Spleen

Hume describes his first, intense response to his consideration of skeptical arguments as "a philosophical melancholy and delirium." It is characterized by a sense of being "confounded," of being in the most deplorable cognitive situation possible, "utterly depriv'd of the use of every member and faculty" (THN 269). This sense leads directly to a willingness to reject all belief and argumentation. Reason alone, he remarks, is "incapable of dispelling these clouds"—presumably because reason alone cannot find serious fault with any of the skeptical arguments surveyed or vindicate itself against its own imputation of imperfection.

Although reason alone cannot overcome it, however, the state of philosophical melancholy and delirium is not a psychologically stable one. Nature itself, Hume observes, supplants this bent of mind in either of two ways: (i) by "relaxing" it directly in the course of time, or (ii) by allowing some "avocation and lively impression" of the senses to divert one's attention from the arguments that originally produce it. Hume's most famous example of such an avocation is, of course, a game of backgammon. Commentators sometimes write as though such diversions constituted the entirety of Hume's proposed solution to the problem of skepticism. In fact, the situation is much more complex. Although diversions do naturally supplant skepticism, in Hume's view, they do not by themselves constitute the solution to the central problem that skeptical arguments pose within the *Treatise*—namely, the problem of determining whether those arguments permit a recommitment to reason and philosophy or instead require an abandonment of the *Treatise*'s own project of inquiry. Having the psychological capacity to overcome or supplant philosophical melancholy and delirium is, in his view, a prerequisite for reaching a satisfactory solution to that problem; it is not the solution itself.

Time and diversions of attention necessarily produce a natural return to an indolent belief in the "general maxims of the world" that allows one to carry on the common affairs of life. In one important respect, however, the mood accompanying this indolent belief differs from the mood preceding philosophical inquiry, for the encounter with philosophical melancholy and delirium leaves behind it a "splenetic" emotional residue. This residue involves a desire to renounce all philosophy, because philosophy is viewed as responsible for having produced the unpleasant state of philosophical melancholy and delirium in the first place. In this splenetic state of mind, the positive cultivation of reason through philosophy appears to be a way of torturing oneself to no good purpose, and hence something best avoided.

Ambition, Superstition, and the Title Principle

Hume reports that the mood of philosophical melancholy and delirium is psychologically unstable, naturally giving way to indolence and spleen. He also reports, however, that the state of indolence and spleen is itself psychologically unstable. As the temporal distance from melancholy and delirium increases, spleen comes gradually to be outweighed by a renewed sense of curiosity about fundamental topics:

> I cannot forbear having a curiosity to be acquainted with the principles of moral good and evil, the nature and foundation of government, and the cause of those several passions and inclinations, which actuate and govern me. I am uneasy to think I approve of one object, and disapprove another; call one thing beautiful, and another deform'd; decide concerning truth and falshood, reason and folly, without knowing upon what principles I proceed. I am concern'd for the condition of the learned world, which lies under such a deplorable ignorance in all these particulars. (THN 271)

This curiosity, when it becomes optimistic, feeds an ambition to contribute "to the instruction of mankind" and to acquire "a name by my inventions and discoveries." This ambition, in turn, provides a natural motive to philosophize. Hume writes: "[S]hou'd I endeavor to banish [these sentiments] by attaching myself to any other business or diversion, I *feel* I shou'd be a loser in point of pleasure; and this is the origin of my philosophy" (THN 271).

Reflection on human weakness produces a second motive to philosophize. Because we cannot long forbear inquiring into topics that lie beyond "that narrow circle of objects, which are the subject of daily conversation and action," Hume holds, we are obliged to choose a guide to the pursuit of these topics. The only practical alternatives are "superstition"—that is, organized religion—and philosophy. Philosophy is to be preferred on two practical grounds, in Hume's view. First, philosophy is a more agreeable guide, because it generally produces more modest opinions and less disturbing sentiments than does superstition. Second, it is a safer guide, because "errors in religion are dangerous . . . [while] those in philosophy [are] only ridiculous" (THN 272).[21]

Thus, the natural course of our thoughts and sentiments leads to a return to reasoning and philosophy. When it does so, Hume notes, we find ourselves believing and acting as if in accordance with the following normative epistemic principle:

> Where reason is lively, and mixes itself with some propensity, it ought to be assented to. Where it does not, it can never have any title to operate upon us. (THN 270)

This principle, which I will call the "Title Principle," differs from the normative principle of "rejecting all refin'd and elaborate reasoning" that Hume has already considered and rejected. Unlike that principle, the Title Principle allows us to accept refined and elaborate reasoning on philosophical topics that interest us, because—as he has just noted—we have a propensity to attend to, and follow, reasoning of just that kind. The Title Principle allows us to reject those trivial suggestions of the imagination that are "changeable, weak, and irregular," because "lively" reflective reasoning does not sustain but instead undermines these suggestions. However, it allows us to accept those principles of the imagination that are "permanent, irresistible, and universal"—such as inductive inference and the belief in continued and distinct existences—because even lively reason that mixes with our propensities cannot ultimately destroy their force. Finally, the Title Principle can be adopted without fear of self-contradiction, for endorsement of the principle results from (i) our desires for knowledge, reputation, and a safe and agreeable guide to topics beyond the narrow circle of everyday objects, together with (ii) simple reasoning about the best means of satisfying those desires. This simple reasoning is itself entirely in accordance with the Title Principle. The new principle thus avoids the "false reason" horn of Hume's dilemma in (E11).

The Title Principle also avoids the "no reason" horn of the dilemma. As Hume has already emphasized, the reasoning described in *Treatise* I.iv.1, by which reason would subvert itself through repeated reflection, is not itself "lively" and does not mix itself with any propensity or preference. On the contrary, it is "strained" and remote from our inclinations and interests. Accordingly, the Title Principle recommends that that kind of refined and elaborate reasoning be rejected.

The Skeptical Recommitment to Reason

Thus far, then, the Title Principle has a promising aspect. It is true that it is not a principle that reason alone could have suggested, for no non-question-begging argument shows that reasonings that are lively and mix with some propensity will produce more true conclusions than reasonings that are not. Something other than reason speaks in favor of the principle, however—namely, our natural propensities themselves. No mere reasoning can convince a person who lacks these propensities to accept the Title Principle; as Hume remarks, a reader whose mood is still one of indolence and spleen must "follow his inclination, and wait the returns of application and good humour" before following Hume's "future speculations" (THN 273). Once our inclination to curiosity returns, however, reasoning can lead to the conclusion that the Title Principle will satisfy our resulting desires better than either of the two normative principles of belief rejected in the argument of (E1) through (E11).

In some respects, the situation is similar to that of inductive reasoning, already surveyed in chapter 4. There we saw that, although no argument can initially establish the Uniformity Thesis (i.e., that unobserved cases resemble observed cases), the human instinct of custom or habit leads us to reason and believe in accordance with it (i.e., as though we accepted it) anyway. When we finally come to turn inductive reasoning on itself, however, such reasoning can be made to speak in its own favor. That is, because inductive reasoning has succeeded in the past, it leads us to infer that it will meet our needs in the future—especially if it is improved by reflectively adopted rules. Similarly, reason cannot initially establish the reliability of the Title Principle, but human nature leads us to reason and believe in accordance with it anyway. Once we do so, the Title Principle can be made to speak in its own favor, for reasoning that is in accordance with the principle leads naturally to the conclusion that continued reasoning in accordance with the principle will best satisfy our curiosity, gratify our ambition, and protect us from the dangerous and disturbing excesses of superstition.

One difficulty remains for Hume. Although there is much to be said in favor of the Title Principle, we must still determine whether our commitment to it can withstand the force of skeptical argumentation. While he does not hold that skeptical arguments actually extinguish all belief, he does conclude from his survey of skeptical arguments that human reason has "many infirmities," for human reason often leads to outcomes that fill us with doubt rather than confidence, especially when it examines its own fundamental mechanisms. Can we consistently accept the Title Principle in the face of what reason intimates about its own apparent weakness?

Hume's answer to this question is affirmative. His reason is that a true skeptic

"will be diffident of his philosophical doubts, as well as of his philosophical conviction" (THN 273). That is, if human reason judges itself to be imperfect, then reason itself tells us that we must discount to some extent the very skepticism to which
it leads us. It gives us, for example, a basis on which to doubt whether the dependence of belief on the seemingly trivial mechanisms by which ideas are enlivening
counts seriously against their reliability; we have a basis to doubt whether the
mechanism by which we acquire belief in continued and distinct existence is not,
after all, a veridical one; we have a basis to doubt the seriousness of the cognitive
illusion of necessary connections in nature; we have a basis to doubt the accuracy
of the conclusion of the "modern philosophers" concerning the unreality of secondary qualities, despite the seeming justness of their argument; and we have a
basis to doubt whether reason unaided by special features of the imagination would
indeed extinguish all belief, and a basis to discount the significance of the fact even
if it would. Accordingly, the skeptic will "never refuse any innocent satisfaction,
which offers itself" on account of either his doubts or convictions (THN 273).

A comparison with Descartes may be useful at this point. Descartes begins the
Meditations by offering grounds for thinking that the senses are imperfect sources
of information. He concludes by arguing that, although subject to imperfections
and infirmities, they are nevertheless to be trusted—on the whole—when regulated
by reason. His conclusion depends partly on the nature of his sensory data and
partly on his reasoning about them. Hume begins *Treatise* I.iv.7 by offering grounds
for thinking that reason is subject to imperfections and infirmities, raising difficulties for itself that it cannot entirely resolve. He concludes *Treatise* I.iv.7 by arguing
that reason should nevertheless be trusted—on the whole—when regulated by
other propensities of human nature. His conclusion depends partly on reasoning
and partly on the nature of his other propensities.

Hume concludes, "[I]f we are philosophers, it ought only to be upon sceptical
principles, and from an inclination which we feel to the employing ourselves after
that manner" (THN 270). His commitment to reason and philosophy is made
"upon sceptical principles" partly because it is made in the acknowledged presence
of arguments that tend "to give us a notion of the imperfections and narrow limits
of human understanding" (ATHN 657). He can even freely admit that "perhaps we
are still in too early an age of the world to discover any principles, which will bear
the examination of the latest posterity" (THN 273), and that a true system or set of
opinions "perhaps, is too much to be hop'd for" (THN 272). But the word 'perhaps'
is essential to both of these remarks. For having vindicated the Title Principle as a
principle of epistemic evaluation and prescription, he can conclude that it is
"proper we shou'd in general indulge our inclination in the most elaborate philosophical researches, notwithstanding our sceptical principles" (THN 273). To
indulge in such researches is to acquire beliefs, and to have beliefs is, of course,
also to believe that those beliefs are true. Indeed, even expressions of complete cer-
titude are still permissible—because irresistible—when subject to Hume's caveat
that such expressions "imply no dogmatical spirit, nor conceited idea of my own
judgment, which are sentiments that I am sensible can become no body, and a
sceptic still less than any other" (THN 274).

Hume's commitment to reason and philosophy is also made "upon sceptical principles" in a deeper way. Not only is it made in the acknowledged presence of arguments that tend "to give us a notion of the imperfections and narrow limits of human understanding," it in fact *depends* on that notion and could not be made satisfactorily without it, in his view. Any attempt to ground a commitment to reason solely on reason's own self-reflection, he holds, leads not to commitment but to the annihilation of all belief. It is the very awareness of reason's imperfections that helps us to discount reason's own tendency to produce devastating self-reflective results, and so to commit ourselves fully to the Title Principle on practical grounds. Thus, we are aided in committing ourselves to reason and its results by facing forthrightly the limits of our cognitive mechanisms. Hume's system is precisely what Passmore judged to be impossible: a "science founded on scepticism."

Skepticism and Commitment after the *Treatise*

The concluding section of the *Enquiry concerning Human Understanding* is, like the concluding section of the *Treatise*, devoted to the topic of skepticism. The *Enquiry's* discussion of the topic differs in a number of respects from that of the *Treatise*, however. For example, Hume introduces several new classifications of species of skepticism, omits any mention of several skeptical arguments found in the earlier work, and introduces several others not found there. The *Enquiry* concludes with an endorsement of what he calls "mitigated" or "academical" skepticism. To what extent do these differences involve a different solution to the fundamental problem of skepticism and commitment to reason?

Three Subjects of Consequent Skepticism

Hume begins Section XII of the *Enquiry* by distinguishing between "antecedent" and "consequent" skepticism. Antecedent skepticism is skepticism arising prior to an investigation of our faculties, while consequent skepticism is that which arises after such an investigation. A moderate antecedent skepticism, he remarks, amounts simply to an appropriate methodological caution and impartiality. However, a radical antecedent skepticism—conceived as an initial unwillingness to accept any beliefs or rely on any of our faculties until their reliability has been deduced from principles that cannot possibly be erroneous[22]—is uncalled for and self-defeating. If we are to inquire at all, he holds, we must begin by provisionally accepting the results of using our cognitive faculties and then proceed to investigate and assess these faculties by applying them to themselves. All of the skeptical arguments that Hume goes on to consider in the *Enquiry* are examples of consequent skepticism, as are all of the skeptical arguments of *Treatise* I.iv.7. Although he does not employ the antecedent/consequent distinction in the *Treatise*, it is evident from our previous outlines that each of his five skeptical arguments involves some application of the results of his investigations into the workings of the human understanding.[23]

Hume divides the skeptical arguments of the *Enquiry* into three categories: (i) skepticism concerning the senses, broadly construed; (ii) skepticism concerning demonstrative or what he now also calls "abstract" reasoning; and (iii) skepticism concerning probable or nondemonstrative reasoning, which he now calls "moral" reasoning, or "reasoning concerning matters of fact."

Hume cites three skeptical arguments concerning the senses. The first is the argument based on the occurrence of sensory errors and illusions. He dismisses this argument (which he calls "trite") as being "of easy solution," because it shows only that the senses cannot be trusted implicitly; it does not tend to show that the senses are always or usually in error, nor does it tend to show that they cannot be corrected by reasoning about their operations. The second and third skeptical arguments concerning the senses are, in essence, the arguments of (A7) through (A26) and (B1) through (B25), respectively. He characterizes the second argument as showing that

> [T]he opinion of external existence . . . if rested on natural instinct [in the manner of the "vulgar"], is contrary to reason, and if referred to reason [in the manner of the "philosophical"], is contrary to natural instinct, and at the same time carries no rational evidence with it, to convince an impartial enquirer. (EHU §123)

He characterizes the third argument as showing that the opinion of an external existence "is contrary to reason: at least, if it be a principle of reason, that all sensible qualities are in the mind, not in the object."

Hume cites only one argument for skepticism concerning demonstrative or "abstract" reasoning. This argument concerns the fact that "geometry or the science of quantity" uses seemingly flawless demonstrative reasoning to reach such "paradoxical conclusions" as the infinite divisibility of extension and time. Hume tries to block the demonstration of these paradoxical conclusions in *Treatise* I.ii by means of his account of extension as composed of extensionless *minima sensibilia* (see chapter 3); accordingly, he does not cite the existence of these paradoxical conclusions as a basis for skepticism in the *Treatise*. In the *Enquiry*, in contrast, he does cite them as a basis for skepticism, but he adds a footnote offering a "hint" that a reformed account of our ideas of the parts of extension might "avoid these absurdities and contradictions" (EHU §124n). As this footnote shows, his concern at this stage of the *Enquiry* is not with the final epistemic evaluation of the skeptical arguments that he surveys but rather with their psychological power to produce doubt and uncertainty.

Finally, Hume cites two skeptical objections to probable reasoning, one "popular" and one "more philosophical." The popular objection cites the wide range of inconsistent opinions held among different individuals, and sometimes even by the same individual. He immediately dismisses this objection as "weak." Once again, however, this is not an epistemic evaluation but a psychological observation; he explains that the objection is weak because it in fact has little tendency to weaken our belief or produce skeptical sentiments. This, in turn, is because, "in common life, we reason every moment concerning fact and existence," so that "any popular objections, derived from thence, must be insufficient to destroy that evidence" (EHU §126). That is, because the objection draws its premises from common life, it leads the mind immediately back into the consideration of common life, where we cannot refrain from employing probable reasoning. The second and more philosophical objection relies on the conclusions of *Enquiry* IV and V that the underlying mechanism of inductive inference is "nothing but custom or a certain instinct of our nature"—to which he adds that such an instinct, "like other instincts, may be fallacious and deceitful" (EHU §127). This argument (as noted in chapter 4) is itself an inductive argument, appealing to experience of other instincts. He treats this argument as more skeptically efficacious than the popular argument, because it draws the mind's attention away from ordinary topics of everyday life onto the inner workings of its own cognitive processes.

Of his five arguments for skepticism in *Treatise* I.iv.7, then, Hume in the *Enquiry* retains and separates two aspects of the first (concerning inductive inference and the origin of belief in continued and distinct existence), while dropping another (concerning memory); he retains the second (concerning the "contradiction" of the modern philosophy); and he omits the third (concerning the illusion of real necessary connections),[24] the fourth (concerning reason's subversion of belief), and, consequently, the fifth (concerning the status of refined and elaborate reasoning) entirely. At the same time, he adds an argument from paradoxical conclusions concerning infinite divisibility, and he also mentions briefly the "trite" skeptical arguments based on sensory illusions and the "weak" popular argument against probable reasoning based on the prevalence of disagreements about matters of fact.

There is also a striking difference in Hume's manner of presenting skeptical arguments. Whereas the *Treatise* presents the arguments dramatically and in the first person, reporting vividly on Hume's own skeptical sentiments and moods, the *Enquiry* takes a far more detached and third-person approach, often personifying reason itself as the subject or bearer of skeptical sentiments. Both works, however, focus in their initial presentation of the arguments on the psychological consequences of skeptical arguments, deferring the question of their epistemic evaluation until after all of the skeptical arguments have been presented.

Skeptical Commitment to Reason in the Enquiry

The *Enquiry* differs from the *Treatise* not only in its list of skeptical arguments and in the manner in which it presents them but also in several aspects of its discussion of them. Most obviously, perhaps, the *Enquiry* emphasizes a distinction between what it calls "Pyrrhonian" or "excessive" skepticism, on the one hand, and "academical" or "mitigated" skepticism, on the other. But although the terms themselves do not occur in the *Treatise*, similar kinds of skepticism do. By "Pyrrhonian skepticism," Hume simply means extreme doubt or loss of belief, which corresponds closely to the state of "readiness to reject all belief and reasoning" that the *Treatise* describes as an aspect of "philosophical melancholy and delirium."[25] Academical or mitigated skepticism, as described in the *Enquiry*, has two aspects or "species." The first consists in "a degree of doubt, and caution, and modesty, which in all kinds of scrutiny and decision, ought for ever to accompany a just reasoner" (EHU §129). This caution, resulting from an awareness of "the strange infirmities of human understanding, even in its most perfect state," corresponds to the "scepticism" and willingness to proceed "upon sceptical principles" that Hume endorses at the end of Book I of the *Treatise*. The second consists in a "limitation of our enquiries to such subjects as are best adapted to the narrow capacity of human understanding." It may initially appear that this limitation is incompatible with Hume's stated willingness, near the end of *Treatise* I.iv.7, to pursue topics beyond our "narrow circle" of everyday objects. However, the topics beyond our "narrow circle of objects" include "the principles of moral good and evil, the nature and foundation of government, . . . the cause of . . . passions and inclinations," and other elements that constitute parts of Hume's own science of man. Mitigated skepticism does not proscribe these topics; rather, it proscribes only determinations "with regard to the origin of worlds, and the situation of nature, from, and to eternity" (EHU §130). It is precisely on these latter topics that the determinations of religion are particularly dangerous, and the moderation of philosophy—particularly Hume's own skeptical philosophy—is most to be preferred.

A second evident difference between the two works is that the *Enquiry* contains no explicit statement of the Title Principle. The Title Principle approves specifically of reasoning that is "lively, and mixes itself with some propensity." By doing so, it allows its adherents to reject some, but not all, "refin'd and elaborate reasoning," and so to ignore reason's tendency to subvert all belief by reflective self-application. The *Enquiry*, however, contains no statement of the problem of reason's subversion of belief or, accordingly, of the problem of the status of refined and elaborate reasoning to which that subversion gives rise. Presumably Hume omits these problems because he has lost at least some confidence in the initial plausibility of his argument that reason *would* subvert all belief (see note 19), but perhaps he omits them only because he deems the arguments too complicated and out of the way for the purposes of the *Enquiry*. In either case, the result is that Hume has no need in the *Enquiry* to present the full Title Principle or to defend its distinction between kinds of reasoning. It is sufficient for his purposes in the *Enquiry* to justify a general return to philosophy and reasoning after the consideration of skeptical arguments and the intense but temporary skepticism that they produce.

There are further differences as well. As in the *Treatise*, Hume argues in the *Enquiry* that a return from intense skepticism to reason and philosophy is a natural consequence of human nature. As in the earlier work, he offers a reflective justification for this return on the grounds that it produces immediate pleasure and serves as a practical antidote to superstition. Indeed, the avoidance of superstition is the principal goal of the entire *Enquiry*, as *Enquiry* I ("Of the different Species of Philosophy") makes clear. Missing in the later work, however, is his (perhaps unseemly) invocation of his personal ambition for a literary reputation as a practical justification for returning to reason and philosophy. Missing, too, is the explicit reflection that awareness of reason's infirmities can lead us to be skeptical of our skeptical doubts, as well as of our philosophical convictions. (Although Hume could easily have expressed such a reflection in the *Enquiry*, he may have judged it no longer necessary, especially in light of his omission of the *Treatise's* fourth and fifth skeptical arguments .)

Despite these differences, however, skeptical arguments create fundamentally the same problem in both the *Treatise* and the *Enquiry*: how can we endorse our own faculties in the light of what skeptical arguments seem to show us about the imperfection of those very faculties? His solution to that problem, while simplified in the *Enquiry*, also remains fundamentally the same: it is not reason alone that provides us with a basis on which to endorse its own operations, for reasoning alone simply leads us into skepticism; instead, reason augmented by our desires and inclinations provides the basis for an endorsement of reason. Reason is ultimately a kind of natural activity, one that leads us to approve at least most of its own operations when we reflect on them in the light of our desires and felt needs. Although skeptical sentiments may sometimes be produced anew by an intense consideration of skeptical arguments, we need not, and psychologically cannot, require ourselves to remain in such a state. On the contrary, Hume holds, we can and must reflectively approve of our own commitment to reason after all, even as we are permanently — and usefully — chastened by our assessment of its infirmities of operation and limits of scope. Furthermore, we can and must approve of our own attempts to refine and improve reason by reflecting on its apparent successes and failures in the past. That chastened commitment to self-refining reason and its products, made in full awareness of the nature and weakness of our underlying cognitive mechanisms, is manifest not only in the *Treatise*, the *Enquiries*, and Hume's other writings but in the conduct of his life. It was, above all else, what he wished to convey to us.

Notes

Introduction

1. For the standard book-length account of Hume's life, see Mossner, 1954.

2. This understanding of 'philosophy' remains closely related to the term's original etymology, according to which philosophy is "love of wisdom." To have wisdom, one must know many truths, but one must also know the significance and proper use of the truths that one knows, and one must know, as well, the importance of the questions one asks. Because philosophical questions, by definition, include those on whose answers either the knowledge or the significance of many important truths depends, as well as those that play a crucial role in the evaluation of other important questions, philosophical questions play an especially central role in the acquisition of wisdom. Although there are no doubt as many possible motivations for philosophizing (some honorable and some dishonorable) as there are for most other human activities, the most direct motivation to philosophize—the one most essentially related to the nature of the activity itself—is the love of wisdom. One can certainly philosophize without a love of wisdom, but one can hardly love wisdom without seeking to philosophize. Indeed, philosophy encompasses many of the questions that every thinking and autonomous person must eventually face in the course of deciding how to believe and how to act. Just as no one who needs to navigate and manipulate his or her physical environment can avoid being to some extent a physicist, and no one who seeks to get along with other people can avoid being to some extent a psychologist, so no truly reflective person can avoid being to some extent a philosopher.

3. The term 'cognitive science' is widely used to designate an interdisciplinary study of cognitive (and quasi-cognitive) processes that draws on psychology, philosophy, neurophysiology, computer science, electrical engineering, and linguistics, among other fields. Obviously, many of these disciplines were unknown or not distinguished from others in Hume's time, and the boundaries even of those that were distinguished were quite different from what they are today. I use the term here simply to designate any principled attempt to investigate and understand cognitive processes, without regard to disciplinary boundaries.

4. Absent from this list of philosophical topics are, of course, a number of topics to which Hume devoted considerable attention, including the passions, aesthetics, political allegiance, property, and natural religion. In consequence, the present book focuses primarily on Book I of *A Treatise of Human Nature* and on *An Enquiry concerning Human Under-*

standing. Only to a lesser extent does it focus on Books II and III of the *Treatise* and on *An Enquiry concerning the Principles of Morals,* and it does not explicitly address the *Dialogues concerning Natural Religion* at all. I hope to extend my treatment of Hume's philosophy to these further topics and works in another volume.

Chapter 1

1. Specifically, I address the question concerning the impression/idea distinction later in chapter 1, the question concerning the simple/complex distinction in chapter 3, and the question concerning the sensation/reflection distinction in chapter 10.

2. Cf. Kemp Smith, 1941, p. 137; cf. also pp. 459–463. For a fuller account of several largely unhelpful interpretations of Hume's distinction of two senses of 'imagination', see Wilbanks, 1968.

3. The passage states that "the first Capacity of Humane Intellect, is, That the mind is fitted to receive the Impressions made on it; either, through the *Senses,* by outward Objects; or by its own Operations, when it *reflects* on them" (ECHU II.i.24). Locke also uses the term 'intellectual faculties' to mean cognitive faculties, the term 'intellectual being' to signify a being with human or higher cognitive abilities, and the term 'intellectual world' in opposition to the term 'material world'; he never writes, however, of "intellectual ideas."

4. I owe this suggestion to Elijah Millgram.

5. In the first *Enquiry,* Hume calls the latter kind of reasoning "moral." He does so not because it is restricted to ethics (it is not) but because it is predominant in daily human life.

6. This passage is cited, and its significance for Hume's methodology discussed, in Stroud, 1977, pp. 4–6.

7. Berkeley's later doctrine that we have "notions" of minds, volitions, and relations, even though we do not strictly perceive them, may be thought to constitute an exception to conceptual empiricism. But to say that we do not "perceive" these things is, for Berkeley, simply to say that we do not technically have "ideas" of them and not to say that we do not encounter them. On the contrary, he speaks of knowing the mind "by a reflex act" (TDHP III.232) and comprehending our own existence "by inward feeling or Reflection" (PHK §89) "immediately" or "intuitively" (TDHP II.231). (In this view of nonideational mental self-apprehension Berkeley seems to follow Malebranche, who maintains that we need not and do not have an idea of ourselves, since we experience ourselves directly.) And our notions of God and other minds, in turn, are in his view simply analogical applications of our notion of ourselves (TDHP II.231). Having a "notion," for Berkeley, is thus not a matter of having a concept whose content is not provided by experience; rather, it is a nonrepresentational reflexive action of the mind by which it knows itself, its volitions, and the relations of its ideas directly.

8. I use the term 'explanatory empiricism' in this connection because 'empiricism' is commonly used to denote a contrast with "rationalism," and because the doctrine is part of an interrelated constellation of views common among philosophers classified as empiricists, not because the view is directly connected with a view of experience or of the "empirical."

9. Locke's remarks about substrata occur in the first edition of the *Essay;* the chapter on identity was added for the second edition, in response to a suggestion by William Molyneux.

10. First, unlike the appeal to underlying metaphysical substrata, the second alternative is perfectly intelligible: we can conceive of immaterial souls having location but lacking extension, and of their activity of thinking, which we know by reflection. Second, Locke grants that immaterial souls are the likely actual causes of our thinking, and hence of our *being* persons. In fact, it is even likely that their identity is *correlated* with personal identity, for "the

more probable Opinion is, that this consciousness is annexed to, and the Affection of one individual immaterial Substance" (ECHU II.xxvii.25).

Locke also offers a parallel argument regarding what it means to say of two individuals that they belong to the same species or kind. He rejects one alternative—namely, scholastic "substantial forms"—as something "wholly unintelligible . . . whereof we have scarce so much as any obscure, or confused Conception in general" (ECHU III.vi.10), and a something "they know not what" (ECHU III.iii.17); it thereby leads to conceptual skepticism. He rejects another, more intelligible and scientific alternative—namely, similarity of constitution of the "primary qualities of the insensible [submicroscopic] parts"—as requiring states of affairs that we cannot know to be realized; it thereby leads to epistemological skepticism. And he adopts an alternative—satisfaction of a checklist of sensible qualities determined by our own ideas of the species—that critics would regard as conflating species membership itself with mere evidence of species membership. Indeed, since Locke's account of species membership occurs in the first edition of the *Essay*, whereas the account of personal identity first appears in the second edition, it is likely that the former provided Locke's model for the latter.

11. As we will have occasion to note in chapter 5, "definition" for Hume is the attempt to specify in some fashion the idea or ideas for which a term stands (generally in connection with Hume's theory of abstract ideas). For the positivists, in contrast, "definition" was a matter of providing an alternative locution that is "logically equivalent" in a very fine-grained sense, licensing substitution of the one term for the other without "change of meaning" in a wide variety of contexts. In consequence, the positivists' version of reductive empiricism was less "psychological" than Hume's and had, in many ways, more stringent requirements for success.

Chapter 2

1. It should be noted that the actual formulation of the principle at THN 4 is less than explicit about the doctrine that the correspondence and representation at issue requires resemblance, and the actual formulation at EHU §13 does not mention the restriction to simple impressions and simple ideas. However, the contexts of the two passages leave no doubt about Hume's intentions in either case.

2. Flew, 1961, pp. 25–26, ellipses in original; see also Flew, 1986, pp. 9–25; Bennett, 1971, pp. 225–234; and Merrill, 1976, p. 137.

3. The objection that this treatment of the ideas of space and time violates the Copy Principle is reasonably explicit in Kemp Smith, 1941, chap. 14, which has no doubt influenced many other commentators. For perhaps the most recent example, concerning time in particular, see Johnson, 1989.

4. More specifically, since he asserts that impressions and ideas are alike in content, differing only with respect to their degree of force and liveliness, he could not treat the Copy Principle as a priori without allowing the causal properties of different degrees of force and liveliness to be knowable a priori, contrary to his fundamental principle about causal relations. And although the priority of impressions over ideas might seem more *natural* than the converse, Hume would certainly explain this seeming naturalness as the result of our pervasive experience with such analogous phenomena as reverberation and decay, as well as our pervasive experience of instances of the Copy Principle itself. (See, for example, his similar explanation of the apparent a priori character of communication of motion by impulse, at EHU §24.)

5. This parallel claim, incidentally, seems somewhat overstated if taken as a claim about

the actually occurring ideas of individuals. For a person might sometimes experience a particular impression without ever being moved to form a corresponding idea. (If nothing else, the person might die first.)

6. In the *Enquiry* version of the argument, it should be noted, the Resemblance Thesis is not so explicitly distinguished, with the result that Hume's challenge to provide a counterexample is applied directly to the Copy Principle as a whole; the *Enquiry* also cites the idea of God as an example of an alleged counterexample that will fail. The *Enquiry* version is otherwise very similar to the *Treatise* version.

7. It may be tempting to suppose that, because Hume does not specifically refute skepticism about other minds, and because he is a conceptual reductionist about some other topics, including causation, he should therefore be interpreted as a proto-logical behaviorist. To succumb to this interpretive temptation would, of course, be an error. Logical behaviorism is entirely foreign to Hume's thought (see chapter 8).

8. A somewhat similar situation occurs in Pears, 1990, pp. 24–27. Pears suggests that Hume could modify the Copy Principle so as to allow a mechanism for generating ideas through "lateral connections." In the case of the missing shade of blue, these lateral connections would presumably be relations of natural resemblance. Pears claims, however, that such a modification would contradict Hume's "atomism." But where does Hume state a version of atomism that is incompatible with such a modification, or with the doctrine of natural resemblance that he sets out in the Appendix? There is no such version of atomism to be found in Hume. Certainly Hume's atomistic claim that all complex representations are ultimately composed of simple representations does not constitute such a version, for it is entirely compatible with the doctrine of natural resemblance, and even *requires* that doctrine, as Hume insists in the passage just cited (THN 637).

9. The similarity between imagining the missing shade of blue and "blending" impressions of reflection was suggested to me by William E. Morris.

10. The general point that the missing shade of blue is a special case with a special explanation is also made in Russow, 1980. For an explanation of Hume's willingness to accept the missing shade of blue similar to that presented here, see Fogelin, 1984, as well as Garrett, 1985.

11. Hence, it follows that an idea of time is an idea that requires some time for an individual to have.

12. The idea of "real existence"—that is, the idea of existence outside the mind—appears to be a mode of the simple idea of existence for Locke, although his treatment of it is too brief to permit certainty about the point.

13. See Wright, 1983, pp. 101–107. Wright takes Hume's thesis about the idea of the vacuum to entail the inconceivability of a world that is not a plenum. Accordingly, he takes the passage cited previously from THN 639 to represent Hume's explicit acceptance of a hypothesis that Hume's own theory of ideas rules out as inconceivable. Wright concludes that Hume admits the inadequacy of his own theory of ideas. No such conclusion is needed on the interpretation proposed here.

Chapter 3

1. Kemp Smith's criticism is endorsed in Zabeeh, 1973, p. 78n.

2. It should be noted that, in addition to the strong sense of the term 'inseparable', as it is used in the Separability Principle, Hume also sometimes uses a weaker sense of 'inseparable', according to which any two distinct perceptions that are in fact constantly causally conjoined are "inseparable" (e.g., THN 93, THN 237, and THN 300). The context makes these

uses quite easy to distinguish. The situation is similar to that of the term 'impossible', which Hume also uses in easily distinguishable stronger and weaker senses (see chapter 7). Indeed, since 'inseparability' can be defined as "the impossibility of separation," the ambiguity of the former term can be reduced to the ambiguity of the latter.

3. See, for example, Hendel, 1925, p. 113; Laird, 1932, pp. 27–28; Bennett, 1971, p. 225; and Stroud, 1977, p. 20.

4. As Jonathan Bennett has pointed out to me, Locke is not entirely consistent about the simplicity of the idea of space. Although Locke always classifies it as a simple idea, he also writes of the ideas of space and duration: "[N]one of the distinct ideas we have of either is without all manner of composition: It is the very nature of both of them to consist of parts: But their parts being all of the same kind, and without the mixture of any other idea, hinder them not from having a place amongst simple ideas" (ECHU II.xv.9). Yet as Bennett also notes, this kind of composition is exactly what Locke elsewhere (ECHU II.xii.5) declares to be sufficient to make an idea a "simple mode," which is a kind of *complex* idea.

This situation is comparable to that of *Essay* II.xxi.3. There, Locke "confesses" that the idea of power—which he always classifies as simple—nevertheless *"includes in it some kind of relation,"* a state of affairs that should suffice for classifying it as complex, since he regards all ideas of relation as complex. He goes on to say, however, that *all* of our simple ideas include some kind of relation, and he mentions among others the idea of extension, which he says involves relation because of the composition of spatial parts. He then concludes that we should not allow this to prevent us from classifying the idea of power (or, presumably, any of his other examples) as simple.

Interpreting the Lockean idea of space as complex would bring him much closer to Hume. However, Locke lacks a conception of Humean *minima sensibilia*. Instead, he says that simple modes of space involve a repetition of a *length*, and he denies that we conceive of any smallest length or any other genuine simple of which an idea of space would be composed. In what follows, therefore, I take him at his word in classifying the idea of space itself as a simple idea.

5. This explains how the otherwise similar ideas of "space" and "extension" differ. Any idea of more than one *minimum sensibilium*—however distributed or arrayed—is an idea of space, but only when *minima sensibilia* are *contiguous* do we have an idea of extension.

6. Another difference between Hume and Locke is that Hume regards every shade of a color as a different simple perception (as is evident from his discussion of the missing shade of blue), whereas Locke regards particular shades of colors as simple *modes* of them, and hence as complex ideas.

7. I assume that the shade of black in question is not so dark as to be "complete darkness," which Hume regards as equivalent to the absence of visual perception (THN 55–58), and I am also excluding, of course, any impressions of a colored background.

8. Tweyman, 1974, mentions in passing the incompatibility of spatial complexity with the simplicity of perceptions in Hume. Bennett, 1971, p. 242, recognizes spatial simplicity as an element in Hume's notion of simplicity, but he seems to regard Hume as inconsistently or incoherently combining it with Locke's conception of simplicity. The question of how Hume handles spatial complexity in terms of his simple/complex distinction appears to be raised, but not answered, in Laird, 1932; Laing, 1932; and T. H. Green's introduction to the *Treatise* in Green and Grose, 1874–1875. Kemp Smith, 1941, notes in his discussion of Hume's views on space that Hume regards the ideas of extension and space as complex, and he follows Hume in calling the *minima sensibilia* simple, but he draws no further conclusion and does not really discuss Hume's initial simple/complex distinction.

9. See chapter 8.

10. That simple perceptions can resemble each other in various respects, according to

Hume, and that the respects must be distinguished by distinctions of reason, has also been recognized in Russow, 1980, although she does not directly address the objection that the admission of such distinctions is inconsistent with the Separability Principle. Russow does, however, see an inconsistency in Hume's use of the simple/complex distinction: "[I]n the light of his remarks about the white globe, it seems to follow that the colour-of-the-apple-plus-the-shape-of-the-apple is a simple idea, but that the colour alone, being inseparable from the shape, is not. . . . Hume's general tendency to talk about colours *per se* as simple ideas is not consistent with his considered analysis" (p. 345).

But on my interpretation, Hume is not guilty of any inconsistency on this point, since, in his view, single simple impressions of a given color are unextended, and hence *not* impressions of any shape. Russow is perhaps misled by Hume's remark (cited previously): "'Tis certain that the mind wou'd never have dream'd of distinguishing a figure from the body figur'd, as being in reality neither distinguishable, nor different, nor separable; did it not observe, that even in this simplicity there might be contain'd many different resemblances and relations" (THN 25).

However, it is clearly a *relative* simplicity that Hume intends here; he is only pointing out that there is no complexity *of the sort under discussion*—that is, no complex made up of a figure and a "body figur'd." For on no reasonable interpretation can Hume regard every perception of a *body* as a simple perception. In addition to the fact that ideas of most bodies will include ideas of sounds, smells, and tangible qualities, many if not all perceptions of bodies are composed of perceptions of constituent bodies.

11. Russow, 1980, objects that Hume's doctrine about the "unanalyzability" of resemblances entails that Hume will be unable to distinguish between resemblance and other relations. But no such conclusion follows. Each (abstract) idea of a particular relation will consist of an idea of a related pair (or triple, etc.) together with a "custom" to call up ideas of other related pairs (triples, etc.). Ideas of different relations will involve different classes of pairs (triples, etc.) and hence will be distinguishable from each other. It is true that unanalyzable relations will be indefinable—one will be able to convey the idea of resemblance as opposed to that of contiguity, for example, only by pointing out *resembling* pairs (triples, etc.) as opposed to *contiguous* ones, so as to produce the correct "custom" in the mind of the hearer. And it is also true that Hume characterizes all ideas of relations as complex (THN 13). However, that would be an embarrassment to Hume only if his simple/complex distinction were—like Locke's—intended to be coextensive with the indefinable/definable distinction (as MacNabb and Bennett claim it is). But we have already seen that Hume's distinction is not Locke's, and as we will see in chapter 5, Hume does not insist that all complex ideas are definable. Hume regards the ideas of relations as complex simply because any idea that serves as the abstract idea of a relation must be an idea of a *pair*, *triple*, and so on, and therefore cannot be simple.

12. For more about this argument, see chapter 5.

13. Concerning the difference between impressions and ideas, see also THN 1 and THN 96.

14. Note that Locke, unlike Hume, cannot accept this principle without qualification. For Locke's theory of abstract ideas permits thought with indeterminate ideas, even though ideas in actual experience (i.e., what Hume calls impressions) cannot be indeterminate. Hence there is at least a sense, for Locke, in which abstraction allows even those ideas that are "necessarily connected" to be separated in thought—although this separability cannot be taken to indicate a similar separability of the ideas as they would occur in actual experience. Mandelbaum's restricted version of the Separability Principle does thus have some application to Locke, but not to Hume.

15. For a specific example of this charge, see Merrill, 1976, p. 140. Stroud, 1977, p. 20, along

with many others, expresses somewhat more general qualms about the alleged vagueness imported into Hume's system by the vagueness, carelessness, or inconsistency of the distinction.

16. For Descartes's discussion of the difference between real distinctions, modal distinctions, and distinctions of reason (also called "conceptual distinctions"), see PP §§60–62.

17. Berkeley, who was a far better mathematician than Hume, also denied infinite divisibility in favor of *minima sensibilia* and was much clearer about the mathematical implications of his position. See Fogelin, 1988, for an excellent discussion of this topic.

Chapter 4

1. For the clearest statement and most detailed elaboration of this point, see Baier, 1991.

2. Baier, 1991, pp. 93–99, suggests that *Treatise* I.iii. 15 ("Rules by which to judge of causes and effects") involves a reflexive inductive endorsement of induction. While it is clear that these rules are rules for engaging in induction, and that they are produced and justified by their inductive success, any overall inductive endorsement of induction is at best implicit.

3. For an earlier version of this interpretation, see Beauchamp and Mappes, 1975.

4. It may be suggested that *Treatise* I.iv.1 ("Of scepticism with regard to reason"), at least, uses 'reason' in a narrower or more restricted sense. Both demonstrative and probable reasoning are subjected to skeptical arguments in that section, however, so there is no reason to suppose that the term 'reason' in the section title has a restricted sense. The discussion of "reason" in the first few paragraphs of the section does concern demonstrative reasoning in particular. Hume accomplishes this restriction not by using the term 'reason' itself in a new and narrower sense, however, but by limiting the scope of his discussion in his first sentence ("In all demonstrative sciences . . ."). The argument of *Treatise* I.iv.1 is discussed at length in chapter 10.

5. Although the scope of Hume's sense of 'reason' corresponds closely to Locke's, his account of the mechanism of probable reasoning differs markedly. According to Locke, probable reasoning involves coming to perceive "the appearance of such an Agreement or Disagreement, by the intervention of Proofs, whose connexion is not constant and immutable, or at least is not perceived to be so, but is, or appears for the most part to be so, and is enough to induce the Mind to *judge* the Proposition to be true, or false, rather than the contrary" (ECHU IV.xv.1).

Perceiving this "seeming" or "for the most part" agreement or disagreement of ideas through probable argument, like perceiving the real agreement or disagreement of ideas through demonstrative reasoning, always involves some further ideas that serve as intermediaries. In Humean causal inference, however, we often infer the effect from the cause, or vice versa, without any intermediaries. Thus, Hume writes: "As we can thus form a proposition, which contains only one idea, so we may exert our reason without employing more than two ideas, and without having recourse to a third to serve as a medium betwixt them" (THN 96–97n).

6. Fogelin, 1985, describes Hume as giving a "no-argument" argument (that is, an argument that there is no argument of a certain kind). On my interpretation, the conclusion of Hume's famous argument is a kind of "no-argument" conclusion.

7. The conclusion that there is no non-question-begging reasoning to support the reliability of induction might itself be paraphrased as a claim that induction is "unreasonable," "irrational," and "unwarranted"—but only if the latter terms are understood in a much more restricted and literal-minded sense than is intended by the traditional skeptical interpretations. So understood, the "unreasonableness" of induction would not entail that inductive arguments lack epistemic value.

8. For one influential example, see Winters, 1979, pp. 20–35.

Chapter 5

1. The *Enquiry* version of the first definition omits the *Treatise* version's reference to spatial contiguity, a reference that the *Treatise* itself treats as problematic (since some causes and effects are not spatially located at all) (THN 75 and 75n). The *Enquiry* version of the second definition omits the *Treatise* version's reference to the inference from an impression to a lively idea, and it also lacks the *Treatise* version's implication that the psychological determination must operate in both directions, that is, from idea of effect to idea of cause, as well as from idea of cause to idea of effect.

2. Among those who more or less explicitly endorse the answer "both" are Richards, 1966; MacRae, 1969, pp. 486–491; Beauchamp and Rosenberg, 1981, chap. 1; Pears, 1990; and Baier, 1991. Among those who more or less explicitly endorse the answer "only C1" are Robinson, 1962; Ducasse, 1966, p. 142; and Capaldi, 1975; see also Basson, 1958, pp. 74–76. Among those who more or less explicitly endorse the answer "only C2" are Church, 1935, pp. 81–86; and Botwinick, 1980, pp. 92–98. Among those who more or less explicitly endorse the answer "neither" are Anderson, 1966, chap. 15; Robison, 1977; Hanfling, 1979, pp. 501–514; Wright, 1983, chap. 4; Livingston, 1984, p. 158; Flew, 1986, p. 74, and also 1961, p. 124; Craig, 1987, chap. 2; and Strawson, 1989.

3. See also Flew, 1961, p. 123.

4. See Kemp Smith, 1941, p. 401; and Ducasse, 1966. Another version of the circularity objection, involving "necessary connexion," may be found in Whitehead, 1969, p. 163.

5. Hanfling, 1979; Wright, 1983; Livingston, 1984; and Strawson, 1989. See also Craig, 1987, chap. 2.

6. These questions are: "For what reason we pronounce it *necessary*, that every thing whose existence has a beginning, shou'd also have a cause"; and "Why we conclude, that such particular causes must *necessarily* have such particular effects; and what is the nature of that *inference* we draw from the one to the other, and of the *belief* we repose in it?" (THN 78).

7. As I have argued in chapter 3, however, Hume does not draw his simple/complex distinction in the same way that Locke draws his.

8. For more on the simple/complex distinction in Locke and Hume, see chapter 3.

9. For another, rather different, attempt to apply Hume's theory of abstract ideas to the topic of his analysis of causation, see Robison, 1982.

10. Hume writes of a comparison between two ideas. There is no reason why his theory could not be expanded, however, to include relations with any number of relata, involving a comparison of any number of ideas. For simplicity of exposition, and because the causal relation as Hume conceives it is a two-membered relation, I will not make this natural expansion here.

11. In fact, he writes concerning the relational terms 'inheritance' and 'contract' that "these terms . . . stand for ideas infinitely complicated; and to define them exactly, a hundred volumes of laws, and a thousand volumes of commentators have not been found sufficient" (EPM §161). The "infinite complexity" is, presumably, not within the particular abstract ideas associated with the two terms, for Hume insists elsewhere that the mind cannot have ideas with an infinite number of parts; rather, the infinite complexity is in the membership of the terms' revival sets.

12. Incidentally, this seeming indifference to whether necessary connection is a *relation between* causes and effects or a relational *quality of* causes reflects Locke's previous indifference to any distinction between ideas of relations and ideas of relational qualities. It is also manifest in Hume's willingness to say both that C1 and C2 define 'a cause' and that they define "the relation of cause and effect."

13. The *idealization* of the observer in these respects need not imply that the observer is an "ideal" one in any other respects. See Sayre-McCord, 1994.

14. Similarly, when Hume discusses the belief-enhancing capacity of "cause and effect" in the case of religious relics (EHU §43), what matters for belief-enhancement is not whether the object was *actually* used by a saint but whether we *take* it to have been used by a saint.

15. For a tentative step in the direction of such an interpretation, see Robinson, 1966.

16. This point was first suggested in Robison, 1977, and made again in greater detail in Robison, 1982. See also Jacobsen, 1984.

17. Indeed, even actually unobserved shapes are easily classified, simply by imagining them.

18. Fogelin, 1985, chap. 4, makes this point.

Chapter 6

1. The principles cited actually state a doctrine of universal causation limited to "beginnings of existence." They thus entail unrestricted universal causation only if every event can be construed as the beginning of existence of something, if only of the instantiation of a property. I assume that Hume makes this assumption.

2. It thus shows how the second of the two "neighboring fields" that Hume proposed to explore in *Treatise* I.iii.2 serves to provide the answer to the first neighboring field. These two neighboring fields are described in chapter 5.

3. Stroud does not distinguish between "determinism" and "the doctrine of necessity" in Hume, and he seems to use the two terms interchangeably. Hume's own formulation of the doctrine under discussion at this point (i.e., (N), that "human actions can be traced up, by a necessary chain, to the Deity") is potentially ambiguous between (i) the doctrine of necessity, as we have characterized it, and (ii) an application to human actions of strict determinism. However, it seems clear from Hume's introduction to the discussion that he is raising theological problems with respect to the "doctrine of necessity" in general. These problems only become more acute, of course, if the doctrine of necessity is strengthened to include universal causation and/or strict determinism, and some of Hume's rhetoric in attempting to pose the problems as dramatically as possible is suggestive of these additional doctrines as well.

4. For a more detailed account of Hume's theory of moral judgment, see chapter 9.

5. See Adams, 1975. I owe this way of putting the solution to Jonathan Bennett.

6. For the distinction between first-order desires and second-order desires concerning which first-order desires should be motivating, see Frankfurt, 1971. Frankfurt calls the freedom to obtain whatever the objects of one's first-order desires might be "freedom of action." He calls the freedom to be moved by whatever first-order desires one wills to be moved by "freedom of will." In these terms, Hume's concept of liberty is really a concept of "freedom of action." Hume provides no concept of "freedom of will," in Frankfurt's sense.

Chapter 7

1. It also plays the same role in the expanded definition he offers in a footnote: "a transgression of a law of nature by a particular volition of the Deity, or by the interposition of some invisible agent" (EHU §90n). Although the restriction to volitions of the Deity or an invisible agent accurately captures the class of cases in which Hume is most interested, the restriction plays no role in Hume's argument of Part i, which is presumably why it appears only in a footnote.

2. In contrast, it is not entirely clear from Hume's discussion (THN 95–97) whether the assurance produced by a *demonstration* is a matter of an idea coming to possess vivacity at all (and hence whether it is a matter of "belief" in Hume's technical sense), or whether it is just a matter of coming to *conceive of* (or recognize that one is conceiving of) particular ideas standing in those relations that the conclusion of the demonstration describes.

3. In the *Treatise*, Hume mentions "several kinds" of probability of causes. That described here is the only kind he discusses in the *Enquiry*, however, and it is—not coincidentally— the only kind that bears directly on his treatment of miracles. The other kinds depend not on comparing different views derived from experiments but on an imperfection in the habit or custom by which we make inferences concerning an unobserved case—that is, on an imperfection in the ability of the impression to produce a full measure of vivacity in the idea that constitutes our conclusion. This imperfection is due either to an insufficient number of experiments or to a variability in the outcome of those experiments.

4. The step labeled "(16)" actually occurs in Hume's text in the sentence prior to (12). However, since its claim about "proof against proof" clearly depends on (15), I have placed it here.

5. Annette Baier first called the relevance of this passage to my attention.

6. It has been objected that, because he denies our access to, or conception of, any real necessary connections in nature, and defines 'cause' in terms of constant conjunction, Hume has no right to the modal notion of "unalterable" experience. Presumably, however, he would simply define causal modalities in terms of constant conjunction. When he writes of an "unalterable" experience, he may simply mean that, however we try, we find that we— and others whose testimony about such matters has achieved the status of proof—fail to produce a counterexample. Furthermore, Jonathan Bennett has pointed out that Hume sometimes uses 'unalterable' nonmodally—that is, simply as a synonym for 'unchanging'.

7. It may be suggested that Hume relies on an absolute, rather than a subjective, sense of 'miracle' in his previously cited footnote, when he claims that "the raising of a feather, when the wind wants ever so little of a force requisite for that purpose, is as real a miracle, though not so sensible with regard to us" (EHU §90n). To this suggestion, I have two replies. First, it would not be surprising if Hume *did* occasionally use the term in an absolute sense, since (as we have seen) he does not clearly distinguish the absolute sense of 'cause' (and related terms) from the subjective sense, for reasons having to do with his theory of abstract ideas. The important point, for our purposes, is that we can and must interpret the terms 'proof', 'law of nature', and 'miracle' as being consistently used in the subjective sense throughout the course of his *argument*. The footnote in question does not contribute any premises to the argument. Second, however, the use of 'miracle' in the footnote is entirely compatible with a subjective reading. For Hume's point is that "a miracle may be either discoverable by men or not"—that is, an event's being a miracle does not entail either that the event is easily observable or that it is not. On a subjective reading, Hume would thus be claiming that a proposed motion of a feather under certain circumstances could rightly play the *cognitive role of* a miracle if it would violate a "law of nature" (concerning the sufficiency of forces) for which we have a proof, whether the motion itself would be easily sensible by us or not. In contrast, the most obvious versions of an absolute reading would be incompatible with Hume's use of the term in the footnote, since on those versions, as we have seen, *no* miracles can be "discoverable by men."

I do not claim that Hume could not *develop* a version of an absolute sense in which miracles would sometimes be discoverable. For example, he might define a "law of nature" as a regularity for which there is at most one exception, objectively speaking, and a "miracle" as a violation of such a law. However, the fact that he makes no effort to develop such a definition in "On Miracles" suggests that his thinking is being governed throughout that section by the subjective sense. The subjective sense is also strongly suggested by the context provided by the rest of the footnote, which is concerned with the question of what can be "denominated" or "esteemed" a miracle. Tom Reed brought home to me the need to reconcile this footnote from *Enquiry* §90n with my claim that Hume uses 'miracle' subjectively in "On Miracles."

8. Indeed, as we have noted, he appears in his deduction of (28) to go further, holding that proofs entirely obviate, or "annihilate," considerations of probability. Such a position has considerable plausibility. For example, if we are told only that an evenly weighted six-sided die with four blue faces and two red faces was thrown, we will affirm (with probability) that a blue face turned up. If we are then shown a videotape of the throw resulting in a red face turning up, however, and our past experience provides us with a proof of the reliability of videotapes, then we will regard it as *proven* that a red face turned up, the prior probability of a blue face notwithstanding, for the basis of our previous belief was merely probability, whereas now we have a proof. In terms of Humean cognitive psychology, the firm belief resulting from the proof would simply destroy the hesitating belief resulting from the probability. This may occur even when the number of concurring experiments for the probability exceeds the number of experiments supporting the proof. For the cognitive conflict will be between the *outcomes* of the proof and the probability, and by hypothesis, the proof produces a higher degree of vivacity for its outcome than the probability does.

9. Given human psychology as Hume understands it, it would be a miracle if *reasonable* and *reflective* individuals did not do so. This is the point of his ironic concluding remark that "the Christian Religion not only was at first attended with miracles, but even at this day cannot be believed by any reasonable person without one" (EHU §101).

Chapter 8

1. For a description of Locke's theory of personal identity, see chapter 1.

2. The idea may be fairly complex because, although the mind cannot hold an idea of every member of the bundle at once, it may well hold ideas of a number of perceptions—impressions and ideas related to various sense modalities, as well as impressions of reflection and their ideas—at one time. Thus, the idea that serves as the abstract idea of the self may be an idea of a fairly complex perception.

3. Furthermore, he allows (THN 84) that vivacity, once obtained, may persist in a long-standing belief, even though no memory of the "impression" that was its source remains.

4. For a similar view, see Passmore, 1952, pp. 82–83. An older version of Robison's explanation—a version that also bears some resemblance to Kemp Smith's—is found in the common complaint that a perception or bundle of perceptions cannot be aware of itself. That this is not Hume's problem should already be apparent. Humean perceptions are not "aware of themselves," although every occurrence of a perception is an occurrence of sentience. For a perception to become itself an *object* of thought is for an idea of it to occur. For a bundle of perceptions to be "thinking of itself" is simply for an abstract idea of the self to occur within the bundle. See Pike, 1967, pp. 159–165.

5. Stroud's discussion occurs at pp. 118–140. Here is a clear statement of his interpretation: "It is therefore clear that Hume's explanation of the origin of the idea of the self or mind is not necessarily deficient in failing to give an account of how a certain idea arises from certain 'data', but that it leaves completely unintelligible and mysterious the fact that those 'data' are as they are. . . . [W]e find it simply taken as a fact about the Universe of perceptions that the range of reflective vision of any one of them does not extend to all the rest. . . . What accounts for the fact that one cannot survey in the same way *all* the perceptions there are?" (p. 138).

Some have read Stroud as asking, for Hume, "[H]ow we know which perceptions to survey?" But this is a misreading of Stroud's interpretation. There is no need to determine which perceptions to survey; some perceptions simply get surveyed (that is, cause certain later memory perceptions). The object of Stroud's complaint is only that there are many bundles, each of whose causal discreteness has itself no causal explanation.

6. One may well wonder, of course, why "objects" that are so "changeable and inconstant" in their parts are taken to have enduring identities in the first place. Presumably Hume's answer is that even successions with quickly changing parts can be taken to have enduring identities when (i) they rate highly on "reference of parts to a common end," (ii) rate highly on "sympathy and interaction of parts," and (iii) undergo changes of parts that are for the most part regular and predictable, with earlier parts passing away as they are replaced by new ones.

7. He implies, in fact, that in a "real connexion," the existence of one object in some way entails or is impossible without the existence of the other. It is tempting to suppose that Hume's usage is influenced at least partly by Descartes's use of the term 'real distinction' to mark the distinction between conceptually independent objects (i.e., substances). Technical uses of 'real connexion' occur at THN 168, 178, 259, and 636. A nontechnical use occurs at THN 452.

8. That those are the only spatial relations that perceptions can be known to have is clear from *Treatise* I.ii and *Treatise* I.iv.5 (see also THN 253). If Hume were to follow Berkeley—and the analogy of his own views about space—by holding that perceptions in different minds are strictly not parts of the same temporal ordering, then of course the contradiction I have ascribed to Hume would only become more acute, since *no* two perceptions could be said to be nonsimultaneous except as the *result* of bundling. Hume need not hold this view, however.

9. "The comparison of the theatre must not mislead us. They are the successive perceptions only, that constitute the mind; nor have we the most distant notion of the place, where these scenes are represented. . . ." (THN 253).

Chapter 9

1. 'Moral evaluation' is, of course, my term and not Hume's. I use the term for both mental and linguistic evaluations of morality—that is, for both evaluative thoughts and evaluative statements. Commentators often use the term 'moral judgment' for this purpose, but this term has connotations that beg the central question of whether moral evaluations are propositional. I will use the term 'moral judgment' later in a more restricted sense that is, I believe, also Hume's sense of that term.

2. See, for example, Flew, 1966; and Ardal, 1977 and 1989. This option is also considered in Harrison, 1978; and Mackie, 1980.

3. Harrison cites such passages as THN 471, cited subsequently in this chapter. See also Árdal, 1989, chap. 7.

4. All of these possibilities are considered in Harrison, 1978; and Mackie, 1980. For defense of (i), see Hunter, 1962. Norton, 1982; and Swain, 1992, defend (iii).

5. Of course, the Copy Principle requires that *any* ideas used in moral evaluations must have a source in impressions, no matter what the nature of those evaluations may be. If moral evaluations could be reached strictly by inference from nonmoral premises, it would therefore follow that moral evaluations rely only on ideas that are copied from impressions that are not distinctively moral.

6. Good accounts of the correction of moral sentiments occur in Hearn, 1976, and Swain, 1992.

7. It is also, arguably, because our conception of the *character being evaluated* is more vivid (see THN 581).

8. While emphasizing the variability of sentiments due to nearness and remoteness, Hume notes also at THN 583 that "all sentiments of blame and praise are variable, according to . . . the present disposition of the mind." Although he does not amplify this statement, he may well mean that sympathy and hence moral sentiments also vary with one's changing levels of such things as happiness or unhappiness, ease or anxiety, attention or self-absorption. Most of his subsequent remarks about "correcting" interpersonal and intrapersonal variability of our sentiments resulting from difference of situation are also applicable to "correcting" interpersonal and intrapersonal variability resulting from differences in present mental disposition in this sense.

9. As we have seen in chapters 3 and 5, resemblance is sometimes, but not always, a matter of having the same kind of simpler parts in common (THN 637). Where the resemblance among the particular instances in the revival set is of this kind, definitions of abstract ideas will still be relatively easy to provide; when it is not, definition may become more difficult or impossible. The particular instances in the revival set of the relational term 'cause', for example, do not all have simpler parts in common, which is one of the reasons why Hume finds it difficult—although not ultimately impossible—to define.

10. It might be argued that the ability to survey mental characteristics requires, for Hume, the formation of abstract ideas of them, and hence—because abstract ideas depend on the existence of general terms—at least some general terms for such characteristics. This seems debatable to me, however.

11. A *lively* idea of a person or feature of character that included a copy of a moral sentiment as a part would presumably be a (false) belief that the object existed with the moral sentiment as one of its qualities or parts. Mackie, 1980, proposes that we interpret Hume as treating all ordinary moral evaluations as being false beliefs of this kind.

12. Each has an obvious corresponding definition of 'vice'. Both definitions of virtue and vice are evident in the *Treatise* as well, though they are not so explicitly labeled as definitions.

13. For discussion of the ambiguities in both definitions, see chapter 5 and also chapter 7.

14. It is important not to be misled by the comma in this quotation into reading "which can be discover'd by the understanding" as a nonrestrictive clause. Hume, like most of his contemporaries, very often uses commas to introduce restrictive clauses. The convention against doing so is a later innovation.

15. Hume uses both of the terms 'induction' and 'deduction' simply as synonyms for 'inference'. He does not make either the earlier (Baconian) nor the later (contemporary) distinction between induction and deduction.

16. There is independent evidence that the "is/ought" passage was added as an afterthought to *Treatise* III.i.1, which formerly ended with Hume's previous paragraph.

17. Thus, he is not saying that the understanding has nothing to do with moral evaluation; he is saying only that if one had to choose between saying that morality is an object of taste or that it is an object of the understanding, one would have to choose the former. Compare this with his remark in *Treatise* I "*that belief is more properly an act of the sensitive, than of the cogitative part of our natures*" (THN 183). Here Hume does not mean that belief is *not* an act of the cogitative part of our natures—if belief itself is not such an act, then, very little is left that could be—but rather that it is more important to recognize it as an act of the sensitive part.

Chapter 10

1. As Baier, 1991, astutely notes, the sequence of passions described in *Treatise* I.iv.7 serves, among other purposes, to introduce the topic of Book II of the *Treatise*, which is the passions. Chapter 1 of Baier's book is perhaps the most detailed previous account of *Treatise* I.iv.7. While I am much indebted to that work, my account differs in a number of ways that should be evident. Among the most important is that Baier sees Hume as ultimately enlarging the sense of 'reason' to include various propensities within its scope, whereas I see him as arguing for the need to supplement reason with other aspects of human nature but as using the term 'reason' univocally throughout his works to designate the inferential faculty.

2. There is an analogy here with Descartes, who also offered skeptical arguments for the ultimate purpose of grounding and reconfirming our commitments to reason, to philosophy, and to his own cognitive psychology. Although he employs some false premises, I believe that Descartes's strategy, too, is a generally coherent one (and is not, for example, viciously circular). The strategies and the conceptions of reason involved are, of course, radically different in the two cases.

3. The remark that this quality is "trivial and so little founded on reason" occurs after the discussion of the understanding and immediately precedes Hume's references to the senses and memory. It is reasonably clear, however, that it is meant to apply to all three. Hume's phrase "the quality, by which the mind enlivens some ideas beyond others" clearly refers to all three. Moreover, Hume has previously characterized the idea-enlivening process of "the senses" as seemingly trivial and as not founded on reason, in *Treatise* I.iv.2.

4. I will not outline these arguments (THN 188–193), because they are complex and no conclusion of the present chapter turns on their structure or content.

5. Except where otherwise indicated, I am throughout this chapter using 'probable' in the broad sense opposed to demonstration, rather than in the narrow sense opposed to proof (THN 124). Later references to the "probability of causes," of course, concern probability in the narrower sense.

6. Hume does allow (THN 196–197) that we sometimes engage in "reasonings" by which we infer the continued and distinct existence of some object so that it can serve as a cause for some event, in accordance with a causal maxim already adopted. This is not the primary mechanism by which we acquire beliefs in continued and distinct existences, however. Hume claims, moreover, that "this inference arises from the understanding, and from custom in an indirect and oblique manner," because it also depends on the occurrence of other mental operations that are *not* operations of reason.

7. Note that Hume here follows the practice of most of his predecessors in treating memory as a function of the imagination. In *Treatise* I.i.3, he had treated the memory and imagination as two different representational faculties (see chapter 1).

8. According to the *Oxford English Dictionary*, "fallacious" in the eighteenth century could mean "disappointing expectations," as well as "deceitful."

9. Accordingly, when Hume characterizes the philosophical view as "liable to the same difficulties" as the vulgar view (THN 218), he is referring only to their shared causal dependence on imaginative illusions, which he has just finished explaining. The philosophical view is not, in his view, subject to easy empirical falsification—a "difficulty" (to put it mildly) that he had noted much earlier.

10. It might be suggested that there is no difference between this *evaluative* sense of theoretical skepticism and a *prescriptive* skepticism of similar degree. It is certainly possible, however, to be a theoretical skeptic in the evaluative sense while refraining from making the recommendations that are definitive of the prescriptive skeptic. Indeed, such a position would arguably be *justified*, if (i) certain unworthy beliefs were known to be psychologically

inevitable, and (ii) "ought" implied "can." In such circumstances, it would be false that one should reject the unworthy beliefs in question. Fogelin himself makes this quite clear.

11. Hume adds the phrase "or more properly speaking" because in his view the senses alone, or narrowly construed, do not produce the opinion of the continued and distinct existence of bodies. As *Treatise* I.iv.2 argues at length, this opinion results instead from the imagination operating on the deliverances of the senses.

12. This would be a rather Kantian alternative. In the *Prolegomena to Any Future Metaphysics*, Kant compares his philosophy to Locke's by noting that Locke denies that secondary qualities are really in bodies, while Kant denies not only the ultimate reality of secondary qualities but also that of primary qualities. The ascription of a temporally continued existence to things-in-themselves would, of course, be un-Kantian.

13. In the first *Enquiry*, Hume comments that matter without primary or secondary qualities is "a notion so imperfect, that no sceptic will think it worth while to contend against it" (EHU §123).

14. Note that the Conceivability Criterion of Possibility ("Whatever is conceivable is possible"—see chapter 1) states a sufficient condition for possibility, not a necessary condition. Inconceivability is evidence of impossibility only when we have the relevant ideas and find that they cannot be combined. Hume consistently allows that there may be objects or qualities that are inconceivable to us because we lack the required ideas. However, one of the four corollaries that he draws from his account of causation is that "we can never have *reason* to believe that an object exists, of which we cannot form an idea" (THN 172; emphasis added).

15. This version is more general because it applies to all decreases, and not just to decreases of parts. Hume cannot easily construe degrees of belief as literal *parts* of belief, because they are not separable from the ideas whose vivacity they constitute. He does, however, tend to think of the vivacity of probable beliefs as produced by the accumulation or reinforcement of separate ideas or impressions, each with its own degree of vivacity (see the discussion of probability in chapter 7).

16. Thus, he rephrases his final conclusion one page later by stating that "the very same principles [i.e., natural operations], which make us form a decision upon any subject, and correct that decision by a consideration of our genius and capacity . . . when carried further, and apply'd to every new reflex judgment, must . . . utterly subvert all belief and opinion" (THN 183–184).

17. For a further account of Hume's use of the skeptical argument to reinforce his psychology of belief, see Morris, 1989.

18. A similar line of reflection is suggested, as a corrective to Hume's argument, in Karlsson, 1990.

19. Of course, it might be that reason itself would find some way to reconcile the results of these operations—or that reflection on the conflict would convince us that one or the other operation had not been an operation of reason alone but had involved the "irruption of other causes." Perhaps an awareness of such conflicts and concern over their significance contributed to Hume's decision to omit discussion of this skeptical argument from the first *Enquiry*.

20. This policy of refraining from attention to skeptical implications until the time is right to deal with them is perhaps analogous in some respects to Descartes's refraining from returning his attention to the "evil demon" doubt until after he has completed the argument for God's existence and nondeception—an argument that, once completed, is meant to be capable of blocking the doubt.

21. Hume notes that there are "in England, in particular, many honest gentlemen" who have "carried their thoughts very little beyond those objects, which are every day expos'd to their senses" (THN 272). Neither ambition nor the need for a guide to matters outside daily

action will motivate them to philosophize, but presumably they are not particularly likely to fall into philosophical melancholy and delirium in the first place.

22. Hume identifies this radical antecedent skepticism with Descartes's method of hyperbolic doubt.

23. Fogelin, 1985, suggests that Hume's treatments of inductive inference and reason's reflective subversion of belief are examples of antecedent rather than consequent skepticism, because they involve appeals to circularity and infinite regress, respectively, which he conceives as a priori considerations (p. 7). This seems to me to underestimate the extent to which Hume intends his arguments of *Treatise* I.iii.6 and I.iv.1 to turn on his discoveries concerning how reason, as a human cognitive faculty, actually functions. See, for example, (1), (2), (4), (5), (8), and (10) of the argument outlined in chapter 4, and (D1), (D4), (D5), (D6), (D7), (D12), (D13), (D15), and (D20) of the present chapter. Hume conceives of antecedent skepticism as skepticism adopted for methodological reasons, as opposed to reasons based in knowledge of our faculties.

24. He does discuss this topic thoroughly in *Enquiry* VII, of course, and he does briefly mention in *Enquiry* XII that our only idea of the causal relation is that "of two objects, which have been frequently *conjoined* together" (EHU §237). This remark is part of his explanation of skepticism concerning the cognitive mechanism of induction, however, rather than a distinct skeptical topic.

25. Indeed, Hume uses the term 'Pyrrhonian' in the *Abstract* in the course of summarizing the *Treatise's* discussion of this kind of doubt (ATHN 657).

References

Adams, Ernest, 1975. *The Logic of Conditionals* (Dordrecht: D. Reidel).

Ahern, Dennis, 1975. "Hume on the Evidential Impossibility of Miracles." In *Studies in Epistemology*, edited by Nicholas Rescher (Oxford: Blackwell).

Alston, William, and Jonathan Bennett, 1988. "Locke on People and Substances," *The Philosophical Review*, vol. 97, no. 1 (January), pp. 25–46.

Anderson, Robert F., 1966. *Hume's First Principles* (Lincoln: University of Nebraska Press).

Árdal, Páll S., 1977. "Another Look at Hume's Account of Moral Evaluation," *Journal of the History of Philosophy*, vol. 15, no. 4 (October), pp. 408–421.

_____, 1989. *Passion and Value in Hume's Treatise*, 2nd ed. (Edinburgh: Edinburgh University Press).

Arnold, N. Scott, 1983. "Hume's Skepticism about Inductive Inferences," *Journal of the History of Philosophy*, vol. 21, no. 1 (January), pp. 31–55.

Baier, Annette, 1991. *A Progress of Sentiments* (Cambridge: Harvard University Press).

Basinger, David, and Randall Basinger, 1986. *Philosophy and Miracle: The Contemporary Debate* (Lewiston/Queenston: Edwin Mellen Press).

Basson, A. H., 1958. *David Hume* (London: Pelican).

Beauchamp, Tom L., 1979. "Self Inconsistency or Mere Self Perplexity?" *Hume Studies*, vol. 5, no. 1 (April), pp. 37–44.

Beauchamp, Tom L., and Thomas Mappes, 1975. "Is Hume Really a Sceptic about Induction?" *American Philosophical Quarterly*, vol. 12, no. 2 (April), pp. 119–129.

Beauchamp, Tom L., and Alexander Rosenberg, 1981. *Hume and the Problem of Causation* (Oxford: Oxford University Press).

Beckwith, Francis J., 1989. *David Hume's Argument against Miracles: A Critical Analysis* (Lanham, Md.: University Press of America).

Bennett, Jonathan, 1971. *Locke, Berkeley, Hume: Central Themes* (Oxford: Oxford University Press).

_____, 1984. *A Study of Spinoza's Ethics* (Indianapolis: Hackett).

Biro, John I., 1976. "Hume on Self-Identity and Memory," *The Review of Metaphysics*, vol. 30, no. 1 (September), pp. 19–38.

_____, 1979. "Hume's Difficulties with the Self," *Hume Studies*, vol. 5, no. 1 (April), pp. 45–54.

Botwinick, Aryeh, 1980. *Ethics, Politics and Epistemology: A Study in the Unity of Hume's Thought* (Lanham, Md.: University Press of America).

Bricke, John, 1980. *Hume's Philosophy of Mind* (Princeton: Princeton University Press).

Broad, C. D., 1916–1917. "Hume's Theory of the Credibility of Miracles," *Proceedings of the Aristotelian Society*, n.s. 17, pp. 77–94. Reprinted in *Human Understanding: Essays in the Philosophy of David Hume*, edited by Alexander Sesonke and Noel Fleming (Belmont: Wadsworth, 1965).

Broughton, Janet, 1983. "Hume's Skepticism about Causal Inferences," *Pacific Philosophical Quarterly*, vol. 64, no. 1 (January), pp. 3–18.

Burns, R. M., 1981. *The Great Debate on Miracles: From Joseph Glanville to David Hume* (Lewisburg: Bucknell University Press).

Capaldi, Nicholas, 1975. *David Hume: The Newtonian Philosopher* (Boston: Twayne).

Church, Ralph, 1935. *Hume's Theory of the Understanding* (Ithaca: Cornell University Press).

Coleman, Dorothy, 1988. "Hume, Miracles, and Lotteries," *Hume Studies*, vol. 14, no. 2 (November), pp. 328–346.

Craig, E. J., 1987. *The Mind of God and the Works of Man* (Oxford: Clarendon Press).

DeWitt, Richard, 1985. "Hume's Probability Argument of I,iv,1," *Hume Studies*, vol. 11, no. 2 (November), pp. 125–140.

Ducasse, C. J., 1966. "Critique of Hume's Conception of Causality," *Journal of Philosophy*, vol. 63, no. 6 (March 17), pp. 141–148.

Flage, Daniel, 1987. *Berkeley's Doctrine of Notions: A Reconstruction Based on His Theory of Meaning* (London: Croom Helm).

_____, 1990. *David Hume's Theory of Mind* (London: Routledge and Kegan Paul).

Flew, Antony, 1959. "Hume's Check," *Philosophical Quarterly*, vol. 9, no. 34 (January), pp. 1–18.

_____, 1961. *Hume's Philosophy of Belief* (London: Routledge and Kegan Paul).

_____, 1966. "On the Interpretation of Hume." In *Hume: A Collection of Critical Essays*, edited by V. C. Chappell (Garden City, N.Y.: Doubleday).

_____, 1986. *David Hume: Philosopher of Moral Science* (Oxford: Basil Blackwell).

Fogelin, Robert J., 1984. "Hume and the Missing Shade of Blue," *Philosophy and Phenomenological Research*, vol. 45, no. 2 (December), pp. 263–271.

_____, 1985. *Hume's Skepticism in the Treatise of Human Nature* (London: Routledge and Kegan Paul).

_____, 1988. "Hume and Berkeley on the Proofs of Infinite Divisibility," *The Philosophical Review*, vol. 97, no. 1 (January), pp. 47–70.

_____, 1990. "What Hume Actually Said about Miracles," *Hume Studies*, vol. 16, no. 1 (April), pp. 81–86.

Frankfurt, Harry, 1971. "Freedom of the Will and the Concept of a Person," *The Journal of Philosophy*, vol. 68, no. 1 (January), pp. 5–20.

Garrett, Don, 1981. "Hume's Self-Doubts about Personal Identity," *The Philosophical Review*, vol. 90, no. 3 (July), pp. 337–358.

_____, 1985. "Simplicity and Separability in Hume's Empiricism," *Archiv für Geschichte der Philosophie*, vol. 67, no. 3 (September), pp. 270–288.

_____, 1990. "Truth, Method, and Correspondence in Spinoza and Leibniz," *Studia Spinozana*, vol. 6, pp. 13–43.

_____, 1991. "Spinoza's Necessitarianism." In *God and Nature: Spinoza's Metaphysics*, edited by Yirmiyahu Yovel (Leiden: Brill).

_____, 1993. "The Representation of Causation and Hume's Two Definitions of 'Cause'," *Noûs*, vol. 27, no. 2 (June), pp. 167–190.

Green, T. H., and T. H. Grose, 1874–1875. *The Philosophical Works of David Hume*, 4 vols., (London: Longmans Green).

Hambourger, Robert, 1980. "Belief in Miracles and Hume's *Essay*," *Noûs*, vol. 14, no. 4 (November), pp. 587–604.

Hanfling, Oswald, 1979. "Hume's Idea of Necessary Connexion," *Philosophy*, vol. 54, no. 210 (October), pp. 501–514.

Harrison, Jonathan, 1978. *Hume's Moral Epistemology* (Oxford: Clarendon Press).

Hearn, Thomas, 1973. "Árdal on the Moral Sentiments in Hume's *Treatise*," *Philosophy*, vol. 48, no. 185 (July), pp. 288–292.

_____, 1976. "General Rules and the Moral Sentiments in Hume's *Treatise*," *Review of Metaphysics*, vol. 30, no. 1 (September), pp. 57–72.

Hendel, Charles, 1925. *Studies in the Philosophy of David Hume* (Princeton: Princeton University Press).

Hickenlooper, Susan, 1992. "Hume on Liberty and Necessity," unpublished.

Hunter, Geoffrey, 1962. "Hume on Is and Ought," *Philosophy*, vol. 37, no. 140 (April), pp. 148–152.

Imlay, Robert A., 1981. "Hume's 'Of Scepticism with regard to reason': A Study in Contrasting Themes," *Hume Studies*, vol. 7, no. 2 (November), pp. 121–136.

Jacobsen, Anne Jaap, 1984. "Does Hume Hold a Regularity Theory?" *History of Philosophy Quarterly*, vol. 1, no. 1 (January), pp. 75–91.

Johnson, Oliver, 1989. "Time and the Idea of Time," *Hume Studies*, vol. 15, no. 1 (April), pp. 205–219.

Karlsson, Mikael, 1990. "Epistemic Leaks and Epistemic Meltdowns: A Response to William Morris on Scepticism with Regard to Reason," *Hume Studies*, vol. 16, no. 2 (November), pp. 121–130.

Kemp Smith, Norman, 1941. *The Philosophy of David Hume* (London: MacMillan).

Kripke, Saul, 1980. *Naming and Necessity* (Cambridge, Mass.: Harvard University Press).

Laing, B. M., 1932. *David Hume* (London: Oxford University Press).

Laird, John, 1932. *Hume's Philosophy of Human Nature* (London: Methuen).

Levine, Michael P., 1989. *Hume and the Problem of Miracles: A Solution* (Dordrecht: Kluwer).

Lewis, C. S., 1947. *Miracles: A Preliminary Study* (New York: MacMillan).

Livingston, Donald, 1984. *Hume's Philosophy of Common Life* (Chicago: University of Chicago Press).

Mackie, J. L., 1980. *Hume's Moral Theory* (London: Routledge and Kegan Paul).

_____, 1982. *The Miracle of Theism* (Oxford: Clarendon Press).

MacNabb, D. G. C., 1951. *David Hume: His Theory of Knowledge and Morality* (London: Hutchinson).

MacRae, Robert, 1969. "Hume on Meaning," *Dialogue* (Canada), vol. 8, no. 3 (December), pp. 486–491.

Mandelbaum, Maurice, 1974. "The Distinguishable and the Separable: A Note on Hume and Causation," *Journal of the History of Philosophy*, vol. 12, no. 2 (April), pp. 242–247.

Merrill, Kenneth, 1976. "Hume, Whitehead, and Philosophic Method." In *David Hume: Many-Sided Genius*, edited by Kenneth Merrill and Robert W. Shahan (Norman: University of Oklahoma Press).

Morris, William Edward, 1989. "Hume's Scepticism about Reason," *Hume Studies*, vol. 15, no. 1 (April), pp. 39–60.

Mossner, Ernest Campbell, 1954. *The Life of David Hume* (Austin: University of Texas Press).

Nathanson, Stephen, 1976. "Hume's Second Thoughts on the Self," *Hume Studies*, vol. 2, no. 1 (April), pp. 36–45.

262 References

Norton, David Fate, 1982. *David Hume: Common-Sense Moralist, Sceptical Metaphysician* (Princeton: Princeton University Press).

Owen, David, 1987. "Hume versus Price on Miracles and Prior Probabilities: Testimony and the Bayesian Calculation," *The Philosophical Quarterly*, vol. 37, no. 147 (April), pp. 187–202.

Passmore, John A., 1952. *Hume's Intentions* (Cambridge: Cambridge University Press).

Patten, S. C., 1976. "Hume's Bundles, Self-Consciousness, and Kant," *Hume Studies*, vol. 2, no. 1 (April), pp. 59–64.

Pears, David, 1975. *Questions in the Philosophy of Mind* (London: Duckworth).

———, 1990. *Hume's System: An Examination of the First Book of His Treatise* (Oxford: Oxford University Press).

———, 1993. "Hume on Personal Identity," *Hume Studies*, vol. 19, no. 2 (November), pp. 289–299.

Penelhum, Terence, 1975. *Hume* (New York: St. Martin's Press).

———, 1987. "Hume on Liberty and Necessity," presented to the Sâo Paulo Hume Conference, Sâo Paulo, Brazil.

Pike, Nelson, 1967. "Hume's Bundle Theory of the Self: A Limited Defense," *American Philosophical Quarterly*, vol. 4, no. 2 (April), pp. 159–165.

Richards, Thomas J., 1966. "Hume's Two Definitions of 'Cause'." In *Hume: A Collection of Critical Essays*, edited by V. C. Chappell (Garden City, N.Y.: Doubleday Anchor).

Robinson, J. A., 1962. "Hume's Two Definitions of 'Cause,'" *The Philosophical Quarterly*, vol. 12. Reprinted in *Hume: A Collection of Critical Essays*, edited by V. C. Chappell (Garden City, N.Y.: Doubleday Anchor, 1966), pp. 129–147.

———, 1966. "Hume's Two Definitions of 'Cause' Reconsidered." In *Hume: A Collection of Critical Essays*, edited by V. C. Chappell (Garden City, N.Y.: Doubleday Anchor), pp. 162–168.

Robison, Wade, 1974. "Hume on Personal Identity," *Journal of the History of Philosophy*, vol. 12, no. 2 (April), pp. 181–193.

———, 1977. "Hume's Causal Scepticism." In *David Hume: Bicentennary Papers*, edited by G. P. Morice (Austin: University of Texas Press).

———, 1982. "One Consequence of Hume's Nominalism," *Hume Studies*, vol. 8, no. 2 (November), pp. 102–118.

Russow, Lilly-Marlene, 1980. "Simple Ideas and Resemblance," *Philosophical Quarterly*, vol. 30, no. 121 (October), pp. 340–350.

Sayre-McCord, Geoffrey, 1994. "Why Hume's Observer Isn't Ideal—and Shouldn't Be," *Social Philosophy and Policy*, vol. 11, no. 1 (winter), pp. 202–228.

Sobel, J. H., 1987. "On the Evidence of Testimony for Miracles: A Bayesian Reconstruction of David Hume's Analysis," *Philosophical Quarterly*, vol. 37, no. 147 (April), pp. 166–186.

Sorenson, Roy A., 1983. "Hume's Skepticism concerning Reports of Miracles," *Analysis*, vol. 43, no. 1 (January), p. 60.

Stove, D. C., 1973. *Probability and Hume's Inductive Scepticism* (Oxford: Clarendon Press).

Strawson, Galen, 1989. *The Secret Connexion: Causation, Realism, and David Hume* (Oxford: Clarendon Press).

Strawson, P. F., 1952. *Introduction to Logical Theory* (London: Methuen and Co.).

Stroud, Barry, 1977. *Hume* (London: Routledge and Kegan Paul).

———, 1978. "Hume and the Idea of Causal Necessity," *Philosophical Studies*, vol. 33, no. 1 (January), pp. 39–59.

Swain, Corliss, 1992. "Passionate Objectivity," *Noûs*, vol. 26, no. 4 (December), pp. 465–490.

Swinburne, Richard, 1970. *The Concept of Miracle* (London: MacMillan).

Tweyman, Stanley, 1974. "Hume on Separating the Inseparable," in *Hume and the Enlightenment*, edited by C. L. Read (Edinburgh: University of Edinburgh Press).

Whitehead, Alfred North, 1969. *Process and Reality* (New York: The Free Press).

Wilbanks, Jan, 1968. *Hume's Theory of Imagination* (The Hague: Martinus Nijhoff).

Wilson, Fred, 1983. "Hume's Sceptical Argument against Reason," *Hume Studies*, vol. 9, no. 2 (November), pp. 90–129.

_____, 1989. "The Logic of Probabilities in Hume's Argument against Miracles," *Hume Studies*, vol. 15, no. 2 (November), pp. 255–275.

Winkler, Kenneth P., 1991. "The New Hume," *The Philosophical Review*, vol. 100, no. 4 (October), pp. 541–580.

Winters, Barbara, 1979. "Hume on Reason," *Hume Studies*, vol. 5, no. 1 (April), pp. 20–35.

Wright, John P., 1983. *The Sceptical Realism of David Hume* (Minneapolis: Minnesota University Press).

Yandell, Keith E., 1990. *Hume's "Inexplicable Mystery": His Views on Religion* (Philadelphia: Temple University Press).

Zabeeh, Farhang, 1973. *Hume, Precursor of Modern Empiricism* (The Hague: Martinus Nijhoff).

Index